Management

Edited by K.M. Pirkle
University of Georgia

A Customized Version of Creating Effective Organizations

Fifth Edition By
David J. Cherrington and W. Gibb Dyer

Cover image © 2009 by Shutterstock, Inc.

Kendall Hunt
publishing company

www.kendallhunt.com
Send all inquiries to:
4050 Westmark Drive
Dubuque, IA 52004-1840

Copyright © 2009 by K.M. Pirkle

ISBN 978-0-7575-6962-3

Kendall/Hunt Publishing Company has the exclusive rights to reproduce this work, to prepare derivative works from this work, to publicly distribute this work, to publicly perform this work and to publicly display this work.

All rights reserved. No part of this publication may be reproduced, stored in a retrieval system, or transmitted, in any form or by any means, electronic, mechanical, photocopying, recording, or otherwise, without the prior written permission of the copyright owner.

Printed in the United States of America
10 9 8 7 6 5 4 3 2

Contents

- **Chapter 1** The Nature of Management — 1
- **Chapter 2** The Basics of Planning and Project Management — 17
- **Chapter 3** Strategy — 45
- **Chapter 4** International Management — 65
- **Chapter 5** The Nature of Entrepreneurship — 81
- **Chapter 6** Organizational Design — 91
- **Chapter 7** Leadership — 113
- **Chapter 8** Analyzing Individual Behavior — 133
- **Chapter 9** Performance Management — 155
- **Chapter 10** Effective Groups and Teams — 177
- **Chapter 11** Managerial Control — 199
- **Chapter 12** Operations and Services Management — 217
- **Appendix A** — 233
- **Appendix B** — 269
- **Index** — 281

The Nature of Management

What Is Management?

To begin, we examine the concepts that form the base of this book.

Management is an activity or process. More specifically, management is the process of assembling and using sets of resources in a goal-directed manner to accomplish tasks in an organizational setting. This definition can be subdivided into its key parts:

1. Management is a process: It involves a series of activities and operations, such as planning, deciding, and evaluating.
2. Management involves assembling and using sets of resources: It is a process that brings together, and puts into use, a variety of resources: human, financial, material, and informational.
3. Management involves acting in a goal-directed manner to accomplish tasks: It is an activity with a purpose and direction. The purpose or direction may be that of the individual, the organization, or, usually, a combination of the two. It includes one's efforts to complete activities successfully and to achieve particular levels of desired results.
4. Management involves activities carried out in an organizational setting: It is a process undertaken in organizations by people with different functions intentionally structured and coordinated to achieve common purposes.

In addition to being "a process" or set of activities, management can also have several other meanings. The term sometimes designates a particular part of the organization: the set of individuals who carry out management activities. Thus, some may use the phrase "the *management* of IBM decided..." or "the management of University Hospital developed a new personnel policy...." Often, when the term is used this way, it does not necessarily refer to all members of management but rather to those who occupy the highest-level positions within the organization (top management).

Another similar use of the term is to distinguish a category of people (that is, "management") from those who are members of collective bargaining units ("union" members or, more informally, "labor") or those who are not involved in specific managerial activities, whether or not they are union members ("nonmanagement employees" or "rank-and-file employees"). The term *member* refers to any person (any employee) in an organization without regard to that individual's place in the organization. In this book, we use the term *manager* to refer to anyone who has designated responsibilities for carrying out managerial activities, and *managing* to refer to the process of completing those activities.

However, *management* is too complex a concept for any one definition to capture accurately. Next, we explain several of the challenges with which managers must deal.

Managerial Challenges

Managers face a number of challenges on a regular basis. The nature of the environment in which managers operate requires that they manage change effectively. Managers are responsible for managing resources—financial, human, and otherwise. To ensure that their organization is competitive and survives in a rapidly changing environment, they must

Hitt, Michael, Black, Stewart, Porter, Lyman W., *Management*, 2nd edition, © 2008. Reprinted by permission of Pearson Education, Inc., Upper Saddle River, NJ.

manage strategically. Because of the major changes occurring rapidly in the business world today, managers must be entrepreneurial and innovative. Essentially, they must continuously find ways to create more value for customers than do competitors. Managers' activities take place within organizations. Although managers are the primary "drivers" of their organizations, organizations put boundaries on what managers can and cannot do. We examine each of these challenges next.

Managing Change

Managing change is the most persistent, pervasive, and powerful challenge with which all managers have to deal, regardless of the organizations for which they work or where they're located. No matter how new or experienced managers are, they will be confronted with both the need for change and the opportunity to create change. Not making any changes is unlikely to be an option. As a Greek philosopher once wrote many centuries ago, "Change alone is unchanging,"[1] and that statement remains appropriate today.

Managing change is no simple task, especially because most people naturally resist change. Thus, managers must find ways to gain the employees' acceptance of change in order to implement it effectively. To gain acceptance, it is useful for managers to create "small wins." For example, the manager might implement the change in one smaller area and make it successful. This success then makes the change legitimate in the eyes of the employees.[2] Two of the major causes of change with which managers must deal are new technology and globalization.

Technology

No managers in today's world can ignore the impact of technology and the way it affects their jobs and firms. Technology developments often force managers to make changes—whether they want to or not. The Internet is a case in point. The Internet has had far-reaching effects on how managers do their jobs.

The introduction of a new technology often leads to the development of new products and new processes for accomplishing tasks. The Internet has created many opportunities to market products differently, to reach distant markets, and to communicate internally and externally in more effective ways. Therefore, it has provided many opportunities for managers. Yet, they must identify these opportunities and find ways to exploit them. If they do not, competitors are likely to do so and take market share from them. Essentially, the Internet has increased the speed of change, the flow of information, the competitive reach into international markets, and the amount of competition in all markets.

Because the Internet provides information, it has served as a catalyst for the continued development of other technologies and information about them. It has placed an emphasis on the importance of knowledge and has increased the importance of human capital (the holder of the knowledge). It has helped many small and medium-sized firms to enter and compete in international markets, thereby enhancing globalization.[3]

Globalization

Globalization is the development and observation of the increasing international and cross-national nature of everything from politics to business. No longer can managers ignore what happens in the rest of the world because events in other countries tend to affect their organizations. Global events will almost certainly affect the goals that managers set, the decisions they make, and how they must coordinate and lead the work of other people.

The opening of many world markets (e.g., in China), the development of free trade agreements (such as the General Agreement on Tariffs and Trade—GATT, and the North American Free Trade Agreement—NAFTA), growing economies around the world, and increases in technology that facilitate global partnerships and competition have all contributed greatly to increasing globalization.[4] Opening of markets to foreign firms coupled with economic development increases market opportunities but simultaneously leads to greater global competition. In order to compete effectively in global markets, firms have sought increasingly to outsource activities to people and firms in lower-cost countries like India and China.[5]

Globalization promotes greater involvement in international markets. Thus, firms moving into international markets increasingly need to learn about different cultures and the institutional environments in these markets.[6] Some firms have facilitated this learning process by developing multicultural management teams. These teams have managers who speak different languages and have knowledge about the markets and environments in different regions of the world in which the firms operate.[7] Because of the complexities of operating in multiple countries and regions, some firms focus their international operations in one or a few specific regions of the world. In this way, they can develop the knowledge of the culture, markets, and institutions to operate there effectively.[8]

Managing Resources

A major part of a manager's job is to manage the resources of the organization. The manager must ensure the efficient use of resources but also use the resources in ways that maximize the achievement of the organization's goals. Among the resources important to managers are financial capital, human capital, physical resources (buildings and equipment, for example), and technology. They build and manage a portfolio of resources.[9] To build the portfolio, they have to acquire and develop the resources needed to complete the organization's tasks. For example, managers need to recruit and select the best employees possible to join the organization. After becoming employees, managers need to continually develop the employees' knowledge and skills.[10] As they do so, the employees' value to the organization increases. This implies that managers need to be effective in evaluating people's skills in order to select the best and to know what skills they need to develop. Managers must also design and implement the means to promote learning in the organization.[11]

Once they have the portfolio of resources, managers have to then allocate and coordinate these resources to accomplish the required tasks of the organization.[12] Managers are also responsible for developing and implementing a strategy to use the organization's capabilities to accomplish its goals.[13] One of the major dimensions of coordination is the relationship with others, especially other managers in the organization and with the employees managed. So, managers' interpersonal and communication skills are paramount in this process. We conclude that managers largely get things done with and through people in the organization. As a result, how they manage human capital is critical to their success.

Xerox CEO Anne Mulcahy is largely credited with turning around that company's performance. But Mulcahy argues that it was Xerox's employees who were critical to the turnaround in the company's performance. She stated that ". . . attracting them, motivating them, keeping them—making Xerox an employer of choice—is critical to our drive back to greatness."[14] These comments suggest that staffing the organization with the best human capital possible and further developing the knowledge and skills of employees is critical for the success.[15] This conclusion emphasizes the importance of managing the organization's resources (especially the people) to its ability to compete and survive in an increasingly competitive environment.[16]

Managing Strategically

Managerial challenges create an incredibly complex, dynamic, and competitive landscape in which most managers must operate. To survive and perform well in such an environment, managers throughout the organization need to manage strategically.[17] Managers at the top of the organization—CEOs such as Meg Whitman at eBay—establish goals and formulate a strategy for the firm to achieve those goals. To accomplish the goals, the company must effectively implement the strategy, which requires managers at all levels of the organization to set and accomplish goals that contribute to the organization's ultimate performance.

The increasing globalization and the enhanced use of technology have contributed to greater changes emphasizing the importance of knowledge to organizational success.[18] The importance placed on the intellectual capital of the organization requires managers to use their portfolio of resources effectively.[19] Of primary importance are intangible resources such as the employees and the firm's reputation. Managers are responsible for building an organization's capabilities and then leveraging them through a strategy designed to give it an advantage over its competitors. They usually do this by creating more value for their customers than competitors.[20]

BMW managers, for example, developed a strategy to use the firm's excellent research and development (R&D) capabilities to design and manufacture several new automobiles with the goal of increasing U.S. sales by 40 percent by 2008. The top managers at BMW made this decision at a time when other automobile manufacturers were reducing R&D expenditures to control costs. Capitalizing on its strengths and using them strategically to offer consumers more and better auto designs so far has given BMW an advantage over its competitors and contributed to its superior performance.[21]

Managers are responsible for forming the strategies of the major units within the organization as well. Because people in the organization have to implement the strategy, managers must focus heavily on the human factor. As they implement their strategies, they will encounter conflicting conditions. Often this means managing multiple situations simultaneously and remaining flexible to adapt to changing conditions. Additionally, achieving an organization's goals requires that managers commit themselves to always being alert to how they can improve and strengthen strategies in advancing the organization's vision. Finally, the dynamic competitive landscape entails substantial change. To adapt to this change, managers should be innovative and entrepreneurial; they should search continuously for new opportunities.

Managing Entrepreneurially

Managers should regularly search for new opportunities in the current marketplace or identify ideas that could create new markets.[22] Entrepreneurship involves identifying new opportunities and exploiting them. Thus, managers must be entrepreneurial. Entrepreneurial activity is not limited to new, small firms, however. Managers in large firms need to be entrepreneurial and create new businesses as well. Developing new businesses requires that the lead person, and perhaps others, take entrepreneurial actions. Given the amount of change and innovation encountered in most industries and countries, businesses cannot survive without being entrepreneurial.[23]

To be entrepreneurial, managers must develop an entrepreneurial mind-set. An entrepreneurial mind-set is a way of thinking about businesses that emphasizes actions to take advantage of uncertainty.[24] With an entrepreneurial mind-set, managers can sense opportunities and take actions to exploit them. Uncertainty in the environment tends to level the "playing field" for both large and smaller organizations and for resource-rich and resource-poor ones. Anyone can identify opportunities and exploit them to achieve a competitive advantage. This is how Microsoft beat its competitors, who were at one time larger and more powerful. To develop an entrepreneurial mind-set, managers must first be alert to new ideas and use them to create value for customers.[25]

Both large and small firms and new and established firms can be entrepreneurial. For reasons described earlier, they not only can be, they must be to survive. The original Polaroid, once an entrepreneurial company and a market leader in instant photography, no longer exists because it lost its entrepreneurial nature, and market share winnowed away with the development of digital photography technology (the firm that bought the rights to the Polaroid name is struggling). As a whole, small and new firms tend to be more entrepreneurial but often lack the ability to sustain this advantage. On the other hand, large, established firms are good at using their size to gain an advantage and sustaining their positions as long as new, rival products don't enter the market. However, larger firms have a more difficult time being entrepreneurial.[26]

Historical Approaches to Management

While many think that management is a very new concept, it is not. Even ancient civilizations encountered managerial challenges and found ways to cope with them. More than 1,000 years ago, Chinese leaders searched for an effective means of governing a large organization (government) and expressed the importance of open communications and consideration of people's needs. Additionally, Chinese leaders discussed the value of specialized labor, hiring and promotions based on merit, and the need to clearly describe jobs.[27] The modern field of strategic management owes its origins to an ancient Chinese warrior, Sun Tsu, and his book, *The Art of War*.

Management was practiced in many parts of the world many years ago. For example, consider how the pyramids were designed and built in Egypt so long ago. Completing these "wonders of the world" required a significant amount of planning, organization, and management of labor. Likewise, 2,000 years ago, the Roman Empire required effective management to build major monuments and an extensive network of roads and viaducts. Additionally, the development and spread of the Catholic Church throughout the world required a significant amount of planning, organization, and directing of people's efforts and activities.

The origins of what is often referred to as "modern management" are found in the Industrial Revolution, which began in England in the mid-eighteenth century and later spread to the United States and other geographic regions of the world. While many have contributed to the development of management thought and practices, Fredrick W. Taylor (1856–1915), an American engineer, is often credited as the "father of modern management." Taylor's work on linking workers' incentives to their performance provided an important base for motivation theory applied to the workplace. He argued that pay was only part of the reward and that employees should be provided regularly with feedback on their performance. His primary legacy is the principles of scientific management that form the base for many of the different functions, roles, and activities of managers that we explore in this book.[28] Recent research proclaims that scientific management was a sophisticated theoretical approach that contributed to other fields as well as institutional economics.[29]

Many other people have contributed to our notion of modern management theory and practice over the course of the last two centuries as well. Among them are Frank and Lillian Gilbreth, who developed the beginnings of time and motion studies to determine the most efficient manner in which to complete tasks. Alfred P. Sloan (former CEO of General Motors) and Chester Barnard (an executive of AT&T) both contributed to our knowledge of how to build an efficient and effective organization. While Sloan focused on the formal aspects of organizing such as the functions and divisions, Barnard emphasized the social characteristics of organizing such as cooperation, building common purpose, and the importance of communication. Mary Parker Follett and Douglas McGregor focused on the importance and value of leadership in organizations. Follett espoused principles related to the importance of integration and treating employees as partners. Similarly, McGregor is best known for promoting "Theory Y" leadership practices with positive assumptions about human nature in which positive leadership can bring forth greater efforts and levels of achievement from employees. And, Abraham Maslow and Frederick Herzberg made major contributions to our knowledge of motivation that are present in managerial practices today. Maslow is best known for his "hierarchy of needs" theory and Herzberg for proposing the independence of motivators and hygiene factors. Both of these individuals' ideas led to the concept of job enrichment used to design tasks that more effectively motivate employees and use more of their skills.[30]

What Do Managers Do?

There are several ways to examine managers' jobs aside from observing what managers do. Over the years, several systems have been developed to classify (a) managerial functions, (b) the roles in which managers operate, and (c) the characteristics and dimensions of managerial jobs. These typologies can provide useful ways to examine the varied nature of managerial jobs and responsibilities. In effect, they provide a road map for understanding what management is.

One way to think about the question "What do managers do?" is to analyze the work of managers according to the different functions that they perform. The first such classification system dates back at least 80 years, and, after more than eight decades, this system remains widely used by management scholars and writers.[31] A variation of this traditional typology forms the basis for the general sequencing of the chapters in this book (as well as most other textbooks on the subject of management). The four principal managerial functions most applicable to modern organizations are planning, organizing, directing, and controlling.

Planning

Planning involves estimating future conditions and circumstances and, based on these estimations, making decisions about what work the manager does and all of those for whom she or he is responsible. This function involves at least three distinct levels or types: strategic planning, which addresses strategic actions designed to achieve the organization's long-range goals;[32] tactical planning, which translates strategic plans into actions designed to achieve specific and shorter-term goals and objectives;[33] and operational planning, which identifies the actions needed to accomplish the goals of particular units of the organization or particular product lines in their respective markets.[34]

Planning is important in large and small organizations and in new and established companies. It may be even more important in new and small businesses because they rarely have the slack resources necessary to overcome major mistakes.[35] Firms that do not plan are frequently unprepared for unexpected events. When unexpected events occur, the firms' performance suffers, and they may have to take extraordinary actions.[36] Thus, planning is a highly important managerial function.

Organizing

To conduct managerial work, resources must be integrated systematically, and this function is labeled organizing. It involves identifying the appropriate structure of relationships among positions, and the people occupying them, and linking that structure to the overall strategic direction of the organization. Because today's world is basically full of uncertainties and ambiguities, organizing is a critical function of managers. At its most basic level, the purpose of this managerial function is the attempt to bring order to the organization. Without it, chaos would ensue.

Most people think of the organization structure as represented by the organization chart. And, an organization chart informs others about some portions of the formal structure. Yet, organizing involves much more. For example, decisions about what units should be represented on the firm's project teams are a part of organizing.[37] The degree of autonomy granted to these units is a managerial organizing decision. Often firms producing modular products also have autonomous modular organization units.[38] Such units are becoming more common when integrating units from acquired businesses[39] and when establishing international subsidiaries.[40] As a result, the organizing function of management is complex and challenging.

Nestlé S.A. has had a "flat," or decentralized, organizational structure since its founding a century ago. This structure gives Nestlé's local country managers around the world a great deal of autonomy to satisfy customers in different markets. As a result, the company has achieved a significant amount of success using this structure. However, in recent times, Nestlé management has recognized that the decentralized structure has caused it to develop costly duplicate units and capabilities. The CEO of Nestlé, Peter Brabeck-Letmathe, spoke about the need for efficiencies and identified recent projects designed to reduce costs while maintaining excellence and the flexibility needed to deal with the uncertainties of operating in global markets.

Directing

This function has typically had a number of different labels over the years. Directing is the process of attempting to influence other people to attain the organization's objectives. It heavily involves leading and motivating those for whom the manager is responsible, interacting with them effectively in group and team situations, and communicating in ways that are highly supportive of their efforts to accomplish their tasks and achieve organizational goals. Directing has several dimensions including leadership, motivation, communication, and the management of groups or teams among others.

Leaders must develop effective relationships with their followers, and their actions should result in fair outcomes for them, often referred to as justice.[41] Leaders can have a significant impact on an organization's outcomes—for example, on its innovation and performance.[42] Thus, the leadership exhibited by managers is highly important. Managers use leadership actions to manage change (to transform organizations and units).[43] A critical function for managers as leaders is to motivate their employees to be highly productive. To do so requires that the managers understand the individuals whom they manage and use the tools at their disposal to individualize the rewards for the employees tied to their performance.[44] Many managers focus their activities on directing teams in the current organizational environment. Thus, as leaders, they must find ways to direct the team while simultaneously motivating individuals, empowering both the teams and each individual member of the team.[45] For these reasons, directing is a challenging responsibility for managers.

Controlling

The word *controlling* sometimes has a negative connotation. Yet, control is a necessary and important managerial function. The essence of this function is to regulate the work of those for whom a manager is responsible.[46] Managers can accomplish control in several different ways, including setting standards of performance for employees in advance, monitoring ongoing (real-time) performance, and, especially, assessing the performance of employees on completed tasks. The results of these evaluations are then fed back into the manager's planning process. However, controlling employee behavior is a difficult task. If managers do not take great care in this process, they can elicit some unexpected and undesirable behaviors. Therefore, they must apply controls carefully and effectively.[47] Although they might want to avoid controls that are too tight for their employees, managers must also be careful to avoid overly loose controls. The lack of effective controls can lead to negative outcomes such as the Enron affair. Thus, managers must achieve a *balanced* set of controls.

Therefore, it is important to consider these four managerial functions as parts of a reciprocal and recurring process, as illustrated in Exhibit 1.1.

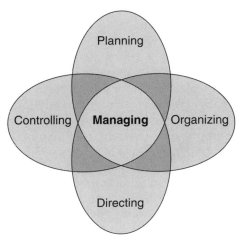

Exhibit 1.1 ■ Managerial Functions

Managerial Roles

Some years ago, the Canadian scholar Henry Mintzberg proposed another approach to understanding managerial work.[48] Mintzberg based his classification system on research regarding how managers spend their time at work, primarily with regard to the roles they play. This way of viewing managers' work activities complements the functional approach; it provides additional understanding and insights on what managers do.

Mintzberg's typology of managerial roles entails three major categories—interpersonal, informational, and decisional—each of which contains specific roles. Together, there are 10 such roles in this typology, as shown in Exhibit 1.2 and described in the following sections.

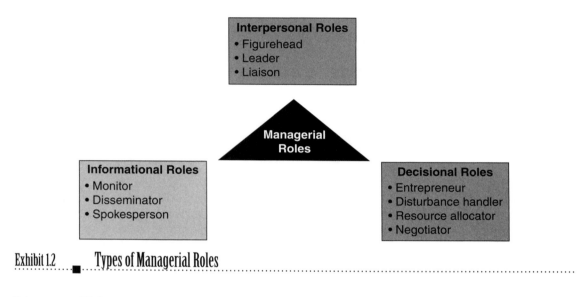

Exhibit 1.2 Types of Managerial Roles

Interpersonal Roles

Interpersonal roles are composed of three types of behavior and are derived directly from the manager's formal authority granted by the organization. They are:

1. *The Figurehead Role* This set of behaviors involves an emphasis on ceremonial activities, such as attending a social function, welcoming a visiting dignitary, or presiding at a farewell reception for a departing employee. A familiar term for this role of representing the organization, borrowed from the military, is "showing the flag." Over time, this behavior is important and is a necessary component of a manager's job. For example, the dean of a business school often finds it necessary to participate in figurehead activities such as commencement ceremonies, which are important for the long-term benefit of the school.
2. *The Leader Role* This role involves influencing or directing others. It is the set of responsibilities people typically associate with a manager's job, as the organization gives the manager formal authority over the work of other people. To the extent that managers are able to translate this authority into actual influence, they are exercising leadership behavior. A manager demonstrates leadership behavior when, for example, a newly appointed project team leader gathers her handpicked team members together and discusses the vision and goals for the team and how to accomplish them.
3. *The Liaison Role* This role emphasizes the contacts that a manager has with those outside the formal authority chain of command. These contacts include not only other managers within the organization but also many external individuals such as customers, suppliers, government officials, and managers from other organizations. It also emphasizes lateral interactions, as contrasted with vertical interpersonal interactions of a manager, and it highlights the fact that an important part of a manager's job is to serve as an integrator for his or her own unit and other units or groups. The liaison role applies to the situation where a marketing manager interacts with key customers to learn about their reactions to new product ideas.

Informational Roles

This set of roles builds on the interpersonal relationships that a manager establishes, and it underlines the importance of the network of contacts built up and maintained by the manager.[49] The three specific informational roles are the following:

1. *The Monitor Role* This type of behavior involves extensive information-seeking in which managers engage to remain aware of crucial developments that may affect their units and their own work. Such monitoring typically deals with spoken and written information and "soft" as well as "hard" facts. A manager attending an industry conference who spends considerable time in informal lobby and cocktail lounge conversations in order to gather data on current developments in the industry provides an example of this role.
2. *The Disseminator Role* A manager not only receives information but also sends it. This often includes information that the receiver wants but otherwise has no easy access to without the help of the manager. A supervisor who learns about the firm's reorganization plans affecting his or her department and conveys that information to his subordinates is acting in a disseminator role.
3. *The Spokesperson Role* A manager is frequently called upon to represent the views of the unit for which he or she is responsible. At lower management levels, this typically involves representing the unit to other individuals or groups within the organization; at higher management levels, this typically involves an external component, presenting the organization's activities and concerns to external constituents, such as customers and suppliers.[50] When the manager of the western region meets with other regional managers and presents the views of his region's sales personnel about how well a proposed new sales incentive plan is working, he is functioning in a spokesperson role.

Decisional Roles

The final category in the typology of roles relates to the decision-making requirements of a manager's job. There are four such decisional roles:

1. *The Entrepreneurial Role* Managers not only make routine decisions in their jobs but also frequently engage in activities that explore new opportunities or start new projects. Such entrepreneurial behavior within an organization often involves a series of small decisions that permit ongoing assessment about whether to continue or abandon new ventures. Playing this role often involves some risk, but the sequence of decisions usually limits this risk. Suppose, for example, that a lower-level production manager comes up with an idea for a new organizational sales unit. She then discusses the idea with her colleagues and, based on their reactions, modifies it and presents it to upper-level management. Such a manager is playing an entrepreneurial role that goes beyond her regular responsibilities.
2. *The Disturbance Handler Role* Managers initiate actions of their own, but they must also respond to problems or "disturbances." In this role, a manager often acts as a judge, problem solver, or conflict manager. The goal of such actions is to stop small problems from developing into larger ones. If a manager faces a situation in which employees cannot agree about who will do a particularly unpleasant but necessary task, the manager must settle the matter. In doing so, he or she is functioning as a disturbance handler.
3. *The Resource Allocator Role* Because resources must be managed efficiently in organizations and slack rarely exists, an important responsibility of managers is deciding how to distribute the resources. Such allocation decisions have a direct effect on the performance of a unit and indirectly communicate information to employees about the relative importance of the firm's activities. The manager of front desk services for a large resort hotel who decides how many and which clerks to assign to each shift is operating in a resource allocator role.
4. *The Negotiator Role* Managers are often called upon to make accommodations with other units or other organizations (depending on the level of the management position). In this decisional situation, managers are responsible for knowing what resources they can or cannot commit to particular negotiated solutions. A manager who serves on a negotiating team to establish a new joint venture with another company functions in the negotiator role.

Decisional roles are particularly important in managerial responsibilities. Managers are expected to make decisions, and many of them have important performance implications. For example, managers have to decide when to develop and take new products to the market, when to develop new ventures, when to hire and lay off employees, and so forth. They are expected to make these decisions efficiently, with due speed but also comprehensively.[51] Frequently, there are no clearly correct paths to follow. Rather, decisions often require that managers exercise reasonable judgment and use their education, training, and experience.[52]

This typology of managerial work roles emphasizes the considerable variety of behaviors required by managers. Certainly, the extent to which any particular role is important varies considerably from one managerial job to another. The front-line supervisor of a group of bank tellers is likely to have a different mix of roles than the bank's executive vice president. Nevertheless, the 10 roles help to understand the total set of activities that managers usually have to perform over time.

Managerial Job Dimensions

Analyzing the dimensions of managerial jobs provides additional insight about the work. A British researcher, Rosemary Stewart, developed one particular approach.[53] Stewart proposed that three dimensions characterize a managerial job, regardless of its level and type of unit in an organization:

- the demands made on it;
- the constraints placed on it; and
- the choices permitted in it.

Analyzing managerial jobs in this way not only provides further understanding of what managers do but also permits direct comparisons of different jobs; for example, how the position of "manager of information systems" compares with that of "marketing vice president" or "plant manager."

Demands

This dimension of management refers to what the holder of a particular managerial position must do. "Demands" involve two types: activities or duties to carry out and the standards or levels of minimum performance to meet. Demands can come from several sources, such as the organization, the immediate boss, or the organization of work activities. Typical types of demands include such behavior as attending required meetings, adhering to scheduled deadlines, following certain procedures, and the like. No doubt, for example, Meg Whitman has sales and performance targets to meet in her CEO position at eBay.

Constraints

"Constraints" are factors that limit a manager's response to various demands. One obvious constraint for any manager is the amount of time available for an activity. Other typical constraints include budgets, technology, the attitudes of subordinates, and legal regulations. All managerial jobs have constraints. Consequently, managers need to develop a good understanding of how to minimize or overcome these constraints.

Choices

This dimension underscores the fact that despite demands and constraints, managers always have the opportunity to exercise discretion. Thus, a manager regularly makes choices about what to do or not do, how to complete tasks, and which employees will participate in projects, among others. Frankly, discretion is an important part of managerial jobs. How they exercise it and the quality of the judgments that they make largely determine their effectiveness as managers. In her present and past managerial positions, Meg Whitman has faced a multitude of choices about how to make staffing decisions, how to demonstrate leadership, how to respond to changing market conditions affecting Internet use, and the like.

Exhibit 1.3 illustrates these three job dimensions for two different managerial jobs, a project team manager in a manufacturing company and a manager of a medium-sized fast-food restaurant. Although both are managerial jobs, their demands and constraints are quite different. Some of the choices permitted, however, are similar. The combination of the three dimensions determines the requirements to be a manager.

Exhibit 1.3 Two Managerial Jobs with Different Demands, Constraints, and Choices

	Job A: Project Team Manager	Job B: Fast-Food Restaurant Manager
Demands	■ Develop new product with strong market appeal ■ Hold formal weekly progress meeting with boss ■ Frequent travel to other company sites	■ Maintain attractive appearance of restaurant ■ Keep employee costs as low as possible ■ Meet standards for speed of service
Constraints	■ 12-month deadline for product development ■ Project budget limit of $1 million ■ No choice in selecting team members	■ Most employees have limited formal education ■ Few monetary incentives to reward outstanding performance ■ Federal and state health and safety regulations
Choices	■ The organizational structure of the project team ■ Sequencing of project tasks ■ Budget allocations	■ Selection of employee to promote to supervisor ■ Scheduling of shifts and assignments ■ Local advertising promotions

What Skills Do Managers Need?

Similar to other human activity, managing involves the exercise of skills, that is, highly developed abilities and competencies. Managers develop these skills through a combination of aptitude, education, training, and experience. Three types are critical for managerial tasks, particularly for the leadership component of management: technical, interpersonal, and conceptual (see Exhibit 1.4).

Technical
- Specialized knowledge (including when and how to use the skills)

Interpersonal
- Sensitivity
- Persuasiveness
- Empathy

Conceptual
- Logical reasoning
- Judgment
- Analytical ability

Exhibit 1.4 ■ Manager's Skills

Technical Skills

Technical skills involve having specialized knowledge about procedures, processes, equipment and include the related abilities of knowing how and when to use that knowledge. Research shows that these skills are especially important early in managerial careers (see Exhibit 1.5), when leading lower-level employees and gaining their respect is often part of a manager's job. In addition, technical skills seem to be particularly critical in many successful entrepreneurial start-up firms, such as those involving Steve Jobs and

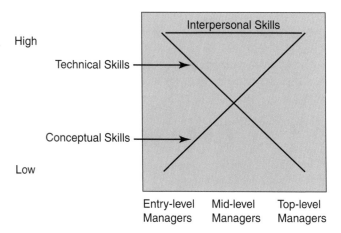

Exhibit 1.5 ■ Relative Importance of Managerial Skills at Different Organizational Levels

Steve Wozniak at Apple Computer or Bill Gates at Microsoft. Technical skills, whether in an entrepreneurial venture or in a larger organization, are frequently necessary but usually are not sufficient for managing effectively. An overreliance on technical skills may actually reduce a manager's overall effectiveness. The first Apple computer designed and built by Jobs and Wozniak required their technical skills to start the fledgling company. However, as Apple grew, their technical skills became relatively less important because they employed technical specialists. Jobs and Wozniak were not, however, always readily able to exchange those technical skills for other, equally impressive leadership skills. As a result, the company had to search for other managerial talent, and did so with mixed success. After gaining considerable managerial experience in other business endeavors, Jobs subsequently returned to lead Apple in the late 1990s with the assistance of other able managers.

Interpersonal Skills

Interpersonal skills such as sensitivity, persuasiveness, and empathy are important at all levels of management, although particularly so at lower and middle levels. A longitudinal study of career advancement conducted at AT&T found evidence that such skills, measured early in careers, were important in predicting advancement in managerial ranks 20 years later. However, a lack of these skills may prematurely limit managerial advancement even when other skills exist, but these skills alone are unlikely to guarantee managerial success. As the management researchers suggested, "The charming but not brilliant find that the job gets too big and the problems too complex to get by on interpersonal skills [alone]."[54]

Conceptual Skills

Often called cognitive ability or cognitive complexity, conceptual skills such as logical reasoning, judgment, and analytical abilities are a relatively strong predictor of managerial effectiveness. These skills are often a major determinant of who reaches the highest management levels of the organization. A clear example of someone who was selected for a CEO job precisely because of his conceptual skills is Jack Welch, the former CEO at General Electric. Welch was appointed to the top position at GE in 1981 and immediately set out to restructure the organization with the objective of making it more globally competitive. Over time and after several major changes in the organization, he reduced a significant amount of GE's bureaucracy and developed a more flexible organization. He also changed GE's corporate culture to one based on the greater empowerment of employees.

Endnotes

1. G. Davenport (trans. 1976). *Herakleitos and Diogenes*. Pt. 1. Fragment 23.
2. T. Reay, K. Golden-Biddle, and K. Germann. "Legitimizing a New Role: Small Wins and Microprocesses of Change." *Academy of Management Journal* 49 (2006): 977–996.
3. M. A. Hitt, B. W. Keats, and S. M. DeMarie. "Navigating in the New Competitive Landscape: Building Strategic Flexibility and Competitive Advantage in the 21st Century." *Academy of Management Executive* 12 no. 4 (1998): 22–42.
4. Ibid.
5. T. L. Friedman. *The World Is Flat* (New York: Farrar, Straus and Giroux. 2005).
6. M. A. Hitt. V. Franklin, and H. Zhu. "Culture, Institutions and International Strategy." *Journal of International Management* 12 (2006): 222–234.
7. Y. Luo and O. Shenkar. "The Multinational Corporation as a Multilingual Community: Language and Organization in a Global Context." *Journal of International Business Studies* 37 (2006): 321–339.
8. K. Meyer, "Globalfocusing: From Domestic Conglomerates to Global Specialists," *Journal of Management Studies* 43 (2006): 1109–1144.
9. D. G. Sirmon, M. A. Hitt, and R. D. Ireland. "Managing Firm Resources in Dynamic Environments to Create Value: Looking Inside the Black Box." *Academy of Management Review* 32 (2007): 273–292.
10. S. Thornhill. "Knowledge. Innovation and Firm Performance in High- and Low-Technology Regimes." *Journal of Business Venturing* 21 (2006): 687–703.
11. J. Salk and M. A. Lyles. "Gratitude Nostalgia and What Now? Knowledge Acquisition and Learning a Decade Later," *Journal of International Business Studies* 38 (2007): 19–26.
12. D. Tan and J. T. Mahoney. "Why a Multinational Firm Chooses Expatriates: Integrating Resource-based, Agency and Transaction Costs Perspectives." *Journal of Management Studies* 43 (2006): 457–484.
13. A. K. Gupta, K. G. Smith, and C. E. Shalley, "The Interplay Between Exploration and Exploitation." *Academy of Management Journal* 49 (2006): 693–706; D. Lavie, "Capability Reconfiguration: An Analysis of Incumbent Responses to Technological Change." *Academy of Management Review* 31 (2006): 153–174.
14. A. M. Mulcahy. From Survival to Success: Leading in Turbulent Times, speech in the U.S. Chamber of Commerce Leadership Series, Washington, D.C., www.uschamber.com, April 2, 2003.
15. R. E. Ployhart, "Staffing in the 21st Century: New Challenges and Strategic Opportunities," *Journal of Management* 32 (2006): 868–897.
16. M. A. Hitt, L. Bierman. K. Uhlenbruck, and K. Shimizu. "The Importance of Resources in the Internationalization of Professional Service Firms: The Good, the Bad and the Ugly." *Academy of Management Journal* 49 (2006): 1137–1157.
17. M. A. Hitt, R. D. Ireland, and R. E. Hoskisson. *Strategic Management: Competitiveness and Globalization* (Cincinnati. OH: Southwestern Publishing Co., 2007).
18. A. S. DeNisi, M. A. Hitt, and S. E. Jackson. "The Knowledge-Based Approach to Sustainable Competitive Advantage," in S. E. Jackson, M. A. Hitt, and A. S. DeNisi (eds.). *Managing Knowledge for Sustained Competitive Advantage* (San Francisco, CA: Jossey-Bass, 2003).
19. S. L. Newbert. "Empirical Research on the Resource-Based View of the Firm: An Assessment and Suggestions for Future Research." *Strategic Management Journal* 28 (2007): 121–146.
20. Sirmon, Hitt, and Ireland. "Managing Firm Resources in Dynamic Environments to Create Value."
21. G. Edmondson. C. Palmeri, B. Grow, and C. Tierney. "BMW Will Panke's High-Speed Approach Hurt the Brand?" *Business Week*, June 9, 2003, 57–60.
22. R. A. Baron, "Opportunity Recognition as Pattern Recognition: How Entrepreneurs 'Connect the Dots' to Identify New Business Opportunities." *Academy of Management Perspectives* 20 (2006): 104–119: J. M. Howell, C. M. Shea, and C. A. Higgins. "Champions of Product Innovations: Defining, Developing, and Validating a Measure of Champion Behavior." *Journal of Business Venturing* 20 (2005): 641–661.

23. M. A. Hitt, R. D. Ireland, S. M. Camp, and D. S. Sexton. *Strategic Entrepreneurship: Creating a New Mindset* (Oxford, UK: Blackwell Publishing, 2002).
24. R. McGrath and I. MacMillan. *The Entrepreneurial Mindset* (Boston: Harvard Business School Press, 2000).
25. R. D. Ireland, M. A. Hitt, and D. G. Sirmon, "A Model of Strategic Entrepreneurship: The Construct and Its Dimensions." *Journal of Management* 29 (2003): 963–989.
26. Ibid.
27. V. P. Rindova and W. H. Starbuck, "Ancient Chinese Theories of Control." *Journal of Management Inquiry* 6 (1997): 144–159.
28. D. A. Wren and R. G. Greenwood. *Management Innovators: The People and Ideas That Have Shaped Modern Business* (New York: Oxford University Press, 1998).
29. S. Wagner-Tsukamoto. "An Institutional Economic Reconstruction of Scientific Management: On the Lost Theoretical Logic of Taylorism." *Academy of Management Review* 32 (2007): 105–117.
30. Ibid.
31. S. J. Carroll and D. J. Gillen, "Are Classical Management Functions Useful in Describing Managerial Jobs and Behavior," *Academy of Management Review* 12 (1987): 39–51.
32. V. F. Misangyi. H. Elms, T. Greckhamer, and J. A. LePine. "A New Perspective on a Fundamental Debate: A Multilevel Approach to Industry. Corporate and Business Unit Effects." *Strategic Management Journal* 27 (2006): 571–590.
33. S. Brown and K. Blackmon. "Aligning Manufacturing Strategy and Business-Level Competitive Strategy in New Competitive Environments: The Case for Strategic Resonance." *Journal of Management Studies* 42 (2005): 793–815.
34. G. Dowell. "Product Line Strategies of New Entrants in an Established Industry: Evidence from the U.S. Bicycle Industry." *Strategic Management Journal* 27 (2006): 959–979.
35. S. Shane and F. Delmar. "Planning for the Market: Business Planning Before Marketing and the Continuation of Organizing Efforts," *Journal of Business Venturing* 19 (2004): 767–785.
36. J. L. Morrow, D. G. Sirmon, M. A. Hitt, and T. R. Holcomb. "Creating Value in the Face of Declining Performance: Firm Strategies and Organizational Recovery," *Strategic Management Journal* 28 (2007): 271–283.
37. M. Lindgren and J. Packendorff, "What's New in New Forms of Organizing? On the Construction of Gender in Project-based Work," *Journal of Management Studies* 43 (2006): 841–866.
38. G. Hoetker, "Do Modular Products Lead to Modular Organizations?" *Strategic Management Journal* 27 (2006): 501–518.
39. S. Karim, "Modularity in Organizational Structure: The Reconfiguration of Internally Developed and Acquired Business Units," *Strategic Management Journal* 27 (2006): 799–823.
40. A. W. Harzing, "Geographical Distance and the Role and Management of Subsidiaries: The Case of Subsidiaries Down-Under." *Asia-Pacific Journal of Management* 23 (2006): 167–185.
41. B. Erdogan, R. C. Liden, and M. L. Kraimer. "Justice and Leader-Member Exchange: The Moderating Role of Organizational Culture," *Academy of Management Journal* 49 (2006): 395–406.
42. D. S. Elenkov and I. M. Manev. "Top Management Leadership and Influence on Innovation: The Role of Sociocultural Context," *Journal of Management* 31 (2005): 381–402; R. T. Sparrowe, B. W. Soetjipto, and M. L. Kraimer. "Do Leaders' Influence Tactics Relate to Members' Helping Behaviors? It Depends on the Quality of the Relationship," *Academy of Management Journal* 49 (2006): 1194–1208.
43. R. F. Piccolo and J. A. Colquitt. "Transformational Leadership and Job Behaviors: The Mediating Role of Core Job Characteristics." *Academy of Management Journal* 49 (2006): 327–340.
44. P. Steel and C. L. Konig, "Integrating Theories of Motivation." *Academy of Management Review* 31 (2006): 889–913.
45. P. Balkundi and D. A. Harrison. "Ties. Leaders and Time in Teams: Strong Inference About Network Structure's Effects on Team Viability and Performance." *Academy of Management Journal* 49 (2006): 49–68: A. Srivastava, K. M. Bartol, and E. A. Locke,

"Empowering Leadership in Management Teams: Effects on Knowledge Sharing. Efficacy and Performance." *Academy of Management Journal* 49 (2006): 1239–1251.
46. T. R. Tyler and S. L. Blader. "Can Business Effectively Regulate Employee Conduct? The Antecedents of Rule Following in Work Settings," *Academy of Management Journal* 49 (2006): 1143–1158.
47. B. E. Litzky, K. A. Eddleston, and D. L. Kidder, "The Good, the Bad, and the Misguided," *Academy of Management Perspectives* 20 (2006): 91–103.
48. H. Mintzberg. "The Manager's Job: Folklore and Fact, *Harvard Business Review* 5 no. 4 (1975): 49–61.
49. G. K. Lee, "The Significance of Network Resources in Race to Enter Emerging Product Markets: The convergence of Telephony Communications and Computer Networking, 1989–2001," *Strategic Management Journal* 28 (2007): 17–37.
50. J. H. Dyer and N. W. Hatch. "Relation-specific Capability and Barriers to Knowledge Transfers: Creating Advancement Through Network Relationships," *Strategic Management Journal* 27 (2006): 701–719.
51. T. Talaulicar, J. Grundei, and A. V. Werder, "Strategic Decision Making in Start-ups: The Effect of Top Management Team Organization and Processes on Speed and Comprehensiveness," *Journal of Business Venturing* 20: 519–541.
52. E. Dane and M. G. Pratt. "Exploring Intuition and Its Role in Managerial Decision Making." *Academy of Management Review* 32 (2007): 33–54.
53. R. Stewart. "A Model for Understanding Managerial Jobs and Behavior." *Academy of Management Review* 7 (1982): 7–13.
54. M. W. McCall and M. M. Lombardo. *Off the Track* (Greensboro. NC: Center for Creative Leadership, 1983).

The Basics of Planning & Project Management 2

The Changing Workplace

Nintendo: "Wii Will Rock You"

Nintendo's legendary videogame designer Shigeru Miyamoto is lying face down on the floor in Kyoto, Japan, hobbled by a right cross and struggling to regain his composure. The man some credit with the very existence of the $30 billion videogame industry, the Walt Disney of our generation, has taken one blow to the face too many. I'm standing over the creative force behind Donkey Kong, Super Mario, Nintendogs and his latest worldwide sensation, the Wii. I goad him to get up for the rest of his beating.

Clearly, one of us is taking our boxing match a bit too seriously. After all, it's not really Miyamoto who has crumbled but rather his avatar—his Mii, in Nintendo parlance. "Ohhh" is about all the man can muster as the clock runs out. Miyamoto puts down his controller and concedes defeat to finish a photo shoot. I may have beaten him at his own game, but we both know who's the real winner here. Nintendo's newest contraption has performed exactly as designed, creating yet another Wiivangelist, this time a gloating *gaijin* 5,000 miles from home who not only got up off the couch to play a videogame but actually worked up a sweat. With this little victory Miyamoto and company gather more momentum in their quest to conquer worthier competition. . . .

Nintendo is churning out over a million units a month and still can't meet demand. At the Nintendo World store in New York City's Rockefeller Center, shipments arrive nightly. In the wee hours customers begin lining up around the block. Doors open at nine, and a few hours later the consoles are gone. In the world's gadget epicenter, Tokyo's Akihabara district, shopkeepers complain about the lack of inventory. Wii displays are covered with SOLD OUT signs, while piles of PlayStation3 boxes carry a different message: 5 percent OFF. Even the Nintendo of America company store near Seattle sees lines of employees, visitors and contractors. . . .

It's not unusual for a new game console to sell out during its pre-Christmas introduction, only to see sales dwindle come January. But six months after the Wii's launch, sales are accelerating. Nintendo sold 360,000 boxes in the U.S. in April [2007], 100,000 more than in March. That's two Wiis for every Xbox 360 and four for every PlayStation3. While Sony and Microsoft lose money on hardware in hopes of seeding the market with their consoles, analysts say Nintendo makes about $50 on every unit. It may not sound like much, but the company plans to sell 35 million of these things over the next few years. That's $1.75 billion in potential profit. . . .

More difficult to comprehend is how a company founded 118 years ago as a maker of playing cards in Kyoto came to be pummeling Microsoft and Sony. The answer has something to do with reinvention. From industry-changing arcade machines to handhelds, 3-D graphics to immersive game play, Nintendo has shown a knack for leapfrogging its industry. Sure, some initiatives failed—a toy vacuum cleaner, a taxi service, a chain of "love hotels"—but the company rarely fails to surprise. And if the Wii shortage demonstrates anything, it's that this time, in changing perceptions of gaming, Nintendo has surprised even itself.

In a quieter moment Miyamoto ponders that ability to chart a new course. "How Nintendo has been able to create one surprise after another is a big question even for me," he says. "I'd like to know the answer."

The word "Nintendo" is an amalgamation of three symbols: *nin*, meaning "leave to"; *ten*, for "heaven"; and *do*, "company." The most common translation in Kyoto is "the company that leaves to heaven." What that means is open to debate. It could be a resignation to fate, as in "The company's destiny is in heaven's hands." But it's clear from a series of exclusive interviews with several executives over three months in Japan and the U.S. that little is left to chance. Another translation might be "Take care of every detail, and heaven will take care of the rest."

The man who oversees every detail is president and CEO Satoru Iwata. Iwata, 47, started as a developer for a firm Nintendo bought in 2000. Since taking over in 2002 he has westernized Nintendo, instituting

(continued)

From Kreitner. *Custom POD: Preset Edition Management 10e with Student Study Guide and Crisis Management Chapter*, 10E. © 2007 South-Western, a part of Cengage Learning, Inc. Reproduced by permission. www.cengage.com/permissions.

performance-based raises and a retirement age of 65. To hear suppliers and contractors talk, working with Nintendo is both frustrating and inspirational. It can be Wal-Mart-esque, driving down prices by playing parts manufacturers against one another while challenging them to be more creative. Employees talk breathlessly about loving their jobs while grumbling about hectic schedules. Everyone flies commercial. The one person permitted in first class, Iwata himself, has been known to slog to London and back in one day for a press conference. No hotel required.

In short, Iwata has made Nintendo as efficient as a bullet train and as stingy as a bento box. The company's 3,400 employees generated $8.26 billion in revenue last year, or $2.5 million each. While exchange rates and fiscal calendars complicate comparisons to U.S. companies, let's do it anyway. Over roughly the same time frame, Microsoft employees generated $624,000 each; Google's performed 50 percent better, at $994,000, though still less than half as well as Nintendo employees. Nintendo's profits reached almost $1.5 billion, or $442,000 per employee, last year, compared with Microsoft's $177,000 and Google's $288,000.

Such gaudy numbers aren't the result of mere penny-pinching. Mainly they're a product of the strategic course Iwata has set. When he took over, PlayStation2 was king, and Microsoft, with its Xbox, was challenging Sony in a technological arms race. But Iwata felt his competitors were fighting the wrong battle. Cramming more technology into consoles would only make the games more expensive, harder to use, and worst of all, less fun. "We decided that Nintendo was going to take another route—game expansion," says Iwata, seated on the edge of a leather chair, leaning over green tea in a three-piece suit, a strip of gray emerging along the part in his thick hair. He has an easy command of English but speaks through an interpreter. "We are not competing against Sony or Microsoft. We are battling the indifference of people who have no interest in videogames."

Source: Excerpted from Jeffrey M. O'Brien, "Wii Will Rock You," *Fortune* (June 11, 2007): 82–92. © 2007 Time Inc. All rights reserved.

There is an old saying in management circles about the need to plan: "Organizations that fail to plan, plan to fail." Nintendo is a consistent winner because it formulates detailed plans and carries them out with diligence. But even Nintendo can't eliminate uncertainty in the global marketplace, as evidenced by inventory shortages in the face of unexpectedly high demand for its Wii game systems. Yes, amid all the uncertainty, even *success* can be a problem for today's planners.

Planning is the process of coping with uncertainty by formulating future courses of action to achieve specified results. Planning enables humans to achieve great things by envisioning a pathway from concept to reality. The greater the mission, the longer and more challenging the pathway. For example, imagine the challenges awaiting Starbucks. In 2006, *Fortune* magazine reported Howard Schultz's ambitious growth plan: "the head of the world's largest coffee-shop chain said he plans to more than triple the number of stores, to 40,000, with half in the U.S. and half overseas."[1] Planning is a never-ending process because of constant change, uncertainty, new competition, unexpected problems, and emerging opportunities.[2]

Because planning affects all downstream management functions (see Exhibit 2.1), it has been called the primary management function. With this model in mind, we shall discuss uncertainty, highlight five essential aspects of the planning function, and take a close look at management by objectives and project planning. We shall also introduce four practical tools (flow charts, Gantt charts, PERT networks, and breakeven analysis).

Coping with Uncertainty

Ben Franklin said the only sure things in life are death and taxes. Although this is a gloomy prospect, it does capture a key theme of modern life. We are faced with a great deal of uncertainty. Organizations, like individuals, are continually challenged to accomplish something in spite of general uncertainty.[3] Organizations meet this challenge largely through planning. As a context for our discussion of planning in this and the following chapter, let us explore environmental uncertainty from two perspectives: (1) types of uncertainty and (2) organizational responses to environmental uncertainty.

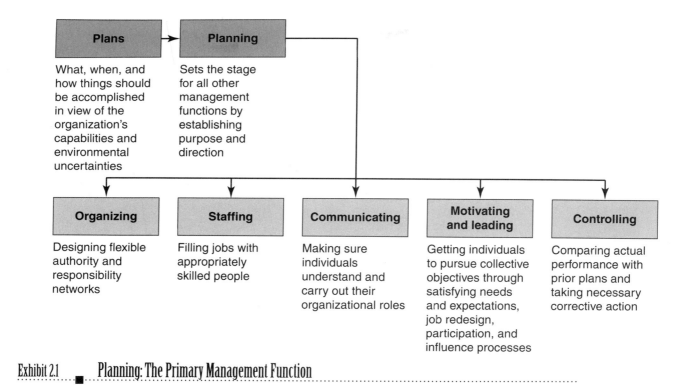

Exhibit 2.1 ■ Planning: The Primary Management Function

Three Types of Uncertainty

Through the years, *environmental uncertainty* has been a catch-all term among managers and researchers. However, research indicates that people actually perceive three types of environmental uncertainty: state uncertainty, effect uncertainty, and response uncertainty. State uncertainty occurs when the environment, or a portion of the environment, is considered unpredictable. A manager's attempt to predict the *effects* of specific environmental changes or events on his or her organization involves effect uncertainty. Response uncertainty is inability to predict the *consequences* of a particular decision or organizational response.[4]

A simple analogy can help us conceptually sort out these three types of uncertainty. Suppose you are a golfer, and on your way to the course you wonder whether it is going to rain; this is *state uncertainty*. Next, you experience *effect uncertainty* because you are not sure whether it will rain hard enough, if it does rain, to make you quit before finishing nine holes. Soon you begin weighing your chances of making par if you have to adjust your choice of golf clubs to poor playing conditions; now you are experiencing *response uncertainty*. Each of the three types of perceived uncertainty could affect your golfing attitude and performance. Similarly, managers are affected by their different perceptions of environmental factors. Their degree of uncertainty may vary from one type of uncertainty to another. A manager may, for example, be unsure about whether a key employee is about to quit (considerable state uncertainty) but very sure that productivity would suffer without that individual (little effect uncertainty).[5]

Organizational Responses to Uncertainty

Some organizations do a better job than others of planning amid various combinations of uncertainty. This is due in part to differing patterns of response to environmental factors beyond the organization's immediate control. As outlined in Table 2.1, organizations cope with environmental uncertainty by adopting one of four positions vis-a-vis the environment in which they operate. These are the positions taken by defenders, prospectors, analyzers, and reactors,[6] and each position has its own characteristic impact on planning.

Table 2.1 Different Organizational Responses to an Uncertain Environment

Type of Organizational Response	Characteristics of Response
1. Defenders	Highly expert at producing and marketing a few products in a narrowly defined market
	Opportunities beyond present market not sought
	Few adjustments in technology, organization structure, and methods of operation because of narrow focus
	Primary attention devoted to efficiency of current operations
2. Prospectors	Primary attention devoted to searching for new market opportunities
	Frequent development and testing of new products and services
	Source of change and uncertainty for competitors
	Loss of efficiency because of continual product and market innovation
3. Analyzers	Simultaneous operations in stable and changing product/market domains
	In relatively stable product/market domain, emphasis on formalized structures and processes to achieve routine and efficient operation
	In changing product/market domain, emphasis on detecting and copying competitors' most promising ideas
4. Reactors	Frequently unable to respond quickly to perceived changes in environment
	Make adjustments only when finally forced to do so by environmental pressures

Source: Adapted from *Organizational Strategy, Structure, and Process,* by Raymond E. Miles and Charles C. Snow. Copyright © 1978, McGraw-Hill Book Company, p. 29.

Defenders

A defender can be successful as long as its primary technology and narrow product line remain competitive. But defenders can become stranded on a dead-end road if their primary market seriously weakens. A prime example of a defender is Harley-Davidson, which sold its recreational vehicle division and other nonmotorcycle businesses to get back to basics. Harley-Davidson enjoys such fierce brand loyalty among Hog riders that many sport a tattoo of the company's logo. Can you imagine a Coca-Cola or a Wal-Mart tattoo? But Harley-Davidson runs the risk of having its narrow focus miss the mark in an aging America. Specifically, the median age of Harley buyers rose from 35 in 1987 to 46 in 2002. Harley-Davidson is therefore seeking to lure younger riders who prefer sleek bikes away from Honda and other Japanese rivals.[7]

Prospectors

Prospector organizations are easy to spot because they have a reputation for aggressively making things happen rather than waiting for them to happen. But life is challenging for prospectors such as Amazon.com Inc.:

> In some ways, Amazon is the ultimate example of transformation. Despite constant criticism, Amazon CEO Jeffrey P. Bezos quickly moved the company beyond books to other media, then to electronics, and just about everything else. Now Bezos is working on his next diversification play: offering other businesses spare computing and storage capacity, as well as leftover space in Amazon's huge distribution centers. The strategy has yet to deliver

> *meaningful revenues, or any profits. But as Bezos will tell you, it reflects a never-ending need to search for the next source of tech growth.*[8]

Prospectors (or pioneers) traditionally have been admired for their ability to gain what strategists call a *first-mover advantage*. In other words, the first one to market wins. Following the Internet crash, when many dot-com pioneers were the first to go bankrupt, the first-mover advantage was given a second look. Two researchers, one from the United States and the other from France, recently offered this insight about both industrial and consumer goods companies: "... we found that over the long haul, early movers are considerably *less* profitable than later entrants. Although pioneers do enjoy sustained revenue advantages, they also suffer from persistently *high* costs, which eventually overwhelm the sales gains."[9] Prospectors need to pick their opportunities very carefully, selecting those with the best combination of feasibility and profit potential. This is especially true for entrepreneurs starting small businesses.[10]

Analyzers

An essentially conservative strategy of following the leader marks an organization as an analyzer. It is a "me too" response to environmental uncertainty. Analyzers let market leaders take expensive R&D risks and then imitate or build upon what works. This slower, more studied approach can pay off when the economy turns down and prospectors stumble. A classic example is Israel's Teva Pharmaceuticals, a maker of generic drugs that sell for much less than brand-name drugs:

> *You may never have heard of the Israeli company. But you could very well be taking one of its drugs. One in every 15 prescriptions in the U.S. is a Teva product, making the company this country's largest drug supplier. With $3.3 billion in revenues, it sells more than 450 drugs in North America, Europe, and Israel—everything from antibiotics to heart medicines....*
>
> *Chief executive Israel Makov doesn't have any illusions about turning Teva into a brand-name producer.... His goal is to double sales every four years by remaining largely a maker of me-too medications.*[11]

Although analyzers such as generic drug companies may not get a lot of respect, they perform the important economic function of breaking up overly concentrated industries. Customers appreciate the resulting lower prices, too.

Reactors

The reactor is the exact opposite of the prospector. Reactors wait for adversity, such as declining sales, before taking corrective steps. They are slow to develop new products to supplement their tried-and-true ones. Their strategic responses to changes in the environment are often late. An instructive example in this area is Kodak:

> *Kodak continues to grapple with one of the harshest corporate transitions of the past decade. Its 100-year-old film business is waning in the face of digital photography, which exploded [in 2003]....*
>
> *The company cautiously moved into digital photography in the mid-1990s but never made the transition away from film. Now, it might be too late.*
>
> *"Kodak saw this coming," says Michael Raynor, co-author of management best-seller* The Innovator's Solution. *But instead of driving a transition earlier and building up a digital business, it's now "leaping on a train when it's going 70 miles per hour," Raynor says.*[12]

Not surprisingly, Kodak's global workforce has been cut by one-third (about 31,000 employees) over the last decade.[13] According to one field study, reactors tended to be less profitable than defenders, prospectors, and analyzers.[14]

Balancing Planned Action and Spontaneity in the Twenty-First Century

In the obsolete command-and-control management model, plans were considered destiny. Top management formulated exacting plans for every aspect of operations and then kept everything under tight control to "meet the plan." All too often, however, plans were derailed by unanticipated events, and success was dampened by organizational inflexibility. Today's progressive managers see plans as general guidelines for action, based on imperfect and incomplete information. Planning is no longer the exclusive domain of top management; it now typically involves those who carry out the plans because they are closer to the customer. Planning experts, who recommend *strategic agility*,[15] say managers need to balance planned action with the flexibility to take advantage of surprise events and unexpected opportunities. A good analogy is to an improvisational comedy act.[16] The stand-up comic has a plan for the introduction, structure of the act, some tried-and-true jokes, and closing remarks. Within this planned framework, the comic will play off the audience's input and improvise as necessary. Accordingly, 3M Corporation had a plan for encouraging innovation that allowed it to capitalize on the spontaneous success of the Post-it Note.[17] Planning should be a springboard to success, not a barrier to creativity.

The Essentials of Planning

Planning is an ever-present feature of modern life, although there is no universal approach. Virtually everyone is a planner, at least in the informal sense. We plan leisure activities after school or work; we make career plans. Personal or informal plans give purpose to our lives. In a similar fashion, more formalized plans enable managers to mobilize their intentions to accomplish organizational purposes. A plan is a specific, documented intention consisting of an objective and an action statement. The objective portion is the end, and the action statement represents the means to that end. Stated another way, objectives give management targets to shoot at, whereas action statements provide the arrows for hitting the targets. Properly conceived plans tell *what*, *when*, and *how* something is to be done.

In spite of the wide variety of formal planning systems that managers encounter on the job, we can identify some essentials of sound planning. Among these common denominators are organizational mission, types of planning, objectives, priorities, and the planning/control cycle.

Organizational Mission

To some, defining an organization's mission might seem to be an exercise in the obvious. But exactly the opposite is true. Some organizations drift along without a clear mission. Others lose sight of their original mission. Sometimes an organization, such as the U.S. Army Corps of Engineers, finds its original mission no longer acceptable to key stakeholders. In fact, the Corps is stepping back from its tradition of building dams and levees, in favor of more environmentally sensitive projects. It has tackled "a 30-year, $7.8 billion restoration of the Florida Everglades"[18] that will involve tearing down levees to restore the natural flow of the Kissimmee River. Periodically redefining an organization's mission is both common and necessary in an era of rapid change.

A clear, formally written, and publicized statement of an organization's mission is the cornerstone of any planning system that will effectively guide the organization through uncertain times. The satirical definition by Scott Adams, the Dilbert cartoonist, tells us how *not* to write an organizational mission statement: "A Mission Statement is defined as a long, awkward sentence that demonstrates management's inability to think clearly."[19] This sad state of affairs, too often true, can be avoided by a well-written mission statement that does the following things:

1. *Defines* your organization for key stakeholders
2. Creates an *inspiring vision* of what the organization can be and can do
3. Outlines *how* the vision is to be accomplished
4. Establishes key *priorities*
5. States a *common goal* and fosters a sense of togetherness
6. Creates a *philosophical anchor* for all organizational activities
7. Generates *enthusiasm* and a "can do" attitude
8. *Empowers* present and future organization members to believe that *every* individual is the key to success[20]

A good mission statement provides a focal point for the entire planning process. When Vincent A. Sarni took the top job at PPG, the large glass and paint company, he created a document he called "Blueprint for the Decade." In it he specified the company's mission and corporate objectives for such things as service, quality, and financial performance.

> *Sarni ... trudged from plant to plant preaching the virtues in his Little Blue Book. "My first two or three years I always started with a discussion of the Blueprint," he says. "I don't have to do that anymore. The Blueprint's on the shop floor, and it has meaning."*[21]

Types of Planning

Ideally, planning begins at the top of the organizational pyramid and filters down. The rationale for beginning at the top is the need for coordination. It is top management's job to state the organization's mission, establish strategic priorities, and draw up major policies. After these statements are in place, successive rounds of strategic, intermediate, and operational planning can occur. Exhibit 2.2 presents an idealized picture of the three types of planning, as carried out by different levels of management.

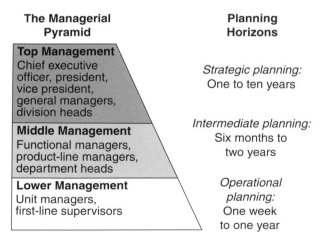

Exhibit 2.2 — Types of Planning

Strategic, Intermediate, and Operational Planning

Strategic planning is the process of determining how to pursue the organization's long-term goals with the resources expected to be available.[22] A well-conceived strategic plan communicates much more than general intentions about profit and growth. It specifies *how* the organization will achieve a competitive advantage, with profit and growth as necessary by-products. Intermediate planning is the process of determining the contributions that subunits can make with allocated resources. Finally, operational planning is the process of determining how specific tasks can best be accomplished on time with available resources. Each level of planning is vital to an organization's success and cannot effectively stand alone without the support of the other two levels.

Planning Horizons

As Exhibit 2.2 illustrates, planning horizons vary for the three types of planning. The term planning horizon refers to the time that elapses between the formulation and the execution of a planned activity. As the planning process evolves from strategic to operational, planning horizons shorten and plans become increasingly specific. Naturally, management can be more confident—and hence more specific—about the near future than about the distant future.

Note, however, that the three planning horizons overlap, their boundaries being elastic rather than rigid. The trend today is toward involving employees from all levels in the strategic planning process. Also, it is not uncommon for top and lower managers to have a hand in formulating intermediate plans. Middle managers often help lower managers draw up operational plans as well. Hence Exhibit 2.2 is an ideal instructional model with countless variations in the workplace.

Objectives

Just as a distant port is the target or goal for a ship's crew, objectives are targets that organization members steer toward. Although some theorists distinguish between goals and objectives, managers typically use the terms interchangeably. A goal or an objective is defined as a specific commitment to achieve a measurable result within a given time frame. Many experts view objectives as the single most important feature of the planning process. They help managers and entrepreneurs build a bridge between their dreams, aspirations, and visions and an achievable *reality*. Dan Sullivan, a consultant for entrepreneurs, explains:

> *[Objectives and goals] should be achievable by definition. If you are setting functional goals, at useful increments, they should be both real and realizable. The distance between where you actually are now and your goal can be measured objectively, and when you achieve your goal, you know it. Think of the distinction this way: no matter how fast you run toward the horizon, you'll never get there, but if you run more quickly toward a goalpost, you will get there faster. Sounds simplistic, but I'm constantly amazed at how many people—and entrepreneurs in particular—confuse their goals with their ideals.*[23]

It is important for present and future managers to be able to write good objectives, to be aware of their importance, and to understand how objectives combine to form a means-ends chain.

Writing Good Objectives

An authority on objectives recommends that "as far as possible, objectives [should be] expressed in quantitative, measurable, concrete terms, in the form of a written statement of desired results to be achieved within a given time period."[24] In other words, objectives represent a firm commitment to accomplish something specific. A well-written objective should state what is to be accomplished and when it is to be accomplished. In the following sample objectives, note that the desired results are expressed *quantitatively*, in units of output, dollars, or percentage of change.

- To increase subcompact car production by 240,000 units during the next production year
- To reduce bad-debt loss by $50,000 during the next six months
- To achieve an 18 percent increase in Brand X sales by December 31 of the current year

For actual practice in writing good objectives and plans, see the Action Learning exercise at the end of this chapter.

The Importance of Objectives

From the standpoint of planning, carefully prepared objectives benefit managers by serving as targets and measuring sticks, fostering commitment, and enhancing motivation.[25]

- *Targets.* As mentioned earlier, objectives provide managers with specific targets. Without objectives, managers at all levels would find it difficult to make coordinated decisions. People quite naturally tend to pursue their own ends in the absence of formal organizational objectives.
- *Measuring sticks.* An easily overlooked, after-the-fact feature of objectives is that they are useful for measuring how well an organizational subunit or individual has performed. When appraising performance, managers need an established standard against which they can measure performance. Concrete objectives enable managers to weigh performance objectively on the basis of accomplishment, rather than subjectively on the basis of personality or prejudice.
- *Commitment.* The very process of getting an employee to agree to pursue a given objective gives that individual a personal stake in the success of the enterprise. Thus objectives can be helpful in encouraging personal commitment to collective ends. Without individual commitment, even well-intentioned and carefully conceived strategies are doomed to failure.
- *Motivation.* Good objectives represent a challenge—something to reach for. Accordingly, they have a motivational aspect. People usually feel good about themselves and what they do when they successfully achieve a challenging objective. Moreover, objectives give managers a rational basis for rewarding performance. Employees who believe they will be equitably rewarded for achieving a given objective will be motivated to perform well.

The Means-Ends Chain of Objectives

Like the overall planning process, objective setting is a top-to-bottom proposition. Top managers set broader objectives with longer time horizons than do successively lower levels of managers. In effect, this downward flow of objectives creates a means-ends chain. Working from bottom to top in Exhibit 2.3, supervisory-level objectives provide the means for achieving middle-level objectives (ends) that, in turn, provide the means for achieving top-level objectives (ends).

The organizational hierarchy in Exhibit 2.3 has, of course, been telescoped and narrowed at the middle and lower levels for illustrative purposes. Usually, two or three layers of management would separate the president and the product-line managers.

Another layer or two would separate product-line managers from area sales managers. But the telescoping helps show that lower-level objectives provide the means for accomplishing higher-level ends or objectives.

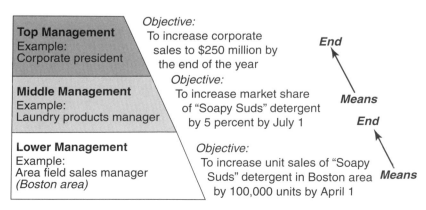

Exhibit 2.3 — **A Typical Means-Ends Chain of Objectives**

Priorities (Both Strategic and Personal)

Defined as a ranking of goals, objectives, or activities in order of importance, priorities play a special role in planning. By listing long-range organizational objectives in order of their priority, top management prepares to make later decisions regarding the allocation of resources. Limited time, talent, and financial and material resources need to be channeled into more important endeavors and away from other areas in proportion to the relative priority of the areas. Establishment of priorities is a key factor in managerial and organizational effectiveness. Strategic priorities give both insiders and outsiders answers to the questions "Why does the organization exist?" and "How should it act and react during a crisis?" An inspiring illustration of the latter occurred for American Express after the September 11, 2001, terrorist attacks:

> *The hundreds of ad hoc decisions made by [new CEO Kenneth I.] Chenault and his team were guided by two overriding concerns: employee safety and customer service. AmEx helped 560,000 stranded cardholders get home, in some cases chartering airplanes and buses to ferry them across the country. It waived millions of dollars in delinquent fees on late-paying cardholders and increased credit limits to cash-starved clients. . . .*
>
> *Most telling, Chenault gathered 5,000 American Express employees at the Paramount Theater in New York on Sept. 20 for a highly emotional "town hall meeting." During the session, Chenault demonstrated . . . poise, compassion, and decisiveness.*[26]

The A-B-C Priority System

Despite time-management seminars, day planners, and computerized "personal digital assistants," establishing priorities remains a subjective process affected by organizational politics and value conflicts.[27] Although there is no universally acceptable formula for carrying out this important function, the following A-B-C priority system is helpful.

- A. "Must do" objectives *critical* to successful performance. They may be the result of special demands from higher levels of management or other external sources.
- B. "Should do" objectives *necessary* for improved performance. They are generally vital, but their achievement can be postponed if necessary.
- C. "Nice to do" objectives *desirable* for improved performance, but not critical to survival or improved performance. They can be eliminated or postponed to achieve objectives of higher priority.[28]

Home Depot uses an interesting and effective color-coded variation of this approach. According to *Business Week:* ". . . when a to-do list for managers arrives electronically, it is marked in green. If it isn't done by the set date, it changes to red—and district managers can pounce."[29]

The 80/20 Principle

Another proven priority-setting tool is the 80/20 principle (or Pareto analysis, as mentioned in Chapter 2). "The 80/20 principle asserts that a minority of causes, inputs, or effort usually leads to a majority of the results, outputs, or rewards."[30] Care needs to be taken not to interpret the 80/20 formula too literally—it is approximate. Managers can leverage their time by focusing on the *few* people, problems, or opportunities with the *greatest* impact. Consider this situation, for example:

> *Market Line Associates, an Atlanta financial consultancy, estimates that the top 20% of customers at a typical commercial bank generate up to six times as much revenue as they cost, while the bottom fifth cost three to four times more than they make for the company.*[31]

For profit-minded banks and other businesses, all customers are not alike. Indeed, ING Bank, the U.S. subsidiary of the Dutch insurance giant ING, "'fires' about 3,600 of its 2 million customers every year. Ditching clients who are too time-consuming saves the company at least $1 million annually."[32] How would business purists who say, "The customer is always right," feel about this practice?

Avoiding the "Busyness" Trap

These two simple yet effective tools for establishing priorities can help managers avoid the so-called *busyness trap*.[33] In these fast-paced times, managers should not confuse being busy with being effective and efficient. *Results* are what really count. Activities and speed, without results, are an energy-sapping waste of time. By slowing down a bit, having clear priorities, and taking a strategic view of daily problems, busy managers can be successful *and* "get a life."[34]

Finally, managers striving to establish priorities amid lots of competing demands would do well to heed Peter Drucker's advice—that the most important skill for setting priorities and managing time is simply learning to say "no."

The Planning/Control Cycle

To put the planning process in perspective, it is important to show how it is connected with the control function. Exhibit 2.4 illustrates the cyclical relationship between planning and control. Planning gets things headed in the right direction, and control keeps them headed in the right direction (see Ethics: Character, Courage, and Values). Basically, each of the three levels of planning is a two-step sequence followed by a two-step control sequence.

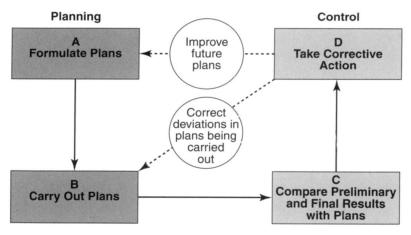

Exhibit 2.4   The Basic Planning/Control Cycle

The initial planning/control cycle begins when top management establishes strategic plans. When those strategic plans are carried out, intermediate and operational plans are formulated, thus setting in motion two more planning/control cycles. As strategic, intermediate, and operational plans are carried out, the control function begins. Corrective action is necessary when either the preliminary or the final results deviate from plans. For planned activities still in progress, the corrective action can get things back on track before it is too late. Deviations between final results and plans, on the other hand, are instructive feedback for the improvement of future plans. The broken lines in Exhibit 2.4 represent the important sort of feedback that makes the planning/control cycle a dynamic and evolving process. Our attention now turns to some practical planning tools.

Management by Objectives and Project Planning

In this section we examine a traditional planning technique and a modern planning challenge. Valuable lessons about planning can be learned from each.

Management by Objectives

Management by objectives (MBO) is a comprehensive management system based on measurable and participatively set objectives. MBO has come a long way since it was first suggested by Peter Drucker in 1954 as a means of promoting managerial self-control.[35] MBO theory[36] and practice subsequently mushroomed and spread around the world. In one form or another, and under various labels, MBO has been adopted by most public and private organizations of any significant size. For example, at Cypress Semiconductor Corporation, the San Jose, California, electronics firm, computerization paved the way for high-tech MBO. T. J. Rodgers, the company's founder and chief executive officer, explains:

> *All of Cypress's 1,400 employees have goals, which, in theory, makes them no different from employees at most other companies. What makes our people different is that every week they set their own goals, commit to achieving them by a specific date, enter them into a database, and report whether or not they completed prior goals. Cypress's computerized goal system is an important part of our managerial infrastructure. It is a detailed guide to the future and an objective record of the past. In any given week, some 6,000 goals in the database come due. Our ability to meet those goals ultimately determines our success or failure. . . .*
>
> *I developed the goal system long before personal computers existed. It has its roots in management-by-objectives techniques I learned in the mid-1970s at American Microsystems.*[37]

The common denominator that has made MBO programs so popular in management theory and practice is the emphasis on objectives that are both *measurable* and *participatively set*.

The MBO Cycle

Because MBO combines planning and control, the four-stage MBO cycle corresponds to the planning/control cycle outlined in Exhibit 2.4. Steps 1 and 2 make up the planning phase of MBO, and steps 3 and 4 are the control phase.

1. *Step 1: Setting objectives.* A hierarchy of challenging, fair, and internally consistent objectives is the necessary starting point for the MBO cycle and serves as the foundation for all that follows. All objectives, according to MBO theory, should be reduced to writing and put away for later reference during steps 3 and 4. Consistent with what was said earlier about objectives, objective setting in MBO begins at the top of the managerial pyramid and filters down, one layer at a time.

    MBO's main contribution to the objective-setting process is its emphasis on the participation and involvement of people at lower levels. There is no place in MBO for the domineering manager ("Here are the objectives I've written for you") or for the passive manager ("I'll go along with whatever objectives you set"). MBO calls for a give-and-take negotiation of objectives between the manager and those who report directly to him or her.[38]

2. *Step 2: Developing action plans.* With the addition of action statements to the participatively set objectives, the planning phase of MBO is complete. Managers at each level develop plans that incorporate objectives established in step 1. Higher managers are responsible for ensuring that their direct assistants' plans complement one another and do not work at cross-purposes.

3. *Step 3: Periodic review.* As plans turn into action, attention turns to step 3, monitoring performance. Advocates of MBO usually recommend face-to-face meetings between a manager and his or her people at three-, six-, and nine-month intervals. (Some organizations, such as Cypress, rely on shorter cycles.) These periodic checkups permit those who are responsible for a particular set of objectives to reconsider them, checking their validity in view of unexpected events—added duties or the loss of a key assistant—that could make

them obsolete. If an objective is no longer valid, it is amended accordingly. Otherwise, progress toward valid objectives is assessed. Periodic checkups also afford managers an excellent opportunity to give their people needed and appreciated feedback.

4. *Step 4: Performance appraisal.* At the end of one complete cycle of MBO, typically one year after the original goals were set, final performance is compared with the previously agreed-upon objectives. The pairs of superior and subordinate managers who mutually set the objectives one year earlier meet face to face once again to discuss how things have turned out. MBO emphasizes results, not personalities or excuses. The control phase of the MBO cycle is completed when success is rewarded with promotion, merit pay, or other suitable benefits and when failure is noted for future corrective action.

After one round of MBO, the cycle repeats itself, with each cycle contributing to the learning process. A common practice in introducing MBO is to start at the top and to pull a new layer of management into the MBO process each year. Experience has shown that plunging several layers of management into MBO all at once often causes confusion, dissatisfaction, and failure. In fact, even a moderate-sized organization usually takes five or more years to evolve a full-blown MBO system that ties together such areas as planning, control, performance appraisal, and the reward system. MBO programs can be facilitated by using off-the-shelf software programs. Such programs offer helpful spreadsheet formats for goal setting, timelines, at-a-glance status boards, and performance reports. MBO proponents believe that effective leadership and greater motivation—through the use of realistic objectives, more effective control, and self-control—are the natural by-products of a proper MBO system.[39]

Strengths and Limitations of MBO

Any widely used management technique is bound to generate debate about its relative strengths and weaknesses, and MBO is no exception.[40] Present and future managers will have more realistic expectations for MBO if they are familiar with both sides of this debate. The four primary strengths of MBO and four common complaints about it are compared in Exhibit 2.5.

This debate will probably not be resolved in the near future. Critics of MBO, such as the late quality expert W. Edwards Deming, point to both theoretical and methodological flaws.[41] Meanwhile, MBO advocates insist that it is the misapplication of MBO, not the MBO concept itself, that leads to problems. In the final analysis, MBO will probably work when organizational conditions are favorable and will probably fail when those conditions are unfavorable. A favorable climate for MBO includes top-management commitment, openness to change, Theory Y management, and employees who are willing and able to shoulder greater responsibility.[42] Research justifies putting *top-management commitment* at the top of the list. In a review of 70 MBO studies, researchers found that "when top-management commitment was high, the average gain in productivity was 56 percent. When such commitment was low,

Strengths	Limitations
• MBO blends planning and control into a rational system of management.	• MBO is too often sold as a cure-all.
• MBO forces an organization to develop a top-to-bottom hierarchy of objectives.	• MBO is easily stalled by authoritarian (Theory X) managers and inflexible bureaucratic policies and rules.
• MBO emphasizes end results rather than good intentions or personalities.	• MBO takes too much time and effort and generates too much paperwork.
• MBO encourages self-management and personal commitment through employee participation in setting objectives.	• MBO's emphasis on measurable objectives can be used as a threat by overzealous managers.

Exhibit 2.5   MBO's Strengths and Limitations

the average gain in productivity was only 6 percent."[43] A strong positive relationship was also found between top-management commitment to MBO program success and employee job satisfaction.[44] The greater management's commitment, the greater the satisfaction.

Project Planning and Management

Project-based organizations are becoming the norm today. Why? Concept-to-market times are being honed to the minimum in today's technology-driven world.[45] Typically, cross-functional teams of people with different technical skills are brought together on a temporary basis to complete a specific project as swiftly as possible. According to the 240,000-member Project Management Institute, "A project is a temporary endeavor undertaken to achieve a particular aim."[46] Projects, like all other activities within the management domain, need to be systematically planned and managed. What sets project planning/management apart is the *temporary* nature of projects, as contrasted to the typical ongoing or continuous activities in organizations. Projects may be pursued within the organization or performed for outside clients. When the job is done, project members disband and move on to other projects or return to their usual work routines. Time is usually of the essence for project managers because of tight schedules and deadlines. For example, put yourself in the shoes of the executive project manager at book publisher Scholastic faced with the following challenge:

> *Print 12 million copies of the highly anticipated* Harry Potter and the Deathly Hallows—*a record first printing in publishing—and deliver them to thousands of retailers around the U.S.*
>
> *The daunting part was synchronizing shipments to arrive no more than a day (or hours) before the scheduled July 21 [2007] 12:01 a.m. release—to minimize the risk of someone's leaking the book's ending.*
>
> *Even before author J. K. Rowling delivered the manuscript . . . [in early 2007], Scholastic was in full battle planning. Executives from its manufacturing and logistics divisions were meeting with printers and trucking companies to make sure they could deliver on the tight turnaround required to get the book to fans before summer vacation ended.*[47]

Project management is the usual thing on Hollywood movie sets and at construction companies building homes, roads, and skyscrapers. But it is newer to manufacturers, banks, insurance companies, hospitals, and government agencies. Unfortunately, much of this Internet-age project management leaves a lot to be desired. For example, consider the dismal track record for information technology (IT) projects, typically involving conversion of an old computer system to new hardware, software, and work methods.

> *Most large IT projects are delivered late and over budget because they are inefficiently managed. A study by the Hackett Group, a Hudson, Ohio–based benchmarking firm, found that the average company completes only 37 percent of large IT projects on time and only 42 percent on budget.*[48]

A broader and deeper understanding of project management is in order.

Project managers face many difficult challenges. First and foremost, they work outside the normal organizational hierarchy or chain of command because projects are ad hoc and temporary. Consequently, they must rely on excellent "people management skills" instead of on giving orders.[49] Those skills include, but are not limited to, communication, motivation, leadership, conflict resolution, and negotiation.

Project *planning* deserves special attention in this chapter because project managers have the difficult job of being both intermediate/tactical and operational planners. They are responsible for both the big picture and the little details of their project. A project that is not well planned is a project doomed to failure. So let us take a look at the project life cycle, project management software, the six roles project managers play, and guidelines for project managers.

The Project Life Cycle

Every project, from developing a new breakfast cereal to staging a benefit rock concert, has a predictable four-stage life cycle. As shown in Exhibit 2.6, the four stages are conceptualization, planning, execution, and termination. Although they are shown equally spaced in Exhibit 2.6, the four stages typically involve varying periods of time. Sometimes the borders between stages blur. For example, project goal setting actually begins in the conceptualization stage and often carries over to the planning stage. During this stage, project managers turn their attention to facilities and equipment, personnel and task assignments, and scheduling. Work on the project begins in the execution stage, and additional resources are acquired as needed. Budget demands are highest during the execution stage because everything is in motion. To some, the label "termination" in stage 4 might suggest a sudden end to the project. But more typically, the completed project is turned over to an end user

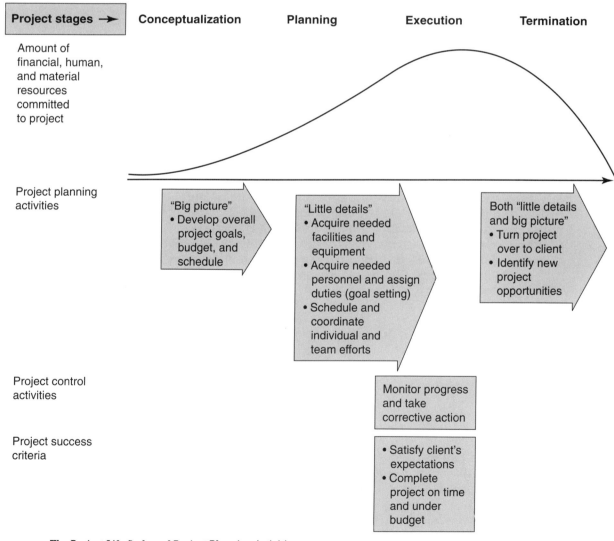

Exhibit 2.6 The Project Life Cycle and Project Planning Activities

Source: *Adapted in part from Exhibit 1.2 and discussion in Jeffrey K. Pinto and O. P. Kharbanda,* Successful Project Managers: Leading Your Team to Success *(New York: Van Nostrand Reinhold, 1995), pp. 17–21.*

(for example, a new breakfast cereal is turned over to manufacturing) and project resources are phased out.[50]

Project Management Software

Recall from our earlier discussion of the basic planning/control cycle (Exhibit 2.4) how planning and control are intertwined. One cannot occur without the other. The same is true for project planning. Making sure planned activities occur when and where appropriate and taking corrective action when necessary can be an overwhelming job for the manager of a complex project. Fortunately, a host of computer software programs can make the task manageable. But which one of the many available programs—such as Microsoft Project for Windows—should a project manager use? Thanks to project management experts, we have a handy list of screening criteria for selecting the right tool. Judging from the list that follows, the overriding attributes of good project management software packages are *flexibility* and *transparency* (meaning quick and up-to-date status reports on all important aspects of the project).[51]

- Identify and ultimately schedule need-to-do activities
- Ability to dynamically shift priorities and schedules, and view resulting impact
- Provide critical path analysis
- Provide flexibility for plan modifications
- Ability to set priority levels
- Flexibility to manage all resources: people, hardware, environments, cash
- Ability to merge plans
- Management alerts for project slippage
- Automatic time recording to map against project
- Identification of time spent on activities[52]

Six Roles Played by Project Managers

In a recent study, interviews with 40 project managers (and their clients) revealed what it takes to be effective.[53] The managers studied were working with outside clients on IT projects involving software development, systems integration, and technical support. In addition to the key role of "implementer," effective project managers played the roles of entrepreneur, politician, friend, marketer, and coach (see Table 2.2). Each role has its own set of challenges and appropriate strategies for meeting those challenges. It takes a highly skilled and motivated person to play all these roles successfully in today's business environment. As one project management educator put it.

> *In today's harsh business economy, executives want to know one thing about any project management initiative: "What's the value?" More than ever, every dollar invested must be justified, and every initiative must deliver tangible results.*[54]

Project Management Guidelines

Project managers need a working knowledge of basic planning concepts and tools, as presented in this chapter (see Window on the World). Beyond that, they need to be aware of the following special planning demands of projects.

- *Projects are schedule-driven and results-oriented.* By definition, projects are created to accomplish something specific by a certain time. Project managers require a positive attitude about making lots of quick decisions and doing things in a hurry. They tend to value results more than process.
- *The big picture and the little details are of equal importance.* Project managers need to keep the overall project goal and deadline in mind when attending to day-to-day problems and personnel issues. This is difficult because distractions are constant.

Table 2.2 Roles, Challenges, and Strategies for Effective Project Managers

Project Manager Role	Challenges	Strategies
Implementer	—Effectively plan, organize, and accomplish the project goals.	—Extend this role to include the newly identified roles described.
Entrepreneur	—Navigate unfamiliar surroundings. —Survive in a "sink or swim" environment. —Manage the unexpected.	—Build relationships with a number of different stakeholders. —Use persuasion to influence others. —Be charismatic in the presentation of new approaches.
Politician	—Understand two diverse corporate cultures (parent and client organizations). —Operate within the political system of the client organization.	—Align with the powerful individuals. —Obtain a senior/politically savvy client sponsor to promote and support the project.
Friend	—Determine the important relationships to build and sustain outside the team itself. —Be a friend to the client.	—Build friendships with key project managers and functional managers. —Identify common interests and experiences to bridge a friendship with the client.
Marketer	—Access client corporate strategic information. —Understand the strategic objectives of the client organization. —Determine future business opportunities.	—Develop a strong relationship with the primary client contact and with top management in the client organization. —Align new ideas/proposals with the strategic objectives of the client organization.
Coach	—Blend team members from multiple organizations. —Motivate team members without formal authority. —Reward and recognize team accomplishments with limited resources.	—Identify mutually rewarding common objectives. —Provide challenging tasks to build the skills of the team members. —Promote the team and its members to key decision makers.

Source: From *Academy of Management Executives*, 2004, by Sheila Webber and Marie Torti. Reprinted by permission. Permission conveyed through Copyright Clearance Center.

- *Project planning is a necessity, not a luxury.* Novice project managers tend to get swept away by the pressure for results and fail to devote adequate time and resources to project planning.
- *Project managers know the motivational power of a deadline.* A challenging (but not impossible) project deadline is the project manager's most powerful motivational tool. The final deadline serves as a focal point for all team and individual goal setting.[55]

Graphical Planning/Scheduling/Control Tools

Management science specialists have introduced needed precision into the planning/control cycle through graphical analysis. Three graphical tools for planning, scheduling, and controlling operations are flow charts, Gantt charts, and PERT networks. They can be found in project management software programs.

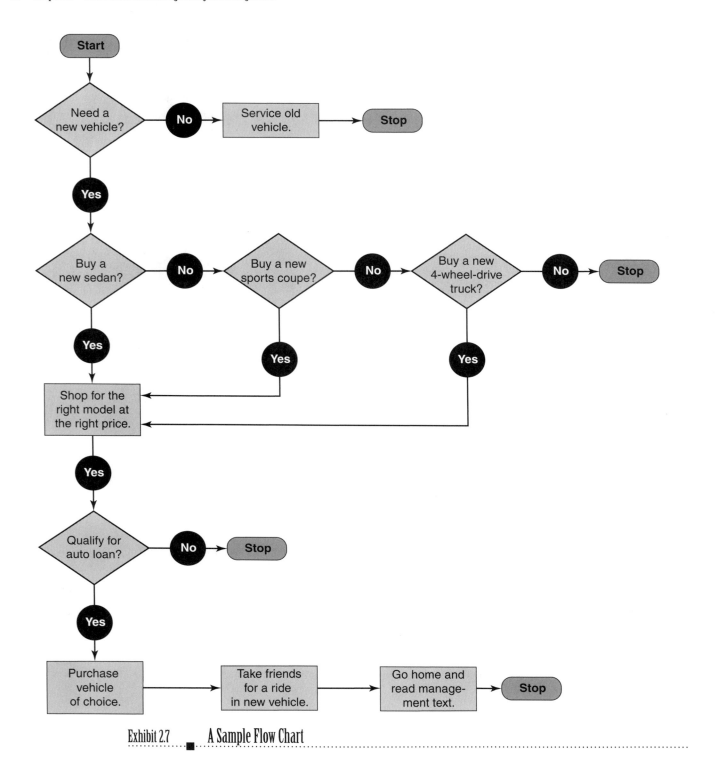

Exhibit 2.7 ■ A Sample Flow Chart

Sequencing with Flow Charts

Flow charts have been used extensively by computer programmers for identifying task components and by TQM (total quality management) teams for *work simplification* (eliminating wasted steps and activities). Beyond that, flow charts are a useful sequencing tool with broad application.[56] Sequencing is simply arranging events in the order of their actual or desired occurrence. For instance, this book had to be purchased before it could be read. Thus the event "purchase book" would come before the event "read book" in a flow chart for completing assignments in this course.

A sample flow chart is given in Exhibit 2.7. Note that the chart consists of boxes and diamonds in addition to the start and stop ovals. Each box contains a major event, and each diamond contains a yes-or-no decision.

Managers at all levels and in all specialized areas can identify and properly sequence important events and decisions with flow charts of this kind. User-friendly computer programs make flow-charting fun and easy today. Flow charts force people to consider all relevant links in a particular endeavor, as well as their proper sequence. This is an advantage because it encourages analytical thinking. But flow charts have two disadvantages. First, they do not indicate the time dimension—that is, the varying amounts of time required to complete each step and make each decision. Second, the use of flow charts is not practical for complex endeavors in which several activities take place at once.

Scheduling with Gantt Charts

Scheduling is an important part of effective planning. When later steps depend on the successful completion of earlier steps, schedules help managers determine when and where resources are needed. Without schedules, inefficiency creeps in as equipment and people stand idle. Also, like any type of plan or budget, schedules provide management with a measuring stick for corrective action. Gantt charts, named for Henry L. Gantt, who developed the technique, are a convenient scheduling tool for managers.[57] Gantt worked with Frederick W. Taylor at Midvale Steel beginning in 1887 and helped refine the practice of scientific management. A Gantt chart is a graphical scheduling technique historically used in production operations. Things have changed since Gantt's time, and so have Gantt chart applications. Updated versions like the one in Exhibit 2.8 are widely used today for planning and scheduling all sorts of organizational activities. They are especially useful for large projects such as moving into a new building or installing a new computer network.[58]

Exhibit 2.8 also shows how a Gantt chart can be used for more than just scheduling the important steps of a job. Filling in the timelines of completed activities makes it possible to assess *actual* progress at a glance. Like flow charts, Gantt charts force managers to be analytical as they reduce jobs or projects to separate steps. Moreover, Gantt charts improve on flow charts by allowing the planner to specify the time to be spent on each activity.

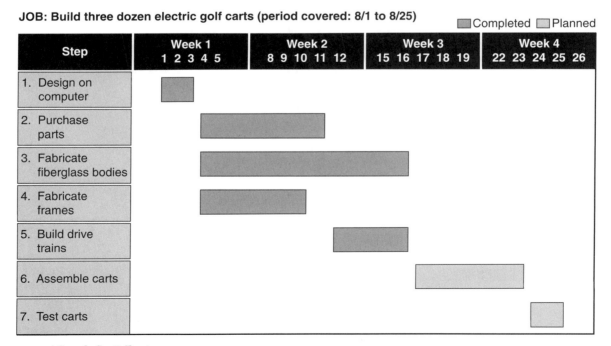

Exhibit 2.8   A Sample Gantt Chart

A disadvantage Gantt charts share with flow charts is that overly complex endeavors are cumbersome to chart.

PERT Networks

The more complex the project, the greater the need for reliable sequencing and scheduling of key activities. Simultaneous sequencing and scheduling amounts to programming. One of the most widely recognized programming tools used by managers is a technique referred to simply as PERT. An acronym for Program Evaluation and Review Technique (PERT) is a graphical sequencing and scheduling tool for large, complex, and nonroutine projects.

History of PERT

PERT was developed in 1958 by a team of management consultants for the U.S. Navy Special Projects Office. At the time, the navy was faced with the seemingly insurmountable task of building a weapon system that could fire a missile from the deck of a submerged submarine. PERT not only contributed to the development of the Polaris submarine project but also was credited with helping to bring the system to combat readiness nearly two years ahead of schedule. News of this dramatic administrative feat caught the attention of managers around the world. But, as one user of PERT reflected, "No management technique has ever caused so much enthusiasm, controversy, and disappointment as PERT."[59] Realizing that PERT is not a panacea, but rather a specialized planning and control tool that can be appropriately or inappropriately applied, helps managers accept it at face value.[60]

PERT Terminology

Because PERT has its own special language, four key terms must be understood.

- *Event.* A PERT event is a performance milestone representing the start or finish of some activity. Handing in a difficult management exam is an event.
- *Activity.* A PERT activity represents work in process. Activities are time-consuming jobs that begin and end with an event. Studying for a management exam and taking the exam are activities.
- *Time.* PERT times are estimated times for the completion of PERT activities. PERT times are weighted averages of three separate time estimates: (1) *optimistic time* (T_o)—the time an activity should take under the best of conditions; (2) *most likely time* (T_m)—the time an activity should take under normal conditions; and (3) *pessimistic time* (T_p)—the time an activity should take under the worst possible conditions. The formula for calculating estimated PERT time (T_e) is

$$T_e = \frac{T_o + 4T_m + T_p}{6}$$

- *Critical path.* The critical path is the most time-consuming chain of activities and events in a PERT network. In other words, the longest path through a PERT network is critical because if any of the activities along it are delayed, the entire project will be delayed accordingly.[61]

PERT in Action

A PERT network is shown in Exhibit 2.9. The task in this example, the design and construction of three dozen customized golf carts for use by physically challenged adults, is relatively simple for instructional purposes. PERT networks are usually reserved for more complex projects with hundreds or even thousands of activities. PERT events are coded by circled letters, and PERT activities, shown by the arrows connecting the PERT events, are coded by number. A PERT time (T_e) has been calculated and recorded for each PERT activity.

Before reading on, see if you can pick out the critical path in the PERT network in Exhibit 2.9. By calculating which path will take the most time from beginning to end, you will see that the critical path turns out to be A-B-C-F-G-H-I. This particular chain of activities and events will require an estimated 21.75 workdays to complete. The overall duration of the project is dictated by the critical path, and a delay in any of the activities along this critical path will delay the entire project.

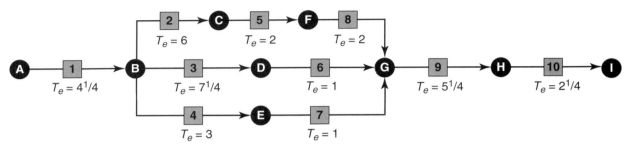

Exhibit 2.9 — A Sample PERT Network

Positive and Negative Aspects of PERT

During the 50 years that PERT has been used in a wide variety of settings, both its positive and its negative aspects have become apparent.

On the plus side, PERT is an excellent scheduling tool for large, nonroutine projects, ranging from constructing an electricity generation station to launching a space vehicle. PERT is a helpful planning aid because it forces managers to envision projects in their entirety. It also gives them a tool for predicting resource needs, potential problem areas, and the impact of delays on project completion. If an activity runs over or under its estimated time, the ripple effect of lost or gained time on down-stream activities can be calculated. PERT also gives managers an opportunity, through the calculation of optimistic and pessimistic times, to factor in realistic uncertainties about planning horizons.

On the minus side, PERT is an inappropriate tool for repetitive assembly-line operations in which scheduling is dictated by the pace of machines. PERT also shares with other planning and decision-making aids the disadvantage of being only as good as its underlying assumptions. False assumptions about activities and events and miscalculations of PERT times can render PERT ineffective. Despite the objective impression of numerical calculations, PERT times are derived rather subjectively. Moreover, PERT's critics say it is too time-consuming: A complex PERT network prepared by hand may be obsolete by the time it is completed, and frequent updates can tie PERT in knots. Project management software with computerized PERT routines is essential for complex projects because it can greatly speed the graphical plotting process and updating of time estimates.

Break-Even Analysis

In well-managed businesses, profit is a forethought rather than an afterthought. A widely used tool for projecting profits relative to costs and sales volume is break-even analysis. In fact, break-even analysis is often referred to as cost-volume-profit analysis. By using either the algebraic method or the graphical method, planners can calculate the break-even point, the level of sales at which the firm neither suffers a loss nor realizes a profit. In effect, the break-even point is the profit-making threshold. If sales are below that point, the organization loses money. If sales go beyond the break-even point, it makes a profit. Break-even points, as discussed later, are often expressed in units. An example is Europe's Airbus Industrie's huge 555-passenger commercial airliner that went into service in 2007. The break-even point for the $300 million double-deck A380 reportedly is about 250 units.[62]

From a procedural standpoint, a critical part of break-even analysis is separating fixed costs from variable costs.

Fixed versus Variable Costs

Some expenses, called fixed costs, must be paid even if a firm fails to sell a single unit. Other expenses, termed variable costs, are incurred only as units are produced and sold. Fixed costs are contractual costs that must be paid regardless of the level of output or sales. Typical examples include rent, utilities, insurance premiums, managerial and professional staff salaries, property taxes, and licenses. Variable costs are costs that vary directly with the firm's production and sales. Common variable costs include costs of production (such as labor, materials, and supplies), sales commissions, and product delivery expenses. As output and sales increase, fixed costs remain the same but variable costs accumulate. Looking at it another way, fixed costs are a function of *time* and variable costs are a function of *volume*. You can now calculate the break-even point.

The Algebraic Method

Where the following abbreviations are used,

FC = total fixed costs
P = price (per unit)
VC = variable costs (per unit)
BEP = break-even point

the formula for calculating break-even point (in units) is

$$BEP(\text{in units}) = \frac{FC}{P - VC}$$

The difference between the selling price P and per-unit variable costs VC is referred to as the contribution margin. In other words, the contribution margin is the portion of the unit selling price that falls above and beyond the variable costs and that can be applied to fixed costs. Above the break-even point, the contribution margin contributes to profits.

Variable costs are normally expressed as a percentage of the unit selling price. As a working example of how the break-even point (in units) can be calculated, assume that a firm has total fixed costs of $30,000, a unit selling price of $7, and variable costs of 57 percent (or $4 in round numbers).

$$BEP(\text{in units}) = \frac{30{,}000}{7 - 4} = 10{,}000$$

This calculation shows that 10,000 units must be produced and sold at $7 each if the firm is to break even on this particular product.

Price Planning

Break-even analysis is an excellent "what-if" tool for planners who want to know what impact price changes will have on profit. For instance, what would the break-even point be if the unit selling price were lowered to match a competitor's price of $6?

$$BEP(\text{in units}) = \frac{30{,}000}{6-4} = 15{,}000$$

In this case, the $1 drop in price to $6 means that 15,000 units must be sold before a profit can be realized.

Profit Planning

Planners often set profit objectives and then work backwards to determine the required level of output. Break-even analysis greatly assists such planners. The modified break-even formula for profit planning is

$$BEP(\text{in units}) = \frac{FC + \text{desired profit}}{P - VC}$$

Assuming that top management has set a profit objective for the year at $30,000 and that the original figures above apply, the following calculation results:

$$BEP(\text{in units}) = \frac{30{,}000 + 30{,}000}{7 - 4} = 20{,}000$$

To meet the profit objective of $30,000, the company would need to sell 20,000 units at $7 each.

The Graphical Method

If you place the dollar value of costs and revenues on a vertical axis and unit sales on a horizontal axis, you can calculate the break-even point by plotting fixed costs, total costs (fixed + variable costs), and total revenue. As illustrated in Exhibit 2.10, the break-even point is where the total costs line and the total sales revenue line intersect.

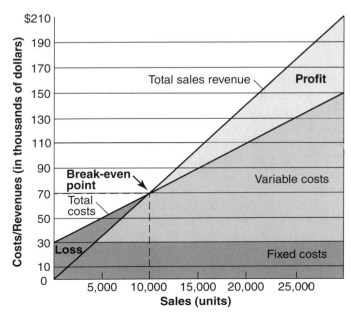

Exhibit 2.10 ■ Graphical Break-Even Analysis

Although the algebraic method does the same job, some planners prefer the graphical method because it presents the various cost-volume-profit relationships at a glance, in a convenient visual format.

Break-Even Analysis: Strengths and Limitations

Like the other planning tools discussed in this chapter, break-even analysis is not a cure-all. It has both strengths and limitations.

On the positive side, break-even analysis forces planners to acknowledge and deal realistically with the interrelatedness of cost, volume, and profit. All three variables are connected such that a change in one sends ripples of change through the other two. As mentioned earlier, break-even analysis allows planners to ask what-if questions concerning the impact of price changes and varying profit objectives.

The primary problem with break-even analysis is that neatly separating fixed and variable costs can be very difficult. General managers should enlist the help of accountants to isolate relevant fixed and variable costs. Moreover, because of complex factors in supply and demand, break-even analysis is not a good tool for setting prices. It serves better as a general planning and decision-making aid.

■ Endnotes

1. David Stires, "A Darker View of Starbucks," *Fortune* (November 13, 2006): 197.
2. See Darrell Rigby, "A Growing Focus on Preparedness," *Harvard Business Review*, 85 (July–August 2007): 21–22.
3. For example, see John Carey, "Shell: The Case of the Missing Oil," *Business Week* (January 26, 2004): 45–46; and Sarah Bartlett, "What We Didn't Plan For," *Inc.*, 27 (January 2005): 74–81.
4. Based on discussion in Frances J. Milliken, "Three Types of Perceived Uncertainty About the Environment: State, Effect, and Response Uncertainty," *Academy of Management Review*, 12 (January 1987): 133–143. Also see Hugh Courtney, *20/20 Foresight: Crafting Strategy in an Uncertain World* (Boston: Harvard Business School Press, 2001): chp. 2. Uncertainty and fear are discussed in Jerry Useem, "A Brief History of Fear," *Fortune* (September 3, 2007): 84–86.
5. For related reading, see Peter Coy and Jack Ewing, "Where Are All the Workers?" *Business Week* (April 9, 2007): 28–31; and Jennifer Schramm, "Coping with Tight Labor," *HR Magazine*, 52 (June 2007): 192.
6. See Raymond E. Miles and Charles C. Snow, *Organizational Strategy, Structure, and Process* (New York: McGraw-Hill, 1978), p. 29. A validation of the Miles and Snow model can be found in Stephen M. Shortell and Edward J. Zajak, "Perceptual and Archival Measures of Miles and Snow's Strategic Types: A Comprehensive Assessment of Reliability and Validity," *Academy of Management Journal*, 33 (December 1990): 817–832. Also see the four articles accompanying David J. Ketchen, Jr., "Introduction: Raymond E. Miles and Charles C. Snow's *Organizational Strategy, Structure, and Process*," *Academy of Management Executive*, 17 (November 2003): 95–96.
7. Data from Joseph Weber, "Harley Investors May Get a Wobbly Ride," *Business Week* (February 11, 2002): 65.
8. Spencer E. Ante, "The Info Tech 100," *Business Week* (July 2, 2007): 64. For related reading about prospectors, see Fernando F. Suarez and Gianvito Lanzolla, "The Role of Environmental Dynamics in Building a First Mover Advantage Theory," *Academy of Management Review*, 32 (April 2007): 377–392; Rita Gunther McGrath and Thomas Keil, "The Value Captor's Process: Getting the Most out of Your New Business Ventures," *Harvard Business Review*, 85 (May 2007): 128–136; and Cliff Edwards, "The Road to WiMax," *Business Week* (September 3, 2007): 58–64.
9. William Boulding and Markus Christen, "First-Mover Disadvantage," *Harvard Business Review*, 79 (October 2001): 20–21 (emphasis added). Also see Jim Collins, "Best Beats

First," *Inc.*, 22 (August 2000): 48–52; and Kevin Maney, "Impregnable 'First Mover Advantage' Philosophy Suddenly Isn't," *USA Today* (July 18, 2001): 3B.
10. See Thomas Stemberg, "Treat People Right and They Will Eat Nails for You, and Other Lessons I learned Building Staples into a Giant Company," *Inc.*, 29 (January 2007): 75–77; Pat Regnier, "Getting Rich in America," *Money*, 36 (July 2007): 74–77; and Chuck Salter, "Girl Power," *Fast Company*, no. 118 (September 2007): 104–112.
11. David Stires, "Rx for Investors," *Fortune* (May 3, 2004): 170. For more on analyzers, see Eric Bonabeau, "The Perils of the Imitation Age," *Harvard Business Review*, 82 (June 2004): 45–54; and Owen Thomas, "The 800-Lb. Copycat," *Business 2.0*, 5 (September 2004): 100.
12. Kevin Maney, "Kodak to Lay Off 15,000, Cut Manufacturing Capacity," *USA Today* (January 23, 2004): 4B.
13. Based on data in Ben Dobbin, "Kodak Cutting More Workers," *Arizona Republic* (January 23, 2004): D1–D2.
14. For details, see Jeffrey S. Conant, Michael P. Mokwa, and P. Rajan Varadarajan. "Strategic Types, Distinctive Marketing Competencies and Organizational Performance: A Multiple Measures Based Study," *Strategic Management Journal*, 11 (September 1990): 365–383. Also see Shaker A. Zahra and John A. Pearce II, "Research Evidence on the Miles-Snow Typology," *Journal of Management*, 16 (December 1990): 751–768.
15. See Yves L. Doz and Mikko Kosonen, "The New Deal at the Top," *Harvard Business Review*, 85 (June 2007): 98–104.
16. Based on Mary M. Crossan, Henry W. Lane, Roderick E. White, and Leo Klus, "The Improvising Organization: Where Planning Meets Opportunity," *Organizational Dynamics*, 24 (Spring 1996): 20–35.
17. See Michael Arndt, "3M's Rising Star," *Business Week* (April 12, 2004): 62–74.
18. "$1.4B Authorized to Restore Everglades," *USA Today* (December 12, 2000): 15A. For an update, see Brian Skoloff, "Water Again Flowing into Florida's Big Lake," *USA Today* (July 26, 2007): 4A.
19. Scott Adams, "Dilbert's Management Handbook," *Fortune* (May 13, 1996): 104.
20. Based on R. Duane Ireland and Michael A. Hitt, "Mission Statements: Importance, Challenge, and Recommendations for Development," *Business Horizons*, 35 (May–June 1992): 34–42. Also see V. Kasturi Rangan, "Lofty Missions, Down-to-Earth Plans," *Harvard Business Review*, 82 (March 2004): 112–119.
21. Bill Saporito, "PPG: Shiny, Not Dull," *Fortune* (July 17, 1989): 107.
22. See George Stalk, Jr. "Curveball: Strategies to Fool the Competition," *Harvard Business Review*, 84 (September 2006): 114–122.
23. Dan Sullivan, "The Reality Gap," *Inc.*, 21 (March 1999): 119.
24. Anthony P. Raia, *Managing by Objectives* (Glenview, Ill.: Scott, Foresman, 1974), p. 24.
25. For an excellent and comprehensive treatment of goal setting, see Edwin A. Locke and Gary P. Latham, *Goal Setting: A Motivational Technique That Works!* (Englewood Cliffs, N.J.: Prentice-Hall, 1984). Also see Gary P. Latham and Edwin A. Locke, "Enhancing the Benefits and Overcoming the Pitfalls of Goal Setting," *Organizational Dynamics*, 35, no. 4 (2006): 332–340.
26. John A. Byrne and Heather Timmons, "Tough Times for a New CEO," *Business Week* (October 29, 2001): 66.
27. For example, see Eric Krell, "The Best of Times," *HR Magazine*, 52 (May 2007): 48–52.
28. Raia, *Managing by Objectives*, p. 54.
29. Brian Grow, "Thinking Outside the Big Box," *Business Week* (October 25, 2004): 70.
30. Richard Koch, *The 80/20 Principle: The Secret of Achieving More with Less* (New York: Currency Doubleday, 1998), p. 4. Also see Gail Johnson, "Squeaky Wheels," *Training*, 41 (June 2004): 20.
31. Diane Brady, "Why Service Stinks," *Business Week* (October 23, 2000): 126.
32. Elizabeth Esfahani, "How to Get Tough with Bad Customers," *Business 2.0*, 5 (October 2004): 52.
33. See Barbara Moses, "The Busyness Trap," *Training*, 35 (November 1998): 38–42; "The Time Trap," *Inc.*, 26 (June 2004): 42–43; and Nanci Hellmich, "Most People Multitask, So Most People Don't Sit Down to Eat," *USA Today* (September 30, 2004): 8D.
34. See Steven Berglas, "Chronic Time Abuse," *Harvard Business Review*, 82 (June 2004): 90–97; Michael C. Mankins, "Stop Wasting Valuable Time," *Harvard Business Review*, 82

(September 2004): 58–65; Catherine Arnst, "We'll Get Around to It Later," *Business Week* (January 29, 2007): 10; and Kerry Sulkowicz, "Your Procrastinatin' Heart," *Business Week* (March 12, 2007): 18.

35. See Peter F. Drucker, *The Practice of Management* (New York: Harper & Row, 1954). For a short update on Drucker, see Thomas A. Stewart, "Effective Immediately," *Harvard Business Review*, 82 (June 2004): 10.
36. As an indication of the widespread interest in MBO, more than 700 books, articles, and technical papers had been written on the subject by the late 1970s. For a brief history of MBO, see George S. Odiorne, "MBO: A Backward Glance," *Business Horizons*, 21 (October 1978): 14–24. An excellent collection of readings on MBO may be found in George Odiorne, Heinz Weihrich, and Jack Mendleson, *Executive Skills: A Management by Objectives Approach* (Dubuque, Iowa: Wm. C. Brown, 1980). Also see Henry H. Beam, "George Odiorne," *Business Horizons*, 39 (November–December 1996): 73–76.
37. T. J. Rodgers, "No Excuses Management," *Harvard Business Review*, 68 (July–August 1990): 87, 89.
38. For related reading, see Philippe Haspeslagh, Tomo Noda, and Fares Boulos, "It's Not Just About the Numbers," *Harvard Business Review*, 79 (July–August 2001): 65–73.
39. For example, see Jan P. Muczyk and Bernard C. Reimann, "MBO as a Complement to Effective Leadership," *Academy of Management Executive*, 3 (May 1989): 131–139.
40. An interesting study of the positive and negative aspects of MBO may be found in Robert C. Ford and Frank S. McLaughlin, "Avoiding Disappointment in MBO Programs," *Human Resource Management*, 21 (Summer 1982): 44–49. Positive research evidence is summarized in Robert Rodgers and John E. Hunter, "Impact of Management by Objectives on Organizational Productivity," *Human Resource Management*, 76 (April 1991): 322–336.
41. For a critical appraisal of MBO core assumptions, see David Halpern and Stephen Osofsky, "A Dissenting View of MBO," *Public Personnel Management*, 19 (Fall 1990): 321–330. Deming's critical comments may be found in W. Edwards Deming, *Out of the Crisis* (Cambridge, Mass.: MIT Press, 1986), pp. 23–96; and Dennis W. Organ, "The Editor's Chair," *Business Horizons*, 39 (November–December 1996): 1.
42. See Richard Babcock and Peter F. Sorensen Jr., "An MBO Check-List: Are Conditions Right for Implementation?" *Management Review*, 68 (June 1979): 59–62.
43. Robert Rodgers and John E. Hunter, "Impact of Management by Objectives on Organizational Productivity," *Journal of Applied Psychology*, 76 (April 1991): 322.
44. See Robert Rodgers, John E. Hunter, and Deborah L. Rogers, "Influence of Top Management Commitment on Management Program Success," *Journal of Applied Psychology*, 78 (February 1993): 151–155.
45. For an excellent resource book, see James P. Lewis, *Fundamentals of Project Management*, 3rd ed. (New York: AMACOM, 2007).
46. Project Management Institute, "What Is a Project?" **www.pmi.org**, p. 1.
47. Dean Foust, "Harry Potter and the Logistical Nightmare," *Business Week* (August 6, 2007): 9. Also see Karen Stewart, "Planning a Conference?" *Training*, 44 (April 2007): 31–35.
48. Louisa Wah, "Most IT Projects Prove Inefficient," *Management Review*, 88 (January 1999): 7. Also see Jennifer Gill, "Smart Questions for Your Tech Consultant," *Inc.*, 29 (January 2007): 45.
49. See Dave Zielinski, "Soft Skills, Hard Truths," *Training*, 42 (July 2005): 18–23; Ed Gash, "More Training Than Camp," *Training*, 43 (December 2006): 7; and George B. Graen, Chun Hui, and Elizabeth A. Taylor, "Experience-Based Learning About LMX Leadership and Fairness in Project Teams: A Dyadic Directional Approach," *Academy of Management Learning and Education*, 5 (December 2006): 448–460.
50. For related insights, see Martin Walfisz, Peter Zackariasson, and Timothy L. Wilson, "Real-Time Strategy: Evolutionary Game Development," *Business Horizons*, 49 (November–December 2006): 487–498.
51. See recent issues of *Project Management Journal*.
52. Excerpted from a list of 26 attributes in "4.1 Software Attributes," **www.project-manager.com.**

53. Based on Sheila Simsarian Webber and Maria T. Torti, "Project Managers Doubling as Client Account Executives," *Academy of Management Executive*, 18 (February 2004): 60–71. Also see Sheila Simsarian Webber and Richard J. Klimoski, "Client-Project Manager Engagements, Trust, and Loyalty," *Journal of Organizational Behavior*, 25 (December 2004): 997–1013.
54. Jimmie West, "Show Me the Value," *Training*, 40 (September 2003): 62.
55. See Dan Carrison, "Fueling Deadline Urgency," *HR Magazine*, 48 (December 2003): 111–115; Tammy Galvin, "Managing Projects," *Training*, 41 (January 2004): 12; and Yukika Awazu, Kevin C. Desouza, and J. Roberto Evaristo, "Stopping Runaway IT Projects," *Business Horizons*, 47 (January–February 2004): 73–80.
56. One example of the application of a flow chart is Sharon M. McKinnon, "How Important Are Those Foreign Operations? A Flow-Chart Approach to Loan Analysis," *Financial Analysts Journal*, 41 (January–February 1985): 75–78.
57. For examples of early Gantt charts, see H. L. Gantt, *Organizing for Work* (New York: Harcourt, Brace and Howe, 1919), chp. 8.
58. Gantt chart applications can be found in Conkright, "So You're Going to Manage a Project," p. 64; and Andrew Raskin, "Task Masters," *Inc. Tech* 1999, no. 1 (1999): 62–72.
59. Ivars Avots, "The Management Side of PERT," *California Management Review*, 4 (Winter 1962): 16–27.
60. Additional information on PERT can be found in Nancy Madlin, "Streamlining the PERT Chart," *Management Review*, 75 (September 1986): 67–68; Eric C. Silverberg, "Predicting Project Completion," *Research Technology Review*, 34 (May–June 1991): 46–49; Robert L. Armacost and Rohne L. Jauernig, "Planning and Managing a Major Recruiting Project," *Public Personnel Management*, 20 (Summer 1991): 115–126; T. M. Williams, "Practical Use of Distributions in Network Analysis," *Journal of the Operational Research Society*, 43 (March 1992): 265–270; and Hooshang Kuklan, "Effective Project Management: An Expanded Network Approach," *Journal of Systems Management*, 44 (March 1993): 12–16.
61. Adapted in part from John Fertakis and John Moss, "An Introduction to PERT and PERT/Cost Systems," *Managerial Planning*, 19 (January–February 1971): 24–31.
62. See "Airbus Sees End to A380 Cancellations," *USA Today* (November 24, 2006): 5B.

Strategy

Discovering a Mission

If you want to be an entrepreneur and create your own company, what are the first steps you must take? This chapter describes the concept of strategy, and explains the kinds of decisions you need to make to create a successful company. An effective organization begins with a mission that identifies what it is striving to become and a strategy that explains how it plans to succeed. Organizations are created for a purpose and they function more effectively when all stakeholders clearly understand the organization's mission and strategy. Strategy refers to the goals and set of policies designed to achieve competitive advantage in a particular marketplace. Competitive advantage refers to the ability to transform inputs into goods and services, at a maximum profit on a sustained basis, better than competitors.

The central insight of this chapter can be stated simply: to create a successful company, you must identify a product or service that you can provide in a competitive market and do it better than your competitors. The probability that your company will be profitable increases as you have a clear vision about the product or service you want to provide; you know how it will benefit customers, other companies, and society; you choose an attractive industry in which to compete; you provide a superior product or service in terms of cost and/or quality; you have few, or no, competitors; your product or service cannot be easily imitated by competitors; and few, if any, substitutes can replace the demand for your product or service.

The Value of Mission Statements

An organization is formed when someone has a vision or idea about the kind of product or service the company ought to provide, and this becomes the firm's mission. Even nonprofit organizations must have a shared understanding of what the organization is trying to accomplish and how it will improve the lives of people. Most organizations were started as small, family-run businesses by a founder who had such a vision. Even large corporations originally started as small companies with a vision of a founder. Effective organizations all have a powerful shared vision that evolves and is refined through wide participation. It is the power of a shared mission that usually inspires and unites people more than the charisma of a leader.

A mission statement explains the essence of an organization—why it exists, what it wants to be, who it serves, and why it should continue. It is based on the organization's assumptions about its purpose, its values, its distinctive competencies, and its place in the world. The focus of a mission statement should be realistic and credible, the language should be well articulated and easily understood, and the direction should be ambitious and responsive to change. It should orient the group's energies and serve as a guide to action. It should also be consistent with the organization's values.

Writing Mission Statements

Effective organizations usually have a written mission statement that defines success for the company. These statements help to focus the energies of their members by answering such questions as "Why does our organization exist?", "What business are we in?", "What values will guide us?" Organizational goals and objectives are usually derived from the mission statement, but they are more specific. While mission statements are not measurable, goals and objectives ought to be.

From *Creating Effective Organizations,* 5th edition by David J. Cherrington and W. Gibb Dyer. Copyright © 2009 by Kendall/Hunt Publishing Company. Reprinted by permission.

Although there are no commonly accepted guidelines for writing mission statements, the following elements are usually found in carefully crafted statements:

1. *A purpose statement:* This statement explains what the organization seeks to accomplish and why it deserves the commitment of members and support of the public. Purpose statements try to answer such questions as "How is the world going to be different?" and "What is going to change?" and "How will things be better?"
2. *The business statement:* This statement identifies the organization's business activities or functions, such as to produce and transport alfalfa (for a ranch), or to construct affordable housing for first-time home owners (for a construction firm).
3. *Values statements:* These statements explain the values and beliefs that members hold in common and try to follow. Some of the most common values statements include a commitment to customer service, innovation, diversity, creativity, integrity, and personal development.

Useful mission statements should:

1. identify the purposes of the organization clearly enough that measurable objectives can be derived from them. A clear formulation of the firm's objectives will enable progress toward them to be measured;
2. differentiate the firm from other companies in the industry and establish its individuality and uniqueness;
3. define the business of the company with respect to its activities and products;
4. identify and explain the firm's relationships and obligations to all relevant stakeholders;
5. explain how it will contribute to society and the betterment of people well enough to be exciting and inspiring.

Example

A segment of Hewlett-Packard's mission statement illustrates these characteristics:"Hewlett-Packard Company designs, manufactures, and services electronic products and systems for measurement, computing, and communication used by people in industry, business, engineering, science, medicine, and education. HP's basic business purpose is to accelerate the advancement of knowledge and improve the effectiveness of people and organizations. The company's more than 25,000 products include computers and peripheral products, electronic test and measurement instruments and systems, networking products, medical electronic equipment, instruments and systems for chemical analysis, handheld calculators, and electronic components."[1]

Selecting a Strategy

Organizations operate in a dynamic environment; external and internal forces change continually. To use a sports metaphor, both the playing field and the rules of the game are constantly being revised for organizations. Products that were popular yesterday may be obsolete today; reliable customers who were satisfied last week may buy from a competitor this week; and last month's suppliers may have gone out of business.

Strategy involves a combination of the goals and plans to achieve competitive advantage, and the methods of implementing them. To use another sports metaphor, a strategy is a game plan. Strategy has generally been used in a military context to refer to the coordinated action plans a military unit intends to use to defeat its enemy. The deployment of troops, the timing of the attack, and the means of deception are all part of military strategy.

Organizations create generic strategies to help them succeed in a dynamic and competitive environment. These generic strategies share several important characteristics:

- They promote the mission and goals the organization is striving to achieve.
- They have a long-term focus that extends beyond the immediate time horizon.
- They define the action plans the organization intends to follow to achieve its mission and goals.
- They recognize explicitly the impact of the external environment, especially the reactions of competitors.

The Role of Strategy

An organization's strategy determines the direction it will go, and serves to unite the energies of many people and departments in a unified effort. Good strategies help organizational leaders make consistent and effective decisions. They also communicate expectations and coordinate the actions of the members. For example, decisions about product quality and where they will be marketed are important strategic decisions. An organization that decides to produce high-quality products and compete in the markets of industrialized nations is pursuing a much different strategy from a company that decides to produce inferior products and sell them in underdeveloped countries. Such was the case with the Korean company Daewoo Group, which decided to focus its markets in the third world because of criticism regarding its poor quality and poor after-sales service.[2]

Strategy is about winning and succeeding. In a business organization, strategy is about profits; it explains how the firm plans to make money now and in the future. A good strategy helps it to remain profitable and continue to grow. Firms that have a sustained competitive advantage are able to provide above-average profits for their investors; firms that do not have a sustained competitive advantage or that are not competing in an attractive industry earn at best only average profits, and seldom survive. Strategies are also important to nonprofit companies, such as hospitals, universities, and government agencies, since they compete with other organizations for clients and resources. Every organization needs to have a strategy that is consistent with its mission. Managers try to position their companies so that they can gain a relative advantage over their rivals. This positioning requires a careful evaluation of the competitive forces that dictate the rules of competition in each industry.

The goal of strategy is to find a competitive environment where a company has imperfect competition. As shown in Exhibit 3.1, such an environment occurs when there are few, if any, competitors (allowing one firm to operate as a monopoly); numerous suppliers and buyers (making it easy to obtain supplies and sell products at advantageous prices); asymmetric information (preventing the dissemination of information to all parties); heterogeneous products (allowing a firm to specialize in specific products); and barriers to entry (making it difficult for other firms to provide competitive products). Firms that have the good fortune to compete in markets that have imperfect competition generally obtain supernormal profits. This situation is much more favorable than one with perfect competition: numerous sellers and buyers, perfect information, homogeneous products, and no barriers to entry or exit. Firms that compete in conditions of perfect competition have difficulty earning anything more than average or below-average profits.

The Goal of Strategy: Imperfect Competition — Exhibit 3.1

Perfect Competition	Imperfect Competition
■ Numerous sellers and buyers	■ Few competitors, numerous suppliers and buyers
■ Perfect information	■ Asymmetric information
■ Homogeneous products	■ Heterogeneous Products
■ No barriers to entry or exit	■ Barriers to entry
Average or below-average profits	Supernormal Profits

> **Example**
>
> *Wal-Mart earned supernormal profits through imperfect competition with a strategy of locating stores in small towns where customers can purchase many low-cost, high-quality items in one location. Wal-Mart's competitive advantage is sustainable primarily because of its natural geographic monopoly and positioning, and secondarily because of its operational efficiencies. Competitors rationally decline to enter towns where Wal-Mart stores are located because Wal-Mart is already there with an optimally efficient store, there is no feasible way to increase local demand, and a second store would create substantial overcapacity such that neither store would make money.*

> **Example**
>
> *A fast-food restaurant that sells hamburgers near a college campus would not likely earn above-average profits if there were dozens of other fast-food outlets within a short distance. Although this location might have many potential customers, they tend to be price-sensitive and informed; they will buy wherever they can get the best value for their money. If any restaurant started to earn significant profits, other restaurants would imitate it and new restaurants would be waiting to enter the same market. Other competitors also have access to the same suppliers.*

Three Grand Strategies

Companies tend to rely on one of these three grand strategies to achieve a competitive edge: cost leadership (being the low-cost producer), differentiation (having a unique product in a large market), and focus (having a unique product in a narrow market).[3]

Cost Leadership

Gaining a competitive advantage through cost leadership involves selling your products and services at a lower cost. This is usually achieved by technological innovations that improve the efficiency of operations, or using low-cost labor that reduces the costs of production. Success with this strategy requires that the organization be the cost leader, not merely one of the contenders for that position. Furthermore, the products and services being offered must be perceived as comparable to, or better than those offered by rivals. Companies that have used this strategy successfully include Southwest Airlines, Wal-Mart, and Canadian Tire.

> **Example**
>
> *Southwest Airlines has achieved a significant competitive advantage in the airline industry by offering low-cost fares to customers. Other airlines have been forced to match these low-cost fares, but in doing so they have not achieved the same level of profitability. Southwest has been able to sustain its competitive advantage because it has lower costs (by eliminating reservations, check-in, and baggage handling) and higher revenues per plane (by faster turnaround times that keep the planes flying longer).*

Differentiation

A differentiation strategy involves providing unique products and services in ways that are widely valued by buyers. This can be achieved by providing exceptionally high quality, extraordinary service, innovative designs, technological capability, or an unusually positive brand image. Whatever attribute the company chooses to establish, its uniqueness must be different from those offered by rivals and significant enough to justify its price premium. Exaggerated advertising claims and the customary hyperbole that borders on sheer deceit provide evidence that many firms rely on this strategy. Firms that have succeeded in finding a unique differentiating factor include Maytag on reliability, Mary Kay Cosmetics on distribution, and Nordstrom on customer service.

Example

Toyota Motors has succeeded in differentiating itself from its competitors by gaining a reputation of exceptional quality in its cars. The Toyota Camry, for example, is widely recognized as a very well-built car with excellent reliability and dependability. Consequently, it sells at a substantial premium above other cars of similar size, and the depreciation on the price of a used Camry is also much less than normal.

Example

In the mid-1980s, Delta Airlines' market researchers found that customers, particularly business customers, were strongly influenced to choose a particular airline by the airline's frequent-flyer program. Consequently, Delta tried to differentiate itself within the airline industry by offering a special program. To motivate customers to choose Delta, they established an exclusive arrangement with American Express that allowed customers to receive triple miles when they flew on Delta with tickets purchased with an American Express card. Unfortunately, Delta failed to anticipate how easily and quickly this strategy could be imitated by its competitors.

Focus Strategy

A focus strategy aims at either a cost advantage or a differentiation advantage in a narrow market segment. Companies that use this strategy select a defined segment of an industry—such as a particular product, a specific kind of end-use buyer, a defined distribution channel, or a limited geographical location—and target its strategy to serve them to the exclusion of others. This strategy is also known as a niche strategy, since the firm seeks to compete in a niche of the larger market. The goal is to exploit a narrow segment of a market by appealing specifically to it. The success of a focus strategy may depend on how narrow the segment is. If the segment is too large, the strategy may suffer because of a lack of focus and uniqueness. But an extremely small segment may limit a company's success until it expands to other segments.

Example

Benmark Inc. of Atlanta, Georgia, specializes in providing unique medical and life insurance benefits for the banking industry, because that industry has liquid assets that can be used advantageously for insurance, tax reduction, and investment purposes. Focusing on one industry allows Benmark to develop targeted services and a social network that facilitates sales. Since bankers tend to know and interact with each other, many sales leads come from referrals. Bank executives tend to make deliberate and rational decisions based on careful cost analyses. Consequently, Benmark uses complex financial data that executives in other industries avoid.

Strategy Formulation

Selecting the right competitive strategy is vital to a firm's success. This decision determines how it is positioned in its industry. Strategy formulation is not a systematic process that advances sequentially from one action plan or objective to another, although it is less chaotic in some organizations than others. Strategy formulation is a dynamic process that is evolutionary in nature and subject to change as external forces change. Since strategy focuses on the future and the future is uncertain, strategy needs to be flexible and ready to respond to revised conditions.

The *strategic management process* involves an analysis of both internal and external factors to identify sources of competitive advantage. This popular approach to strategy development is often called the SWOT method, which stands for Strengths, Weaknesses, Opportunities, and Threats. Decision makers should examine the organization's competitive advantages relative to its internal strengths and weaknesses, its external opportunities and threats, and potential competitor actions. The six steps of the strategic management process are illustrated in Exhibit 3.2.

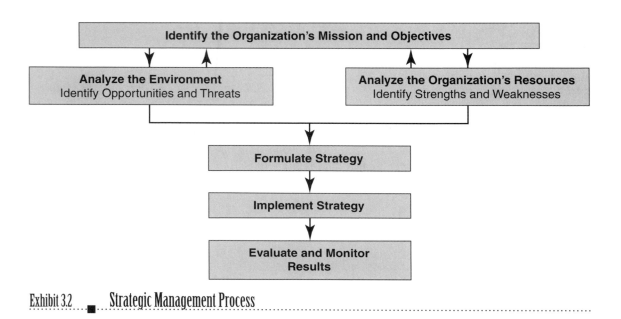

Exhibit 3.2 ■ Strategic Management Process

1. The first step is to identify the organization's mission and decide, "What business are we in?" This step forces management to identify carefully the scope of its products or services. Sometimes it is just as important to know what businesses they *do not* want to pursue as what they *do* want to pursue.
2. The second step is to analyze the external environment and identify the opportunities it wants to pursue and threats it wants to avoid. This process, called environmental scanning, involves anticipating and interpreting changes in the environment, and usually requires screening diverse information to detect emerging trends. Companies that do a good job of environmental scanning generally achieve higher profits and revenue growth than companies that don't.
3. The third step, which occurs simultaneously and interactively with the second step, is to analyze the organization's resources and identify its strengths and weaknesses. What are its skills and abilities? What unique knowledge and patents does it possess? Has it been successful at developing new and innovative products or services? What is its reputation for quality? The unique skills or resources that give an organization a competitive edge are called its core competency. Conversely, those resources that an organization lacks or activities that the firm does not do well are its weaknesses.

4. The fourth step is to combine the external and internal analyses and formulate an overall generic strategy for the organization to follow, plus functional strategies for each organizational function. These functional strategies need to be aligned with the generic strategy so that the entire organization is united.
5. The fifth step is implementation. Even good strategies must be implemented properly or they will not succeed. Good implementation usually requires competent leaders who have the vision to know which direction to pursue, and the trust of the members to encourage their involvement.
6. The sixth step is to evaluate and monitor the organization's results and maintain its competitive advantage. Long-term success with any strategy requires that the advantage be sustainable. That is, it must withstand both the actions of competitors and the evolutionary changes in the industry. This is a difficult challenge since technology changes continually, customer preferences are not stable, and competitors continually imitate successful organizations.

The SWOT approach to strategy formulation assumes that decision makers carefully analyze an organization's strengths, weaknesses, opportunities, and threats as they decide its future. This approach is a very proactive way to develop a strategy and it appears very clean and logical. However, it is not characteristic of the reactive way most organizational strategies develop.

Rather than creating a unified strategy based on a systematic analysis of the environment, most organizations formulate their strategies in response to problems. For example, a competitive threat, such as the sudden introduction of inexpensive competing products, might first cause a company to reduce its price, then segment itself as a quality producer, then pursue a different product line, or finally seek to enter a different market.

Both proactive and reactive methods of strategy formulation are appropriate depending on the circumstances. In a stable environment, a proactive method can be used effectively to move the organization toward its long-term objectives. In an unstable environment, however, strategies need to be more flexible and responsive to change. There is a fine line between weak strategies that fail to proactively set the future course of the organization versus rigid strategies that are inflexible and unable to reactively adapt to change.

Example

The history of US Steel illustrates how one company failed to adapt to competitive forces. When foreign steel companies began selling cheaper steel in the United States, US Steel adopted a series of strategies to help it survive, but each one failed. First it relied on the loyalty of its customers to continue buying higher-priced steel. Next it lowered its prices. Then it lobbied for protective tariffs and embargoes. Then it tried various cost-cutting and technological improvements. Then it merged with Marathon Oil and became USX. When the merger failed to produce large profits, it was divested and returned to US Steel. Finally, it acquired the assets of other bankrupt steel companies and continues to produce steel, but only slightly more than it produced in 1901 when it was founded. The demise of US Steel, which reigned for many years in the early twentieth century as America's largest company, represents a significant strategy failure.

Analyzing the Firm

Aligning the Organization

To survive in a dynamic environment, organizations must be prepared to diagnose their opportunities and revise their strategies. Choosing the right strategy usually makes the difference between success and failure. But good strategies depend on good alignment and

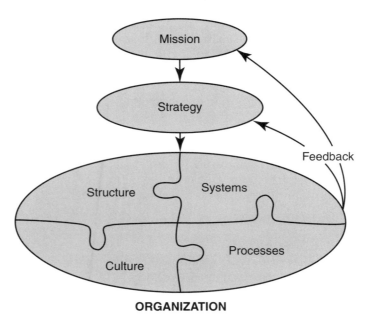

Exhibit 3.3 — **Designing Effective Organizations**

implementation; new strategies require corresponding changes throughout the organization. Exhibit 3.3 shows how the events that transpire within an organization are a consequence of its mission and strategy. If we want to make organizations more effective, the mission and strategy must be aligned with four organizational characteristics: structure, systems, culture, and processes.

Many strategies have failed because the organization's structure, control systems, and reward systems were not adequately designed to implement the strategies. The vital relationship between strategy and organizational structure has been recognized at least since 1920, when DuPont and General Motors implemented innovative multi-divisional structures that created separate product divisions. Each product division acted like an independent profit center. These multidivisional structures were needed to match the strategic changes in the organizations due to their size, managerial control, and reward systems.

Structure

Structure refers to the fixed relationships of the organization, such as how jobs are assigned to departments, who reports to whom, and how the jobs and the departments are arranged in an organizational chart. Strategies and structures must be aligned. An intended strategy has a substantial impact on how a firm is structured, which in turn affects its strategy. For example, a strategy that attempts to diversify responsibility for decision making by creating independent profit centers or autonomous work teams requires a multidivisional structure. However, a multidivisional structure would be highly inappropriate for a firm that had a strategy that required central coordination and tight control. Likewise, a small firm following a single-business strategy requires a simple structure in which the owner-manager makes all major decisions and monitors all activities, while the staff merely serve as an extension of the manager's authority. The impact of different organizational structures on profitability and effectiveness is examined in Chapter 13.

Systems

Systems refer to the patterned activities that keep an organization operating. Chapter 1 identified six essential subsystem activities: procurement, production, disposal, human resource, adaptive, and managerial. Organizational strategies need to be aligned with their

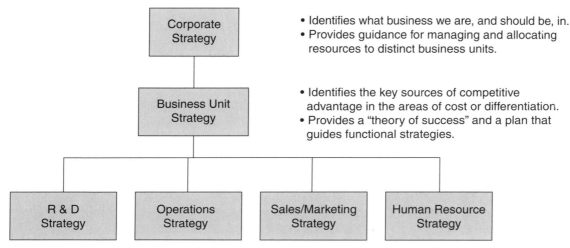

Exhibit 3.4 ■ Multiple Levels of Strategic Analysis

subsystem activities, as illustrated in Exhibit 3.4. The strategy of the corporation must be aligned with the strategies of each business unit, which in turn should be aligned with the functional strategies of each subsystem.

Example

A bank in the southeast made the strategic decision to change from an institutional bank to a consumer bank. This decision required the bank to establish numerous branch offices in neighborhoods, to make banking services more convenient. This generic strategy of growth for the bank had to be aligned with human resource strategies that included aggressive recruiting, careful selection procedures, rapidly rising wages, job creation, and expanded orientation and training.

Example

A tire company discovered that its foreign competitors were manufacturing tires with a new technology that increased productivity, improved quality, and reduced costs. This new technology required fewer workers, which meant that some workers had to be terminated or retired early. But more importantly, the workers who remained had to be well educated and highly trained. The human resource strategies at this tire manufacturer focused on reducing the size of the labor force and retraining those who stayed. High school and college classes were used to help them acquire quantitative skills and learn how to operate computers. The compensation system was also revised to pay workers for their knowledge and to reward new learning.

Culture

Organizational culture refers to the system of shared values and beliefs that influence worker behavior. Each organization creates its own distinctive culture, much as people have distinctive personalities. This culture is based on the values that seem to be widely shared among members of the organization, and they are reflected in the rituals and ceremonies that are held, the traditions that are celebrated, and the stories and myths that are circulated among workers. In times of uncertainty, an organization's culture guides the behavior of members and creates a sense of stability and direction. How culture influences organizational effectiveness is explained further in Chapter 14.

Processes

Organizational processes refer to the interactions among members of the organization. Some of the major organizational processes are the human resource functions of recruiting and staffing that provide the right people in the right jobs at the right time. Other important organizational processes include communication, decision making, leadership, and power. A major consideration in designing an effective structure is ensuring that these processes be accomplished efficiently. For example, effective methods for collecting and communicating useful information need to be integrated within the organizational structure.

Example

Two electronics firms, N.V. Philips (Netherlands) and Matsushita Electric Industrial (Japan) have followed very different strategies and emerged with different organizational capabilities. Philips used a geographic structure to build a worldwide federation of national organizations that are largely autonomous in each country. Product development and production are based on local market conditions and are unique to each country. For example, the furniture-encased televisions sold in the United States were very different in color and style from the TVs sold in other nations. Each national organization took major responsibility for its own financial, legal, and administrative functions. Exhibit 3.5 summarizes these organizational comparisons.

To overtake Philips as the world leader in consumer electronics, Matsushita maintained a centralized structure and leveraged its highly efficient operations in Japan as it expanded overseas. Matsushita adopted a divisional structure: each product line formed a separate division that operated almost like an independent corporation. Product development and engineering occurred in each of the product divisions, spurred by competition among them. As the company expanded overseas, its production, marketing, and sales facilities maintained the culture of a Japanese firm. The company also relied on hundreds of expatriate managers, sent from Japan to facilitate communication and leadership processes in the overseas subsidiaries.

Exhibit 3.5 Contrasting Competitive Strategies

	Philips	Matsushita
Structure	Decentralized federation of autonomous divisions in each country.	Centralized and divisional. Each product line formed a separate division that operated almost like an independent corporation.
Product Development	Determined by local market conditions within each country.	Each division manages its own product development and innovation.
Financial, Legal, and Administrative Functions	Responsibility of each national organization	Central support functions are provided by the home office.

Firm Resources and Core Competencies

Although strategy focuses mostly on the external environment, internal conditions also play a major role in strategy formulation and implementation. This view, referred to as the resource-based theory of the firm, provides a very different focus on the sources of competitive advantage. According to Jay Barney, the person most frequently credited for the resource-based view, sustained competitive advantage results from the ownership and control of resources that are rare, nontradable, nonsubstitutable, valued by the market, and difficult or impossible to imitate.[4] Such resources include physical assets, intangible resources, and organizational capabilities.

Some organizations are able to achieve a sustained competitive advantage and earn above-average profits because they possess unique resources or they have capabilities that provide a competitive edge and cannot be easily imitated. Many inputs to a firm's production process might act as unique resources, such as capital equipment, the skills of individual employees, patents, venture capital, and talented managers. These resources are often categorized as human resources, physical resources, and organizational capital resources. This capability is referred to as its distinctive competence or core capability.

Example

An illustration of a distinctive resource that is rare, nonsubstitutable, and virtually impossible to imitate is Walt Disney's animated characters. Although competitors have attempted to develop their own sets of animated characters, Mickey Mouse, Donald Duck, and other Disney characters are well recognized, very distinctive, and highly admired. Furthermore, Disney has exploited its capability to use these resources in producing universal and timeless entertainment in both animated films and theme parks. For Disney, this capability represents a distinctive competence.

Example

Hayes International is a consulting firm started by Jack L. Hayes, an expert in loss prevention. Although Hayes International hires other consultants and clerical employees, the core competence of this firm is Jack Hayes' forty years of experience in studying employee theft and designing loss-prevention systems. When Jack retires and wants to sell his firm, the purchase price will depend largely on how much of his knowledge and experience he has been able to transfer to others. The core asset of this company is the intellectual property that resides in its founder.

When an organization considers a diversification strategy, it needs to have a clear understanding of its distinctive competence. If the new diversification is able to leverage an existing skill base, the organization will likely achieve high performance. But if the diversification requires acquiring a significantly different skill and knowledge set, it will not likely achieve high performance.

Analyzing the Environment

All organizations must interact with their environment. Organizations depend on the environment to provide the necessary resources and to consume its products. The products must be acceptable to society, and the organization needs to obtain a favorable exchange so that it can recycle the products and convert them into new resources.

The survival of an organization can be threatened by public disapproval. Organizations can be terminated or drastically restricted if society disapproves of the organization's products, the way they are produced, or the organization's failure to comply with social expectations, such as safety requirements, environmental pollution standards, tariff agreements, and other legal requirements. The environment of tobacco companies, for example, has become increasingly hostile because of adverse scientific research, changing social customs, and antismoking laws.

Environmental Sectors

In a broad sense, an organization's environment is infinite and includes everything outside the organization. It is more useful, however, to focus on specific elements that influence it, called the organization's domain, which can be divided into sectors that contain similar elements.[5] Each sector represents an important segment of the environment that potentially influences the survival and effectiveness of the organization. Eight of the most important sectors are shown in Exhibit 3.6. In strategic planning, a firm would want to examine each of these sectors to discover any competitive advantages it could adopt or weaknesses it should avoid.

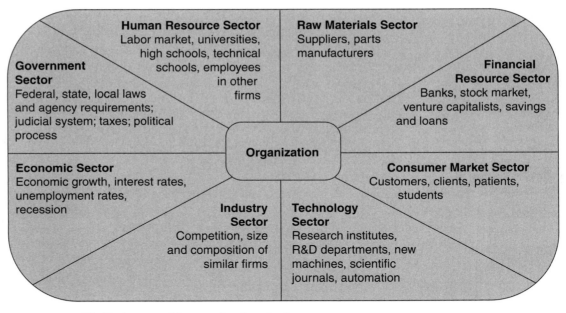

Exhibit 3.6 ■ The Environmental Sectors of an Organization

1. *Human resources sector.* The human resources sector includes the labor market and all the sources from which potential employees may be obtained, including employment agencies, universities, technical schools, and other educational institutions. Employees can also be pirated from other organizations or recruited from foreign labor forces.
2. *Raw materials sector.* Raw materials must be obtained from the external environment. These materials include everything from paper and students for a university, patients for a hospital, iron ore for a steel mill, and insecticide for a farm. The raw materials sector for the auto industry includes a large number of suppliers and parts manufacturers.
3. *Financial resources sector.* Money is an essential input for most organizations, especially new companies. The financial resources sector includes places where financing can be obtained, such as banks, savings and loan institutions, stock markets, and venture capitalists.

4. *Consumer markets.* The outputs produced by the organization must be consumed by customers who purchase the goods and services. This market sector includes the customers, clients, and potential users of the organization's products and services. For example, hospitals serve patients, schools serve students, supermarkets supply homemakers, airlines move travelers, and government agencies serve the public.
5. *Technology sector.* Technology is the use of available knowledge and techniques to produce goods and services. The technology sector includes scientific research centers, universities, and the research and development efforts of other organizations that contribute to new production techniques and the creation of new knowledge.
6. *Industry sector.* An industry encompasses all the organizations in the same type of business, most of which act as competitors to an organization. The size of the industry and the number of other competing firms create a unique industry sector for each organization. An industry dominated by one or two major corporations, such as heavy-equipment manufacturing, is much different from an industry characterized by hundreds of small companies, such as the fast-food industry.
7. *Economics sector.* Organizations are not isolated from economic conditions. The success and effectiveness of an organization is influenced by the health of the overall economy and by such factors as whether the economy is expanding or contracting. Some of the most important aspects of this sector include economic growth, unemployment rates, recessions, inflation rates, and the rate of investment.
8. *Government sector.* The government sector includes all the federal, state, and local laws plus the regulatory agencies that administer these laws, and the judicial system that resolves disputes. This sector also includes the political system and political action committees, and lobbyists who try to change the laws and obtain favorable legislative treatment.

Globalization

We live in a global economy. Every nation participates in the production and consumption of goods and services that move around the globe, crossing economic, cultural, and political boundaries. Globalization has encouraged international integration. For example, financial resources from one country may be used to buy natural resources from another country and make products manufactured in still another country and distributed worldwide. But it has also led to intense competitive pressures for companies everywhere in the world. These conditions force global companies to think seriously about the strategies required to sustain their competitive advantage. Global corporations often provide their foreign suppliers and overseas subsidiaries with business knowledge, management practices, training, and all sorts of other intangible exports that are seldom measured.

One of the most visible indications of increasing globalization is the practice of offshoring, which involves moving jobs from one country to another country where they can be performed less expensively. Many manufacturing and service jobs can be performed equally well anywhere in the world. Therefore, companies can achieve a competitive advantage by moving these jobs to countries where the labor rates are lower. For example, the labor costs of manufacturing workers in China are about one tenth of the labor costs of similar workers in the United States and Europe. Similarly, the costs of operating a call center in India are substantially less than the costs of operating the same call center in the United States and Indian workers can be trained to respond as if they lived in the state next door.

Increased globalization has also led to significant migrations of workers across national boundaries. Within the European Union, workers are free to move wherever they want to find employment and sell their services. Immigration laws in the United States limit the number of immigrants who can enter the country legally; however, many illegal immigrants are also added to the labor pool each year, which significantly influences labor costs and the availability of worker skills.

Industry Analysis

One strategy model focuses on helping firms identify their competitive niche in the external environment by selecting a profitable industry and competing effectively in it. The industrial organization model, or I/O model, suggests that the conditions and characteristics of the external environment are the primary determinants of successful strategies that will help firms earn above-average profits.[6]

Firms face the challenge of finding the most attractive industry in which to compete. Because most firms are assumed to have equal access to similar resources that are mobile across companies, competitiveness generally can be increased only when they find the industry with the highest profit potential and learn how to use their resources to formulate and implement the strategy required by that industry. Michael Porter has developed a five-forces model of competition that identifies the major environmental forces of an industry analysis, as illustrated in Exhibit 3.7.[7] This five-forces model suggests that an industry's profit potential is a function of the interactions among these five forces. Organizations can use this analysis to examine an industry's profit potential and to establish a defensible competitive position, given the industry's structural characteristics. The five forces are suppliers, buyers, rival firms, product substitutes, and the threat of new entrants.

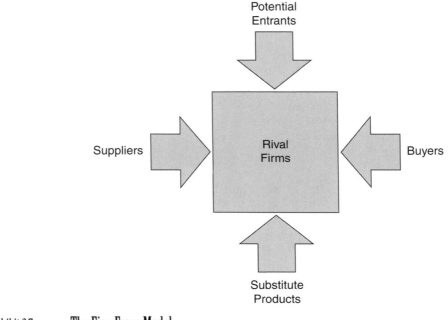

Exhibit 3.7 ■ The Five-Force Model

Source: Adapted from Michael Porter, *Competitive Strategy,* (New York: Free Press, 1980), p. 4.

1. *Suppliers.* Firms depend on their suppliers for materials to which they provide added value. The power of suppliers depends on such factors as how many suppliers are available, whether there are satisfactory substitute supplies, and whether a supplier might choose to integrate forward, such as a bakery deciding to open its own retail outlet.
2. *Buyers.* Firms seek to maximize their revenues, while buyers want to purchase goods at the lowest possible price. The power of buyers increases when there are many competing products, when the products are similar, or when only one or a few buyers purchase the entire output.
3. *Rival firms.* Competition among rivals is stimulated when one or more firms identifies an opportunity to improve their market position or when they feel competitive pressures. Since the firms in an industry are mutually dependent on each other, a competitive

advance by one (such as frequent-flyer mileage in the airline industry) usually precipitates corresponding moves by all of the others. Rivalry is especially strong when most of the firms are equally balanced and feel a need to distinguish themselves, when the market is not expanding and firms fear a loss of market share, and when the products are not unique and can be easily replaced.

4. *Substitute products.* Firms compete against other firms that offer substitute products. Therefore, substitute products place an upper limit on the prices firms can charge, since substitutes will be used whenever the price of the product exceeds the price of the substitute. The threat of substitute products is strong when customers can easily switch to the substitute and when the substitute's quality is high and its costs are low. For example, Nutrasweet is a substitute for sugar, since it performs similar functions, and the price of Nutrasweet provides an upper limit on the price of sugar.

Substitutes do not need to be other products; they can also be other processes or activities that eliminate the need. For instance, the companies that manufacture water meters would discover that the demand for their product could be eliminated if a city decided to charge users a flat monthly fee rather than according to the number of gallons they used. Likewise, California's lawyers who were representing workers in industrial accidents found that the lucrative incentives they anticipated disappeared when that state's supreme court ruled that plaintiffs were not eligible to receive punitive damages for workers' compensation injuries.

5. *New entrants.* New entrants threaten existing competitors by providing additional production capacity. Unless there is a corresponding increase in the demand for additional production, there will likely be price cuts and a corresponding loss of revenues and profits for all firms. Existing competitors try to develop barriers to new entrants, while new entrants seek markets where the barriers are relatively weak. Some of the most challenging entry barriers are inefficient economies of scale for new entrants (small operations do not benefit from large production runs), unrecognized product differentiation (customers are not familiar with the new product), insufficient starting capital (significant funds are needed for a firm's initial resources in physical facilities and inventory), limited access to distribution channels (new firms do not have established relationships with distributors), and historical cost disadvantages (the established competitors have already acquired the most favorable locations, proprietary product technology, and favorable access to raw materials).

Competitor Analysis

In addition to analyzing the overall industry, firms also need to analyze each company with which they directly compete. This assessment, called a competitor analysis, is especially critical for firms facing one or a few powerful competitors. In the airline industry, for example, each airline is vitally interested in what other airlines are doing. Are they changing their routes or prices, are they purchasing new planes or increasing their work force, and are they providing new or improved services or benefits?

Successful companies perform a competitor analysis for each competing firm in their industry. This analysis involves examining each competitor's future objectives, current strategy, assumptions, and capabilities. The kinds of questions involved in this analysis are:[8]

1. *Future objectives:* How do our goals compare to our competitors' goals? What will we emphasize in the future? What are our attitudes and the attitudes of others toward risk?
2. *Current strategy:* How are we currently competing? Does this strategy support changes in the competitive structure?
3. *Assumptions:* Do we assume the future will be volatile or stable? Are we operating under a status quo or are we advancing? What assumptions do our competitors hold about the industry and about themselves?
4. *Capabilities:* What are the strengths and the weaknesses of each competitor? How do we rate compared to our competitors?

An effective competitor analysis requires gathering needed information and data, referred to as competitor intelligence. Information needs to be obtained about each competitor's customers, distribution channels, marketing, sales, advertising, finances, operations, organizational structure, research and development, and strategic plans. Analysts have an obligation to obtain this information in ways that are ethical. Stealing drawings or documents, eavesdropping, and trespassing are unethical and illegal methods of collecting information. However, techniques that are generally considered both legal and ethical include (a) obtaining publicly available information, such as court records, help-wanted ads, annual reports, financial reports of publicly held corporations, and Uniform Commercial Code filings, and (b) attending trade fairs and shows to obtain brochures and advertisements, view the exhibits, and listen to discussions about their products.

The ethics of several intelligence-gathering techniques is questionable even though they are technically legal, such as paying someone to serve as an impostor (such as a student, a management consultant, or a reporter) to obtain inside information, conducting job interviews for jobs that don't exist in hopes that a competitor's employees will apply and volunteer inside information, hiring a competitor's key employees to obtain knowledge about technological innovations, and purchasing a competitor's trash to obtain documents and other inside information. As a general rule, information-gathering techniques ought to respect the right of competitors not to reveal information about their products, operations, and strategic intentions that they do not want divulged. When evaluating the ethics of such cases, the Golden Rule should serve as a useful moral guideline.

Environmental Uncertainty

All organizations function in an uncertain environment, but the uncertainty is much greater for some organizations than for others. Reducing this uncertainty may be important to an organization's effectiveness and survival.

Complexity and Stability

When the environment is uncertain, managers have difficulty predicting external changes and they have to make decisions with insufficient information. Producing viable products requires good information about such things as consumer interests and the availability of resources. Uncertainty also increases the risk of failure and makes it difficult to compute the costs and probabilities associated with different decisions.

Organizational uncertainty is determined by two dimensions: complexity and stability, as shown in Exhibit 3.8. Environmental complexity concerns the number of external elements

Exhibit 3.8 — Framework for Evaluating Environmental Uncertainty

ENVIRONMENTAL STABILITY	ENVIRONMENTAL COMPLEXITY	
	Simple	**Complex**
Stable	Simple + Stable = Low Uncertainty *Examples: Soft drink bottlers, beer distributors, container manufacturers, agricultural farms, auto repair shops.*	Complex + Stable = Low Moderate Uncertainty *Examples: Universities, hospitals, insurance companies, government agencies*
Unstable	Simple + Unstable = High Moderate Uncertainty *Examples: Software companies, fashion clothing, music industry, toy manufacturers*	Complex + Unstable = High Uncertainty *Examples: Airline companies, oil companies, computer firms, aerospace firms, auto industry*

Source: Adapted from Duncan, R., "Characteristics of Organizational Environments and Perceived Environmental Uncertainty," *Administrative Science Quarterly*, vol. 17 (1972): 320.

relevant to an organization. In a simple environment, the organization interacts with only a small number of external elements. For example, a family-operated chicken farm that sells most of its eggs to one food chain has a very simple environment. In a complex environment, however, the organization must interact with a large number of diverse external elements. Automobile companies, for example, interact with hundreds of parts suppliers located in many different countries, plus hundreds of dealerships scattered throughout the world. Furthermore, they interact with countless elements in the human resources sector in acquiring new employees, plus dozens of agencies from the government sector.

How rapidly the environment changes is called environmental stability, and it is stable when it remains relatively unchanged for several years. Some organizations enjoy a very stable environment, such as lead pipe manufacturers, whose pipe and connecting joints have remained virtually unchanged for many years. Other organizations have a very unstable environment, such as the electronics industry, whose products may become obsolete overnight because of technological advances and new scientific discoveries. The actions of competitors and the unpredictability of the market also contribute to making the electronics industry a very unstable environment.

Reducing Uncertainty

Because uncertainty threatens an organization's survival and reduces its effectiveness, organizations use a variety of strategies to reduce environmental uncertainty. Most of these efforts focus on gaining greater control over environmental resources. The first two strategies listed here, however, involve internal changes within the organization.

1. *Changing the organizational structure.* As the environment becomes more complex, the organization needs more buffering departments and boundary spanners. In a stable environment, the internal structure can be centralized and can operate according to fixed rules and procedures. When the environment is unstable, however, the organization's structure must be informal, decentralized, and coordinated by the efforts of many individuals whose specific responsibility is to facilitate this control.
2. *Planning and forecasting.* Organizations can increase their capacity to respond to an unstable environment by forecasting environment changes and creating contingency plans. Planning can soften the adverse impact of external shifts. Organizations that have unstable environments frequently create separate planning departments to help the organization adapt successfully. For example, economic forecasting may not change the economy any more than weather forecasting can change the weather. However, a good economic forecast may be as helpful to organizational planning as a weather forecast is to scheduling a company picnic. An interesting paradox regarding economic forecasts is that their accuracy increases as the environment becomes more stable, but their usefulness increases as the environment becomes more unstable. Although forecasts in an unstable environment are not as accurate, they are nevertheless more useful because they identify the important contingencies and the relationships between them, and forecasts can always be updated.
3. *Mergers and acquisitions.* An effective method to control environmental resources is to buy a controlling interest in an upstream or downstream company that serves as a supplier or consumer. If there is uncertainty about the source of a crucial raw material, this uncertainty can be removed by buying the supplier. For example, steel companies have acquired iron and coal mines, and soft-drink manufacturers have acquired bottle makers. A similar method of controlling environmental resources is through joint ventures and contracts that create a legal and binding relationship between two or more firms. In a joint venture, organizations share the risks and costs associated with large projects. Contracts are designed to provide long-term security for both the supplier and the consumer of raw materials, by tying the consumer and the supplier to specific amounts and prices. For example, McDonald's Corporation will sometimes acquire an entire crop of potatoes to be certain of its supply of french fries.
4. *Cooptation.* Cooptation is any strategy of bringing outside people into the organization and making them feel obligated to contribute because of their organizational involvement. Cooptation occurs when leaders of important environmental sectors are brought

into the organization by having them serve on an advisory committee or a board of directors. Cooptation explains why organizations in more uncertain environments tend to have larger boards of directors—a larger board can reduce uncertainty to a greater degree.[9] Some organizations reduce their resource uncertainty by creating a formal linkage called an interlocking directorate in which the members of the board of directors of one company sit on the board of directors of another company. These individuals influence the policies and decisions of each organization in ways that guarantee interfirm cooperation. Another form of cooptation is to recruit executives from another interdependent organization. For example, companies in the aerospace industry hire retired generals and executives from the Department of Defense to obtain better information about technical specifications and to improve their chances of obtaining defense contracts.

5. *Public relations and advertising.* Organizations spend enormous amounts of money to influence consumer tastes and public opinion. Advertising and public relations activities are designed to reduce uncertainty by providing a stable demand for the company's outputs or a constant level of inputs. Press reports and other news media shape the company's image in the minds of suppliers, customers, and government officials. Hospitals, for example, have begun to advertise their services to attract more patients.

6. *Political activity.* Since government legislation and agency enforcement can exert such a powerful influence on organizations, many of them spend a considerable amount of money on lobbyists and political action committees. These individuals strive to protect the interests of the organization by making members of governing bodies aware of the interests of the organization and the consequences of a proposed bill. Many organizations have formed trade associations for similar purposes, such as the National Association of Manufacturers. By pooling their resources, organizations expect the associations to have a larger voice in lobbying legislators, influencing new regulations, developing public relations campaigns, and blocking unfair competition.

7. *Illegal activities.* Although it is wrong, many organizations resort to illegal activities to control environmental uncertainty. Scarce environmental resources and pressures to succeed, especially from top managers, often lead managers to behave in illegal ways. Some examples of illegal behaviors include payoffs to foreign governments, illegal political contributions, promotional gifts, illegal kickbacks, price fixing, illegal mergers, franchise violations, refusals to bargain in good faith with a union, and espionage in market development and innovations.

Although organizations usually try to adapt to the environment, some try to change and control the environment. This is especially true of large organizations that command large resources. The environment is not fixed. Organizations can adapt when necessary, but they can also neutralize or alter a problematic sector in the environment. Although the potential of significantly influencing the environment is small when organizations act alone, a group of organizations can make a noticeable change within the environment when they are united.

Endnotes

1. http://www.hp.com
2. Steve Glain, "Strategic Move: Daewoo Group Shifts Its Focus to Markets In the Third World," *The Wall Street Journal,* October 11, 1993, p. A1.
3. Michael E. Porter, *Competitive Advantage,* (New York: Free Press, 1985).
4. Jay B. Barney, Organizational Culture: Can it be a Source of Sustained Competitive Advantage?" *Academy of Management Review,* No l. 11, (1986), pp. 656–665; Jay B. Barney, "Firm Resources and Sustained Competitive Advantage," *Journal of Management,* vol. 17 (1991), pp. 99–120.
5. Richard L. Daft, *Organization Theory and Design,* 8th ed. (Mason, OH: Thomson South-Western, 2004), Ch. 1.

6. Michael A. Hitt, R. Duane Ireland, and Robert E. Hoskisson, *Strategic Management: Competitiveness and Globalization.* (Minneapolis: West Publishing, 1995), Ch. 1.
7. Michael E. Porter, *Competitive Strategy: Techniques for Analyzing Industries and Competitors.* (New York: Free Press, 1980); Michael E. Porter, *Competitive Advantage,* (New York: Free Press, 1985).
8. Michael E. Porter, *Competitive Strategy: Techniques for Analyzing Industries and Competitors* (New York: Free Press, 1980), p. 49.
9. Jeffrey Pfeffer, "Size and Composition of Corporate Boards of Directors: The Organization and Its Environment," *Administrative Science Quarterly*, vol. 17 (1972), pp. 218–228.

International Management

4

Globalization

Globalization refers to the flow of goods and services, capital (money), and knowledge across country borders. Globalization enhances the economic interdependence among countries and organizations across countries. [1] According to Thomas Friedman, the author of the popular book, *The World Is Flat*, we are in the third stage of globalization, with the first involving internationalization of countries, the second involving companies moving into international markets, and the current and third stage involving individuals collaborating (and competing) on a global basis.[2] The increasing interdependence among countries, companies, and even individuals across country borders has reduced the influence that national governments can have on their economies.[3]

Increasing globalization has dramatically changed the competitive landscape in recent years for everyone. For example, when coupled with new technology, especially in information systems, small firms now have access to markets and resources in other countries. This has allowed them to compete effectively with larger and often more established firms. Additionally, even firms from economies that are less developed can better compete in international markets as well.[4]

A Manager's Challenge

Globalization

Made in China

As I tucked my seven-year old boy into bed one evening, he said, "Wow, Mommy, I can't believe my bed says 'Made in Canada'. Finally, I have something that doesn't say 'Made in China'." A bit taken aback I asked him why he was so surprised. He calmly began pointing to all of the items in his room that were exported from China. What I did not realize, but my son did, is that a majority of his toys and furniture were made in China. From 1998 to 1999, U. S. imports from China increased $71.2 billion. It is expected that China's trade surplus will exceed $140 billion this year, according to a Chinese government official. So far in 2006 China's exports exceeded imports by $110.0 billion, so what does this mean for the U. S.?

Financial markets are beginning to recognize that the emerging Chinese economy is boosting global growth. Some economists believe that the growing number of products imported from China is one reason inflation has remained low in the United States. This has encouraged banks to keep interest rates low, stimulating U. S. investment and growth. The purchase by China's central bank of billions of dollars of U. S. Treasury bills has also likely kept U. S. interest rates low.

Americans are exporting more goods to China as well. In 2006, these exports were up 20 percent. Some American corporations feel that without China, they would be less efficient, less profitable, and would have to pay lower wages to their workers in the United States. So whether Americans realize it or not, China has had a major impact on the United States' recovery following the country's 2001 recession.

However, China's growing trade surplus—the fact that it exports more than it imports—is becoming a sore point with some of its trading partners, including the United States. U. S. textile lobbyists, for example, are

(continued)

Hitt, Michael, Black, Stewart, Porter, Lyman W., *Management*, 2nd edition, © 2008. Reprinted by permission of Pearson Education, Inc., Upper Saddle River, NJ.

concerned that massive amounts of Chinese imports have cost thousands of Americans their jobs. Collectively these lobbyists have filed a petition to limit the importation of certain clothing products. China is also under some pressure from the United States to increase the value of its currency, the yuan. This would help make China's exports more expensive and U. S. imports into China more competitive.

Finally, U. S. retailers complain it often takes too long to receive Chinese imports, costing them Sales. They feel that, to compete with the European retailers, it's important to replenish Merchandise faster to keep up with current trends. As a result, they are beginning to consider buying some of their merchandise locally.

Sources: D. Cohen, "The Global Reverbs of China and India" *Business Week*, February 9, 2006, www.businessweek.com, P. Bhatnager, "Is made in U.S. A, Back in Vogue?" CNN Money March 1, 2006, www.cnnmoney.com. A, Yeh, "U.S.-China Trade Relations Take a Turn for the Worse". *Financial Times*, November 5,2004, www.ft.com, C. Swann, "Strong Exports Help to Offset U.S. Trade Deficit", *Financial Times*, July 12, 2006, www.ft.com, R. Lenihan, "Value-Conscious Americans Are Long-Time Fans of Chinese Goods." CNN Money, May 22, 2006, www.cnnmoney.com, Editorial, "Don't Blame Job Woes on China", *Business Week* October 13, 2003, www.businessweek.com. The Associated Press, Beijing, "China's Trade Surplus to Extend $140 B." *Business Week,* November 5, 2006, www.businessweek.com.

According to Friedman, globalization has gone beyond the point where small and large companies have moved into international markets. Today, the world is at the point where even individual people are collaborating (and competing) with one another on a global basis.[5] Friedman suggests that the increased globalization has made all of us, regardless of our country of origin, "next-door neighbors"—and competitors.[6]

In the professional services area, many functions have shifted to countries like China and India because their workers have the ability to do a quality job at a much lower cost. Many U.S. firms are outsourcing services such as software development and tax-return preparation to India. Some U.S. companies are sending their U.S. employees to India for surgery because it is less expensive there, and the quality of the care is excellent.

India and China are expected to be major players in the global economy over the next 30 to 40 years. Some have argued that the combined economies of China, India, Brazil, and Russia are likely to be greater than the total economies of the G6 countries (Canada, France, Germany, Japan, United Kingdom, and United States) by the year 2040.[7]

Toyota is an example of a global company that has enjoyed a substantial amount of success internationally. It is poised to become the world's number one automaker. In 2006 alone, General Motors and Ford laid off 46,000 employees while Toyota moved forward opening new plants in the United States and other parts of the world. Over 50 percent of Toyota's sales revenues come from outside of Japan.[8] Toyota has emphasized high quality and reliability and thereby forced many of its competitors to do the same or lose market share. Toyota's employees and managers are strongly encouraged to continuously search for ways to improve the process that reduces the costs of manufacturing cars and increases the quality of the autos manufactured.[9]

Undoubtedly, globalization has both positive and negative effects on most countries as suggested in *The World Is Flat*, mentioned previously. It provides opportunities for companies to expand and grow by entering new foreign markets. It can also improve the economic development of countries. Yet, competition from foreign firms entering their home markets can harm some local companies. Some of the questions about China relate to their effect on U.S.-based firms and their employees in the United States. Competition in U.S. markets from Chinese firms has seriously harmed U.S. furniture and textile firms. Thus, government officials have to weigh the benefits of globalization against the costs. Often these officials are under significant pressure by different constituencies to institute trade barriers that make it more difficult for foreign firms to compete effectively in their home markets.

Understanding a Country's Environment

Wal-Mart, the biggest company in the world, employs over 500,000 employees across the globe. The company serves 49 million customers in international markets via 2,700 stores, and enjoys sales of over $67 billion in international markets.[10] To continue to grow and be profitable, it is important for Wal-Mart to know which markets to enter and how to compete in them. There are two major aspects of a country's environment that managers need to understand: institutions and culture. We discuss each next.

The Country's Institutional Environment

Each country has a distinct institutional environment composed of economic development, political-legal, and physical infrastructure dimensions. The institutional environment consists of the country's rules, policies, and enforcement processes. This, in turn, influences the behavior of the individuals and organizations that operate within the country.[11]

The Economic Development Dimension

Countries vary in their level of economic development. Economic development and growth is vital to most countries because it contributes to better living standards and the health and welfare of citizens.[12] Economic development is important to local and foreign firms as well because it opens up greater market opportunities for them.

Country economies may be classified into developed, emerging, and developing economies. Some countries, such as the United States and Japan, have highly developed economies. Others such as Sudan and El Salvador have less-developed economies. Still others, like China and India, have economies that are not highly developed but are growing rapidly. These economies are classified as emerging.[13] For example, the countries in Western Europe have developed economies, whereas most of the countries in Eastern Europe have emerging economies.

Developed economies tend to be larger than less-developed or emerging economies. They also tend to have more-effective capital markets. In effective capital markets, people and businesses are readily able to borrow money from banks and other financial institutions or raise it by selling shares in stock markets. Developed economies tend to be larger than those in other countries. Emerging economy countries like China often have rapidly growing economies and their capital markets tend to be young and underdeveloped. Finally, the weakest economies exist in developing economies.

The Political-Legal Dimension

This dimension of the institutional environment refers to a country's political risks, regulations, laws, and the enforcement of them. Governments develop laws and policies to govern the behavior of their citizens and organizations operating within the country's boundaries.[14] Among the important regulations that affect businesses are those related to the way foreign firms operate. These regulations include laws that put tariffs and quotas on imported goods, laws that dictate the way employees are treated, and laws dictating how publicly traded firms listed on major exchanges in the country must behave.

For example, after China began to open its markets (partially at least), all foreign firms entering the country were required to form joint ventures with Chinese firms. Foreign firms' behaviors were regulated in order to protect local firms that often lacked the resources and capabilities needed to compete with firms from developed countries. In recent years, the Sarbanes-Oxley Act, often referred to as SOX, enacted by the United States in 2002, was designed to curtail scandals like the ones at Enron and WorldCom. Both domestic and foreign firms registered on U.S. stock exchanges must adhere to the provisions set forth in SOX. For example, all CEOs and CFOs must certify that the financial statements published by the firm are accurate and satisfy the rules set forth by standards in the industry and legal requirements. Almost 1,300 companies restated their earnings in 2005 because of SOX, which is more than any other previous year since records have been maintained.[15]

Primarily, the rules established by the law are intended to make the management of public firms more transparent. Yet, the rules can be excessive and discourage investment from abroad. Furthermore, an increasing amount of companies are going private (buying back their publicly traded stock) in order to avoid having to deal with the costly reporting rules required by the law. Thus, in late 2006, the U.S. Securities and Exchange Commission announced a number of "deregulation" orders designed to make compliance with the law less onerous on businesses.[16] Laws such as SOX play an important role in countries' institutional environments.

Among the important laws are those regarding intellectual property rights. When the laws related to and enforcement of intellectual property rights (e.g., patents) are weak, firms with valuable technologies are reluctant to bring them into the country. And, if they do enter the country's markets, they may not use the valuable technology in the market there or will guard it carefully to ensure their local partners don't access it. However, when barriers to such knowledge exist, they reduce the value of the joint venture, especially to the local partner. Local partners in developing and emerging markets often have goals of learning technological and managerial capabilities from their more-capable foreign partners.[17]

The Physical Infrastructure Dimension

Institutional infrastructure is critical to the operation of businesses within a country because they facilitate business communications and the movement of goods from their source to the ultimate consumer. Physical infrastructure includes the amount and quality of roads and highways, number of telephone lines (per capita), and number of airports, etc. The availability of physical infrastructure often plays an important role in decisions to enter a new international market by a foreign firm because they tend to perform more poorly in countries where the infrastructure is not well developed.[18] Therefore, countries that wish to attract foreign investment must try to develop their physical infrastructure.[19]

Without the physical infrastructure, it is difficult for firms to distribute their products to potential customers. Thus, they either have to sell to smaller markets because they are unable to reach as many potential customers, or they have to distribute their products in much more costly ways. In either case, the firm earns lower profits than it would if the country's physical infrastructure was more well developed.

Importance of the Institutional Environment

Economic growth is vital to most countries because it contributes to the standards of living, health, and welfare of their citizens.[20] Economic growth is important to local and foreign firms as well. Higher rates of economic growth suggest greater market opportunities for all firms and attract new business development and foreign investments in the country's economy.

Beyond the attractiveness of a country's economic development and health, laws, regulations, political stability, and physical infrastructure play important roles in firms' behaviors. In particular, multinational firms seeking to invest in new international markets need to understand these elements of a country's institutional environment. These institutional dimensions can greatly affect a firm's willingness to make direct investments in a country's markets. Furthermore recent research shows that the strong presence of multinational firms in a country strongly influences the development of its institutional environment. For example, the greater number of multinational corporations in a country the greater the pressure on its government to develop and enforce legislation to reduce corruption.[21] The influences are partly because of these firms' effects on the country's economic development and growth. Alternatively, corruption also discourages foreign companies from making major investments in a country.[22] As we will learn later in the chapter, institutional environments have major effects on firms' international strategies and especially affect which countries firms enter.

While institutional forces play an important role in determining firms' behaviors within a country, societal culture plays at least as strong a role. Culture's effects may be more pervasive because of its influence on human behavior. Next, we examine the nature of culture and its effects on individual and firm behaviors.

Culture

Although institutional forces play an important role in terms of how and where businesses globalize, a society's culture is critical. Culture is a learned set of assumptions, values, and beliefs that have been accepted by members of a group and that affect human behavior.[23] Some have referred to culture as a collective programming of the mind that has a powerful effect on individual behavior.[24] Although a culture can exist among any group of people, our focus is on national cultures.

Understanding culture is critical because it can dramatically influence how people observe and interpret the business world around them—for example, whether they see situations as opportunities or threats. A person's culture likely affects his or her opinion about the "right" managerial behavior. For example, only 10 percent of Swedish managers believe they should have precise answers to most questions subordinates ask them, whereas 78 percent of Japanese managers think they should.[25] As this specific example illustrates, culture can contribute to preexisting ways of interpreting events, evaluating them, and determining a course of action.

Cultural Dimensions

The most prominent studies of culture were conducted by Geert Hofstede and by a large number of researchers led by Robert House referred to as GLOBE.[26] Both these complex studies identified at least four prominent dimensions of national culture: power distance, uncertainty avoidance, individualism versus collectivism, and gender focus.

Power distance is the extent to which people accept power and authority differences among people. Power distance is not a measure of the extent to which there are power and status differences in a group. Most countries have richer and poorer citizens, and more and less powerful citizens. Power distance does not suggest whether or not status and power differentials exist in a country but rather the extent to which people in the country accept any differences. In Hofstede's study, people from the Philippines, Venezuela, and Mexico had the highest levels of acceptance of power differences. In contrast, Austria, Israel, and Denmark had the lowest levels of acceptance.

Cultures differ in the extent to which they need things to be clear or ambiguous. This dimension of culture has been labeled uncertainty avoidance. Citizens in nations high in uncertainty avoidance prefer clear norms (rules that govern behavior). Groups high in uncertainty avoidance create structures and institutions to reduce uncertainty. By contrast, groups that are low in uncertainty avoidance prefer to have fewer rules and tend to be more comfortable in ambiguous situations. For example, managers from Sweden, the Netherlands, and the United States are most comfortable with uncertainty. Managers from Indonesia and Japan are least comfortable with high uncertainty.

Individualism is the extent to which people's identities are self-oriented and people are expected to take care of themselves and their immediate families. People from the United States and Great Britain often score high on individual orientations. Individuals from these countries exhibit high emotional independence from organizations and institutions and tend to emphasize and reward individual achievement and value individual decisions. Alternatively, collectivism is the extent to which a person's identity is a function of the group(s) to which the person belongs (his or her family, firm, community, and so forth) and the extent to which group members are expected to look after each other. People from China, Venezuela, and Pakistan have high collective orientations. People from these countries tend to exhibit emotional dependence on organizations and institutions to which they belong, emphasize group membership, and value collective decisions.

Gender focus represents the extent to which people in a country value masculine or feminine traits. Countries emphasizing masculine traits value activities that lead to success, money, and possessions. Alternatively those emphasizing feminine traits value activities that show a caring for others and enhance the quality of life.

Countries such as the United States tend to emphasize masculine traits. In the United States, people often work many hours a week (usually over 60 hours), and take shorter vacations. In other countries that do not emphasize masculine traits, work is often valued less.

Understanding cultures can be valuable for a number of reasons. For example, cultural characteristics can predict how managers will respond to socially responsible actions. Research has shown that managers in cultures that emphasize collectivism and are low in power distance engage in greater amounts of socially responsible activities than cultures with high individualism and high power distance.[27]

Globalization has greatly enhanced the extent to which cultural diversity plays a role in business. As companies globalize and expand their operations around the world, they create an increased opportunity and demand for people from different cultures to effectively interact together. Managers must interact and deal with suppliers, customers, and partners from different cultures. We discuss the management of cultural diversity within companies and relationships across cultures later in this chapter.

Knowing and understanding different institutional environments and cultures is important if managers are to make good strategic decisions about which foreign markets to enter and how to manage operations established in these markets. We examine these strategies next and discuss how different institutional and cultural environments affect the strategies chosen and how to implement and manage them.

International Market-Entry Strategies

Choosing which international markets to enter and how to enter them is critically important to many small-, medium-, and large-sized firms in recent times. With the increasing globalization discussed at the beginning of this chapter, a large number of firms are servicing international markets at their birth. International markets are attractive to firms for several reasons. International markets increase the size of firms' potential markets and their sales revenue. When they sell more products abroad, these firms gain greater economies of scale, which, in turn, increases their potential profit. Firms can also gain access to special resources (e.g., lower-cost labor, valuable raw materials) in some international locations that can help them become more competitive in global markets. These are referred to as location advantages.[28]

The previous information suggests that firms have considerable motivation to enter international markets. Yet, all international markets are not created equal. As stated earlier, countries vary in their institutional environments and cultures. Thus, the attractiveness of countries' markets also varies. First, early in their internationalization efforts, firms prefer to enter markets that have similar institutional environments and similar cultures to their home country. This is because they better understand these environments and thereby take less risk entering these markets. This is important, especially for small firms with less capital, because entering international markets requires resources and learning about the new market and environment rapidly.[29] For these reasons and to reduce potential costs, firms also often cluster their international operations in one or a few geographic regions.[30] As firms gain more experience entering and operating in international markets, they are willing to enter markets where the differences in institutional environments and cultures are greater. Yet, the institutional environments and cultural differences also influence the means by which firms enter new international markets.

Firms can enter new foreign markets in a variety of ways. Each poses different risks and requires different levels and types of resources. Among the ways to enter a new market are by exporting products to the market, licensing products to firms there, either acquiring or creating strategic alliances with local firms, or establishing your own operations in the country. We explore each of these strategies next.

Exporting

The most common way of entering international markets is by exporting goods. This is especially true for smaller firms and for firms initially entering into foreign markets. Exporting involves manufacturing products in a firm's home country and shipping them to a foreign market. It is a popular entry strategy because of the lower capital requirements and risks. Exporting does not require establishing operations in the country, thereby avoiding a large capital investment. However, it does require the exporting firm to establish a means of marketing and distributing its goods within the country. Thus, it may have to combine exporting and strategic alliances with local firms in order to distribute their goods to customers. As a result, the costs of transportation and having to share profits with a local firm can reduce the profits a firm can earn from the international market. Therefore, although an export strategy is less risky, it is unlikely to provide big returns because of its associated costs. If the exporting firm's transportation costs are high, it might be limited to exporting only to countries in close proximity of their home base of operations. Exports are also particularly sensitive to fluctuations in exchange rates.[31]

Licensing

Licensing arrangements allow a local firm in the new market to manufacture and distribute a firm's product. Usually, the licensing contract provides the specifications to maintain quality and the quantity to produce and sell along with the royalty percentages on the sales. In these cases, the licensor has low costs and takes little risk; the licensee takes the major risks. Yet, licensing is unlikely to produce major returns for the licensor unless the potential sales in the new market are large.

The Altria Group, owner of Philip Morris brand cigarettes, is losing sales in the United States due to declining cigarette use. Thus, it is searching for new markets for its products. Recently, it has signed a license agreement with two Chinese firms to manufacture and market cigarettes in China under the Marlboro brand. This arrangement might still be lucrative for the Altria Group because the market for cigarettes in China is large and growing.[32]

Although licensing has advantages, it also has disadvantages. The primary disadvantage is that the licensing firm has little control over its product and the use of its brand in the new market. This underscores how important it is for a firm's licensing contracts to be clear and enforceable. Unfortunately, contracts with Chinese firms often go unenforced. Remember, most of China's legal and regulatory institutions are relatively new. Thus, the Altria Group could experience problems if it doesn't like how China is using the Marlboro brand. Like exporting, licensing is also unlikely to produce big returns for a firm unless sales in the new market are large.

Creating Strategic Alliances

The most popular strategy for international expansion has become strategic alliances. Strategic alliances are cooperative arrangements between two firms in which they agree to share resources to accomplish a mutually desirable goal. Strategic alliances allow firms to share the costs and risks of entering new markets, and they provide the opportunity for firms to access resources they do not have. As such, it also allows them to sometimes learn new capabilities from their partners.[33] In this way, alliances can contribute to a firm's ability to maintain or increase its competitiveness in global markets.

Moreover, strategic alliances allow firms to outsource functions they once did in-house to other companies abroad. Although the strategy can give a firm access to better and cheaper service functions, it isn't always problem free.

Strategic alliances allow firms to outsource functions that they completed in-house previously. A Manager's Challenge explains the advantages and disadvantages of outsourcing. In general, outsourcing allows firms to gain access to better and often cheaper performance of functions. In this way, firms can compete better in international markets and even to enter and compete in some markets where they could not compete previously. The vignette also suggests one of the problems of outsourcing alliances. The differences in culture and language can lead to a less than satisfactory performance. For example, Dell experienced problems after it outsourced its customer support function to India. It received a substantial number of complaints and bad publicity that probably resulted in lost sales.

Not all strategic alliances are successful. A large number of them fail. Yet equity-based alliances, such as joint ventures whereby companies share risks and rewards, tend to be more successful because the firm has more voice in and control of the activities completed by the alliance or venture. Trust also seems to be an important factor in the success of an alliance.[34] So is the way in which firms manage alliances. As such, many firms are establishing alliance management functions to increase the success because of the large number of strategic alliances firms are forming.[35]

A country's institutional environment affects the decision to enter its markets and the means chosen to enter. In addition to the particular institutions in place, the stability of the institutions is of interest to foreign firms. Uncertainty in the institutional environment can stunt economic growth, making markets less desirable.[36] At the very least, firms entering uncertain institutional environments need to do so in ways that lower their risk. Forming strategic alliances to share resources and risks is one way of doing so.[37] Uncertainty in the country's institutional environment also affects the type of alliance formed and the type of partner desired. For example, in uncertain environments, firms look for short-term partners. In more stable institutional environments, firms select alliance partners with whom they can work over the long term. In Other words, they seek long-term returns from their alliance partnerships.[38]

Acquisitions

Acquisitions of local firms made by foreign firms to enter a new international market are referred to as cross-border acquisitions. The number of cross-border acquisitions has increased in recent years. Such acquisitions are more common among non-U.S. firms. For example, the number of cross-border acquisitions by European firms has grown dramatically in recent years. Even firms from emerging market countries have used this strategy as exemplified by the Chinese firm Lenova's acquisition of IBM's laptop computer business.

In recent years, approximately 40 percent to 50 percent of acquisitions made worldwide are cross-border acquisitions.[39] Acquisitions of a local firm in order to enter a new foreign market have several advantages. For one, they provide a fast way to enter a market. Operations in the new market are immediate with the acquired firm's customers, facilities, and relationships (e.g., with suppliers, government units, etc.). It generally represents the largest new market entry of the different alternatives. Wal-Mart entered the United Kingdom and Germany using acquisitions of local firms in those countries.[40]

Cross-border acquisitions are sometimes controversial with the local public or government. Such was true when CNOOC, the large Chinese petroleum company, attempted to acquire Unocal, a large U.S.-based oil company. CNOOC withdrew its bid because of objections from many in the U.S. Congress. Thus, there are disadvantages to cross-border acquisitions as well.

Cross-border acquisitions usually entail many of the potential advantages of acquisitions made within a firm's own home country. But if there are problems with a cross-border acquisition, they can be severe. For example, a common problem in acquisitions is the challenge of integrating two previously independent companies. Differences in the corporate cultures between the acquiring and acquired firms make integration difficult. Yet, cross-border acquisitions face a double-layered cultural integration problem.[41] Integration requires overcoming differences in corporate culture and national culture. Outside of selecting the right target, integration is the largest reason for the failure of acquisitions.[42]

Costs are another major disadvantage of cross-border acquisitions. It has become common for acquiring firms to pay a premium (more than market value) for target firms. Yet, premiums may be a larger problem in cross-border acquisitions because the acquiring firms frequently have less information on the target than in domestic acquisitions. And, research has shown that premiums are highest in host countries known for having a large amount of corruption.[43]

Therefore, if acquiring firms make the correct choice of target and do not overpay for the acquisition, it can be a positive opportunity to enter a new foreign market. Yet, the acquiring firm still must achieve integration, and that is likely to present a challenge.

Establishing New, Wholly Owned Subsidiaries

Some firms prefer to establish a new, wholly owned subsidiary to enter a new international market. When a company creates a wholly owned subsidiary in a foreign country, it makes a direct investment to establish a business that it solely owns and controls there. Such a subsidiary is often called a "Greenfield venture."

Greenfield ventures afford the firm maximum control over the operations. Firms such as Starbucks—those with strong intangible resources including a good brand name, human capital, and so forth—may prefer Greenfield ventures to enter international markets because it allows them to buffer these assets from current and potential competitors in the new market.[44]

Greenfield ventures are often complex and expensive to launch. To maintain that control requires that the firm not only build its own facilities, it must establish relationships with suppliers, build distribution networks within the foreign country, and foster a positive relationship with potential consumers. Thus, they must attract customers from existing competitors or convince new customers to buy their product. Firms establishing Greenfield ventures must learn about the national culture and institutional environment—on their own. If the cultural distance or institutional distance between the home and host countries is high, a firm may experience difficulties establishing a new wholly owned subsidiary or making one that they establish to be successful. Therefore, the risks of establishing these subsidiaries can be quite high.[45]

With the development of the Chinese economy and the significant amount of cross-border trade between Western country firms and Chinese firms, UPS is establishing new wholly owned subsidiaries in Shanghai and FedEx is doing the same in Guangzhou. The firms entered the markets with Greenfield investments because they needed to ensure fast and reliable service and the desire to maintain control over their logistics operations.[46]

While wholly owned subsidiaries are valuable and allow firms to control their operations, they are risky and not always successful. EBay entered the China market with a partial acquisition of Eachnet.com in 2002 followed by a full buyout of the company in 2003, paying a total of $180 million for the company. In 2005, eBay invested over $100 million in marketing for its wholly owned Chinese subsidiary. Even with the acquisition, eBay was unable to manage the Chinese marketplace and fend off competition. Its primary competitor in China, Taobao, took market share from eBay's subsidiary. While Meg Whitman, CEO of eBay, has touted the Chinese market and eBay's Chinese subsidiary as a future growth engine for the company, in December 2006, eBay announced it was shutting down its main Web site in China and forming a joint venture with Tom Online, Inc., to operate in the Chinese market. Analysts said eBay lost market share because the company neither understood the Chinese market and culture nor quickly countered Taobao's challenge.[47] Now, eBay will use a Chinese partner to help it navigate the challenging Chinese market.

The decisions to enter foreign markets, what markets to enter, and how to enter them are very important. Yet, the management of international operations also affects their success. In the following sections, we explore the management of these international operations, first examining the corporate approach used. We then examine how to manage across cultures with emphasis on managing cross-cultural teams.

Managing International Operations

Companies must choose the manner in which they manage their international subsidiaries, and these choices carry important meaning for the management and flow of resources and information throughout the international operations in the company. Of critical importance is the degree of autonomy granted to the individual subsidiaries to develop and implement their own strategies. One of three different approaches—a global focus, region/country focus, or a transnational focus—reflects the focus of the home office.

Taking a Global Focus

In a globally focused organization, the firm's home office makes major strategic decisions. Thus, the global organization has centralized authority, and the international subsidiaries usually follow the same or a similar strategy in each of their markets. These organizations normally attempt to market a relatively standardized product across geographic markets. Such an approach provides economies of scale and helps to manage the costs and thereby to enhance the profits. Thus, it helps firms to gain returns on innovative products developed in the home country market, especially firms that compete in markets where price is a critical competitive concern. In a globally focused organization, subsidiaries often share resources, allowing the most efficient allocation of resources throughout the company.

While a global focus has several advantages as noted previously, it also has some disadvantages. Because it does not allow the international subsidiary the flexibility to decide how to compete, it may be unable to take advantage of market opportunities when they occur. Furthermore an international subsidiary operating in a globally focused organization does not have the flexibility to react quickly to competitors' strategic moves. As such, they are vulnerable to competitors taking strategic actions with the intent of "stealing" market share in the local market. These international subsidiaries cannot respond easily to changes in customers' needs in the local market. Vodaphone used a global focus but then was unable to respond to local customers' needs in Japan and lost market share. Alternatively, Cemex, the third-largest cement company in the world, uses a global focus successfully. In this case, the type of product sold (e.g., ready mix cement) can largely be standardized. Cemex, headquartered in Mexico, has operations in North America, South America, Asia, and Europe. The centralized approach used by Cemex provides economies of scale and higher returns.[48]

Taking a Region–Country Focus

In an organization using a region–country focus, the primary authority to determine competitive strategy rests with the managers of its international subsidiary based in a region of the world or a specific country. In this way, the region or country managers can tailor their strategies to local market conditions and demands. For example, subsidiaries can design, manufacture, and sell products that best satisfy local market customers. In this sense, subsidiaries can customize products for the local customers as opposed to the home office dictating product features. Thus, this type of organization is highly decentralized. The advantage of this approach is that it is flexible and allows a subsidiary to react quickly to changes in the marketplace. It can respond rapidly to competitors' strategic moves and can also respond quickly to take advantage of new market opportunities identified. It is most effective when the firm's subsidiaries operate in widely different markets indicated by countries with different cultures and different institutional environments. However, such an approach can be expensive for the company because it cannot achieve economies of scale. Furthermore, the diversity of strategies across markets may be difficult to oversee and govern from the home office. In particular, it may be difficult for home-office managers to evaluate the performance of subsidiary managers, especially if it requires assessing the value of the strategy chosen by that manager.

European multinational firms commonly use the region–country focused approach because they are operating in multiple countries with different institutional environments across Europe.[49] Unilever, a well-known European consumer products company, has traditionally used a decentralized approach to manage its international operations.[50]

Taking a Transnational Focus

Two well-known scholars and management consultants, Christopher Bartlett and Sumantra Ghoshal, developed the idea of a transnational organization. They suggest that a transnational organization is one that strives to be simultaneously centralized and decentralized. As such, its goal is to achieve global efficiency while maintaining local market responsiveness. In these organizations, strategic decisions are decentralized. Nonetheless, the organizations usually try to achieve global efficiency by having their subsidiaries share resources. Shared values, trusting relationships, and incentive systems that reward subsidiary managers for the firm's overall performance help facilitate this cooperation.

Effectively managed, this type of an organization often outperforms either of the other two types of organizations. Although it's easier to achieve either global efficiency or local responsiveness than it is to achieve both simultaneously, a company can do it. For example, Nissan CEO Carlos Ghosn used a transnational focus to turn around that automaker's performance. The different business units worked to achieve global efficiency while also maintaining responsiveness to regional markets. Thanks partly to the transnational focus, Nissan is now one of the top performers in the global automobile industry.[51]

While the overall focus, amount of authority delegated to subsidiary managers, and the degree of resource sharing across international subsidiaries are all important, managing diverse units across cultures and multicultural teams is critical to the firm's performance. Therefore, we examine these next.

Managing Across Cultures

In multinational firms with subsidiaries operating in multiple international markets, managers must often oversee, direct, and evaluate employees and other managers from different cultures and institutional environments. Managing people from a single country is a significant challenge; managing people operating in different cultures and institutional environments is often an extreme challenge—one that is very complex. It requires managers to understand cultural differences and how these differences affect employees' attitudes and behaviors.

Perhaps one of the most useful concepts for examining and understanding different countries' cultures is cultural context.[52] Cultural context is the degree to which a situation influences behavior or perception of the appropriateness of behaviors. In high-context cultures, people pay close attention to the situation and its various elements. Key contextual variables determine appropriate and inappropriate behavior. In low-context cultures, contextual variables have much less impact on the determination of appropriate behaviors. In other words, in low-context cultures, the situation may or may not affect what is considered appropriate behavior, but in high-context cultures, the context has a significant influence on this judgment.

For example, in Japan there are five different words for the pronoun *you*. The context determines what form of the pronoun *you* is appropriate for addressing different people. If you are talking to a customer holding a significantly higher title than yours, who works in a large company such as Matsushita, and is several years older, you would be expected to use the term *otaku* when addressing the customer. If you were talking to a subordinate several years younger, *kimi* is the appropriate pronoun.

With this in mind, consider some of the issues related to managing both people who come from low-context and high-context cultures. For example, imagine a team composed of one person each from the United States, Australia, Korea, and Japan. The team meets to discuss a global production problem and report to a senior executive from a client company. For the two people from low-context cultures (the United States and Australia), the phrase "say what you mean, and mean what you say" would not only be familiar to them but appropriate. Consequently, if the senior executive asked if the team could complete a specific task and the team had already discussed the impossibility of the task, the two team members from low-context cultures would most likely say "no." To say "yes" when you mean "no" would not be appropriate regardless of the fact that the senior executive from a client is in the room. These two people would likely view someone who said "yes" when he or she meant "no" with suspicion and at worst as untruthful.

But for the two team members from high-context cultures, the fact that the senior executive from a client is in the room asking the questions influences their perception of the appropriate response. For them, in this situation, saying "yes" when they meant "no" would be entirely appropriate. To say "no" without considering the context would be considered unsophisticated, self-centered, or simply immature.

Imagine then the manager's problem if the American replies that what the client is asking for is not possible while the Korean member of the team says it is. Not only will this confuse the client, but imagine the attributions that the American and Australian are likely to make about their Japanese and Korean team members, and, in turn, what the Korean and Japanese team members probably think of the other two. Without understanding the influence of culture context, the team trust and effectiveness could suffer.

The key issue for managers leading multicultural teams is to recognize that neither high-context nor low-context cultures are correct or incorrect; rather, they are quite different. These differences influence the effectiveness of a manager's behaviors, including their communication, negotiation, decision making, and leadership skills. The previous case helps illustrate the concept and some of its implications. It points out that a lack of awareness of this fundamental dimension of cultural differences can lead to misinterpretations, mistaken attributions, mistrust, and ineffectiveness.

However, managing people working in different countries, cultures, and institutional environments is not the only complex managerial situation managers must confront in multinational enterprises. Even within countries, local workforces are becoming more culturally diverse. This is certainly true in the United States, which is considered a "melting pot" of many cultures. As globalization continues at a rapid pace, it is also becoming increasingly the case in many other countries. Many people of European descent, Asian ethnicities (e.g., Chinese, Korean, Japanese, Vietnamese), African ethnicity, Hispanic ethnicity, etc., coexist, living and working together in the same organizations and in similar jobs. Therefore, managers often have to manage multicultural teams within one organization in one location.

Managing Multicultural Teams

The first type of multicultural team is geographically dispersed across country borders. Although geographically dispersed, they often focus on regular business tasks such as developing new marketing programs and products. Yet, the team interacts somewhat differently than more traditional teams. Instead of face-to-face meetings, members frequently depend on technologically mediated communications, such as e-mail, Internet chat rooms, company intranets, teleconferencing, videoconferencing, and so forth.[53] Often the groups are called virtual teams because of their reliance on electronic communication.

The forms of communication vary in their richness, leaving open the possibility that messages will be misperceived or misunderstood especially because the communications must cross cultures. When problems like this occur, it can disrupt the team's ability to complete its task(s). If misunderstandings occur early in the development team's formation, members may not trust, a characteristic important for the functioning of such teams. Trust is especially important for geographically dispersed multicultural teams because they often lack traditional direct supervision, must work more autonomously, and cannot coordinate with other team members as easily as more traditional teams.[54]

In these international teams, significant responsibility rests with the team manager to ensure effective function. Team managers need to build trust rapidly early in the development of these teams. Building trust rapidly is sometimes referred to as swift trust. Swift trust is the rapid development of trust in teams with positive and reciprocal communications about the team's task activities.[55] To build swift trust, the team manager must help members communicate with one another in a positive way, coordinate their efforts, and quickly eliminate any misunderstandings. To do this, the manager must have significant cultural knowledge and sensitivity in addition to effective managerial skills. The manager builds a unified vision and emphasizes collaborative outcomes with international teams for greatest success.[56]

Developing a Global Mind-set

With the opening of world markets, firms from all over the world are formulating strategies to increase their presence in international markets. As such, these strategies and managers' abilities to manage diverse country operations and people from multiple cultures are critical to firm performance.[57] Because of this global evolution, the competitive terrain is changing in many international markets.⁵⁸ Competing in international markets, managing international operations, and managing multicultural teams requires managers to develop a global mind-set. A global mind-set is a set of cognitive attributes that allows an individual (e.g., manager) to influence individuals, groups, and organizations from diverse sociocultural and institutional environments.⁵⁹ The composition of a team can influence such a mind-set. A. G. Lafley, the CEO of Procter & Gamble, reformulated his top management team so that at least 50 percent of its members came from outside the United States. Lafley's goal was to help his top managers adopt a global mind-set.⁶⁰

While a global mind-set is important for operating multinational enterprises, some have expressed concerns about the globalization trend. As described in the box, globalization has created concerns on the part of some who believe that societies may lose their cultural identities over time. Others doubt this possibility and see the benefits of globalization. In addition to the economic benefits, it also facilitates the development of cultural sensitivity and understanding. There are countries that attempt to form barriers to globalization, refusing to participate in the economic globalization. Unfortunately, such actions will not stop the process. And, as the economic benefits accrue to other countries, the ones that create barriers are harmed the most because they lose out on economic development. Firms and managers that understand the value of unique cultures and institutions can adapt and use cultural differences to advantage. A global mind-set helps them do that.

Jagdish Sheth, a well-known scholar and consultant on international trends, argues that we can expect cultural integration over time—not cultural clashes. Sheth believes that Western cultures will not dominate the globe as some people fear. Rather, he believes Western societies such as the United States will adopt Asian cultural values because of the increase in economic power and influence of China and India and the greater acceptance and willingness by Westerners to assimilate diverse cultures. The United States and Canada, for example, are already multicultural with large minority populations, including ethnic Chinese and Indians. This cultural integration will lead to increased diversity within cultures and geographic regions.⁶¹ As a result, the ability to manage multicultural workforces and serve multicultural consumer markets will continue to be more highly valued. These trends heighten why it's important for managers to develop a global mind-set.

Endnotes

1. M. A. Hitt, R. D. Ireland, and R. E. Hoskisson, *Strategic Management: Competitiveness and Globalization* (Cincinnati, OH: Thomson/South-Western Publishing, 2007); P. Williamson and M. Zeng, "Strategies for Competing in a Changed China," *MIT Sloan Management Review* 45, no. 4 (2004): 85–91.
2. T. L. Friedman, *The World Is Flat* (New York: Farrar, Straus and Giroux, 2005).
3. M. Mandel, "Can Anyone Steer This Economy?" *BusinessWeek,* November 20, 2006, 56–62.
4. M. A. Hitt, H. Li, and W. Worthington, "Emerging Markets as Learning Laboratories: Learning Behaviors of Local Firms and Foreign Entrants in Different Institutional Contexts," *Management and Organization Review* I (2005): 353–380.
5. Friedman, *The World Is Flat.*
6. Ibid.
7. D. Wilson and R. Purushothaman, "Dreaming with BRICs: The Path to 2050". Goldman Sachs Global Economics Paper No. 9, 2003.
8. R. D. Ireland, M. A. Hitt, S. M. Camp, and D. S. Sexton, "Integrating Entrepreneurship and Strategic Management Actions to Create Firm Wealth," *Academy of Management Executive* 46, no. 34 (2001): 49–63.
9. C. Fishman. "No Satisfaction," *Fast Company,* December 2006, 82–92.
10. Wal-Mart International Fact Sheet, www.walmartfacts.com, November 2006.
11. M. A. Hitt, R. M. Holmes, T. Miller, and M. P. Salmador, Modeling country institutional profiles: The dynamics of institutional environments. Paper presented at the Strategic Management Society Conference, November, Vienna, Austria, 2006.

12. S. Chetty, K. Eriksson, and J. Lindbergh, "The Effect of Specificity of Experience on a Firm's Perceived Importance of Institutional Knowledge in an Ongoing Business," *Journal of International Business Studies* 37 (2006): 699–712.
13. R. Hoskisson, L. Eden, C.M. Lau, and M. Wright, "Strategy in Emerging Economies," *Academy of Management Journal* (Special Research Forum on Strategies in Emerging Economies) 433 (2000): 249–67.
14. J. Dunning, "Reevaluating the Benefits of Foreign Direct Investment," *Transnational Corporations* 34 (1994): 23–51.
15. *Business Week*, "The Jury Is Out," December 8, 2006, 106.
16. S. Labaton, "S.E.C. Eases Regulations on Business," *New York Times*, December 14, 2006, www.nytimes.com.
17. M. A. Hitt, M. T. Dacin, E. Levitas, J. -L. Arregle, and A. Borza, "Partner Selection in Developed and Emerging Market Contexts: Resource-based and Organizational Learning Perspectives," *Academy of Management Journal* 434 (2000): 4349–4467.
18. T. Isobe, S. Makino, and D. B. Montgomery, "Resource Commitment, Entry Timing, and Market Performance of Foreign Direct Investments in Emerging Economies: The Case of Japanese International Joint Ventures in China," *Academy of Management Journal* 43 (2000): 468–484.
19. S. M. Lee, "South Korea: From the Land of Morning Calm to ICT Hotbed," *Academy of Management Executive* 17 (2003): 7–18.
20. S. Chetty, K. Eriksson, and J. Lindbergh, "The Effect of Specificity of Experience on a Firm's Perceived Importance of Institutional Knowledge in an Ongoing Business," *Journal of International Business Studies* 37 (2006): 699–712.
21. C. C. Kwok and S. Tadesse, "The MNC as an Agent of Change for Host-Country Institutions: FDI and Corruption," *Journal of International Business Studies* 37 (2006): 767–785.
22. A. Cuervo-Cazurra, "Who Cares About Corruption?" *Journal of International Business Studies* 37 (2006): 807–822.
23. K. Leung, R. S. Bhagat, N. R. Buchan, M. Erez, and C. B. Gibson, "Culture and International Business: Recent Advances and Their Implications for the Future," *Journal of International Business Studies* 36 (2005): 357–378.
24. P. C. Earley, "Leading Cultural Research in the Future: A Matter of Paradigms and Taste," *Journal of International Business Studies* 37 (2006): 922–931.
25. R. Steers and J. S. Black, *Organization Behavior* (New York: HarperCollins, 1994).
26. G. Hofstede, *Culture's Consequences* (Beverly Hills, CA: Sage, 1980): G. Hofstede, *Cultures and Organizations* (Berkshire, U. K.: McGraw-Hill, 1994): R. J. House, P. J. Hanges, et al., *Culture, Leadership and Organizations: The Globe Study of 62 Societies* (Thousand Oaks, CA: Sage, 2004).
27. D. A. Waldman, A. S. de Luque, N. Washburn, R. J. House, et al. "Cultural and Leadership Predictors of Corporate Social Responsibility Values of Top Management: A GLOBE Study of 15 Countries," *Journal of International Business Studies* 37 (2006): 823–837.
28. Hitt, Ireland, and Hoskisson, *Strategic Management*.
29. H. J. Sapienza, E. Autio, G. George, and S. Zahra, "A Capabilities Perspective on the Effects of Early Internationalization on Firm Survival and Growth," *Academy of Management Review* 31 (2006): 914–933.
30. E. Maitland, E. L. Rose, and S. Nicholas, "How Firms Grow: Clustering as a Dynamic Model of Internationalization," *Journal of International Business Studies,* 36 (2005): 435–451.
31. Hitt, Ireland, and Hoskisson, *Strategic Management*.
32. N. Zamiska and V. O'Connell, "Philip Morris in Talks to Make Marlboro in China," *Wall Street Journal,* April 21, 2005, B1–B2.
33. J. S. Harrison, M. A. Hitt, R. E. Hoskisson, and R. D. Ireland, "Resource Complementarity in Business Combinations: Extending the Logic to Organizational Alliances," *Journal of Management* 27(2001): 679–690.
34. J. J. Reuer and M. Zollo, "Termination Outcomes of Research Alliances," *Research Policy* 34 (1) (2005): 101–115.
35. R. D. Ireland, M. A. Hitt, and D. Vaidyanath, "Alliance Management as a Source of Competitive Advantage," *Journal of Management* 28 (2002): 413–446.
36. Chetty, Eriksson, and Lindbergh, "The Effect of Specificity on Experience . . ."

37. Hitt, Dacin, Levitas, Arregle, and Borza, "Partner Selection in Developed and Emerging Market Contexts . . ."
38. M. A. Hitt, D. Ahlstrom, M. T. Dacin, E. Levitas, and L. Svobodina, "The Institutional Effects on Strategic Alliance Partner Selection in Transition Economies: China Versus Russia," *Organization Science* 15 (2004): 173–185.
39. K. Shimizu, M. A. Hitt, D. Vaidyanath, and V. Pisano, "Theoretical Foundations of Cross-border Mergers and Acquisitions: A Review of Current Research and Recommendations for the Future," *Journal of International Management* 10 (2004): 307–353.
40. J. Levine, "Europe: Gold Mines and Quicksand," *Forbes,* April 12, 2004, 76.
41. H. G. Barkema, J. H. J. Bell, and J. M. Pennings, "Foreign Entry, Cultural Barriers and Learning," *Strategic Management Journal* 17 (1996): 151–166.
42. M. A. Hitt, V. Franklin, and H. Zhu, "Culture, Institutions and International Strategy," *Journal of International Management* 12 (2006): 222–234.
43. U. Weitzel and S. Berns, "Cross-border Takeovers, Corruption, and Related Aspects of Governance," *Journal of International Business Studies* 37 (2006): 786–806.
44. A. W. Harzing, "Acquisitions Versus Greenfield Investments: International Strategy and Management of Entry Modes," *Strategic Management Journal* 23 (2002): 211–227.
45. B. Elango, "The Influence of Plant Characteristics on the Entry Mode Choice of Overseas Firms," *Journal of Operations Management* 23 (2005): 65–79.
46. B. Stanley, "United Parcel Service to Open a Hub in Shanghai," *Wall Street Journal,* July 8, 2005, B2; B. Stanley, "FedEx Plans Hub in Guangzhou: Facility to Begin Operation in 2008 as Cargo Industry Tries to Claim Turf in Asia," *Asian Wall Street Journal,* July 14, 2005, A3.
47. D. Lee, "EBay to Enlist a Partner in China," *Los Angeles Times,* December 20, 2006, www.latimes.com; K. Hafner and B. Stone, "EBay Is Expected to Close Its Auction Site in China," *New York Times,* December 19, 2006, www.nytimes.com.
48. Hitt, Ireland, and Hoskisson, *Strategic Management.*
49. A. W. Harzing and A. Sorge, "The Relative Impact of Country of Origin and Universal Contingencies in Internationalization Strategies and Corporate Control in Multinational Enterprises: Worldwide and European Perspectives," *Organization Studies* 24 (2003): 187–214.
50. G. Jones, "Control, Performance and Knowledge Transfers in Large Multinationals: Unilever in the United States, 1945–1980," *Business History Review* 76 (2002): 435–478.
51. J. P. Millikin and D. Fu, "The Global Leadership of Carlos Ghosn at Nissan," *Thunderbird International Business Review* 47, no. 1 (2005): 121–137.
52. E. Hall, *Beyond Culture* (Garden City, NY: Doubleday, 1976): S. A. Zahra, R. D. Ireland, and M. A. Hitt, "International Expansion by New Venture Firms: International Diversity, Mode of Entry, Technological Learning and Performance," *Academy of Management Journal* 43 (2000): 925–950.
53. D. L. Shapiro, S. A. Furst, G. M. Spreitzer, and M. A. Von Glinow, "Transnational Teams in the Electronic Age: Are Team Identity and High Performance at Risk?" *Journal of Organizational Behavior* 23 (2002): 455–467.
54. Y. Shin, "A Person-Environment Fit Model for Virtual Organizations," *Journal of Management,* 30 (2004): 725–743.
55. S. L. Jarvenpaa and D. E. Leidner, "Communication and Trust in Virtual Teams," *Organization Science,* 10 (1999): 791–815.
56. M. A. Hitt, C. C. Miller, and A. Colella, *Organizational Behavior: A Strategic Approach* (Hoboken, NJ: John Wiley & Sons, 2006).
57. M. A. Hitt, L. Tihanyi, T. Miller, and B. Connelly, "International Diversification: Antecedents, Outcomes and Moderators," *Journal of Management* 32 (2006): 831–867.
58. K. E. Meyer, "Global Focus in: From Domestic Conglomerates to Global Specialist," *Journal of Management Studies* 43(2006): 1109–1144.
59. M. Javidan, R. M. Steers, and M. A. Hitt (eds.). *The Global Mindset Advances in International Management,* Volume 19 (Amsterdam: Elsevier Science, 2007).
60. G. Colvin, "Lafley and Immelt: In Search of Billions," *Fortune,* December 11, 2006, 70–72.
61. J. Sheth, "Clash of Cultures or Fusion of Cultures? Implications for International Business," *Journal of International Management* 12 (2006): 218–221.

The Nature of Entrepreneurship

5

People with innovative ideas for new businesses don't always get the chance to turn them into reality. And a good percentage of them are women. Count-Me-In for Women's Economic Independence is trying to turn the tables and give female entrepreneurs a chance to get started. Co-founded by Nell Merlino (who also created Take Our Daughters to Work Day) and Iris Burnett, Count-Me-In provides "microcredit" loans in amounts from $500 to $10,000 to help women start and expand small businesses. Women qualify for the loans by a unique credit scoring system that doesn't hold against them things such as a divorce, time off to raise a family, or age—all things that might discourage conventional lenders. Merlino says: "Women own 38% of all businesses in this country, but still have far less access to capital than men because of today's process," Count-Me-In is out to change all that.[1]

Geneva Francais received a $1,500 loan from Count-Me-In to build storage shelves for her special cooking sauce "Geneva's Splash," brewed and bottled in her kitchen. Francais is a 65-year-old widow. She says: "A bank would not loan a woman money when she is 65 years old. It's as simple as that." Heather McCartney is married to a high school principal in New York. She received a $5,000 loan to expand "Ethnic Edibles," her line of cookies and cookie cutters designed according to traditional African motifs. The money will be used for packaging and marketing.[2]

Think about it. There is so much one can do with creativity and initiative. In fact, this is a chapter of examples. The goal is not only to inform, but to better familiarize you with the nature of entrepreneurship, small business, and new venture creation. The objective is also to stimulate you to consider starting your own business, become your own boss, and make your own special contribution to society. What about it? Can we count you into the world of entrepreneurship and small business?

The Nature of Entrepreneurship

Success in a highly competitive business environment depends on entrepreneurship. This term is used to describe strategic thinking and risk-taking behavior that result in the creation of new opportunities. H. Wayne Huizenga, who started Waste Management with just $5,000 and once owned Blockbuster Video and the Miami Dolphins, describes it this way: "An important part of being an entrepreneur is a gut instinct that allows you to believe in your heart that something will work even though everyone else says it will not. You say, 'I am going to make sure it works. I am going to go out there and make it happen.'"[3]

Who Are the Entrepreneurs?

An entrepreneur is a risk-taking individual who takes action to pursue opportunities others fail to recognize, or may even view as problems or threats. Business entrepreneurs start new ventures that bring to life new products or service ideas. Their stories are rich with ideas for all of us to consider. Although the people in the following examples are different, they share something in common. Each built a successful long-term business from good ideas and hard work.[4]

After a career in sales, Mary Kay Ash "retired" for a month. The year was 1963. When she started to write a book to help women compete in the male-dominated business world, she realized she was writing a business plan. From that plan arose Mary Kay Cosmetics.

From *Management*, 10th edition by John R. Schermerhorn. Copyright © 2009 by John Wiley & Sons, Inc. Reproduced with permission of John Wiley & Sons, Inc.

Launched with an investment of $5,000, the company now operates worldwide and has been named one of the best companies to work for in America. Mary Kay's goal from the beginning was "to help women everywhere reach their full potential."

Want to start an airline? Richard Branson decided he would and called it Virgin Atlantic. His career began in his native England with a student literary magazine and small mail-order record business. Since then he's built "Virgin" into one of the world's most recognized brand names. Virgin Group is a business conglomerate employing some 25,000 people around the globe. It holds over 200 companies, including Virgin Mobile, Virgin Records, and even a space venture—Virgin Galactic. It's all very creative and ambitious—but that's Branson. "I love to learn things I know little about," he says.

With a vision and a $175,000 loan, Earl Graves started *Black Enterprise* magazine in 1970. That success grew into the diversified business information company Earl G. Graves Ltd., including BlackEnterprise.com. Graves grew up in Brooklyn. New York, and at the age of 6 he was selling Christmas cards to neighbors. Today the business school at his college alma mater. Baltimore's Morgan State University, is named after him. Graves says: "I feel that a large part of my role as publisher of *Black Enterprise* is to be a catalyst for black economic development in this country."

In 1973, Anita Roddick was a 33-year-old housewife looking for a way to support herself and her two children. She spotted a niche for natural-based skin and health care products, and started mixing and selling them from a small shop in Brighton, England. The Body Shop has grown to some 1,500 outlets in 47 countries with 24 languages, selling a product every half-second to one of its 86 million customers. Known for her commitment to human rights, the environment, and economic development, Roddick once said: "If you think you're too small to have an impact, try going to bed with a mosquito."

Characteristics of Entrepreneurs

A common image of an entrepreneur is as the founder of a new business enterprise that achieves large-scale success, like the ones just mentioned. But entrepreneurs also operate on a smaller and less-public scale. Those who take the risk of buying a local McDonald's or Subway Sandwich franchise, opening a small retail shop, or going into a self-employed service business are also entrepreneurs. Similarly, anyone who assumes responsibility for introducing a new product or change in operations within an organization is also demonstrating the qualities of entrepreneurship.

Research suggests that entrepreneurs tend to share certain *attitudes and personal characteristics*. The general profile is of an individual who is very self-confident, determined, resilient, adaptable, and driven by excellence.[5] You should be able to identify these attributes in the prior examples. As shown in Exhibit 5.1, typical personality traits and characteristics of entrepreneurs include the following.[6]

- *Internal locus of control:* Entrepreneurs believe that they are in control of their own destiny; they are self-directing and like autonomy.
- *High energy level:* Entrepreneurs are persistent, hard working, and willing to exert extraordinary efforts to succeed.
- *High need for achievement:* Entrepreneurs are motivated to accomplish challenging goals; they thrive on performance feedback.
- *Tolerance for ambiguity:* Entrepreneurs are risk takers; they tolerate situations with high degrees of uncertainty.
- *Self-confidence:* Entrepreneurs feel competent, believe in themselves, and are willing to make decisions.
- *Passion and action orientation:* Entrepreneurs try to act ahead of problems; they want to get things done and not waste valuable time.
- *Self-reliance and desire for independence:* Entrepreneurs want independence: they are self-reliant; they want to be their own bosses, not work for others.
- *Flexibility:* Entrepreneurs are willing to admit problems and errors, and are willing to change a course of action when plans aren't working.

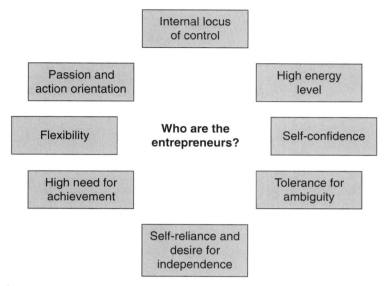

Exhibit 5.1 — Personality Traits and Characteristics of Entrepreneurs

Entrepreneurs also tend to have unique backgrounds and personal experiences.[7] *Childhood experiences and family environment* seem to make a difference. Evidence links entrepreneurs with parents who were entrepreneurial and self-employed. And, entrepreneurs are often raised in families that encourage responsibility, initiative, and independence. Another issue is *career or work history*. Entrepreneurs who try one venture often go on to others. Prior work experience in the business area or industry is helpful.

Entrepreneurs also tend to emerge during certain *windows of career opportunity*. Most start their businesses between the ages of 22 and 45, an age spread that seems to allow for risk taking. However, age shouldn't be viewed as a barrier. When Tony DeSio was 50 he founded the Mail Boxes Etc. chain. He sold it for $300 million when he was 67 and suffering heart problems. Within a year he launched PixArts, another franchise chain based on photography and art.[8]

Finally, a report in the *Harvard Business Review* suggests that entrepreneurs may have unique and *deeply embedded life interests*. The article describes entrepreneurs as having strong interests in creative production—enjoying project initiation, working with the unknown, and finding unconventional solutions. They also have strong interests in enterprise control—finding enjoyment from running things. The combination of creative production and enterprise control is characteristic of people who want to start things and move things toward a goal.[9]

Undoubtedly, entrepreneurs seek independence and the sense of mastery that comes with success. That seems to keep driving Tony DeSio from the earlier example. When asked by a reporter what he liked most about entrepreneurship, he replied: "Being able to make decisions without having to go through layers of corporate hierarchy—just being a master of your own destiny."[10]

Diversity and Entrepreneurship

When economists speak about entrepreneurs they differentiate between those who are driven by the quest for new opportunities and those who are driven by absolute need.[11] Those in the latter group pursue necessity-based entrepreneurship; they start new ventures because they have few or no other employment and career options. Sometimes these are women and minorities who have suffered the "glass ceiling" effect and have found career doors closed.

The National Foundation for Women Business Owners (NFWBO) reports that women own more than 9 million businesses in the United States. As noted earlier, this represents about 38% of all U.S. businesses.[12] Entrepreneurship offers women opportunities to strike out on their own and gain economic independence, providing a pathway for career success that may be blocked otherwise.[13]

The NFWBO also reports that women are starting new businesses at twice the rate of the national average, with most motivated by a new idea or by realizing they could do for themselves what they were already doing for other employers. Among women leaving private-sector employment to work on their own, 33% said they were not being taken seriously by their prior employer; 29% said they had experienced "glass ceiling" issues.[14] In *Women Business Owners of Color: Challenges and Accomplishments*, the NFWBO discusses the motivations of women of color to pursue entrepreneurship because of glass ceiling problems—not being recognized or valued by their employers, not being taken seriously, and seeing others promoted ahead of them.[15]

Career difficulties may help explain why minority entrepreneurship is one of the fastest-growing sectors of our economy. Businesses created by minority entrepreneurs employ more than 4 million U.S. workers and generate over $500 billion in annual revenues. And the trend is upward. In the last census of small businesses, those owned by African Americans had grown by 45%, by Hispanics 31%, and by Asians 24%. Small businesses owned by women also had grown by 24%.[16]

Entrepreneurship and Small Business

The U.S. Small Business Administration (SBA) defines a small business as one with 500 or fewer employees, that is independently owned and operated, and that does not dominate its industry.[17] Almost 99% of American businesses meet this definition, and some 87% employ fewer than 20 persons.

The small business sector is very important in most nations of the world because small businesses offer major economic advantages. In the United States, for example, they employ some 52% of private workers, provide 51% of private-sector output, receive 35% of federal government contract dollars, and provide as many as 7 out of every 10 new jobs in the economy.[18] Smaller businesses are especially prevalent in the service and retailing sectors of the economy. Higher costs of entry make them less common in other industries, such as manufacturing and transportation.

How to Get Started

There are many reasons why entrepreneurs launch their own small businesses. One study reports the following motivations: #1—wanting to be your own boss and control your future: #2—going to work for a family-owned business: and #3—seeking to fulfill a dream.[19] Once a decision is made to go the small business route, the most common ways to get involved are: start one, buy an existing one, or buy and run a franchise—where a business owner sells to another the right to operate the same business in another location. A franchise, such as Subway, Quiznos, or Domino's Pizza, runs under the original owner's business name and guidance. In return, the franchise parent receives a share of income or a flat fee from the franchisee.

Internet Entrepreneurship

Have you started a "dot-com" today? The Internet creates an array of entrepreneurial possibilities. Just take a look at the action on eBay and imagine how many people are now running small trading businesses from their homes.

The SBA says that some 85% of small firms are already conducting business over the Internet.[20] Many of these firms are existing firms that modified traditional ways to pursue new Internet-driven opportunities. For others, the old ways of operating from a bricks-and-mortar retail establishment have given way to entirely online business activities. That's what happened to Rod Spencer and his S&S Sportscards store in Worthington, Ohio. He closed his store, not because business was bad; it was really good. But the nature of the business was shifting into cyberspace. When sales over the Internet became much greater than in-store sales. Spencer decided to follow the world of e-commerce. He now works from his own home with a computer and high-speed Internet connection. This saves the cost of renting retail space and hiring store employees. "I can do less business overall," he says, "to make a higher profit."[21]

Family Businesses

Family businesses, ones owned and financially controlled by family members, represent the largest percent age of businesses operating worldwide. The Family Firm Institute reports that family businesses account for 78% of new jobs created in the United States and provide 60% of the nation's employment.[22]

Family businesses must solve the same problems of other small or large businesses—meeting the challenges of strategy, competitive advantage, and operational excellence. When everything goes right, the family firm is almost an ideal situation—everyone working together, sharing values and a common goal, and knowing that what they do benefits the family. But it doesn't always work out this way—or stay this way, as a business changes hands over successive generations. Indeed, family businesses often face quite unique problems.

"Okay, Dad, so he's your brother. But does that mean we have to put up with inferior work and an erratic schedule that we would never tolerate from anyone else in the business?"[23] This complaint introduces a problem that can all too often set the stage for failure in a family business—the family business feud. Simply put, members of the controlling family get into disagreements about work responsibilities, business strategy, operating approaches, finances, or other matters. The example is indicative of an intergenerational problem, but the feud can be between spouses, among siblings, or between parents and children. It really doesn't matter. Unless family disagreements are resolved to the benefit of the business itself, the firm will have difficulty surviving in a highly competitive environment.

Another common problem faced by family businesses is the succession problem—transferring leadership from one generation to the next. A survey of small and midsized family businesses indicated that 66% planned on keeping the business within the family.[24] But, the management question is: how will the assets be distributed and who will run the business when the current head leaves? Although this problem, is not specific to the small firm, it is especially significant in the family business context. A family business that has been in operation for some time is often a source of both business momentum and financial wealth. Ideally, both are maintained in the succession process. But data on succession are eye-opening. About 30% of family firms survive to the second generation; only 12% survive to the third; and only 3% are expected to survive beyond that.[25]

Business advisors recommend a succession plan—a formal statement that describes how the leadership transition and related financial matters will be handled when the time for changeover arrives. A succession plan should include at least procedures for choosing or designating the firm's new leadership, legal aspects of any ownership transfer, and financial and estate plans relating to the transfer. The foundations for effective implementation of a succession plan are set up well ahead of the need to use it. The plan should be shared and understood among all affected by it. The chosen successor should be prepared, through experience and training, to perform the new role when needed.

Why Small Businesses Fail

Small businesses have a high failure rate—one high enough to be intimidating. The SBA reports that as many as 60 to 80% of new businesses fail in their first five years of operation.[26] Part of this is a "counting" issue—the government counts as a "failure" any business that closes, whether it is because of the death or retirement of an owner, sale to someone else, or the inability to earn a profit.[27] Nevertheless, the fact remains: a lot of small business startups don't make it. And as shown in Exhibit 5.2 on the next page, most of the failures are the result of bad judgment and management mistakes of several types.[28]

Exhibit 5.2 Eight Reasons Why Many Small Businesses Fail

- *Lack of experience*—not having sufficient know-how to run a business in the chosen market or area.
- *Lack of expertise*—not having expertise in the essentials of business operations, including finance, purchasing, selling, and production.
- *Lack of strategy and strategic leadership*—not taking the time to craft a vision and mission, nor to formulate and properly implement a strategy.
- *Poor financial control*—not keeping track of the numbers, and failure to control business finances.
- *Growing too fast*—not taking the time to consolidate a position, fine-tune the organization, and systematically meet the challenges of growth.
- *Insufficient commitment*—not devoting enough time to the requirements of running a competitive business.
- *Ethical failure*—falling prey to the temptations of fraud, deception, and embezzlement.

New Venture Creation

Whether your interest is low-tech or high-tech, online or offline, opportunities for new ventures are always there for the true entrepreneur. To pursue entrepreneurship and start a new business, you need good ideas and the courage to give them a chance. But you must also be prepared to meet and master the test of strategy and competitive advantage. Can you identify a market niche that is being missed by other established firms? Can you identify a new market that has not yet been discovered by existing firms? Can you generate first-mover advantage by exploiting a niche or entering a market before competitors? These are among the questions that entrepreneurs must ask and answer in the process of beginning a new venture.

Life Cycles of Entrepreneurial Firms

Exhibit 5.3 describes the stages common to the life cycles of entrepreneurial companies. It shows the relatively predictable progression of the small business. The firm begins with the *birth stage*—where the entrepreneur struggles to get the new venture established and survive long enough to test the liability of the underlying business model in the marketplace. The firm then passes into the *breakthrough stage*—where the business model begins to work well, growth is experienced, and the complexity of managing the business operation expands significantly. Next comes the *maturity stage*—where the entrepreneur experiences

Birth Stage	Breakthrough Stage	Maturity Stage
• Establishing the firm • Getting customers • Finding the money	• Working on finances • Becoming profitable • Growing	• Refining the strategy • Continuing growth • Managing for success
Fighting for existence and survival	Coping with growth and takeoff	Investing wisely and staying flexible

Exhibit 5.3 Stages in the Life Cycle of an Entrepreneurial Firm

the advantages of market success and financial stability, while also facing the continuing management challenge of remaining competitive in a changing environment.

Entrepreneurs must often deal with substantial control and management dilemmas when their firms experience growth. Including possible diversification or global expansion. They encounter a variation of the succession problem described earlier for family businesses. This time, the problem is transition from entrepreneurial leadership to professional strategic leadership. The former brings the venture into being and sees it through the early stages of life; the latter manages and leads the venture into maturity as an ever-evolving and perhaps still-growing corporate, enterprise. If the entrepreneur is incapable of meeting or unwilling to meet the firm's strategic leadership needs in later life-cycle stages, continued business survival and success may well depend on the business being sold, or management control being passed to professionals.

Writing the Business Plan

When people start new businesses or even start new units within existing ones, they can benefit from a good business plan. This plan describes the details needed to obtain startup financing and operate a new business.[29] Banks and other financiers want to see a business plan before they loan money or invest in a new venture; senior managers want to see a business plan before they allocate scarce organizational resources to support a new entrepreneurial project. There's good reason for this. The detailed thinking required to prepare a business plan can contribute to the success of the new initiative. It forces the entrepreneur to think through important issues and challenges before starting out. Says Ed Federkeil, who founded a small business called California Custom Sport Trucks: "It gives you direction instead of haphazardly sticking your key in the door every day and saying—'What are we going to do?'"[30]

Although there is no single template for a successful business plan, there is general agreement on the framework. Every business plan should have an executive summary, cover certain business fundamentals, be well organized with headings and easy to read, and run no more than about 20 pages in length. In addition to advice you find in books and magazines, there are many online resources available to assist in the development of a business plan.[31]

Choosing the Form of Ownership

One of the important planning choices that must be made in starting a new venture is the legal form of ownership. There are a number of alternatives, and the choice among them requires careful consideration of their respective advantages and disadvantages. Briefly, the ownership forms include the following:

A sole proprietorship is simply an individual or a married couple pursuing business for a profit. This does not involve incorporation. One does business, for example, under a personal name—such as "Tiaña Lopez Designs." A sole proprietorship is simple to start, run, and terminate, and it is the most common form of small business ownership in the United States. However, the business owner is personally liable for business debts and claims.

A partnership is formed when two or more people agree to contribute resources to start and operate a business together. It is usually backed by a legal and written partnership agreement. Business partners agree on the contribution of resources and skills to the new venture, and on the sharing of profits and losses. In a *general partnership*, the simplest and most common form, they also share management responsibilities. A *limited partnership* consists of a general partner and one or more "limited" partners who do not participate in day-to-day business management. They share in the profits, but their losses are limited to the amount of their investment. A *limited liability partnership*, common among professionals such as accountants and attorneys, limits the liability of one partner for the negligence of another.

A corporation, commonly identified by the "Inc." designation in a name, is a legal entity that is chartered by the state and exists separately from its owners. The corporation can be for-profit, such as Microsoft Inc., or nonprofit, such as Count-Me-In, Inc.—a firm helping women entrepreneurs get started with small loans. The corporate form offers two major advantages: (1) it grants the organization certain legal rights (e.g., to engage in contracts), and (2) the corporation becomes responsible for its own liabilities. This separates the owners from personal liability and gives the firm a life of its own that can extend beyond that of its owners. The disadvantage of incorporation rests largely with the cost of incorporating and the complexity of the documentation required to operate an incorporated business.

Recently, the limited liability corporation, or LLC, has gained popularity. A limited liability corporation combines the advantages of the other forms—sole proprietorship, partnership, and corporation. For liability purposes, it functions like a corporation, protecting the assets of owners against claims made against the company. For tax purposes, it functions as a partnership in the case of multiple owners, and as a sole proprietorship in the case of a single owner.

Financing the New Venture

Starting a new venture takes money, and that money often must be raised. Realistically speaking, the cost of a new business startup can easily exceed the amount a would-be entrepreneur has available from personal sources.

There are two major ways an entrepreneur can obtain outside financing for a new venture. Debt financing involves going into debt by borrowing money from another person, bank, or financial institution. This loan must be paid back over time, with interest. It also requires collateral that pledges business assets or personal assets, such as a home, to secure the loan in case of default. Equity financing involves giving ownership shares in the business to outsiders in return for their cash investments. This money does not need to be paid back. It is an investment, and the investor assumes the risk for potential gains and losses. In return for taking that risk, the equity investor gains some proportionate ownership control.

Equity financing is usually obtained from venture capitalists, companies and individuals that make investments in new ventures in return for an equity stake in the business. Most venture capitalists tend to focus on relatively large investments of $1 million or more, and they usually take a management role, such as a board of directors seat, in order to oversee business growth. The hope is that a fast-growing firm will gain a solid market base and be either sold at a profit to another firm or become a candidate for an initial public offering. This "IPO" is when shares of stock in the business are first sold to the public and then begin trading on a major stock exchange. When an IPO is successful and the share prices are bid up by the market, the original investments of the venture capitalist and entrepreneur rise in value. The anticipation of such return on investment is a large part of the venture capitalist's motivation: indeed, it is the business model of the venture capitalist.

When large amounts of venture capital aren't available to the entrepreneur, another important financing option is the angel investor. This is a wealthy individual who is willing to make an investment in return for equity in a new venture. Angel investors are especially common and helpful in the very early startup stage. Their presence can raise investor confidence and help attract additional venture funding that would otherwise not be available. For example, when Liz Cobb wanted to start her sales compensation firm, Incentive Systems, she contacted 15 to 20 venture capital firms. She was interviewed by 10 and turned down by all of them. After she located $250,000 from two angel investors, the venture capital firms got interested again. She was able to obtain her first $2 million in financing and has since built the firm into a 70-plus employee business.[32]

Endnotes

1. Information from "Women Business Owners Receive First-Ever Micro Loans Via the Internet," *Business Wire* (August 9, 2000); Jim Hopkins, "Non-Profit Loan Group Takes Risks on Women in Business," *USA Today* (August 9, 2000), p. 2B; and "Women's Group Grants First Loans to Entrepreneurs," *Columbus Dispatch* (August 10, 2000), p. B2.
2. Ibid.
3. Speech at the Lloyd Greif Center for Enterpreneurial Studies, Marshall School of Business, University of Southern California, 1996.
4. "Information from the corporate Web sites and from The Entrepreneur's Hall of Fame: www.1tbn.com/halloffame.html.
5. For a review and discussion of the entrepreneurial mind, see Jeffry A. Timmons, *New Venture Creation: Entrepreneurship for the 21st Century* (New York: Irwin/McGraw-Hill, 1999), pp. 219–25.
6. See the review by Robert D. Hisrich and Michael P. Peters, *Entrepreneurship*, 4th ed. (New York: Irwin/McGraw-Hill, 1998), pp. 67-70; and Paulette Thomas, "Entrepreneurs' Biggest Problems and How They Solve Them," *Wall Street Journal Reports* (March 17, 2003). pp. R1, R2.
7. Based on research summarized by Hisrich and Peters, op. cit., pp. 70–74.
8. Information from Jim Hopkins, "Serial Entrepreneur Strikes Again at Age 70," *USA Today* (August 15, 2000).
9. Timothy Butler and James Waldroop, "Job Sculpting: The Art of Retaining Your Best People," *Harvard Business Review* (September–October 1999), pp. 144–52.
10. This list is developed from Timmons, op. cit. pp. 47–48; and Hisrich and Peters, op. cit., pp. 67–70.
11. "Smart Talk: Start-Ups and Schooling," *Wall Street Journal* (September 7, 2004), p. B4.
12. *Paths to Entrepreneurship: New Directions for Women in Business* (New York: Catalyst, 1998) and Eve Hayek, "Report Shatters Myths About U.S. Women's Equality" (October 1, 2005); both available on the National Foundation for Women Business Owners Web site: www.nfwbo.org/key.html.
13. Data from Ibid, and "Smart Talk: Start-Ups and Schooling," *Wall Street Journal* (September 7, 2004), p. B4.
14. Data from *Paths to Entrepreneurship: New Directions for Women in Business* (New York: Catalyst, 1998), as summarized on the National Foundation for Women Business Owners Web site: www.nfwbo.org/key.html.
15. National Foundation for Women Business Owners, *Women Business Owners of Color: Challenges and Accomplishments* (1998).
16. Data reported by Karen E. Klein, "Minority Start Ups: A Measure of Progress," *BusinessWeek* (August 25, 2005), retrieved from www.businessweekonline.
17. *The Facts About Small Business 1999* (Washington, DC: U.S. Small Business Administration, Office of Advocacy).
18. See U.S. Small Business Administration Web site: www.sba.gov; and *Statistical Abstract of the United States* (Washington, DC: U.S. Census Bureau, 1999).
19. Information reported in "The Rewards," *Inc. State of Small Business* (May 20–21, 2001), pp. 50–51.
20. "Small Business Expansions in Electronic Commerce," U.S. Small Business Administration, Office of Advocacy (June 2000).
21. Information from Will Christensen, "Rod Spencer's Sports-Card Business Has Migrated to Cyberspace Market place," *Columbus Dispatch* (July 24, 2000), p. F1.
22. Data reported by The Family Firm Institute: www.ffi.org/looking/factsfb.html.
23. Conversation from the case "Am I My Uncle's Keeper?" by Paul I. Karofsky (Northeastern University Center for Family Business) and published at: www.fambiz.com/contprov.cfm?ContProvCode=NECFB[ANGELO]ID= 140.
24. Survey of Small and Mid-Sized Businesses: Trends for 2000 (Arthur Andersen, 2000).
25. Ibid.
26. See U.S. Small Business Administration Web site: www.sba.gov.

27. George Gendron, "The Failure Myth," *Inc.* (January 2001), p. 13.
28. Discussion based on "The Life Cycle of Entrepreneurial Firms," in Ricky Griffin, ed., *Management,* 6th ed. (New York: Houghton Mifflin, 1999), pp. 309–10; and Neil C. Churchill and Virginia L. Lewis, "The Five Stages of Small Business Growth," *Harvard Business Review* (May–June 1993), pp. 30–50.
29. Developed from William S. Sahlman, "How to Write a Great Business Plan," *Harvard Business Review* (July–August 1997), pp. 98–108.
30. Marcia H. Pounds, "Business Plan Sets Course for Growth," *Columbus Dispatch* (March 16, 1998), p. 9; see also the firm's Web site: www.calcustoms.com.
31. Standard components of business plans are described in many text sources such as Linda Pinson and Jerry Jinnett, *Anatomy of a Business Plan: A Step-by-Step Guide to Starting Smart, Building the Business, and Securing Your Company's Future,* 4th ed. (Dearborn Trade, 1999), and Scarborough and Zimmerer, op. cit.; and on Web sites such as: American Express Small Business Services, Business Town.com, and Bizplanlt.com.
32. "You've Come a Long Way Baby," *BusinessWeek: Frontier* (July 10, 2000).

Organizational Design

Why should you learn about organizational structure? This is a good question to ask, since organizational structure is the most abstract and difficult concept to understand in organizational behavior. The answer is very simple: poorly structured organizations contribute to employee burnout and stress; create conflict between work teams; prevent even highly motivated people from succeeding in their work; waste valuable resources, including money and time; fail to serve customers; limit the profitability of the company; and eventually threaten the organization's survival. Moreover, the most immediate and permanent way to revitalize an organization is to redesign its structure. Obviously, it is worth knowing the basic principles of organizational structure and how to adapt them to the appropriate conditions.

Concepts of Organizational Design

Organizations are open social systems that consist of patterned activities, and this chapter explains how these patterned activities are structured. The purpose of organizational structure is to regulate these activities and reduce the variability in human performance, or in other words, control behavior by making it coordinated and predictable.

Controlling the behavior of people in organizations is essential because organizations cannot survive if their members behave in random, unpredictable ways. Such a situation would produce chaos and disorganization. The difference between a well organized and poorly organized group is as dramatic as the difference between the beauty of an orchestra playing a symphony and the noise the musicians produce when they are tuning their instruments. To produce the necessary patterned activities and thereby create an organization, the variability in human behavior must be reduced so that people behave in predictable patterns. Although organizations vary in the amount of control they require from their members, at least some control is inherent in every organization.

The term organizational structure refers to the relatively fixed relationships among the jobs in the organization. The process of creating this structure and making decisions about the relative benefits of alternative structures is called organizational design. Creating an organizational structure involves two issues: (1) differentiation, or creating a division of labor, and (2) integration, or coordinating the different roles created by the division of labor. Therefore, the study of organizational structure examines the manner in which an organization divides labor into specialized tasks and then coordinates them. The five major design decisions that must be made are division of labor, departmentalization, span of control, delegation of authority, and coordinating mechanisms.

Division of Labor

The term division of labor refers to the process of dividing a large task into successively smaller jobs, called job specialization. All jobs are specialized to some degree, since one person can't do everything, but some jobs are considerably more specialized than others. One of the major benefits of specialized activities is that a group of people working together with a division of labor are able to produce more than they could if each member produced the entire product working alone.

The key issue here is how specialized the work should be. Specialization is low when employees perform a variety of tasks and high when each person performs only a single task. The degree of specialization can be represented along a continuum.

From *Creating Effective Organizations*, 5th edition by David J. Cherrington and W. Gibb Dyer. Copyright © 2009 by Kendall/Hunt Publishing Company. Reprinted by permission.

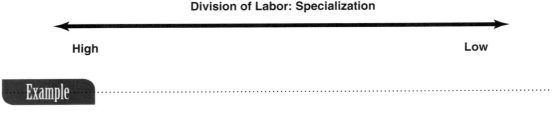

> **Example**
>
> *In a word processing center, the degree of specialization is low if three typists are allowed to edit, type, and proofread the manuscripts they type. However, if each of these functions were assigned to a different individual, the degree of specialization would be high.*

Deciding on the appropriate level of specialization is an important design decision because it greatly influences productivity. It is possible to create jobs that are so highly specialized that the organization suffers from a lack of coordination and at times there isn't enough work to keep everyone busy. Highly specialized jobs can also be extremely boring, yet there are definite advantages to highly specialized jobs.

Departmentalization

Departmentalization is the process of combining jobs into groups or departments. Managers must decide whether the most appropriate structure is to have a homogeneous department with similar jobs or a heterogeneous department with unrelated jobs. Jobs can be grouped according to several criteria; the most popular criteria include function, product, territory, and clientele, as illustrated in Exhibit 6.1.

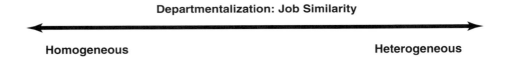

Functional Departmentalization

Functional departmentalization involves grouping jobs that perform similar functions into the same department. For example, all the jobs associated with accounting, such as general ledger accountant, accounts payable clerk, accounts receivable clerk, and cost accountant, could all be combined into an accounting department. Organizing the departments by function would be a homogeneous form of departmentalization, since everyone in the department would share the same specialized skills. Other forms of departmentalization tend to be market-based and more heterogeneous.

Functional departmentalization is the most widely used scheme because in most organizations it is the most effective method. This explains why a typical manufacturing company is departmentalized into production, marketing, finance, accounting, research and development, and human resource departments. Most hospitals are departmentalized in terms of such functions as surgery, nursing, psychiatry, pharmacy, human resource, and housekeeping.

Functional departmentalization has both advantages and disadvantages. Perhaps the most significant advantage is that it promotes skill specialization by having people work together who face similar problems and opportunities. The functional form also permits the maximum use of resources, and encourages the use of specialists and specialized equipment, thereby eliminating duplication of equipment and effort. Communication and performance are usually improved because superiors share expertise with their subordinates.

One disadvantage of functional departmentalization is that it reduces communication and cooperation between departments and fosters a parochial perspective. This narrow orientation limits managers' capacities for coordination, and encourages a short time horizon. Coordination and support across functional departments are often difficult

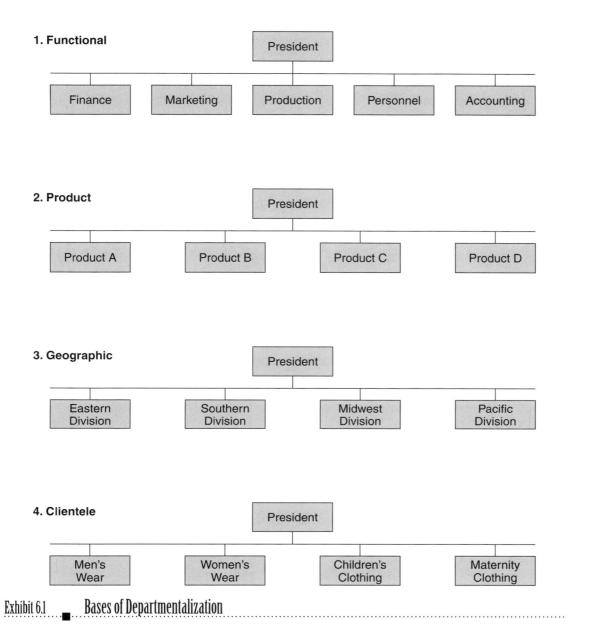

Exhibit 6.1   Bases of Departmentalization

because departments are separated both geographically and psychologically, and members come to view problems only from their limited functional perspectives.

Functional departmentalization also contributes to a problem called suboptimizing. Suboptimizing occurs when one department pursues its own goals and tries to look good at the expense of other departments or of the organization as a whole. Suboptimizing is particularly problematic when departments are rewarded for achieving their own goals. Although departments are expected to serve each other and they should be rewarded for the service they provide, many departmental goals can best be achieved when each department pursues its own selfish interests. Custodial departments, for example, could keep the buildings cleaner if no one used the buildings. Likewise, the accounting and human resource departments could generate better reports if managers from whom the information was obtained spent all their time completing lengthy forms.

Product Departmentalization

Product departmentalization involves grouping jobs that produce similar products, which typically occurs in large firms when it becomes difficult to coordinate the various functional departments. The members of a product-oriented department can develop greater expertise in researching, manufacturing, and distributing a specific product line. Managers have better control over the success or failure of each product if the authority, responsibility, and accountability are assigned according to products. This method is illustrated by the "brand" management structure that Procter & Gamble uses with its major products.

The product form of departmentalization has both advantages and disadvantages, and is often contrasted with the functional form of departmentalization. The major advantage is that it creates greater inter-departmental coordination and focuses the efforts of each department on producing an effective and useful product. Companies organized by product are generally customer-oriented, and their employees tend to be cohesive and involved in their work.

The major disadvantage of organizing by product is that the resources and skills of the organization are not fully employed unless the organization is extremely large. For example, a computer-driven lathe machine that is used for only one product and sits idle much of the time represents an inefficient use of capital resources. Another disadvantage is that product-oriented departments usually lead to increased costs because of duplication of activities, especially staff functions.

Geographic Departmentalization

Organizations use geographic departmentalization when they assign all the activities in an area to the same unit. This method typically occurs when organizations are geographically dispersed and a local manager is assigned to supervise both the functions and products in that area. This method is popular among retail companies that have stores located in many cities. Each store manager is ultimately responsible for recruiting, hiring, training, advertising, selling, and other diverse functions.

The major advantage of geographic departmentalization comes from minimizing problems created by distance, such as difficulties in communicating, observing, and making timely decisions. The disadvantage is that they miss the important advantages of functional and product departmentalization, which would have been superior if distance hadn't precluded them.

Customer Departmentalization

Occasionally the most effective way to combine jobs is to organize them according to the customers who are served. These advantages occur when groups of customers have distinct needs. Many universities, for example, have a separate evening class program or an executive MBA program, because the interests of these students are significantly different from those of the regular day-time students. Many department stores have separate departments for men's clothing, women's clothing, maternity clothing, and children's clothing because the customers served by each department have unique and separate interests.

Each form of departmentalization has both advantages and disadvantages. Therefore, managers are required to balance the strengths and weaknesses of each form and decide which will create the highest efficiency. In most situations, managers use a mixed strategy that combines two or more forms of departmentalization. For example, department stores combine the advantages of customer departmentalization with a functional form of organization among the staff units. The accounting, finance, human resource, and purchasing departments represent functional departmentalization, while the men's clothing, women's clothing, boys' clothing, and maternity departments represent customer departmentalization.

Span of Control

When selecting the span of control, managers decide how many people should be placed in a group under one supervisor; the number can vary along a continuum from few to many.

Span of Control: Number

Few ←————————————————————→ Many

The span-of-control decision has a major influence on the organization's shape and structure. Organizations that use a broad span of control have relatively few hierarchical levels, while a narrow span creates a tall organizational structure, as illustrated in Exhibit 6.2. Each hypothetical structure involves thirty-one positions. A narrow span of control, with only two subordinates per supervisor, produces a tall organizational structure with five hierarchical levels. However, a span of control of five produces a flat organizational structure with only three hierarchical levels.

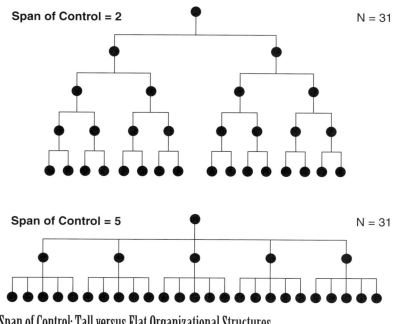

Exhibit 6.2 ■ Span of Control: Tall versus Flat Organizational Structures

A narrow span of control allows for closer control over subordinates and greater personal contact between manager and subordinate. The risk, however, is that a manager with a narrow span of control comes to know only two or three subordinates very well and fails to become acquainted with others in the hierarchy. Consequently, tall organizations often inhibit interpersonal communication within the organization.

During the 1940s and 1950s, management scholars tried to prescribe the ideal span of control. One scholar calculated the geometric increase in the number of relationships a manager must supervise as the span of control increased, and concluded that the maximum span of control should never exceed three or four subordinates.[1] In actual practice, however, several organizations had spans of control greater than twenty, and the groups were supervised quite effectively. Consequently, the "ideal span of control" does not exist; the appropriate span of control varies with the nature of the tasks being performed.[2] Although a range of four to six subordinates is often recommended, a much larger span of control may be appropriate, depending on four situational variables:

1. *Contact required.* Jobs that require frequent contact and a high degree of coordination between supervisor and subordinates should use narrower spans of control. For example, jobs in medical technology often require frequent consultation of team members with a supervisor; therefore, a large span of control would preclude the necessary sharing of ideas and information that typically must occur on an informal basis.
2. *Level of subordinates' education and training.* Large spans of control are appropriate for highly skilled employees and professionals who are well trained. They generally require less supervision because they know their jobs well and they largely supervise themselves.

3. *Ability to communicate.* Instructions, guidelines, and policies can be communicated to employees by a variety of methods. If all the necessary instructions can be written and then disseminated, it would be possible for one manager to supervise a large group. However, as communication becomes more difficult and job-related discussions become more important, a narrower span of control is appropriate to avoid overloading a supervisor.
4. *Nature of the task.* Jobs that are repetitive and stable require less supervision and are more amenable to wide spans of control. For this reason, some field supervisors are able to supervise as many as sixty to seventy-five field hands in harvesting agricultural crops. However, when tasks are changed frequently, a narrower span of control is appropriate.

There seems to be a natural tendency for managers to adopt narrow spans of control, which increases the number of hierarchical levels. However, productivity often increases after organizations have eliminated one or more hierarchical levels of administration, so companies are often encouraged to eliminate hierarchical levels by increasing spans of control.

Delegation of Authority

The fourth design issue concerns the delegation of authority. Decentralization involves distributing power and authority to lower-level supervisors and employees. The more decentralized an organization, the greater the extent to which the rank-and-file employees can participate in and accept responsibility for decisions concerning their jobs and the activities of the organization. Decision-making authority can vary along a continuum from centralized to decentralized.

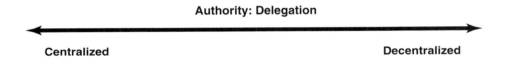

Decentralization often leads to greater organizational effectiveness, since it allows greater autonomy and responsibility among lower-level employees thereby more effectively using an organization's human resources. Supervisors in decentralized organizations typically report higher levels of job satisfaction and involvement, and they tend to be more productive because of increased autonomy and responsibility. A company that is struggling with declining sales may decide to decentralize its management structure to make it more responsive to customers and more conducive to new product development.

In spite of its benefits, however, decentralization is not universally superior and does not always contribute to greater organizational effectiveness. Some organizations have excelled with decentralized decision making while others have fared better with a centralized structure. Several weaknesses of decentralization have been identified suggesting that centralized decision making is sometimes superior.

1. Certain shared functions, especially staff functions, are more difficult to execute under decentralization.
2. Decentralization can create jurisdictional disputes and conflicts over priorities, since each unit essentially becomes an independent area.
3. Decentralization requires greater competence and expertise and greater commitment on the part of decision makers than centralized control does.
4. Decentralized decisions made by many lower-level managers create problems of coordination and integration. A decentralized organization could be very ineffective, because of inadequate coordination and integration.

To design an effective organizational structure, managers must select the optimal balance between centralized and decentralized authority. Power and authority should be decentralized to the extent that organizations use the knowledge and expertise of lower-level participants while maintaining sufficient centralization to ensure adequate coordination and control.[3] Like the other concepts of organizational design, the ideal policy depends on the situation.

Coordinating Mechanisms

Organizations need to process information and coordinate the efforts of their members. Employees at lower levels need to perform activities consistent with top-level goals, and the managers at the top need to know about the activities and accomplishments of people at lower levels. Five primary methods are available for coordinating the activities of members, and these methods vary according to the amount of discretion that workers are allowed.

Coordinating Mechanisms: Personal Discretion

◄───►

Direct Supervision and Rules   **Mutual Adjustment**

1. *Direct supervision.* All work is coordinated by supervisors through rules that are continually monitored, or by specific on-the-job instructions.

Example

A landscaping crew works under the direct supervision of an architect who tells each worker where each shrub and tree should be planted. An orchestra plays under the direct supervision of a conductor who coordinates precisely when everyone plays.

2. *Standardization of work processes.* Routine jobs can be coordinated through standard operating procedures or by the technology itself that regulates the activities. Here, it is the activities that are coordinated.

Example

Assembly line jobs are coordinated by the pace of the line. The workers know what they are required to do and they perform their assigned activities as the products move along the production line.

3. *Standardization of outputs.* When products or services must be produced according to established specifications, these specifications may serve as an adequate basis for coordinating the activities. Individual workers are allowed some discretion in performing the work, provided the output meets the required specifications. Here, it is the outputs that are coordinated.

Example

Construction workers are mostly coordinated by the products they produce. They know how to do the job correctly so that it will pass inspection. They establish their own pace of work and to some extent they are free to vary the order of the activities they perform.

4. *Standardization of skills.* The work of highly skilled and trained employees is typically coordinated by the professional training they have received. What they do and how they do it is based on the skills they were taught in their technical training.

Example

The work of a surgical team is mostly coordinated by having members who perform their jobs according to the ways they were trained. The members rely on each other to do what they were trained to do and this training serves to integrate their actions.

5. *Mutual adjustment.* Activities that are constantly changing and uncertain are coordinated through mutual adjustment, which consists of a constant interchange of informal communication. Here, individuals have the greatest discretion and they coordinate their work through informal meetings, personal conversations, and liaison positions, mutually adjusting to one another's needs. Employees communicate with whomever they need to communicate without regard for formal lines of communication.

Example

Rescue teams, emergency medical technicians, and other groups that respond in crisis situations coordinate their activities through mutual adjustment. Because each situation is unique and unexpected problems arise, the team members are required to continually adjust their plans and coordinate their responses among themselves.

A crucial issue in choosing a coordinating mechanism concerns the need for information and the ways in which information is collected, processed, and disseminated. The type of information collected by a driver's license bureau, for example, is mostly routine information that can be coordinated by rules and procedures. Fashion merchandisers, however, require extensive market information, which they may obtain from a variety of irregular sources and disseminate informally to anyone who needs to know.

Coordinating mechanisms influence the degree of formalization in an organization. The term formalization refers to the degree to which rules and procedures guide the actions of employees. These rules and procedures can be either explicit or implicit. Explicit rules are written in job descriptions, policy and procedures manuals, or office memos. Implicit rules are often unwritten and develop as employees establish their own ways of doing things over time. Although they are unwritten, implicit rules often become standard operating procedures with the same effect on employee behavior as explicit rules.

In a highly formal organization, employees are required to follow strict rules and procedures that tell them exactly how to perform their work. Informal organizations have very few rules and procedures; the employees are largely free to structure their own jobs. Formal organizations tend to rely on direct supervision and standardization of work processes, while informal organizations tend to use mutual adjustment and standardization of skills. An example of a formal structure in a university would be an administrative agency, such as the student loans office, while an example of an informal structure would be an academic department, such as the sociology department.

Matrix Organizational Structures

Some organizations have combined two kinds of departmentalization, functional and product, in an effort to capitalize on the advantages of each. This dual structure, called a matrix structure, simultaneously organizes part of the organization along product lines and part of the organization along functional lines, as illustrated in Exhibit 6.3.

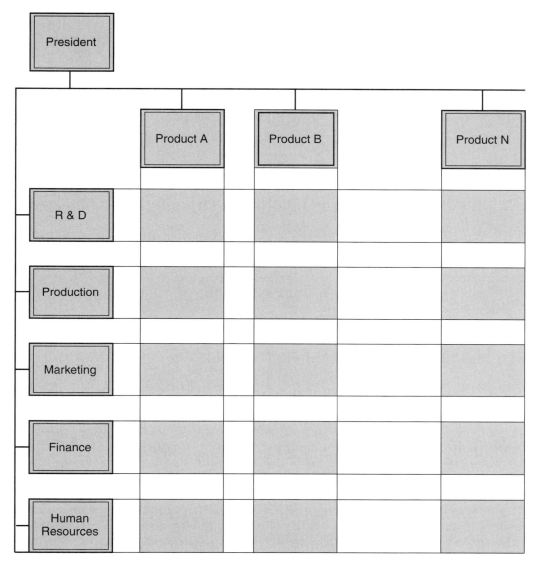

Exhibit 6.3 ■ Matrix Organizational Structure

In a matrix organization, each department reports simultaneously to both product managers and functional managers who have equal authority within the organization. For example, a member of the legal department may be assigned to assist with the development of a specific product and assume the responsibility for all the legal activities associated with the development, production, and distribution of the product. This individual would report to both the product manager and the supervisor of the legal department.

Although dual structures are awkward, they can quickly create new products while retaining the benefits of a functional structure. Consequently, a matrix structure is particularly effective when environmental pressures create a demand for both technical quality (functional) and frequent new products (product). These dual pressures require a dual authority structure to deal with them. A matrix structure is particularly useful in an uncertain environment when frequent external changes and high interdependence between departments require effective linkages between departments inside the organization.

The disadvantage of a matrix structure is that it increases role ambiguity, stress, and anxiety, because people are assigned to more than one department. Matrix structures violate the principle of unity of command. The employees who work in a matrix structure often feel that inconsistent demands are made on them, causing unproductive conflicts that call for short-term crisis management. Occasionally, employees abuse the dual-authority structure by playing one manager against another, thereby generating excuses for their incompetence or inactivity.[4]

Universal Design Theories

The structure of an organization is determined by the five concepts explained earlier: division of labor, departmentalization, span of control, delegation of authority, and coordinating mechanisms. Different combinations of these factors can produce many different organizational structures. Which structure is the most effective? This section describes universal theories of organizational design that were meant to be ideal structures. Unfortunately, a universally superior organizational structure does not exist; the best structure depends on the situation, as explained in the next section.

Mechanistic versus Organic Organizational Structures

Two contrasting types of organizational structure have been recommended as universally appropriate for every organization. These two types differ greatly in the amount of formal structure and control they advocate. Several labels have been used to describe these two types. The labels used in this book are mechanistic versus organic organizational structures.

Mechanistic and organic organizational structures were first described in a classic study by Burns and Stalker.[5] They observed twenty industrial firms in England and discovered that the external environment was related to the internal organizational structure. When the external environment was stable, the internal organization was managed by rules, procedures, and a clear hierarchy of authority. Most managerial decisions were made at the top, and there was strong centralized authority. Burns and Stalker called this a mechanistic organization structure.

Some organizations, those in rapidly changing environments, had a much different organizational structure. The internal organization was much more adaptive, free-flowing, and spontaneous. Rules and regulations were generally not written, and those that were written were often ignored. People had to find their own way within the system and learn what to do. The hierarchy of authority was not clear, and decision-making authority was broadly decentralized. Burns and Stalker called this an organic organizational structure.

A more recent term that is used to describe an organic structure is a virtual work-place; however, this term often implies more than just a flexible workplace. A virtual workplace refers to networks of people in a workplace where work is done anytime and anywhere and not bound by the traditional limitations of time, physical space, job descriptions, title, and hierarchical reporting relationships. It usually involves work that is done through a variety of communication technologies and working styles, such as telecenters, teleworking, hot-desking, and virtual offices. The virtual workplace has become an increasingly preferred workplace for many.[6]

The differences between an organic and a mechanistic organizational structure are illustrated in Exhibit 6.4. In a mechanistic structure, the work is divided into highly specialized tasks that are rigidly defined by a formal job description. In an organic structure, however, most tasks are not so highly specialized; employees are often expected to learn how to perform a variety of tasks, and to frequently adjust and redefine their jobs as the situation changes. In a mechanistic structure, communication patterns follow the formal chain of command between superiors and subordinates. In an organic structure, however, communication is horizontal, and employees talk with whomever they need to in order to do their work.

Mechanistic and organic structures differ in each of the five dimensions of organizational structure, as illustrated in Exhibit 6.5. In addition to having highly specialized jobs,

Exhibit 6.4 — Mechanistic versus Organic Organizational Structures

Mechanistic	Organic
1. Tasks are divided into separate, specialized jobs.	1. Tasks may not be highly specialized, and employees may perform a variety of tasks to accomplish the group's task.
2. Tasks are clearly and rigidly defined.	2. Tasks are not elaborately specified: they may be adjusted and redefined through employee interactions.
3. There is a strict hierarchy of authority and control with many rules.	3. There is an informal hierarchy of authority and control with few rules.
4. Knowledge and control of tasks are centralized, and tasks are directed from the top of the organization.	4. Knowledge and control of tasks are located anywhere in the organization.
5. Communication is vertical throughout the formal hierarchy.	5. Communication is horizontal; employees talk with whomever they need to communicate.

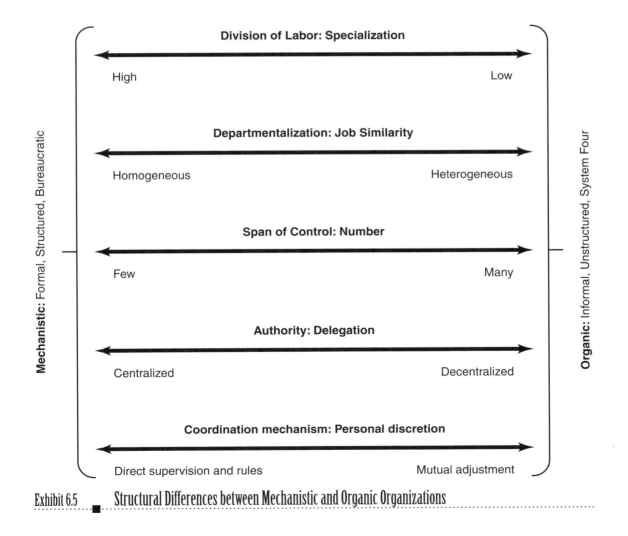

Exhibit 6.5 — Structural Differences between Mechanistic and Organic Organizations

mechanistic structures are characterized by homogeneous departmentalization, a narrow span of control, highly centralized delegation of authority, and coordination through direct supervision and rules. Organic structures are just the opposite: the labor is divided in such a way that the level of specialization is reduced, the jobs are organized into heterogeneous departments, there is a broad span of control, decision-making authority is widely decentralized, and work is coordinated by mutual adjustment. Deciding which structure is best depends on several environmental factors and employee characteristics, as is explained in the later sections.[7]

Bureaucratic Organizational Design

Perhaps the best description of a mechanistic organizational structure is Max Weber's description of bureaucracy.[8] Highly bureaucratic organizations have a very mechanistic organizational structure. Unfortunately, the word "bureaucracy" is associated with a variety of negative feelings. Many people associate bureaucracy with excessive red tape, procedural delays, and organizational inefficiency. These connotations are not consistent with Max Weber's description of bureaucracy. According to Weber, a bureaucracy was a sociological concept that referred to the rational collection of clearly organized activities. The word *bureaucracy* comes from the French word *bureau*, which means "office." In short, a bureaucracy is a collection of carefully organized offices performing specialized functions according to clearly defined rules and procedures. Weber's description of bureaucracy was intended as a description of the ideal form of a large organizational structure. The major attributes of this ideal form were rationality and efficiency. A bureaucratic structure was a well organized collection of offices that combined the efforts of many people using a system of rules and procedures. Weber's description included the following identifying characteristics.

1. *A division of labor based on functional specialization.* All tasks necessary for accomplishing the goals of the organization are divided into highly specialized jobs. Such job specialization allows jobholders to become expert in their jobs and to be held responsible for the effective performance of their duties.
2. *A well-defined hierarchy of authority.* Each officeholder in the organization is accountable to a supervisor. The authority of supervisors is based on expert knowledge and legitimized by the fact that it is delegated from the top of the hierarchy. In this way, a clearly defined chain of command is created.
3. *A system of rules covering the rights and duties of employees.* Each task is performed according to a consistent system of abstract rules to ensure uniformity and coordination of different tasks. Through a system of clearly defined rules, officeholders can eliminate any uncertainty in performing their tasks that is caused by individual differences.
4. *Impersonal relationships.* Each officeholder maintains a social distance from subordinates and clients and conducts the business of the office in a formal, impersonal manner. Strict adherence to the rules and impersonal relationships ensure that personalities do not interfere with the efficient accomplishment of the office's objectives. There should be no favoritism resulting from personal friendships or ingratiating behaviors.
5. *Promotion and selection based on technical competence.* Employment in a bureaucratic organization is based on technical qualifications, and employees are protected against arbitrary dismissal. Similarly, promotions are based on seniority and achievement. Employment in the bureaucracy is viewed as a lifelong career, designed to create loyalty and commitment.
6. *Written communications and records.* All administrative acts, decisions, and rules are recorded in writing. Since verbal conversations and discussions cannot be filed, all decisions, complaints, and administrative acts are to be written and filed. Record keeping provides an organizational memory, and written documents provide continuity over time.

Many of the characteristics that Weber recommended for an ideal bureaucracy seem quite obvious to us today because we are surrounded by organizations that have rules, a division of labor, written documents, and a hierarchy of authority. These characteristics provide an impersonal means of controlling organizations by guaranteeing that dependable work will be performed by qualified employees under the impartial direction of rational supervisors. These rational characteristics, however, were not so obvious a century ago when there were very few large organizations. Most organizations were family operated and characterized by nepotism and unfair treatment. Weber's recommendation of a rational, bureaucratic ideal was intended both to eliminate favoritism and increase organizational efficiency.

Advantages of a Bureaucracy

Bureaucracy has survived and even thrived because its advantages outweigh its disadvantages. The advantages of a bureaucracy stem logically from its ideal characteristics. At its best, a bureaucracy is a smooth-running organization in which decisions and activities are processed efficiently and all members are treated equitably. Seven major benefits have been attributed to bureaucracy, as summarized in Exhibit 6.6.

Exhibit 6.6 Advantages and Disadvantages of Bureaucracies

Advantages	Disadvantages
1. Technical efficiency	1. Rigidity of behavior
2. Elimination of favoritism	2. Bureaucratic personality
3. Predictability of performance	3. Inversion of means and ends
4. Job security	4. Resistance to change
5. Technical competence	5. Peter Principle
6. Minimum direction needed	
7. Avoids impulsive action	

1. *Technical efficiency.* The chief benefit of a bureaucracy is that the activities and functions have been carefully analyzed and rationally organized in a way that creates maximum efficiency. The process of dividing the labor into highly specialized jobs, assigning them to different offices, and coordinating them through a carefully designed system of rules and procedures produces what has sometimes been called machine-like efficiency.
2. *Elimination of favoritism.* By following the correct procedures and administering the rules impartially, clients and officeholders are treated fairly. No one is treated with special favors because of personal friendships or ingratiating behaviors. The rules and procedures are administered without regard to family, wealth, or status. This impartial treatment is consistent with bureaucratic ideals that condemn nepotism, partiality, and capricious judgment.
3. *Predictability in performance.* Strict adherence to clearly defined rules and procedures leads to greater predictability of performance. Both customers and employees know in advance the outcome of a decision. For example, if the vacation policy allows three weeks' paid vacation after five years of service, all employees with at least five years of service can expect to receive a three-week paid vacation.
4. *Job security.* By following the rules and doing what the handbook or procedures manual says they are supposed to do, officeholders are assured that they will not be fired. Such a tenure policy maximizes vocational security. Officeholders tend to view their employment in the organization as a lifelong career. Such an outlook minimizes turnover and engenders a high degree of loyalty and commitment.
5. *Technical competence.* Since officeholders are hired on the basis of their ability rather than on the basis of whom they know, they are highly trained, competent officials.

6. *Minimum direction needed.* Because a bureaucracy has been rationally designed, and the officeholders are trained experts who are expected to follow standard rules and operating procedures, very little day-to-day direction is needed to keep the bureaucracy functioning. Like a carefully designed machine that operates smoothly after it is turned on, a bureaucracy is expected to operate smoothly with little direction or added input.
7. *Avoids impulsive decisions.* Since a bureaucracy operates according to standard operating procedures, it is not possible for an impulsive idea on the part of one officeholder to immediately disrupt the entire bureaucracy. Since they must be coordinated with other officeholders, new ideas and changes cannot be implemented quickly. Although reducing the possibility of impulsive action is sometimes an advantage, it can also be a disadvantage when change is required, which explains why bureaucracies are often associated with red tape and resistance to change.

Disadvantages of Bureaucracy

Although Weber described bureaucracies as ideal structures, they are not without their problems. Over the years, several dysfunctional consequences have been identified. Some of these dysfunctional consequences are not created because the bureaucracy fails to operate properly. Instead, they are created because the bureaucracy is functioning exactly as it should; the problems are inherent to the bureaucratic structure itself. In other words, these problems cannot be solved by having the bureaucracy operate more effectively; a stricter application of bureaucratic principles would exacerbate the problems.

1. *Rigidity of behavior.* In a bureaucracy, officeholders are expected to know the rules and procedures and to follow them precisely. Bureaucracies control individual behavior by demanding strict rule compliance. However, as employees follow the rules more precisely, their behavior becomes more rigid and more insensitive to individual problems. This rigid behavior inevitably leads to conflict with clients and customers. Many times people think their personal situation represents an exception to the rule, and occasionally they are right. Wise bureaucrats know when to deviate from the rules and accept responsibility for their decisions, but bureaucrats who have been intimidated or threatened seek to protect themselves by following the rules. As the level of conflict rises, the dysfunctional consequences of a bureaucratic structure become more obvious. Instead of responding helpfully to the complaints of clients and their demands for individual treatment, bureaucrats respond by following the rules more strictly. By strict adherence to the rules in their handbooks and policy manuals, they are able to defend their actions in the face of conflict, but their client relationships suffer.

Example

Airline passengers have been forced to remain on the planes for more than six hours after they had safely landed, because disruptive conditions prevented them from getting to their assigned gate. They were not allowed to leave the plane even though the toilets were filled, food and water were gone, claustrophobic passengers were freaking out, and mothers had exhausted their supply of diapers and formula. The airline personnel were not willing to deviate from FAA regulations in spite of obvious and intense human suffering.

2. *Bureaucratic personality.* Employees who work in bureaucratic organizations sometimes develop unhealthy personalities that are excessively power-oriented. Officeholders come to believe that moral decisions of right or wrong are defined by higher-level officers and by the rules they are expected to follow. Following the rules becomes more important than the possibly inhumane treatment required by strict rule compliance.

> **Example**
>
> *A pregnant student was required to walk back to her apartment in a storm because she forgot to bring her computer lab pass to show that she is registered in a computer class, even though the person at the desk recognizes her as a class member.*

3. *Inversion of means and ends.* Rigid adherence to rules and regulations often results in situations where the rules become more important than achieving the organization's goals, a condition called means-ends inversion: the means become more important than the end. Although the rules were originally designed to further organizational success, each officeholder comes to see the rules and regulations of that office as the ultimate goal. Bureaucratic activities can become so important that they supplant the purpose for which they were created.

> **Example**
>
> *Advertising campaigns, sales incentives, and other programs are designed to increase sales. But each of these programs can come to be viewed as an end in itself, so that an elaborate awards banquet becomes so important that it dominates everyone's time and attention, and replaces efforts to achieve high sales.*

4. *Resistance to change.* As noted earlier, bureaucracies are intentionally designed to resist rapid change. This resistance is created by several aspects of a bureaucracy. First, officeholders tend to avoid responsibility when they are faced with decisions they prefer not to make. By redefining the problem, most officeholders are able to say, "That's not my job." Second, bureaucrats tend to be isolated from external feedback and outside evaluation. Bureaucracies tend to focus on their own internal functioning to the exclusion of external feedback. Their failure to respond to external evaluation prevents them from making corrective adjustments. Third, bureaucracies are not designed to foster setting or accomplishing goals. Rules and procedures focus the efforts of officeholders on activities rather than outcomes. Opportunities to produce innovative products or services tend to be overlooked because of a preoccupation with bureaucratic procedures. Fourth, bureaucracies move at a painfully slow pace when making complex decisions. The delay occurs because of the number of people who must concur before a decision is made about important issues. After the decision is finally made, there is an additional delay while new rules and procedures for each officeholder are created.

> **Example**
>
> *After the United Auto Workers (UAW) union was created in 1935, it set the standard for other unions in negotiating high wages and plush benefits packages for its members. Known for its aggressive bargaining, it continued to bargain for better labor contracts and protective work rules even when the U.S. auto industry was challenged by foreign competition and it was clear that the auto companies could not survive with their current practices. Although it was eventually willing to accept smaller wage and benefit increases for job guarantees, the labor costs for the auto industry were still more than the auto companies could handle and the membership of the UAW has been reduced to less than a third of what it was earlier.*[9]

5. *The Peter Principle.* The Peter Principle was proposed as a satirical and humorous description of the incompetence that often occurs in bureaucratic organizations.[10] This principle states that in a hierarchy, every employee tends to rise to his or her level of *incompetence.* In a bureaucracy, promotions are supposed to be based on demonstrated ability: the most competent individual at one level is promoted to the next level. The Peter Principle explains, however, that competence at one level does not guarantee competence at the next level. The skills required for a subordinate position are frequently different from those required for success at the next level. Therefore, the most competent individuals at one level are promoted from level to level within the organization until they reach their level of incompetence, at which time they are no longer considered for promotion. An example of the Peter Principle is the promotion of competent technical or sales personnel into administrative positions for which they are ill suited by temperament. According to the Peter Principle, the only effective work that occurs in bureaucracies is performed by individuals who have not yet reached their level of incompetence.

Example

Many school districts have a "promotion from within" policy that advances the best classroom teachers to the position of assistant principal and then principal. However, the skills required to be an excellent teacher of children are much different from the skills needed to supervise other adult teachers. Consequently, many of the assistant principals and principals struggle in their jobs and regret being promoted.

System Four Organizational Structure

Rensis Likert proposed a theory of organizational design, called System Four, that is often considered the opposite of bureaucracy.[11] Likert recommended his System Four as the ideal way to design an organization: extensive research by Likert and others has supported his theory. The central premise of Likert's theory is that there are four kinds of management systems, and these systems vary along a continuum from exploitive and authoritative at one end to participative and group-oriented at the other end. The labels of these four systems and brief descriptions are as follows.

1. *The exploitive-authoritative style,* System One, is characterized by the threat of punishment, hostile attitudes, downward communication, and distrust. Top management makes all the decisions and sets all the goals.
2. *The benevolent-authoritative style,* System Two, is slightly less hostile and threatening, since top management behaves more benevolently, but all decisions, goal setting, and communication are directly under the control of top management.
3. *The consultative style,* System Three, involves greater coordination between upper and lower levels of management. The ideas and interests of lower-level employees are considered, and lower-level employees have a limited opportunity to contribute to the decision making and goal setting.
4. *The participative-group oriented style*, System Four, involves open communication, participative decision making within groups, a decentralized authority structure, broad participation in the goal-setting processes whereby realistic objectives are set, and leadership processes that demonstrate a high level of confidence and trust between superiors and subordinates.

Although Likert did not advocate a specific span of control or form of departmentalization (he admitted that these and other design decisions depended on the situation), he argued that higher-level principles should guide management decisions in the design of an organization. Likert advocated three universal principles: (1) the principle of supportive relationships, (2) the use of group decision making, and (3) the creation of high performance goals.

1. The principle of supportive relationships says that all employees should be treated in ways that build and maintain their sense of personal worth and importance. All interactions between superiors and subordinates must be perceived by subordinates as contributing to their personal worth and to increasing their sense of human dignity. Likert assessed the degree to which relationships are supportive by asking such questions as "How much confidence and trust do you feel your superior has in you?" "To what extent does your boss convey to you a feeling of confidence that you can do your job successfully?" "To what extent is your boss interested in helping you to achieve and maintain a good income?"
2. Likert believed that groups were universally superior to the traditional hierarchical control in decision making and leadership. System Four management involves management by groups and recognizes overlapping group membership; each supervisor also serves as a subordinate in another group at the next level above. Those who hold overlapping memberships are called linking pins. At each hierarchical level, all members of a work group who are affected by the outcome of a decision should be involved in it and it is the leader's responsibility to build an effective team. This principle has important implications for design decisions, since it encourages greater delegation of authority and coordination through the mutual adjustment of self-managing teams.
3. To achieve high levels of organizational performance, Likert argued that both managers and subordinates must have high performance aspirations. However, these high performance goals cannot be imposed on employees. System Four provides a mechanism through group decision making and overlapping group memberships to set high-level goals that satisfy both individual and organizational aspirations. Likert's principle of high performance aspirations is entirely consistent with goal setting theory, as discussed in Chapter 10, and the research supporting the impact of challenging and accepted goals.

Contingency Theories of Organizational Design

Principles of organizational design have shifted from universal design theories to contingency design theories that try to identify the appropriate design features for each situation. Two research studies have contributed greatly to our understanding of contingency design theories. One line of research demonstrates that differences in technology determine the most effective organizational design, while the second suggests that differences in environmental uncertainty and the demands for processing information are the crucial factors. Both of these classic studies produce the same conclusion that the appropriate organizational design depends on the environment and each study identifies an important environmental factor that we need to recognize.

Technology

The first study demonstrated that the appropriate organizational structure is determined by the kinds of technology that it uses. Technology refers to the organization's transformation process and includes the knowledge, skills, abilities, machinery, and work procedures that are used in the transformation process. Every organization has a unique type of technology, and Joan Woodward, a British industrial sociologist, demonstrated that an organization's technology should determine how it is designed.[12] Her research surveyed 100 manufacturing firms on a wide range of structural characteristics, such as span of control, levels of management, ratios of management to clerical workers, decentralized decision making, and management style. Her data also included measures of performance regarding economic success.

When she examined the relationships between structure and performance for all 100 companies, she found no relationships—structure didn't seem to matter. However, when she divided the companies into three categories according to their technology, she found that structure was significantly related to performance: the successful companies in each category had structures that fit their technology. The three technology groups were small-batch manufacturing, such as a printing company; mass-production, such as an assembly-line firm; and continuous-process, such as an oil refinery. In each of the three technology groupings, the successful firms had ratios and numbers that were close to the median, while the unsuccessful firms had ratios and numbers that were much higher or lower than the median. Successful small-batch and continuous-process organizations tended to have organic structures, while successful mass-production organizations tended to have mechanistic structures.

Other research has likewise shown that an organization's structure needs to match the routineness of its processes. Routineness refers to the degree of continuity, automation, and rigidity in the production process; the technology would be considered extremely routine if the production process were totally automated and produced a consistent product. The structural variables most frequently analyzed in technology studies are the degree of centralization, formalization, and specialization, and all three of these variables are positively related to routineness. According to this research, when the technology is highly routine (1) decision making should be centralized, (2) the rules and procedures should be formalized, and (3) the process should be decomposed and performed by specialized people and equipment.[13]

Environmental Uncertainty

The second classic study, by Paul Lawrence and Jay Lorsch, demonstrated that the degree of instability and uncertainty in the environment is another important situational variable that influences organizational structure.[14] The appropriate structure depends on the level of environmental uncertainty. Research fairly consistently indicates that organic structures are more effective in uncertain environments, while mechanistic structures are more effective in stable environments.

Lawrence and Lorsch examined organizations in three industries: plastics, packaged food products, and paper containers. These three industries were selected because significant differences were found in the degree of environmental uncertainty. The environment of the plastics firms was extremely uncertain, because of rapidly changing technology and customer demand. Decisions about new products were required even though feedback about the accuracy of the decisions often involved considerable delay. In contrast, the paper container firms faced a highly certain environment. Only minor changes in technology had occurred in the previous twenty years, and these firms focused on producing high-quality, standardized containers, and delivering them to the customer quickly. The consequences of decisions could be ascertained in a short period. Between these two extremes, the producers of packaged foods faced a moderately uncertain environment.

In analyzing how these firms interacted with their environments, Lawrence and Lorsch identified two key concepts: differentiation and integration. Differentiation is the degree of segmentation of the organizational system into subsystems, which is similar to the concepts of specialization of labor and departmentalization. However, differentiation also considers the behavioral attributes of employees in highly specialized departments. As noted earlier, members of highly specialized functional departments tend to adopt a rather narrow-minded, department-oriented focus that emphasizes the achievement of departmental rather than organizational goals.

The consequence of high differentiation is that greater coordination between departments is required. More time and resources must be devoted to achieve coordination, since the attitudes, goals, and work orientations among highly specialized departments differ so widely. Lawrence and Lorsch developed the concept of integration to refer to this coordinating activity.

Lawrence and Lorsch found that environmental uncertainty was related to the amount of differentiation and integration used in each industry. For example, the firms in the container industry faced a fairly stable environment, so they did not need to be highly differentiated, and they tended to adopt a mechanistic structure. The most successful container companies were organized along functional lines with a highly centralized authority structure. Coordination was achieved through direct supervision with formal written schedules. A bureaucratic structure was consistent with the container industry's degree of environmental certainty.

In the plastics industry, however, where companies face an extremely uncertain environment, the most successful plastics companies adopted organic structures. A highly unstable environment required that these companies have a highly differentiated structure with highly specialized internal departments of marketing, production, and research and development to deal with uncertainty in the external environment. Coordination was achieved through mutual adjustment, ad hoc teams that cut across departments, and special coordinators who served as liaisons between departments. The most successful plastics firms achieved high levels of differentiation and high levels of integration to coordinate them.

Lawrence and Lorsch's study contributes to our understanding of organizational design by showing the effects of environmental uncertainty on organizational structure. When the environment is highly uncertain, frequent changes require more information processing to achieve coordination, so special integrators and coordinating mechanisms are a necessary addition to the organization's structure. These integrators are called liaison personnel, brand managers, or product coordinators. Organizations that face a highly uncertain environment and a highly differentiated structure may have a fourth of their management staff assigned to integration activities, such as serving on committees, on task forces, or in liaison roles. Organizations that face very simple, stable environments may not have anyone assigned to a full-time integration role.

The analysis of Lawrence and Lorsch can be extended from the organizational to the departmental level within an organization. A large firm may need to organize its production department quite differently from its research department. One department may tend toward a mechanistic design and the other toward an organic design. The differences between these two departments are due to the different environments to which the two departments must adapt.

Example

If a marketing department of a large firm faced an extremely unstable environment because of transportation problems across international boundaries, the marketing department would need to adopt an organic structure to respond to rapid developments. In contrast, the production department may face a very stable environment that allows for long production runs of standardized products. In this case, a mechanistic structure with formal bureaucratic procedures would be most appropriate for the production department.

Information Processing

The key integrating concept that explains the relationship between environmental uncertainty, technology, and organizational structure is the way the organization processes information.[15] Information flows into the organization from various environmental sectors, and the organization must respond and adapt to this information. Rapid changes in the external environment result in a greater need for incoming information. The consequence of environmental uncertainty on managers is an increase in the flow of information that leads to a communication overload. In essence, the organization becomes inundated with exceptional cases that require individual attention. As a greater number of nonroutine demands are made on the organization from the environment, managers are required to be more and more involved in day-to-day operations. Problems develop as plans become obsolete and the various coordination functions break down. An effective organization requires a structure that allows it to adapt to such a situation.

Organic structures can deal with greater amounts of uncertainty than mechanistic structures can. Organic structures have more highly connected communication networks that permit the efficient use of individuals as problem solvers and increase the opportunity for feedback. Because highly connected networks do not depend on any one individual, they are less susceptible to information overload or saturation. But while organic structures are able to deal effectively with greater amounts of uncertainty than mechanistic structures, there are costs associated with being able to process more information. Organic structures consume more time, effort, and energy, and are less subject to managerial control. Thus, the benefits of increased efficiency and capacity to process information must be weighed against the costs of less control and greater effort and time.

Organizations in a dynamic and complex environment cannot rely on traditional information processing and control techniques where all information is communicated through a chain of command. Changes in market demand, uncertain resources, and new technology disrupt the organization's plans and require adjustments while the task is being performed. Immediate adjustments to production schedules and job assignments disrupt the organization. Coordination is made more difficult because it is impossible to forecast operations or revise standard operating rules or procedures. Organizations must obtain information that reflects the environmental changes.

Endnotes

1. V. A. Graicunas, "Relationship in Organization," *Bulletin of the International Management Institute*, vol. 7 (March 1933), pp. 39–42; reprinted in Luther H. Gulick and Lyndall F. Urwick (eds.), *Papers on the Science of Administration* (New York: Institute of Public Administration, Columbia University, 1937), pp. 182–187; Arthur G. Bedeian, "Vytautas Andrius Graicunas: A Biographical Note," *Academy of Management Journal*, vol. 17 (1974), pp. 347–349; Lyndall F. Urwick, "V. A. Graicunas and the Span of Control," *Academy of Management Journal*, vol. 17 (1974), pp. 349–354.
2. Kenneth J. Meier and John Bohte, "Span of Control and Public Organizations: Implementing Luther Gulick's Research Design," *Public Administration Review*, vol. 63 (Jan/Feb, 2003), pp. 61–70.
3. Michelle A. Johnston, "Delegation And Organizational Structure In Small Businesses: Influences Of Manager's Attachment Patterns," *Group & Organization Management*, vol. 25 (2000), pp. 4–21.
4. Thomas Sy and Laura Sue D'Annunzio, "Challenges and Strategies of Matrix Organizations: Top-Level and Mid-Level Managers' Perspectives," *Human Resource Planning*, vol. 28 (no. 1, 2005), pp. 39–48; Steven C. Dunn, "Motivation by Project and Functional Managers in Matrix Organizations," *Engineering Management Journal*, vol. 13 (June, 2001), pp. 3–9.
5. T. Burns and G. M. Stalker, *The Management of Innovation* (London: Tavistock Institute, 1961).
6. F. Crandall and M. Wallace, *Work & Rewards in the Virtual Workplace*, (AMACOM, New York, NY, 1998).
7. Timothy DeGroot and Amy L. Brownlee, "Effect of Department Structure on the Organizational Citizenship Behavior—Department Effectiveness Relationship," *Journal of Business Research*, vol. 59 (2006), pp. 1116–1123; Marshall Schminke, "Considering the Business in Business Ethics: An Exploratory Study of the Influence of Organizational Size and Structure on Individual Ethical Predispositions," *Journal of Business Ethics*. vol. 30 (2001), pp. 375–390; Maureen L. Ambrose and Marshall Schminke, "Organization Structure as a Moderator of the Relationship Between Procedural Justice, Interactional Justice, Perceived Organizational Support, and Supervisory Trust," *Journal of Applied Psychology*, vol. 88. (2003), pp. 295–305.

8. Max Weber, *The Theory of Social and Economic Organization*, trans. A. M. Henderson and T. Parsons (New York: Free Press, 1947).
9. Joseph B. White and Jeffrey McCracken, "GM-UAW Deal Ushers in New Era for Auto Industry," *The Wall Street Journal*, 27 September 2007, A1.
10. Lawrence F. Peter and Raymond Hull, *The Peter Principle* (New York: Morrow, 1969); Donald E. Walker, "The Peter Principle: A Simple Put-On About Complex Issues," *Change*, vol. 17 (July-August 1985), p. 11.
11. Rensis Likert, *New Patterns of Management* (New York: McGraw-Hill, 1961); Rensis Likert, *The Human Organization* (New York: McGraw-Hill, 1967).
12. Joan Woodward, *Industrial Organization: Theory and Practice* (London: Oxford University Press, 1965).
13. C. Chet Miller, William H. Glick, Yau-De Wang, and George P. Huber, "Understanding Technology-Structure Relationships: Theory Development and Meta-Analytic Theory Testing," *Academy of Management Journal*, vol. 34 (1991), pp. 370–399; Stephen R. Barley, "The Alignment of Technology and Structure Through Roles and Networks," *Administrative Science Quarterly*, vol. 35 (March 1990), pp. 61–103.
14. Paul R. Lawrence and J. W. Lorsch, *Organization and Environment* (Boston: Harvard Business School, 1967); Paul R. Lawrence and J. W. Lorsch, "Differentiation and Integration in Complex Organizations," *Administrative Science Quarterly*, vol. 12 (1967), pp. 1–47.
15. Michael L. Tushman and David A. Nadler, "Information Processing as an Integrating Concept in Organizational Design," *Academy of Management Review*, vol. 3 (1978), pp. 613–624.

Leadership

Leadership

Leadership is an extremely popular topic in organizational behavior because of the role we assume it plays in group and organizational effectiveness. We assume that the success of a group depends primarily on the quality of leadership. A winning season requires a good coach, a military victory requires a great commander, and a productive work group requires a competent supervisor. Whether they deserve it or not, leaders are usually credited for the group's success and blamed for its failure. When a team has a losing season, the coach is fired, not the team.

The most useful definition of leadership is to view it as the incremental influence one individual exerts on another beyond mechanical compliance with routine directives. Leadership occurs when one individual influences others to do something voluntarily rather than because they were required to do it or they feared the consequences of noncompliance. It is this voluntary aspect of leadership that distinguishes it from other types of influence, such as power and authority. Although leaders may use force or coercion to influence the behavior of followers, they must also have the ability to induce voluntary compliance. By this definition, anyone in the organization can be a leader, whether or not that individual is formally identified as such. Indeed, informal leaders are extremely important to the effectiveness of most organizations.

Managers versus Leaders

Although leadership is similar to management, some writers make a clear difference between these topics to highlight the importance and distinctive nature of leadership.

Managing Things versus Leading People

One contrast between management and leadership focuses on what is influenced: managers manage *things,* while leaders lead *people.*[1] Managers focus their efforts on inanimate objects, such as budgets, financial statements, organization charts, sales projections, and productivity reports. Leaders focus their efforts on people as they encourage, inspire, train, empathize, evaluate, and reward. Leaders build organizations, create organizational cultures, and shape society. Managers focus on internal organizational issues as they maintain bureaucratic procedures and keep organizations running smoothly by solving problems.

It has also been said that *managers are people who do things right, and leaders are people who do the right thing*. This statement suggests that leaders and managers focus on different issues. To manage means to direct, to bring about, to accomplish, and to have responsibility for. The functions of management are planning, organizing, directing, and controlling. The successful manager is viewed as someone who achieves results by following the prescribed activities and maintaining behaviors and products within prescribed limits.

To lead, however, is to inspire, to influence, and to motivate. Effective leaders inspire others to pursue excellence, to extend themselves, and to go beyond their perfunctory job requirements by generating creative ideas. This distinction is somewhat overstated, because effective leaders do a lot of managing, and effective managers need to lead. But it serves to emphasize an important organizational outcome: we desperately need leaders who can create

From *Creating Effective Organizations*, 5th edition by David J. Cherrington and W. Gibb Dyer. Copyright © 2009 by Kendall/Hunt Publishing Company. Reprinted by permission.

an energetic and highly committed work force that is successfully adapting to the demands of a changing environment and competently producing viable products and services.

Controlling Complexity versus Producing Change

Another contrast between management and leadership focuses on maintaining stability versus creating change.[2]

- Management focuses on *controlling complexity*—creating order in the organization, solving problems, and ensuring consistency.
- Leadership focuses on *creating change*—recognizing the dynamic environment, sensing opportunities for growth, and communicating a vision that inspires others.

Exhibit 7.1 Comparison between Leadership and Management

	Leadership	Management
Focus	**Producing useful change**	**Controlling complexity**
Role 1. Deciding what needs to be done	Setting direction Creating a vision and strategy	Planning and budgeting
Role 2. Creating a structure of networks and relationships to get work done	Aligning people with a shared vision Communicating with all relevant people	Organizing and staffing Structuring jobs Establishing reporting relationships Providing training Delegating authority
Role 3. Directing productive work	Empowering people	Solving problems Negotiating compromises
Role 4. Ensuring performance	Motivating and inspiring people	Implementing control systems

Both management and leadership involve influencing others through four common roles: planning, organizing, directing, and controlling. As they perform each of these roles, managers and leaders behave very differently because they focus on different outcomes, as summarized in Exhibit 7.1.

Planning—Deciding What Needs to be Done

Managers decide what to do by planning and budgeting—setting targets and goals for the future, establishing detailed steps for achieving them, and allocating resources to accomplish those plans. Planning and budgeting are the processes managers use to control complexity and produce orderly results; they are not used to create change.

Leadership involves helping an organization achieve constructive change, which requires setting a direction—developing a vision of the future and strategies for producing the changes needed to accomplish the vision.

Organizing—Creating Networks and Relationships to Get Work Done

Managers perform a variety of organizing and staffing activities to create a structure for getting work done. These activities include dividing the work into distinct jobs, staffing the jobs with qualified workers, structuring jobs in defined units, establishing reporting relationships, and delegating authority for following the assigned procedures. By organizing and staffing, managers control a complex environment and create a stable structure for getting work done.

The corresponding leadership activity involves aligning people behind a shared vision of how the organization needs to change. Aligning people involves communicating a new direction to the relevant people who can work "unitedly" and form coalitions with a common vision and sense of direction. Change is not an orderly process, and it will be staggered and chaotic unless many people coalesce and move together in the same direction.

Directing Productive Work

Managers are problem solvers. They tend to view work as an enabling process, involving people with multiple talents and interests that may not coincide with each other or with the interests of the organization. They strive to create an acceptable employment exchange by negotiating agreements that satisfy the expectations of workers and the demands of the organization. Bargaining and compromise are used to establish an agreement, and rewards and punishment are used to maintain it.

Leaders rely on empowering people and letting them work autonomously according to their shared vision. Free to exercise individual initiative and motivated by a sense of ownership, people throughout the organization respond quickly and effectively to new opportunities and problems.

Controlling—Ensuring Performance

Managers ensure performance by implementing control systems—establishing measurable standards, collecting performance data, identifying deviations, and taking corrective action.

Leaders ensure performance by motivating and inspiring people to go above and beyond the formal job expectations. Motivation and inspiration energize people, not by monitoring their behavior as control mechanisms do, but by satisfying basic human needs for fulfillment: accomplishment, recognition, self-esteem, a feeling of control over one's life, and the ability to achieve one's ideals. These feelings touch people deeply and elicit a powerful response.

Control systems are supposed to ensure that normal people perform their work in normal ways, day after day. Managing routine performance is not glamorous, but it is necessary. Leadership that inspires excellence and helps organizations thrive in an uncertain world is glamorous, but it may not be any more necessary than management.

In this theory of leadership, leadership is not necessarily better than management, nor is it a replacement for it. Both functions are necessary in organizations, and some believe that the skills for both functions can be acquired by everyone. Others believe that managers and leaders require very different skills and personalities because they focus on almost opposite behaviors that must therefore be performed by different individuals. This issue is not resolved, and there are data supporting both views.

Transformational Leadership

Another contrast used to highlight a particular kind of leadership is transactional versus transformational leadership.[3] Transactional leaders manage the transactions between the organization and its members; they get things done by giving contingent rewards, such as recognition, pay increases, and advancement for employees who perform well. Employees who do not perform well are penalized. Transactional leaders frequently use the management-by-exception principle to monitor the performance of employees and take corrective actions when performance deviates from the standard.

> **Example**
>
> *Some political observers describe President Gerald Ford as an example of a great transactional leader who did an excellent job of working with Congress and managing the affairs of the United States. During the short time he served as president (1974–1977) he replaced all but two cabinet members and did much to stabilize the operations of many federal agencies, such as the Departments of Labor and Commerce. His justification for pardoning Richard Nixon was to end the political turmoil caused by the impeachment proceedings, so the government could move forward.*

Transformational leadership focuses on changing the attitudes and assumptions of employees and building commitment for the organization's mission, objectives, and strategies. Transformational leaders are described as charismatic, inspirational, and intellectually stimulating, and they show individual consideration for each member. This form of leadership occurs when leaders broaden and elevate the interests of their employees, when they generate awareness and acceptance of the purposes and mission of the group, and when they stir their employees to look beyond their own self-interest for the good of the group. The major differences between transactional and transformational leaders are shown in Exhibit 7.2.

Exhibit 7.2 — Characteristics of Transactional and Transformational Leadership

Transactional Leadership

- Establishes goals and objectives
- Designs work flow and delegates task assignments
- Negotiates exchange of rewards for effort
- Rewards performance and recognizes accomplishments
- Searches for deviations from standards and takes corrective action

Transformational Leadership

- *Charismatic:* Provides vision and sense of mission, gains respect and trust, instills pride
- *Individualized consideration:* Gives personal attention, treats each person individually, coaches and encourages followers
- *Intellectually stimulating:* Promotes learning, shares ideas and insights, encourages rationality, uses careful problem solving
- *Inspirational:* Communicates high performance expectations, uses symbols to focus efforts, distills essential purposes, encourages moral behavior

A result that is attributed to transformational leadership is the empowerment of followers, who are capable of taking charge and acting on their own initiative. Empowerment involves providing the conditions that stimulate followers to act in a committed, concerned, and involved way. The kinds of conditions that contribute to empowerment include providing relevant factual information; providing resources such as time, space, and money; and providing support such as backing, endorsement, and legitimacy. Empowered followers make things happen without waiting for detailed instructions or administrative approvals.

Charismatic leadership is a special kind of influence that is attributed to outstanding and gifted individuals. Followers not only trust and respect charismatic leaders, they also idolize them as great heroes or spiritual figures. Charismatic leadership is evidenced by the amount of trust followers have in the correctness of the leader's beliefs, their unquestioning acceptance of the leader, their willing obedience, and their affection for the leader.

Charismatic leaders are described as people who have a high need for social power, high self-confidence, and strong convictions about the morality of their cause. They establish their influence most importantly by the example they model in their own behavior for followers. They maintain their status by managing their charismatic perception (impression management) to preserve the followers' confidence, by articulating an appealing vision of the group's goals in ideological terms, communicating high expectations for followers, and expressing confidence in their followers.

Example

President Bill Clinton was recognized as a charismatic leader who had the capacity to capture the imagination of his listeners. Even when he was fighting threats of impeachment, he delivered an address before the United Nations that received a standing ovation.[4]

Transformational leaders seek to raise the consciousness of followers by appealing to higher ideals and values such as liberty, justice, equality, peace, and humanitarianism, rather than baser emotions such as fear, greed, jealousy, or hatred. This kind of leadership should be viewed as a priceless national treasure that is sorely needed to rejuvenate society and reform institutions. Many writers have suggested that many social and economic problems, including unemployment and the decline in international competitiveness, stem from insufficient transformational leaders who dream inspired visions and are able to motivate followers to pursue them.

Example

President Franklin D. Roosevelt is often described as a great transformational leader because of the vision and wisdom he shared with Americans during his weekly radio broadcasts that helped the United States overcome a major depression and World War II. President Ronald Regan is another transformational leader because of his charismatic personality, his vision of economic changes, and his boldness in attacking communism.

Empirical support for the importance of transformational leadership comes from research that measured transformational and transactional leadership behaviors.[5] Transformational leadership is superior to transactional leadership in encouraging followers to exert extra effort.[6] Leaders who are rated high on transformational leadership factors have a much larger percentage of employees who say they exert extra effort, than do leaders who are rated low. For example, a study of 186 Navy officers on active duty found that transformational leaders obtained more extra efforts from their subordinates and higher satisfaction than did transactional or laissez-faire leaders.[7] Other research studies have likewise found that transformational leadership is associated with greater leader effectiveness and employee satisfaction.[8]

Studies indicate that transformational leadership can be learned and that it is greatly influenced by the kind of leadership modeled in an organization. Leaders at all levels can be trained to be more charismatic, to be more intellectually stimulating, and to show more individual consideration. Successful training programs have been conducted for a variety of groups, such as first-level supervisors in high-tech computer firms, senior executives of insurance firms, and officers in the Israeli military.[9]

Studies that have examined the relationship between personality and leadership quite consistently find that the Big Five personality traits are only modestly correlated with both transformational and transactional leadership. The best correlations suggest that transformational leaders tend to be a little higher than average on extra-version and emotional stability. But, meta-analyses of hundreds of studies find that even these correlations are, on average, low (.21 and .18 respectively).[10] These low correlations reinforce the idea that transformational and transactional leadership skills are not innate personality attributes but something that can be learned by training and experience.

Leadership Traits

Leadership has been studied at three different levels—the individual, the group, and the organization.

- At the individual level of analysis, leadership studies have focused on the traits of successful leaders.
- At the group level, leadership studies have focused on leadership behaviors of both formal and informal leaders.
- The organizational level of analysis has examined how organizational effectiveness is determined by the interaction between the leader, the follower, and the situation.

The traits of successful leaders have been studied for more than a century. World War I highlighted the need for selecting and training effective leaders, and for the quarter century between World War I and World War II, numerous studies investigated the characteristics of good leaders. These studies are generally referred to as trait studies, because their primary goal was to identify the personal traits of effective leaders.

In general, the trait studies were quite disappointing. Although several traits were frequently associated with effective leaders, the research was weak and sometimes contradictory because of methodological problems associated with identifying good leaders, measuring leader traits, and measuring group effectiveness. Because of weak results, the focus of leadership research shifted from trait studies to contingency studies, which examined more than just the traits of the leader.

The research on leadership traits should not be dismissed too quickly, however. Although the trait studies were disappointing, they were not worthless; when considered as a whole these studies help us understand more about how leaders influence others. Several traits produced a significant difference in leadership effectiveness, but they did not act alone. Four major reviews have surveyed the trait studies, and the results can be summarized in three categories: physical traits, intelligence, and personality traits.[11]

Physical Traits

Trait studies examined such physical factors as height, weight, physique, energy, health, and appearance. To the extent that anything can be concluded regarding the relationship among these factors and leadership, it appears that leaders tend to be slightly taller and heavier, have better health, a superior physique, a higher rate of energy output, and a more attractive appearance.

To illustrate, one early study on the effects of height found that executives in insurance companies were taller than policyholders, that bishops were taller than clergymen, that university presidents were taller than college presidents, that sales managers were taller than sales representatives, and that railway presidents were taller than station agents.[12] Results of this sort, however, have not always been consistent. While one literature review found nine studies showing that leaders tend to be taller, it reported two studies showing that leaders tended to be shorter. Attractiveness and a pleasant appearance were found to be highly correlated with leaders among Boy Scouts; but among groups of delinquent youth, leaders were rated as more slovenly and unkempt than other members.[13]

In summary, studies of personal characteristics are not particularly interesting or useful. The results are generally too weak and inconsistent to use in selecting leaders, nor are they useful for training purposes, because very little can be done to change most of these physical traits. The results seem to say more about cultural stereotypes than they do about leadership. Thus, in unstructured situations we can understand why people who are larger, more attractive, better dressed, and more energetic generally succeed in exerting greater influence than others.

Intelligence

Many studies have investigated the relationship between leadership and intelligence, and they generally agree that leaders are more intelligent than nonleaders. The relationship between intelligence and leadership probably stems from the fact that so many leadership functions depend on careful problem solving, and this is a useful insight into effective leadership. One review of leadership studies reported twenty-three experiments showing that leaders were brighter and had greater levels of intelligence than did their followers. Only five studies reported that intelligence made no difference. In general, it appears safe to conclude that leaders are more intelligent than nonleaders, but again the correlations are small. Obviously, many variables other than intelligence influence leadership effectiveness.[14]

An interesting conclusion from these studies is the suggestion that leaders should be more intelligent than the group, but not by too wide a margin. Members who are significantly brighter than other group members are seldom selected as leaders. Because of their superior intellect, it appears that other group members tend to reject them; they are too different from the rest of the group. People with high IQs tend to have different vocabularies, interests, and goals from those of other group members; these differences create communication and interpersonal relations problems.

Leadership effectiveness also appears to be related to scholarship and knowledge. Leaders generally excel scholastically and receive better-than-average grades. General information, practical knowledge, and simply knowing how to get things done appears to be important for effective leadership and several studies have shown a positive relationship between general knowledge and leadership ability. These results contribute to our understanding of leadership and are potentially useful for both selecting and training leaders.

Personality Traits

Other personality traits appear to be related to leadership, although most of the relationships are not especially strong. A list of the personality traits most frequently associated with leadership is shown in Exhibit 7.3. This list is based on the 1948 review of 124 studies of leadership traits by Ralph Stogdill. This list suggests that the average leader is more social, displays greater initiative, is more persistent, knows how to get things done, is more self-confident, displays greater cooperativeness and adaptability, and possesses greater verbal skills than the average person does. These results also help us understand more about leaders and what they need to do to succeed.

Studies examining emotional adjustment quite consistently found that leaders are more emotionally mature than nonleaders. Rather consistent support was also found for the relationship between leadership and self-confidence or self-esteem. Indeed, the relationship

Exhibit 7.3 — Personality Factors Most Frequently Associated with Effective Leadership

Capacity	Achievement	Responsibility	Participation	Status
Intelligence	Scholarship	Honesty	Activity	Socioeconomic
Alertness	Knowledge	Dependability	Sociability	Position
Verbal facility	Athletic accomplishment	Initiative	Cooperation	Popularity
Originality	Personality adjustment	Persistence	Adaptability	
Judgment		Aggressiveness	Humor	
		Self-confidence		
		Desire to excel		

between self-confidence and leadership generally produced some of the highest correlations of any of the personality traits tested. Honesty or integrity is another characteristic attributed to good leaders. Several studies of the characteristics people admire most in leaders report that honesty and fairness are the most important traits.[15] Unless leaders are honest, no one seems to care much about their visions and goals.

Consequently, it is not correct to conclude that personal characteristics are unrelated to leadership; some characteristics are important, but their relationships are rather complex. Four major reviews have concluded that effective leadership does not depend solely on personality traits. Situational variables are also important and the situation often determines whether a personality characteristic will be positively or negatively associated with effective leadership. Each review concluded that leadership must be examined as an interaction of three variables: characteristics of the leader, characteristics of the subordinates, and the nature of the task.

More recently, research at the individual level has focused on leadership competencies, which refer to specific skills that leaders must be capable of performing at the right times and in the right ways. Three general leadership competencies that have been examined are leadership self-efficacy (being confident in one's ability to lead), leadership flexibility (being open to different perspectives and able to work with diverse people), and goal orientation (maintaining a focus on goal accomplishment).[16] Most leadership competencies, however, are unique to specific professions, such as HR competencies for human resource managers or clinical administrator leadership competencies for nursing.[17]

Leader Behaviors

A second line of leadership research examined leader behaviors in the context of the group and attempted to describe what leaders actually do. These studies examined whether certain ways of behaving were more effective than others: how do effective leaders behave differently from other group members? Most of these studies started in the 1940s and have continued since then.

Authoritarian, Democratic, and Laissez-faire Leadership

The contrasting political systems in the United States and Germany preceding World War II inspired one of the early classic studies of leadership that compared the effects of three leadership styles: authoritarian, democratic, and laissez-faire. Ten-year-old boys who were organized into groups of five boys participated in after-school activities under the leadership of a graduate student trained to provide democratic, autocratic, or laissez-faire leadership. Every six weeks the leaders were rotated among groups so that each group experienced each type of leadership. Under the democratic leaders, group decisions were made by majority vote in which equal participation was encouraged and criticism and punishment were minimal. Under the autocratic leader, all decisions were made by the leader and the boys were required to follow prescribed procedures under strict discipline. Under the laissez-faire leader, the actual leadership was minimized and the boys were allowed to work and play essentially without supervision.[18]

During the 18 weeks of this study, the performance of the boys was observed in order to assess the effects of the three leadership styles. Laissez-faire leadership produced the lowest levels of satisfaction and productivity, while autocratic leadership produced the highest levels of aggressive acts. Democratic leadership seemed to produce the most satisfied groups, who also functioned in the most orderly and positive manner, which is what the researchers hoped to find. However, the effects of the leadership styles on productivity were somewhat mixed, although actual measures of productivity were not obtained. Under autocratic leadership, the groups spent more time in productive work activity and had more work-related conversations, but appeared to be more productive only when the leader was present. When the leader left the room, the amount of work-related activity dropped drastically.

The results of this study were somewhat surprising to the researchers, who had expected the highest satisfaction and productivity under democratic leadership. This study was conducted under the direction of Kurt Lewin, a behavioral scientist who came to America from Germany just prior to World War II. Lewin believed that the repressive, autocratic political climate he had left in Germany was not as satisfying, productive, or desirable as a democratic society. He expected the results of the experiment to confirm his hypothesis. Although the boys preferred a democratic leader, they appeared to be more productive under autocratic leadership.

Other studies have also shown that democratic leadership styles are not always the most productive. In fact, some studies have found that both the satisfaction and the productivity of group members are higher under directive leaders than democratic leaders. For example, a study of 488 managers in a consumer loan company found that employees who had high authoritarianism scores (high acceptance of strong authority relationships) were more satisfied and productive when they worked for supervisors who had little tolerance for freedom.[19] Greater satisfaction with an authoritarian leader was also found in another study of over one thousand workers. This study found that employees who worked independently but were required to have frequent interaction with their superior preferred and were more satisfied with an autocratic leader. Some examples of such employees are fire fighters, police officers, and administrative aides.[20]

Conversely, laissez-faire leadership is not a zero type of leadership, but a destructive type of leadership that is often associated with workplace stressors, bullying at work, and psychological distress. When laissez-faire leaders abdicate the responsibilities and duties assigned to them, they fail to meet the legitimate expectations of others. Not only does their job not get done, but they also prevent others from doing it for them. At least one study has found that leaders who abdicate their responsibility to lead create situations that are characterized by high stress, role conflict, role ambiguity, and conflicts with coworkers.[21]

Production-centered and Employee-centered Leader Behaviors

Following World War II, a group of researchers at the University of Michigan began a series of leadership studies that identified two kinds of leadership behaviors that they called production-centered and employee-centered behaviors. Their research method involved nondirective interviews of supervisors and employees in matched units that performed similar work but differed in their performance levels. The high performing units had employee-centered supervisors who developed a supportive personal relationship with subordinates, avoided punitive behavior, and encouraged two-way communication with subordinates. The low performing units had production-centered supervisors who focused on establishing goals, giving instructions, checking on performance, and structuring the work of the group.[22] These two leader behaviors, which were viewed as opposite ends of a continuum, served as the foundation for the traditional human relations approach to leadership that called for more attention to the needs and interests of employees.

Subsequent research on the relationship between production-centered and employee-centered behaviors found them to be independent dimensions of leadership rather than opposite ends of one leadership continuum. A review of twenty-four studies dispelled a popular myth suggesting that supervisors focus on either production or people, and to the extent that they focus on one, they ignore the other. These studies indicated instead that supervisors can be interested in both production and employees. Therefore, a leader who has a strong production orientation is not necessarily uninterested in the employees, as illustrated in Exhibit 7.4.[23]

Initiating Structure and Consideration

About the same time that the University of Michigan researchers were discovering the production-centered and employee-centered dimensions of leadership, a similar research program at The Ohio State University identified two similar dimensions of leader behavior which they called initiating structure and consideration.[24] These two dimensions were identified from questionnaires similar to the exercise at the end of this chapter that they developed and administered to thousands of employees and supervisors. Initiating structure consisted of leader behaviors associated with organizing and defining the work, the

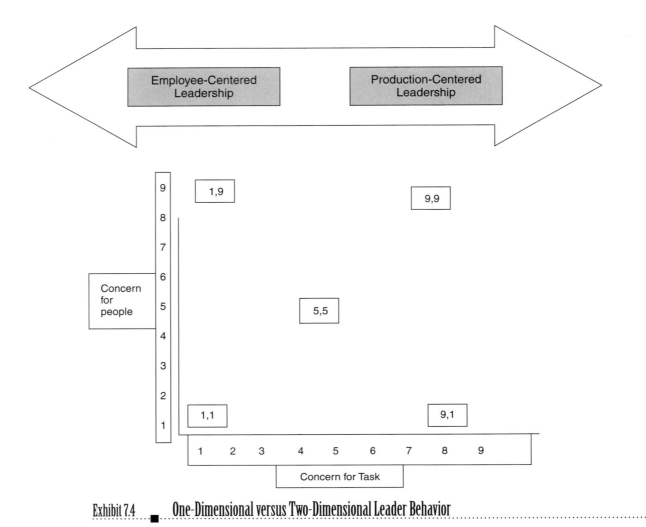

Exhibit 7.4 — One-Dimensional versus Two-Dimensional Leader Behavior

work relationships, and the goals. A leader who initiated structure was described as one who assigned people to particular tasks, expected workers to follow standard routines, and emphasized meeting deadlines. The factor of consideration involved leader behaviors that showed friendship, mutual trust, warmth, and concern for subordinates.

Survey data confirmed that initiating structure and consideration are independent dimensions of leadership behavior. Therefore, a leader could be high on both dimensions, low on both dimensions, or high on one and low on the other. Since both factors are important leader behaviors, the early studies assumed that effective leaders would be high on both dimensions; however, subsequent research failed to support this expectation. The most effective leaders are usually high on both dimensions, but not always. Occasionally other combinations have produced the highest levels of satisfaction and performance, including being high on one scale and low on the other or being at moderate levels on both dimensions.[25]

The Leadership Grid®

Another theory that combines concern for task accomplishment and a concern for people was created by Robert Blake and Jane Mouton using a 9x9 matrix called the Leadership Grid. The concern for production dimension is measured on a nine-point scale and represented along the horizontal dimension, while the vertical dimension measures an individual's concern for people, again using a nine-point scale, as illustrated in Exhibit 7.4. Blake and Mouton assume that the most effective leadership style is a 9,9 style, demonstrating both concern for production and concern for people.[26]

By responding to a questionnaire, individuals place themselves in one of the eighty-one cells on the Leadership Grid. Five different grid positions at the four corners and in the middle are typically used to illustrate different leadership styles:

1,9 Style—Country Club Management: a maximum concern for people with minimum concern for production. This individual is not concerned whether the group actually produces anything, but is highly concerned about the members' personal needs, interests, and interpersonal relationships.

9,1 Style—Authority-Compliance Management: primarily concerned with production and task accomplishment and unconcerned about people. This person wants to get the job done and wants to follow the schedule at all costs.

1,1 Style—Impoverished Management: minimal concern for both production and people. This person essentially abdicates the leadership role.

5,5 Style—Middle-of-the-road Management: a moderate concern for both people and production. This person organizes production to accomplish the necessary work while maintaining satisfactory morale.

9,9 Style—Team Management: a maximum concern for both production and people. This leader wants to meet schedules and get the job done, but at the same time is highly concerned about the feelings and interests of the group members.

The Leadership Grid is popular among managers, and it has been used extensively in management training to help managers move toward a 9,9 style. In spite of its popularity, however, the usefulness of the Leadership Grid has not been consistently supported by research. Most of the available research consists of case analyses that have been loosely interpreted to support it. Empirical research has failed to show that a 9,9 leadership style is universally superior. The demands of the situation, the expectations of other group members, and the nature of the work being performed interact in complex ways that call for a variety of leadership styles. Consequently, the 9,9 leadership style is not always the most effective.

Leader Behaviors as Leadership Roles

Research on leader behaviors helps us understand that both task-oriented and people-oriented leader behaviors are required for effective groups and someone in each group needs to perform these functions effectively. Rather than thinking of leadership strictly in terms of how a formal leader behaves, it is helpful to think of leadership as essential roles performed within a group. This line of thinking implies that leadership consists of essential leader behaviors that can be performed by any group member. The leadership roles of initiating structure and consideration are similar to the work roles and maintenance roles in groups, as explained in Chapter 11. These two roles are necessary for a group to be effective and can be performed either by the formally appointed leader or by other group members.

If a task is already highly structured, or if other group members adequately structure the task themselves, then efforts by the leader to add additional structure are unnecessary and ineffective. Likewise, the maintenance roles of showing consideration and concern for group members may be performed by other group members, thereby eliminating the need for the formal leader to perform this role. Conversely, when the formally appointed leader fails to perform either of these vital leader behaviors, it is not unusual for an informal leader to emerge and perform them to help the group succeed.

Situational Leadership

Research on both leader traits and leader behaviors failed to find one style of leadership that was universally superior. Extensive reviews concluded that effective leadership depended on more than the leader alone; what works well in one situation does not necessarily work well in other situations. These studies concluded that effective leadership depends on a combination of leadership styles, follower characteristics, and environmental factors.

This approach to leadership is referred to as situational leadership theory or contingency theories of leadership.

Five situational leadership theories have received primary attention: (a) Paul Hersey and Ken Blanchard's life cycle theory of leadership, (b) Fred Fiedler's contingency theory of leadership, (c) Robert House's path-goal leadership theory, (d) Victor Vroom and Philip Yetton's decision-making model of leadership, and (e) Robert Tannenbaum and Warren Schmidt's model for choosing a leadership pattern.[27] All of these theories have contributed to our understanding of leadership and their conclusions provide valuable insights for leaders in specific settings. Rather than describing the development and results of each of these theories, they are combined into an integrated model of leadership effectiveness, and only the summary conclusions and applications are presented here. These theories all suggest that leader effectiveness depends on a combination of leader behavior styles, follower characteristics, and environmental factors, as illustrated in Exhibit 7.5.

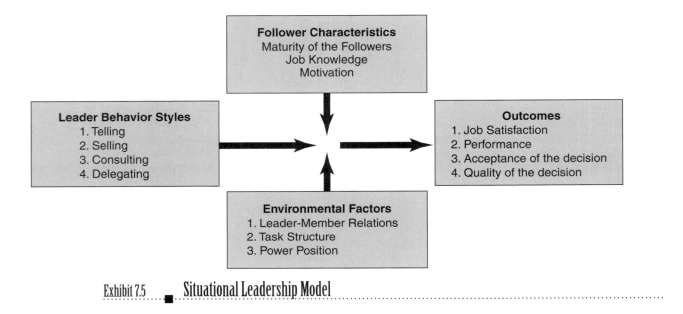

Exhibit 7.5   Situational Leadership Model

Leader Behavior Styles

Leaders can select from among many different styles of leadership and these styles can involve varying levels of interpersonal sensitivity, affiliation, appreciation, and even humor. The most important variable influencing a person's leadership style is the degree to which the leader is willing to allow subordinates to participate in making decisions and directing their own actions. At one extreme is autocratic leadership where all decisions and influence come from the leader, and at the other end of the continuum is democratic leadership where the leader delegates authority to decide and act to the members of a group. This decision is influenced by the leader's value system, especially the value the leader places on participation and involvement by subordinates. The amount of confidence that leaders have in their subordinates, and the leader's ability to handle uncertainty, are also relevant considerations in selecting a leadership style.

When selecting a leadership style, a leader could choose any one of the following patterns that illustrate increasing levels of participation:

1. *Telling:* the leader makes all decisions; he or she simply announces them and tells subordinates what to do. This leadership style is the most autocratic and generally the least preferred by most subordinates. However, it may be appropriate when time is limited and an immediate decision is necessary.
2. *Selling:* the leader presents a tentative decision subject to change and attempts to sell the decision to subordinates. The leader may present ideas and invite questions so that

subordinates feel that their ideas are heard. Most subordinates want their feelings and ideas to be considered: they like having an opportunity to ask questions.
3. *Consulting:* the leader presents the problem to the group and obtains their suggestions and preferences before making the decision. Group participation often yields higher quality ideas than when the leader acts alone. It also reduces resistance when implementing the decision.
4. *Delegating:* the leader may delegate the decision and its implementation to the group and let them handle it on their own, or the leader may join the group and participate as any other member in making and implementing the decision. This style requires great confidence in the ability and motivation of the group and usually requires much more time to make a decision. However, the acceptance of the decision is usually much faster and the implementation is much smoother when the entire group participates.

Involving subordinates in leadership decisions is often a good idea, but not always. To decide which is the most appropriate level of participation, a leader may want to consider the following questions:[28]

- As long as it is accepted, does it make any difference which decision is selected? Are some decisions qualitatively superior to others?
- Do I have enough information to make a high-quality decision, or do subordinates have additional information that ought to be considered?
- Is acceptance of the decision by subordinates crucial to effective implementation? If I make the decision by myself, will they accept it?
- Can I trust subordinates to base their decisions on the best interests of the organization?
- Will subordinates agree on the preferred solution or will there be conflict?
- How much time do we have to make this decision and what are the costs of delaying a decision to involve others?

Follower Characteristics

When selecting a leadership style, the leader should consider such follower characteristics as whether followers have high needs for independence, whether they are ready to assume responsibility for decision making, whether they are interested in the problems, and whether they have enough experience to deal with them. As subordinates gain greater skill and competence in managing themselves, leaders ought to give them more autonomy.[29]

The appropriate leadership style depends primarily on the maturity of the followers. Maturity is defined as the ability and willingness of people to take responsibility for directing their own behavior as it relates to the specific task being performed. An individual or group may demonstrate maturity on some tasks and immaturity on others. Maturity is determined by two components: job maturity (ability) and psychological maturity (willingness). Job maturity is the ability to successfully perform a task and is a function of the follower's job knowledge, training, experience, and skills. Psychological maturity refers to the willingness or motivation to perform the job and is a function of the follower's commitment and confidence.

Telling is an appropriate leadership style for subordinates who have low maturity and are both unable and unwilling to perform the job. Selling is appropriate for followers who are able but unwilling, while consulting is well suited for followers who are willing but unable to do the job. Delegation requires followers who are both able and willing.

Environmental Factors

Many environmental forces influence the appropriate leadership style, including the culture of the organization and its history of allowing subordinates to exercise autonomy, cohesiveness of the group and the degree to which the members work together as a unit, the nature of the problem itself and whether subordinates have the knowledge and experience needed to solve it, and the pressures of time, since group decision making is time-consuming and ineffective in a crisis situation.

Extensive research by Fred Fiedler found that some situations are much more favorable than others for leaders and his results showed that different situations call for different leader behaviors. The environmental factors that have the biggest impact on creating a favorable or unfavorable situation for a leader are:

1. *Leader-member relations:* whether the natural relationships in the situation are friendly and pleasant or unfriendly and unpleasant. A situation that naturally produces friendly relationships with group members is more favorable for a leader.
2. *Task structure:* whether the task is relatively structured and followers know what to do without being told, or unstructured so that the leader must clarify the goals, identify how the task is to be accomplished, and defend the selected solution. Having structured tasks where people know what to do is a more favorable situation for a leader than having to organize a chaotic situation.
3. *Power position:* whether the leader has a strong power position because of official recognition and the ability to administer rewards and punishments, or the leader has a weak power position that is not recognized or accepted. Leaders are in a more favorable position when their status as the leader is recognized and secure than when they have to negotiate or fight for it.

The combination of these three environmental factors determines whether the leader's situation is favorable or unfavorable. The most favorable position for a leader is to have positive leader-member relations, a structured task, and a strong power position. Conversely, the leader is in a very unfavorable situation when the leader-member relations are unpleasant, the task is unstructured, and the leader's power position is insecure. Between these two extremes, of course, are situations of moderate favorableness, which are very important in Fiedler's contingency theory because they call for a very different style of leadership from those of extremely favorable or unfavorable situations.

Fiedler conducted extensive research studies that examined the most effective leadership style in various situations. His research demonstrated that in extremely favorable situations, task-oriented leaders achieve the best results because they focus on getting the work done without worrying too much about their relationships with followers. In these situations, the personal needs of followers are apparently already satisfied and interpersonal sensitivity is unnecessary because there is already a friendly and comfortable situation.

Example

The best leadership style in a professional association, such as the local Society for Human Resource Management, is a task-oriented leader because the situation is very favorable: the members usually like the leaders since they voluntarily chose to join, the leaders are formally elected, and the monthly luncheons are rather structured events. Task-oriented leaders succeed because they simply have to plan the events, advertise them, and keep the members united.

When the situation is extremely unfavorable, the same task-oriented style of leadership again achieves the best results because the job must get done and efforts to act friendly and concerned about followers will not make any difference. A task-oriented leader who simply focuses on getting the work done is more effective than a relationship-oriented leader who spends time fruitlessly trying to build good relationships in an impossible situation.

> **Example**
>
> *The best leadership style for substitute school teachers is a task-oriented style when they face a very unfavorable situation, such as when they are despised by the students, they cannot discipline students effectively, and they have to create their own lesson plans. To succeed in these situations, the substitute teachers must be firm, authoritative, and confident.*

At intermediate levels of favorableness, however, a much different style of leadership is superior. Here, the ideal style is one that is sensitive to the feelings and interests of followers. Interpersonal sensitivity and involvement are important at intermediate levels, since followers need to feel included and relevant. Concern for the group members is apparently a necessary prerequisite for motivating them to perform well.

> **Example**
>
> *In a friendship group of co-workers who eat lunch together every Friday, the leader needs to be sensitive to the interests of group members. This situation is moderately favorable to the leader because, even though there are positive leader-member relations, the task is unstructured and the leader's position is vague. Therefore, the best leader style is one that invites suggestions about where the group wants to go and shows genuine concern for the feelings of each member.*

Determinants of Leadership Effectiveness

Strategies for Improving Leadership

Since the quality of leadership contributes so greatly to the effectiveness of an organization, knowing how to increase leader effectiveness is a serious issue. Improved leader behavior is not a panacea for all organizational problems, but quality leadership is so important that improving the quality of leadership should be an ongoing effort in every organization. Four of the most popular methods of increasing leadership effectiveness include organizational redesign, leadership training, managerial selection and placement, and rewarding leader behavior.

Organizational Engineering

The fastest and sometimes the most effective way to improve leadership is to change the situation so the leaders' skills and orientations match the demands of the situation. When people are placed in situations that are inconsistent with their leadership style, they are generally unsuccessful and they feel very frustrated until they are reassigned. Fiedler's research suggested that the basic leader orientations of most people are rather stable and not easily changed. Therefore, he recommends that organizations engineer the job to fit the manager.[30] This approach is particularly useful when a specific individual is necessary to the organization, yet that person does not possess a compatible leadership style. The job can be changed most easily by changing the degree of task structure or the power position of the leader.

Leadership Training

Although training can help leaders acquire better leadership skills, it is doubtful that such training will change a leader's basic leadership orientation or personality structure. Nevertheless, leadership involves important interpersonal skills that can be acquired through instruction and practice. Leaders can benefit from training in interpersonal skills and management functions—planning, organizing, directing, and controlling. Leaders need to know the differences between transactional and transformational leadership and have an opportunity to practice the skills involved in each kind of leadership. Leadership skills can be acquired through vicarious learning by watching effective leaders and observing how they solve problems and influence people. People who want to learn and who are willing to accept and respond to feedback can improve their leadership skills.

Managerial Selection and Placement

Since basic leadership orientations are not easily changed, companies should select leaders who have leadership styles that fit the situation. Biographical information examining a person's previous leadership experiences can help to predict future leadership effectiveness. Having an organization that is staffed with effective leaders depends far more on good selection than on training.

Rewarding Leader Behavior

Leaders can acquire new leadership skills and learn different leader behaviors if they are sufficiently motivated to experiment and learn. A variety of incentives can reward leaders for learning and developing. Pay increases and promotions are popular incentives that encourage leaders to improve. However, the most powerful incentive is probably the intrinsic satisfaction that comes from greater self-confidence and improved interpersonal relationships between leaders and members.

Reciprocal Influence of Leader and Follower

With thousands of books and articles written about leadership, it is surprising that so little has been written about "followership." We seem to assume that leadership is a one-way process in which leaders influence followers; we overlook the influence in the opposite direction. Only meager efforts have attempted to describe the influence of the group on the leader.

The discussion to this point has assumed that leaders influence followers—that the satisfaction and performance of the followers is caused by the leader's behavior. There are good reasons to reverse this statement, however, and argue that the behavior of the leaders is caused by the performance and satisfaction of the followers. When we acknowledge the leader's capacity to reward the behavior of followers, we should not overlook the capacity of the followers to reward the leader by the ways they perform. For example, organizations reward managers according to the performance of their group. Consequently, the managers of high-performing groups are highly rewarded because of their group's success.

One study has demonstrated the reciprocal nature of influence between leaders and subordinates. In this study, data were collected from first-line managers and two of the supervisors who reported to them. Leaders who were more considerate created greater satisfaction among their subordinates; at the same time, the performance of the subordinates caused changes in the behavior of the leaders. Employees who performed well caused their supervisors to reward them and treat them with greater consideration. Although research on the reciprocal influence between leaders and followers is still rather limited, it is important to remember that leadership may be significantly constrained by the followers.[31]

Some observers contend that the leadership crisis in society is not really caused by bad leaders, but by incompetent or uncooperative followers who fail to complete their work in an active, intelligent, and ethical way. Effective followers are characterized as having (1) personal integrity that demands loyalty to the organization and a willingness to follow their own beliefs, (2) an understanding of the organization and their assigned roles, (3) versatility, and (4) personal responsibility.

Constraints on Leader Behavior

Leaders do not have unlimited opportunities to influence others. Leadership effectiveness is constrained by a variety of factors, such as the extent to which managerial decisions are preprogrammed because of precedent, structure, technological specifications, laws, and the absence of available alternatives. Leadership can also be constrained by a variety of organizational factors limiting the leader's ability either to communicate with or reinforce the behavior of subordinates. The constraints imposed on leaders include external factors, organizational policies, group factors, and individual skills and abilities.

1. *External factors.* Leaders are constrained in what they can do because of economic realities and a host of state and federal laws. For example, leaders are required to pay at least the minimum wage and they are required to enforce safety standards. Leaders who have unskilled followers will have difficulty leading regardless of their leadership style, and the availability of skilled followers is influenced by the external labor market. Some locations have a better supply of skilled employees than others.
2. *Organizational policies.* The organization may constrain a leader's effectiveness by limiting the amount of interaction between leaders and followers or by restricting the leader's ability to reward or punish followers. The history and culture of an organization may limit what a leader is allowed to do and what is considered acceptable.
3. *Group factors.* Group norms are created by the dynamics of the group. If the group is highly cohesive and very determined, it can limit the leader's ability to influence the group. Leaders depend on the cooperation of their groups; a united group has the capacity to blunt or even destroy the influence of a leader.
4. *Individual skills and abilities.* The leader's own skills and abilities may act as constraints, since leaders can only possess so much expertise, energy, and power. Some situations may simply require greater skills and abilities than the leader may possibly hope to possess.

Substitutes for Leadership

While some situations constrain leaders, other situations make leadership unnecessary. These variables are referred to as **leader substitutes** because they substitute for leadership, either by making the leader's behavior unnecessary or neutralizing the leader's ability to influence subordinates. An example of a variable that tends to substitute for leadership is training. Subordinates who have extensive experience, ability, and training tend to eliminate the need for instrumental leadership. Task instructions are simply unnecessary when subordinates already know what to do.

Example

When an ambulance arrives at the emergency room of a hospital, the ER employees do not wait for instructions from a leader before taking action. These employees are highly-trained professionals who have worked in similar situations, even if it has been with different co-workers, and they know what to do because of their training and experience.

Realizing that there are constraints on a leader's behavior and that other factors may serve to neutralize or substitute for the influence of a leader helps explain why the research on leadership has produced such inconsistent results. The inconsistency does not mean that leadership is unimportant; rather, it illustrates the complexity of the world in which leaders are required to function. The complexity of the situation, however, may prevent us from knowing in advance which leadership behaviors will be the most effective.

Leadership is an extremely important function that has an enormous influence on the effectiveness of groups and organizations. Our advice is that you take advantage of leadership opportunities and do your best to learn from them. Don't hesitate or be afraid to be a leader. Leadership skills improve in time with practice and feedback. Even great transformational leaders had to develop their interpersonal skills through successive experiences in which they often failed.

■ Endnotes

1. Warren Bennis, *On Becoming a Leader* (Reading, Mass.: Addison-Wesley, 1989); Warren Bennis, "Why Leaders Can't Lead," *Training and Development Journal*, vol. 43 (April 1989), pp. 35–39; James Kotterman, "Leadership Versus Management: What's the Difference?" *The Journal for Quality and Participation*, vol. 29 (no. 2, 2006), pp. 13–17.
2. John P. Kotter, "What Leaders Really Do," *Harvard Business Review*, vol. 68 (May–June, 1990), pp. 103–111; Abraham Zaleznik, "Managers and Leaders: Are They Different?" *Harvard Business Review*, vol. 70 (March–April 1992), pp. 126–135; A. Zaleznik, "Managers and Leaders: Are They Different?" *Harvard Business Review on Leadership*, Harvard Business School Press, 1988.
3. Bernard M. Bass, "From Transactional to Transformational Leadership: Learning to Share the Vision," *Organizational Dynamics*, vol. 18 (Winter 1990), pp. 19–31; James M. Burns, *Leadership*, (New York: Harper & Row, 1978); Bruce J. Avolio, David A. Waldman, and Francis J. Yammarino, "Leading in the 1990s: The Four I's of Transformational Leadership," *Journal of European Industrial Training*, vol. 15, (no. 4, 1991), pp. 9–16.
4. Paul D. Cherulnik, Kristina A. Donley, Tay Sha R. Wiewel, and Susan R. Miller, "Charisma Is Contagious: The Effect of Leaders' Charisma on Observers' Affect," *Journal of Applied Social Psychology*, vol. 31 (2001), pp. 2149–2159.
5. Bernard M. Bass, *Leadership and Performance Beyond Expectations* (New York: Free Press, 1985); John J. Hater and Bernard M. Bass, "Superiors' Evaluations and Subordinates' Perceptions of Transformational and Transactional Leadership," *Journal of Applied Psychology*, vol. 73 (November 1988), pp. 695–702.
6. Bernard M. Bass, "From Transactional to Transformational Leadership: Learning to Share the Vision," *Organizational Dynamics*, vol. 18 (Winter 1990), pp. 19–31.
7. Francis J. Yammarino and Bernard M. Bass, "Transformational Leadership and Multiple Levels of Analysis," *Human Relations*, vol. 43 (October 1990), pp. 975–995.
8. Ronald J. Deluga, "Relationship of Transformational and Transactional Leadership with Employee Influencing Strategies," *Group and Organization Studies*, vol. 13 (December 1988), pp. 456–467; Joseph Seltzer and Bernard M. Bass, "Transformational Leadership: Beyond Initiation and Consideration," *Journal of Management*, vol. 16 (December 1990), pp. 693–703; William D. Spangler and Lewis R. Braiotta, "Leadership and Corporate Audit Committee Effectiveness," *Group and Organization Studies*, vol. 15 (June 1990), pp. 134–157; David A. Waldman, Bernard M. Bass, and Francis J. Yammarino, "Adding to Contingent-Reward Behavior: The Augmenting Effect of Charismatic Leadership," *Group and Organization Studies*, vol. 15 (December 1990), pp. 381–394; Francis J. Yammarino and Bernard M. Bass, "Transformational Leadership and Multiple Levels of Analysis," *Human Relations*, vol. 43 (October 1990), pp. 975–995.
9. Bernard M. Bass and Bruce J. Avolio, "Developing Transformational Leadership: 1992 and Beyond," *Journal of European Industrial Training*, vol. 14, (no. 5, 1990), pp. 21–27; Micha Popper, Ori Landau, and Ury M. Gluskines, "The Israeli Defense Forces: An Example of Transformational Leadership," *Leadership and Organization Development Journal*, vol. 13, (no. 1, 1992), pp. 3–8; Francis J. Yammarino and Bernard Bass, Transformational Leadership and Multiple Levels of Analysis," *Human Relations*, vol. 43 (October 1990), pp. 975–995.
10. Joyce E. Bono and Timothy A. Judge, "Personality and Transformational and Transactional Leadership: A Meta-Analysis," *Journal of Applied Psychology*, vol. 89 (2004), pp. 901–910.
11. Bernard M. Bass, *Leadership, Psychology, and Organizational Behavior* (New York: Harper & Row, 1960); Cecil A. Gibb, "Leadership," in G. Lindzey and E. Aronson (Eds.), *The Handbook of Social Psychology*, 2nd ed., vol. 4 (Reading, Mass.: Addison-Wesley, 1969); R. D. Mann, "A Review of the Relationships Between Personality and Performance in Small Groups," *Psychological Bulletin*, vol. 56 (1959), pp. 241–270; Ralph M. Stogdill, "Personal Factors Associated with Leadership: A Survey of the Literature," *Journal of*

Psychology, vol. 25 (1948), pp. 35–71; G. Yukl, A. Gordon, and T. Taber, "A Hierarchical Taxonomy of Leadership Behavior: Integrating a Half Century of Behavior Research," *Journal of Leadership and Organizational Studies*, vol. 9 (2002), pp. 15–32; S. J. Zaccaro, (2007). "Trait-based leadership." *American Psychologist, 62,* 6–16.
12. E. B. Gowin, *The Executive and His Control of Men* (New York: Macmillan, 1915).
13. Stogdill, op. cit.
14. Stogdill, op. cit.
15. Shelley A. Kirkpatrick and Edwin A. Locke, "Leadership: Do Traits Matter?" *Academy of Management Executive*, vol. 5 (May 1991), pp. 49–60; J. M. Kouzes and B. Z. Posner, *The Leadership Challenge: How to Keep Getting Extraordinary Things Done in Organizations* (San Francisco: Jossey-Bass Publishers, 1995).
16. David W. Chan, "Leadership and Intelligence," *Roeper Review*, vol. 29 (Spring, 2007), pp. 183–189.
17. *Leadership Competencies for Clinical Managers, The Renaissance of Transformational Leadership.* Edited by Anne M. Baker, Dori Taylor Sullivan, and Michael J. Emery. (Jones and Bartlett Publishers, 2006).
18. Kurt Lewin, R. Lippitt, and R. K. White, "Patterns of Aggressive Behavior in Experimentally-Created Social Climates," *Journal of Social Psychology*, vol. 10 (1939), pp. 271–301.
19. Henry Tosi, "Effect of the Interaction of Leader Behavior and Subordinate Authoritarianism," *Proceedings of the Annual Convention of the American Psychological Association*, vol. 6 part 1 (1971), pp. 473–474.
20. Victor H. Vroom and Floyd C. Mann, "Leader Authoritarianism and Employee Attitudes," *Personnel Psychology*, vol. 13 (1960), pp. 125–140.
21. Anders Skogstad, Stale Einarsen, Torbjorn Torsheim, Merethe Schanke Aasland, and Hilde Hetland, "The Destructiveness of Laissez-Faire Leadership Behavior," *Journal of Occupational Health Psychology*, vol. 12 (2007), pp. 80–92.
22. Daniel Katz, N. Maccoby, and N. C. Morse, *Productivity, Supervision, and Morale in an Office Situation* (Ann Arbor: University of Michigan Survey Research Center, 1950).
23. Peter Weissenberg and M. H. Kavanagh, "The Independence of Initiating Structure and Consideration: A Review of the Evidence," *Personnel Psychology*, vol. 25 (Spring 1972), pp. 119–130.
24. John K. Hemphill, *Leader Behavior Description* (Ohio State Leadership Studies Staff Report, 1950); Ralph M. Stogdill, *Handbook of Leadership* (New York: The Free Press, 1974), Chaps. 11 and 12.
25. E. A. Fleishman, "Twenty Years of Consideration and Structure," in E. A. Fleishman and J. G. Hunt (Eds.), *Current Developments in the Study of Leadership* (Carbondale: Southern Illinois University Press, 1973), pp. 1–40; E. A. Fleishman and E. F. Harris, "Patterns of Leadership Behavior Related to Employee Grievances and Turnover," *Personnel Psychology*, vol. 15 (1962), pp. 43–56.
26. Robert R. Blake and Anne Adams McCanse, *Leadership Dilemmas—Grid Solutions* (Houston: Gulf Publishing, 1991).
27. Paul Hersey, Ken Blanchard, and Dewey E. Johnson, *Management of Organizational Behavior*, 9th ed. (Upper Saddle River, N. J.: Prentice-Hall, 2008); Fred E. Fiedler and Martin M. Chemers, *Leadership and Effective Management* (Glenview, Ill.: Scott, Foresman, 1974); Robert J. House and Terrence R. Mitchell, "Path-Goal Theory of Leadership," *Journal of Contemporary Business* (Autumn 1974), pp. 81–98; Victor H. Vroom and Philip W. Yetton, *Leadership and Decision-Making* (Pittsburgh: University of Pittsburgh Press, 1973); Robert Tannenbaum and Warren H. Schmidt, "How to Choose a Leadership Pattern," *Harvard Business Review*, vol. 51 (May–June, 1973).
28. V. H. Vroom, "Leadership and the Decision-Making Process. *Organizational Dynamics*, vol. 28 (2000), pp. 82–94; Victor H. Vroom and Arthur G. Jago, "The Role of the Situation in Leadership," *American Psychologist*, vol. 62 (2007), pp. 17–24.
29. Seokhwa Yun, Jonathan Cox, and Henry P. Sims, "The Forgotten Follower: A Contingency Model of Leadership and Follower Self-Leadership," *Journal of Managerial Psychology,*" vol. 21 (2006), pp. 374–388.

30. Fred E. Fiedler, "Change the Job to Fit the Manager," *Harvard Business Review*, vol. 43 (1965), pp. 115–122; F. E. Fiedler, "Research on Leadership Selection and Training: One View of the Future," *Administrative Science Quarterly*, vol. 41, (1996), pp. 241–250.
31. Charles N. Green, "The Reciprocal Nature of Influence Between Leader and Subordinate," *Journal of Applied Psychology*, vol. 59 (April 1975), pp. 187–193; Ifechukude B. Mmobousi, "Followership Behavior: A Neglected Aspect of Leadership Studies," *Leadership and Organizational Development Journal*, vol. 12, no. 7 (1991), pp. 11–16.

Analyzing Individual Behavior

Perception

An understanding of perception is important because it has such an enormous impact on understanding individual behavior. No two people share the same reality; for each of us, the world is unique. We cannot understand behavior unless we understand why two people observing the same event can honestly see something entirely different. Furthermore, we need to understand that through our perceptions we are not simply passive observers of the drama of life, but active participants, helping to write the script and play the roles. The behavior of others is influenced by how you perceive them.

The Perceptual Process

Perception is the process of receiving and interpreting environmental stimuli. In a world filled with complex environmental stimuli, our perceptions help us categorize and organize the sensations we receive. We behave according to our interpretation of the reality we see. What we fail to appreciate is that the reality we see is almost never the same as the reality perceived by others. The perceptual process consists of three major components, as shown in Exhibit 8.1: sensation, attention, and perception. These three components are involved in perceiving both physical objects and social events.

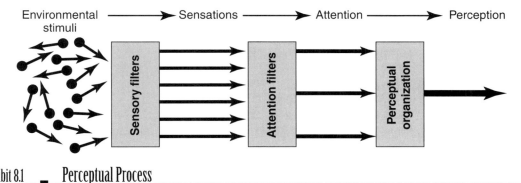

Exhibit 8.1 — Perceptual Process

Sensation

At any given moment we are surrounded by countless environmental stimuli. We are not aware of most of these stimuli, either because we have learned to ignore them, or because our sense organs—sight, smell, taste, touch, and hearing—are not capable of receiving them. Environmental stimuli can only produce sensations in the human body if the body has developed the sensing mechanism to receive them. Whether you are consciously aware of these sensations, however, depends on the next step in the perception process—attention.

Attention

Although we are capable of sensing many environmental stimuli, we attend to only a very small portion of them and ignore the rest. Numerous factors influence the attention process.

1. *Size*. The larger the size of a physical object, the more likely it is to be perceived.

From Creating Effective Organizations, 5th edition by David J. Cherrington and W. Gibb Dyer. Copyright © 2009 by Kendall/Hunt Publishing Company. Reprinted by permission.

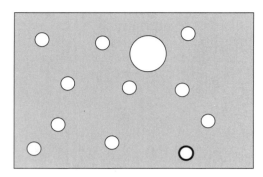

Exhibit 8.2 ■ **The Effects of Size, Intensity, and Contrast on Attention**

2. *Intensity.* The greater the intensity of a stimulus, the more likely it is to be noticed. A loud noise, such as shouting, is more likely to get attention than a quiet voice.
3. *Frequency.* The greater the frequency with which a stimulus is presented, the greater are the chances you will attend to it. This principle of repetition is used extensively in advertising to attract the attention of buyers.
4. *Contrast.* Stimuli that contrast with the surrounding environment are more likely to be selected for attention than stimuli that blend with the environment. The contrast can be created by color, size, or any other factor that distinguishes one stimulus from others, as shown in Exhibit 8.2.
5. *Motion.* Since movement tends to attract attention, a moving stimulus is more likely to be perceived than a stationary object. An animated sign, for example, attracts more attention than a fixed billboard. An object with blinking lights, such as a Christmas tree or sign, attracts more attention than one without blinking lights.
6. *Novelty.* A stimulus that is new and unique will often be perceived more readily than familiar stimuli. Advertisers use the impact of novelty by creating original packaging or advertising messages.

Perception

The process of perception involves organizing and interpreting the sensations we attend to. Visual images, sounds, odors, and other sensations do not simply enter our consciousness as pure, unpolluted sensations. As we attend to them, we consciously try to organize or categorize the sensations into a meaningful perception that somehow makes sense to us.

Although we would like to think of ourselves as open-minded, unbiased, and nonjudgmental in our perceptions, the demands of the situation make it impossible; we are forced to draw quick inferences based on very sparse information. If you were a counselor in a college advisement center and a student came for assistance, you would be required to make rapid inferences based on only limited information. Your recommendations on course loads and elective classes would depend on your perception of the student's situation.

We tend to categorize people using limited pieces of information and then act on this information, even though most of our inferences have not been confirmed. This process is called making perceptual inferences, since we are required to diagnose our situation and make rapid inferences about it from scanty clues.

We cannot wait until we have complete information about each individual before we respond. If we waited until we were fully informed about each person's unique personality and problems, we would never respond. Instead, we develop a system of categories based on only a few pieces of information and use this system to organize our perceptions. For example, college students tend to categorize other college students according to sex, marital status, year in school, and major. If you started a casual conversation with another student, your conversation would likely be much different if you thought that student was a married graduate student majoring in engineering rather than an unmarried freshman majoring in sociology.

The process of grouping environmental stimuli into recognizable patterns is called perceptual organization. Rather than just seeing the stimuli as random observations, we attempt to organize them into meaningful, recognizable patterns. Some of the principles we use to organize these sensations include these:

1. *Figure-ground.* People tend to perceive objects that stand against a background. In a committee meeting, for example, most people see the verbal conversation as *figure*, and fail to attend to the background of nonverbal messages that may be far more meaningful in understanding the group processes.
2. *Similarity.* Stimuli that have common physical traits are more likely to be grouped together than those that do not. Athletic teams wear uniforms to help players recognize their teammates. Some companies that have open floor plans color-code partitions and other furniture to visually define separate functions and responsibilities, such as General Mills, which uses different color schemes to separate the various departments at its headquarters. Because of the principle of similarity, the management style of top managers sets the stage for how the feedback and instructions of middle managers will be perceived by their subordinates.
3. *Proximity.* Stimuli that occur in the same proximity, either in space or in time, are often associated. For example, if you see two people together frequently, you will tend to attribute the characteristics you learn about one individual to the other, until your perceptions become more accurate. An illustration of proximity in time occurs when the boxes in the hall are removed on the same day that you complain about them. You may assume that your complaints led to their removal, without realizing that it would have occurred anyway.
4. *Closure.* Since most of the stimuli we perceive are incomplete, we naturally tend to extrapolate information and project additional information to form a complete picture. For example, a pole placed in front of a stop sign may prevent us from seeing the entire eight-sided figure. But since we have seen many stop signs before, the principle of closure causes us to "see" the complete sign. If we watch an employee work for fifteen minutes and complete the first half of a task, and return twenty minutes later to find the task completed, we attribute the entire task to the employee because of the principle of closure. However, we only saw this person perform half the task, and so our inference about the last half may be incorrect.

Perceiving social events and people is more difficult than perceiving physical objects. If two people disagree about the length of an object, they can measure it. But if they disagree about whether a supervisor is pleased with their work, they may have difficulty verifying which one is right, even if the supervisor's comments were filmed. Although the inferences we make about someone's personality should be based upon the behavior we observe, our perceptions are influenced by a variety of physical characteristics, such as appearance and speech.

The appearance of others influences how we perceive and respond to them, as has been amply demonstrated by the dress-for-success literature. Although many people, especially college students, feel somewhat repulsed by the implications of the research, the data nevertheless show that people who dress in conservative business attire are more likely to be hired, be promoted, make a sale, obtain service, and be treated as someone important.[1] We generally assume that people who are dressed in business suits and uniforms are professional or technical employees performing their assigned functions. Therefore, we tend to respond to them with respect and deference, and willingly comply with their requests. On the other hand, we assume that people dressed in work clothes are lower-level employees, who possess little, if any, authority to tell us what to do. We are more likely to treat them in a discourteous manner.

How people speak also influences our perceptions of them. As we listen to people talk, we make rapid inferences about their personalities, backgrounds, and motives. We notice tone of voice to detect whether individuals are happy, sad, angry, or impatient. We notice the precision and clarity in the messages communicated to us, and we generally assume that a message spoken in a very emphatic and distinct manner is supposed to be carefully attended to. When individuals speak in a particular dialect or accent, we make inferences about their geographic and cultural background. The topics people choose to discuss not only reveal their educational training, but also their personal interests and ways of thinking. In a leaderless group discussion, a female student with a soft, nonassertive voice frequently has difficulty getting the other group members to listen to her ideas. On the other hand, individuals who speak with a distinct, authoritative tone of voice often receive greater credibility than their contributions deserve. A person speaking less than perfect English may be perceived as unintelligent although he or she may be fluent in many languages.

We also draw numerous inferences from nonverbal communications such as eye contact, hand motions, and posture. Sitting up straight, looking the other person in the eye, and nodding your head in agreement indicate to other people that you are interested, and they will perceive you as being friendly and concerned.

The way we organize and interpret environmental stimuli is also influenced by our own characteristics. How we feel about ourselves has an enormous effect on how we perceive others. When we understand ourselves and can accurately describe our own personal characteristics, we can more accurately perceive others. For example, secure people tend to see others as warm rather than cold, and our own sociability influences the importance we attach to the sociability of others. When we accept ourselves and have a positive self-image, we tend to see favorable characteristics in others. We are not as negative or critical about others if we accept ourselves as we are.

Our perceptions are also influenced by our cognitive complexity and our expectations. When we have complex thinking and reasoning structures, we are able to perceive small differences in what we see. Cognitive complexity allows us to differentiate people and events using multiple criteria, which increases the accuracy of our perceptions. Furthermore, we tend to see things that our past experience and personal values have taught us to see. If we are prepared and expecting to see something, we might see it even if it is not there.

McGregor's Theory X versus Theory Y

An excellent illustration of how a perceptual set influences the behavior of managers is provided by Douglas McGregor's Theory X versus Theory Y.[2] McGregor developed his theory at a time when television commercials were contrasting brand X, the ineffective product, with brand Y, the effective one. According to McGregor, *Theory X* represents an outdated, repressive view of human nature that assumes people are lazy, they don't want to work, and management's job is to force or coerce them.
Theory X contains three assumptions:

1. The average human being inherently dislikes work and will avoid it if possible.
2. Because they dislike work, most people must be coerced, controlled, directed, and threatened with punishment to get them to achieve organizational objectives.
3. The average human being prefers to be directed, wishes to avoid responsibility, has relatively little ambition, and wants security above all.

McGregor says employees would behave much differently if managers would adopt a different set of assumptions. In contrast to his pessimistic Theory X view of human nature, McGregor presents a set of six assumptions, which he calls *Theory Y*:

1. The expenditure of physical and mental effort in work is as natural as play or risk. The average human being does not inherently dislike work.
2. External control and the threat of punishment are not the only means of motivating people to achieve organizational objectives. People will exercise self-direction and self-control in the pursuit of objectives to which they are committed.
3. Commitment to objectives is a function of the rewards associated with their achievement. The most significant rewards, the satisfaction of ego and self-actualization needs, can be obtained from effort directed toward organizational objectives.
4. The average human being learns, under proper conditions, not only to accept but also to seek responsibility. Avoidance of responsibility, lack of ambition, and an emphasis on security are generally consequences of experience, not inherent human characteristics.
5. The capacity to exercise a relatively high degree of imagination, ingenuity, and creativity in solving organizational problems is widely, not narrowly, distributed in the population.
6. Under the conditions of modern industrial life, the intellectual potentialities of the average human being are only partially utilized.

According to Theory X, poor performance can be blamed on the employees' failure to demonstrate initiative and motivation. In contrast, Theory Y represents an enlightened view of human nature suggesting that organizational inefficiencies should be blamed on management. If employees are lazy, indifferent, unwilling to take responsibility, uncooperative, or uncreative, these problems indicate that management has failed to unleash the potential of its employees.

These two views of human nature represent significantly different perceptual sets that managers use to perceive the behavior of their subordinates. McGregor explains how these two views cause managers to behave quite differently in response to organizational problems. In his own writing, McGregor uses Theory Y to redesign such management practices as performance appraisal, wage and salary administration, profit sharing, promotions, and participative management.

Perceptual Errors

As we observe people and events, we make countless perceptual errors. This section analyzes six of the most frequent perceptual errors.

Halo Effect

The halo effect refers to the tendency to allow one personality trait to influence our perceptions of other traits. For example, if we see a person smiling and looking pleasant, we may conclude, as one study found, that the person is more honest than people who frown. However, there is no necessary connection between smiling and honesty. One potentially serious application of the halo effect is when it occurs in a performance evaluation. If one particular attribute, positive or negative, colors a supervisor's perception of other unrelated attributes, the performance evaluation process can be extremely unfair and misleading.

Selective Perception

The process of systematically screening out information we don't wish to hear is referred to as selective perception. This process is a learned response; we learn from past experience to ignore or overlook information that is uncomfortable and unpleasant. Occasionally we face stimuli that are so threatening or embarrassing that we refuse to perceive them, and this process is also called perceptual defense.

Implicit Personality Theories

Based on our interactions with many people, we create our own system of personality profiles and use them to categorize new acquaintances. To the extent that our personality profiles are accurate, they facilitate our ability to perceive more rapidly and accurately. Since each person is unique, however, our implicit personality theories can serve at best as only a rough approximation for categorizing people. If we continue to observe carefully, we may find that many of our expectations were not correct.

Projection

The tendency to attribute our own feelings and characteristics to others is called projection. As with other perceptual errors, projection is occasionally an efficient and reasonable perceptual strategy. If we don't like to be criticized, harassed, or threatened, it is reasonable to assume that others would not like it any better. However, projection usually refers to more than just attributing our thoughts and feelings to others. Instead it is used to describe the dysfunctional process of attributing to others the undesirable thoughts and traits we possess but are not willing to admit. In essence, we attribute or project onto others the negative characteristics or feelings we have about ourselves. Projection serves as a defense mechanism to protect our self-concept and makes us more capable of facing others, whom we see as imperfect.

First Impressions

When we meet people for the first time, we form impressions based on limited information that *should* be open for correction on subsequent encounters. Research evidence indicates, however, that first impressions are remarkably stable. In recruiting interviews, for example, it has been found that recruiters form a fairly stable impression of the applicant within the first three or four minutes. Negative first impressions seem to require abundant favorable information to change them, and some recruiters are so opinionated that they refuse to perceive contradictory information.

Allowing first impressions to have a disproportionate and lasting influence on later evaluations is known as the primacy effect. The primacy effect explains why the first few days on the job may have a large impact on the attitudes and performance of new employees. Likewise, the opening comments in a committee meeting may have a lasting impact on the remainder of the group discussion because of the primacy effect.

Stereotyping

The process of stereotyping refers to categorizing individuals based on one or two traits, and attributing other characteristics to them based on their membership in that category. Stereotypes are frequently based on sex, race, age, religion, nationality, and occupation. Although stereotypes help us interpret information more rapidly, they also cause serious perceptual errors. When we create fixed categories based on variables such as sex, race, and age, and resist looking more carefully to confirm our expectations, we make serious perceptual errors that damage ourselves and others.

Since the passage of the Civil Rights Act (1964), significant progress has been made to reduce the use of stereotypes, particularly in hiring new employees. However, we continue to use stereotypes because they serve a useful purpose: they facilitate our rapid perception of others. Occasionally these stereotypes are very useful, especially age and sex stereotypes. For example, it is reasonable to guess that older workers are not as interested in new training programs and opportunities for promotion as younger workers are, because such differences have indeed been documented. Likewise, it may seem reasonable to think that female employees would be less interested in working overtime, since many women, especially those with small children in the home, find working overtime a particular burden. But, even if these assumptions are true in general, they are not necessarily true for a particular person. Some older workers may be very excited about a new training program, and some mothers may be very anxious to work overtime. Although it is impossible to confirm all our stereotypes, we should constantly question the accuracy of our perceptions, and maintain a flexible system of categories.

Discrimination and Prejudice

Illegal discrimination on the basis of race, religion, or sex typically occurs because of prejudice, which is defined as an unreasonable bias associated with suspicion, intolerance, or an irrational dislike for people of a particular race, religion, or sex. To understand the nature of prejudice, it is important to appreciate the psychological impact of individuality and uniqueness. The simple fact that one or two individuals differ significantly from other members of the group will cause them to be perceived and treated differently regardless of whether the differences are on the basis of race, religion, sex, or any other visible characteristic. This can best be illustrated by looking at the letters below.

$$X X x x x X x O x \quad X$$

If you studied this configuration briefly and then attempted to describe it, you would probably say that it consisted of some big and little *X*'s with an *O*. Unless you studied it carefully, you would probably not remember how many big *X*'s and little *x*'s there were or how they were arranged in the configuration, but you would probably remember the *O* and where it was located.

The same process occurs among a group of individuals when one or more individuals differ significantly from the others because of their unique sex or race. They are perceived differently, and they attract more attention, regardless of which race or sex constitutes the majority. This perceptual process occurs simply because the minority stands out from the majority. Three perceptual tendencies explain why minorities experience prejudice within the group: visibility, contrast, and assimilation.[3]

Visibility

When a small percent of the group belong to a particular category, these individuals are more visible. Therefore, if a committee consisted of one female and several males, it is likely that everyone will remember where the woman sat in the committee meeting, what she wore, what she said, and how she voted. The minority tend to capture a larger share of the awareness within that group.

Contrast

When one or more individuals who are different are added to a group, their presence creates a self-consciousness among the dominant group about what makes them a separate class. Each group defines itself partly by knowing what it isn't. Consequently, a polarization and exaggeration of differences occurs, highlighting the differences between the minorities and majorities. Both groups become more aware of their commonalities and their differences, and group processes tend to accentuate the differences by creating stereotypes to separate the two groups.

Assimilation

The third perceptual tendency, assimilation, involves the application of stereotypes and familiar generalizations about a person's social category. Minority group members are not perceived as unique individuals but as representatives of a particular category. In essence, their behavior is assimilated into a stereotype of how members of their particular group are expected to behave. An illustration of assimilation is when a Japanese business executive who is meeting with a group of American executives is asked how other Japanese executives would react to a particular proposal. The question assumes that all Japanese executives respond alike, and that one person can represent them all.

Assimilation and contrast appear to be a function of how much effort people are willing to make to form accurate impressions. While some people challenge their assumptions and seek additional information, others label behavior and ignore uniqueness.

Prejudice and discrimination occur in a variety of settings and range in intensity from very innocent and unintended to very injurious and nasty. Some of the most obvious forms of racism and sexism include name-calling and slurs directed toward a specific individual. Such cruel behavior is considered entirely unacceptable in today's organizations; it is both immoral and illegal. Other forms of prejudice and discrimination, however, are much more subtle because the acts are not directed toward a specific individual and are often said in jest. Such behavior, however, is still considered inappropriate. Jokes and other comments that reflect negatively on another person's race or sex are both insulting and demeaning to everyone.

The Self-Fulfilling Prophecy

An interesting application of biased perceptions is the self-fulfilling prophecy, also called the Pygmalion effect.[4] We are not passive observers of our own social worlds, but active forces in shaping those worlds. To an important extent we create our own social reality by influencing the behavior we observe in others. The self-fulfilling prophecy explains how the expectations in the mind of one person about how others should behave are communicated in a variety of ways, until these individuals actually behave in the way expected. However, the self-fulfilling prophecy involves more than just one person having strong

```
           The Perceiver                          The Target Person

    1. Tentative expectancy
       (I'm told he is friendly.)
                                    →
                                        2. Ambiguous behavior
                                           (could be seen as friendly)
    3. Expectancy Confirmed      ←
       by perceptual
       confirmation (He does
       seem quite friendly.)
              ↓
    4. Warm friendly
       overtures
       (expectancy-behavior
       link)                        →
                                        5. Warm friendly
                                           response
                                           (behavior-behavior link)
    6. Expectancy further        ←
       strengthened by
       behavioral confirmation
       (I was right. He really is
       friendly.)
                                    →
                                        7. Self-concept change (I really
                                           am a friendly person.)
```

Exhibit 8.3 ■ **A Social Interaction Sequence in Which both Perceptual and Behavioral Confirmation Create the Self-fulfilling Prophecy**

Source: Adapted from Edward E. Jones, "Interpreting Interpersonal Behavior: The Effects of Expectancies." *Science*, Vol. 234, (3 October 1986), p. 43.

expectancies that influence the behavior of others. As illustrated in Exhibit 8.3, this process requires that:

- the expectation in the mind of the perceiver influences how the behavior of the target person is interpreted—the perceiver "sees" what he/she expects to see;
- thinking that the expectations are true, the perceiver then treats the target person differently;
- because of the differential treatment, the target person's behavior changes to confirm the perceiver's expectation;
- the perceiver views this behavior as unsolicited evidence that the expectancy was right all along.

Example

A teacher was told that certain randomly selected students in her class were expected to make significant academic improvements that school year, based on the results of a fake test. At the end of the year, the performance of these randomly selected students was much greater than the other students, much to the surprise of the teacher when she was told about the experiment.

The self-fulfilling prophecy has been demonstrated in several experiments with both children and adults.[5] Four elements have been proposed to explain why the self-fulfilling prophecy occurs.

1. *Input.* Individuals who are expected to do well receive better ideas and suggestions than people who are expected to do poorly. As the quantity and quality of information

increase, it helps them perform better, and communicates a sense of urgency and importance about the task.
2. *Output expected.* Specific comments about how much individuals are expected to achieve help them establish realistic levels of aspiration and higher performance goals.
3. *Reinforcement.* Individuals from whom high performance is expected tend to be rewarded more frequently when they achieve their performance goals. Individuals from whom low performance is expected usually perform poorly and are not reinforced. *But even if they perform well, they may not be rewarded, because their supervisors feel threatened or irritated that their expectations are disconfirmed.*
4. *Feedback.* Managers who communicate high performance expectations typically provide greater feedback. This feedback occurs more frequently, and usually contains specific suggestions for improvement.

The self-fulfilling prophecy normally starts when the expectations are planted in the mind of the leader. However, the expectations can also be communicated directly to the actor. The self-fulfilling prophecy has been recommended as a valuable strategy for improving organizational performance. The key is to start the sequence by creating positive expectations in managers and workers for themselves and the organization. Expectations can originate with upper management or a consultant, and must be both challenging and realistic. This strategy works best with new beginnings—before either the manager or workers have prior expectations about performance.

When new employees are introduced into an organization, the self-fulfilling prophecy contributes importantly to their career success. Some have argued that the expectations of managers may be more important than the skills and training of the new trainees in determining their success.[6] An analysis of management training programs suggests that the self-fulfilling prophecy is particularly crucial to the success of new managers.

Personality

Behavior has traditionally been explained as a combination of personality and environmental forces, as expressed by the formula: $B = fn(P, E)$. This formula suggests that our behavior at any given time is a combination of unique personality traits and the demands of the environment.

Personality traits refer to enduring characteristics that describe an individual's attitudes and behavior. Examples are friendliness, dominance, aggressiveness, and shyness. These traits are thought to be quite stable over time such that friendly people usually act friendly and welcome new associations. However, research has also shown that situational forces exert a much larger impact on behavior than personality factors. Indeed, several reviews of the research literature suggest that correlation coefficients are almost always less than .30 between any measured personality variable and actual behavior.[7] Most people find this quite surprising, because they believe the way we behave is a direct reflection of our personalities—friendly people are friendly, and aggressive people are aggressive. However, the evidence indicates that in a friendly environment everyone will be friendly, and in an aggressive environment even passive people will push back when they are pushed long enough. This tendency to overestimate the influence of personality in understanding human behavior is called the fundamental attribution error.

Although the impact of personality on behavior is usually rather small, it is not insignificant. Occasionally personality factors are sufficiently strong to overcome all environmental forces. Furthermore, over time people have an opportunity to create their own situations that match their personalities. Attribution theory examines how we assign responsibility to the person and the situation.

Attribution Theory

When we perceive social events, part of the perceptual process includes assigning responsibility for behavior. Are people responsible for their own behavior because of their personal characteristics, or were they forced to behave as they did because of the situation? The assignment of responsibility and the cognitive processes we use to understand why people act as they do are known as attribution theory.[8]

According to attribution theory, the assignment of responsibility stems from our observations of people over time. For example, if we observe a group of people attempting to use a word processor and find that many of them have difficulty getting the printer to function properly, we perceive the problem as being caused by the situation. But if only one person has difficulty with the printer, we attribute the cause of the problem to that individual's personal skills or abilities. Studies on attribution theory have generated the following conclusions:

1. When we observe someone else's behavior, we tend to overestimate the influence of personality traits and underestimate situational influences.
2. When we explain our own behavior, we tend to overestimate the importance of the situation and underestimate our own personality characteristics.

The explanation for these contrasting conclusions is that as actors we are more aware of the differing situations we face, and therefore we attribute our behavior to these differing situations. But since we are not as knowledgeable about the variety of situations others face, we overlook the situation and attribute their behavior to their personalities. This explanation has been confirmed by a study showing that when observers had empathy for another person, they were more likely to take the actor's perspective and were better able to notice situational causes for the actor's behavior. Conversely, distant observers tended to only notice personality characteristics.[9]

3. As we observe others in casual situations, we tend to attribute their successes to personality traits, such as effort and ability, and their failures to external factors, such as the difficulty of the task.

It is not clear why we attribute success to the person and failure to the situation in casual situations, but apparently this tendency does not extend to an organizational setting. In fact, studies of attribution in organizations suggest that the results are the opposite.

4. In evaluating the performance of employees, poor performance is generally attributed to internal personal factors, especially when the consequences are serious.

A study of nursing supervisors found that they were more likely to hold their employees accountable for poor performance as performance problems became more serious.[10] The behavior of subordinates reflects on their managers; therefore, when subordinates do well, managers are quick to accept partial credit for success; but when problems occur, they are quick to blame subordinates to exonerate themselves.

5. Employees tend to attribute their successes to internal factors and their failures to external causes.

Because of our need to maintain a positive self-image, we attribute our own successes to our personal skills and abilities. When we fail, however, we blame external causes.

Big Five Personality Model

Over the years, dozens of personality traits have been identified and numerous scales have been developed to measure them. Extensive research has attempted to associate the various personality dimensions with political behavior, leadership talent, interpersonal skills, and various pro-social behaviors. More recently, efforts have been made to consolidate these results and simplify our understanding of personality. The result has been the identification of five broad personality traits that seem to be conceptually different and empirically distinct. These five personality dimensions are called the Big Five Model:

1. *Conscientiousness* represents the degree to which an individual is dependable or inconsistent, can be counted on or is unreliable, follows through on commitments or reneges, and keeps promises or breaks them. Those who rate high on conscientiousness

are generally perceived to be careful, thorough, organized, persistent, achievement oriented, hardworking, and persevering. Those who score lower on this dimension are more likely to be viewed as inattentive to detail, uncaring, disrespectful, not interested or motivated, unorganized, apt to give up easily, and lazy.

2. *Agreeableness* measures the degree to which people are friendly or reserved, cooperative or guarded, flexible or inflexible, trusting or cautious, good-natured or moody, softhearted or tough, and tolerant or judgmental. Those scoring high on the first element of these paired traits are viewed as agreeable and easy to work with, while those rating low are viewed as more disagreeable and difficult to work with. Being too agreeable could cause people to be too accommodating, however, and others may take advantage of this weakness.

3. *Emotional stability* (versus Neuroticism) characterizes the degree to which people are consistent or inconsistent in how they react to certain events, they react impulsively or weigh their options before acting, and they take things personally or look at the situation objectively. Those who rate high on emotional stability are viewed as generally poised, calm, able to manage their anger, secure, happy, and objective. Those who rate low are more likely to be anxious, depressed, angry, insecure, worried, and emotional.

4. *Openness to experience* characterizes the degree to which people are interested in broadening their horizons or limiting them, learning new things or sticking with what they already know, meeting new people or associating with current friends and co-workers, going to new places or restricting themselves to known places. Individuals who score high on this factor tend to be highly intellectual, broad-minded, curious, imaginative, and cultured. Those who rate lower tend to be more narrow-minded, less interested in the outside world, and uncomfortable in unfamiliar surroundings and situations. Professionals who are open to experience are more willing to contemplate on feedback for personal development.

5. *Extroversion* represents the degree to which people are outgoing, social, assertive, active, and talkative. The opposite is introversion, which refers to those who are shy, antisocial, passive, and quiet. Extroversion or introversion, in itself, is not necessarily bad, but extremes at both ends of the spectrum can be equally dysfunctional. A person who is too outgoing could be perceived as overbearing, and a person who is too reserved would lack the skills to relate to others.

These five personality dimensions are somewhat related to work-related behaviors and how well people perform on the job.[11] For example, jobs involving conflict situations, such as customer relations, are generally performed better by people who measure high in agreeableness. And, people with high emotional stability tend to work better in high stress situations than those who score high on neuroticism. However, these correlations are generally too small to be useful in employee selection and placement. The best trait for predicting job performance and organizational citizenship behaviors has been conscientiousness. This dimension appears to be a valuable personal attribute that is relevant to a broad range of jobs. Conscientious employees set higher personal goals for themselves, are more highly motivated, and have higher performance expectations than employees with low conscientiousness.

Other Personality Dimensions

Three additional personality traits that contribute to our understanding of individual differences in organizations are the locus of control, self-esteem, and self-efficacy.

Locus of Control

The locus of control refers to the degree to which individuals believe that their actions influence the rewards they receive in life. Individuals with an internal locus of control believe that the rewards they receive are internally controlled by their own actions, whereas individuals with an external locus of control believe external forces such as luck, chance, or fate control their lives and determine their rewards and punishments.[12] If an unexpected opportunity for advancement were presented to two people, the externally controlled individual would probably attribute it to luck or being in the right place at the right time. The internally controlled individual would be more inclined to attribute the opportunity to hard work, effort, and knowledge. As with other personality factors, however, people vary along a continuum and cannot be neatly placed into one category or the other.

Individuals behave differently depending on whether they believe their rewards are internally or externally controlled. In contrast to externals, internals believe that how hard they work will determine how well they perform and how well they will be rewarded. Consequently, internals generally perceive more order and predictability in their job-related outcomes, and usually report higher levels of job satisfaction.[13] Since managers are required to initiate goal-directed activity, it is not surprising that they tend to be internally controlled.

In times of upheaval and disruption, externals generally experience more frustration and anxiety than internals and are less able to cope with the situation. A study of how people responded to a flood following a hurricane found that externals were more concerned than internals about coping with their own tension and frustration. They tended to withdraw from the task of rebuilding and to express bitterness and aggression about the "rotten hand" they had been dealt. Internals, on the other hand, went immediately to the task of acquiring new loans, gathering new resources, and rebuilding their homes and businesses. Obviously, no one could have prevented the storm from happening, but the internals had faith that an active, problem-solving response could determine whether the flood would be a conclusive tragedy or only a temporary setback.[14]

The locus of control is determined largely by an individual's past experiences. Internals are the product of an environment where their behaviors largely decided their outcomes, while externals experienced futility in trying to set their own rewards. Child-rearing practices are thought to have an important influence on the development of locus of control: an internal locus of control is created by predictable and consistent discipline, by parental support and involvement, and by parental encouragement of autonomy and self-control. Some evidence also suggests that the locus of control can be influenced over a long period of time by the way employees are reinforced at work. At least one study has shown that the locus of control becomes more internal as a result of exposure to a work environment where important rewards are consistently associated with individual behavior.[15]

Self-Esteem

Our self-concept is presumed to be a particularly human manifestation, and refers to our own conscious awareness of who we are. We see ourselves relative to others, and form evaluative impressions about our skills, abilities, and behaviors. Our self-concept is a collection of the attitudes, values, and beliefs we have acquired about ourselves from our unique experiences. We form opinions about our behavior, ability, appearance, and overall worth as a person from our own observations and the feedback we receive from others.

Over time, our accumulated experiences establish our self-concept. This self-concept determines how we feel about ourselves, and influences how we respond to others. Individuals with high self-esteem are generally more creative, independent, and spontaneous in their interactions with others. Because of their positive feelings about themselves, they can concentrate on the issues at hand and focus on new and original ideas without being as concerned about how people feel about them. On the other hand, people with low self-esteem tend to feel overly concerned about the evaluations of others, which dilute their ability to concentrate on problems and to think creatively. Their low self-esteem often causes them to withdraw from the task or social situation.

Extensive research has shown that the behaviors of individuals are consistent with their self-concepts. Students, for example, who see themselves as competent academic achievers quite consistently perform better in school than students who don't. Individuals with high self-esteem are generally more accurate in their perceptions of social situations than those with low self-esteem.[16]

Problems of low self-esteem are often attributed to inadequate positive reinforcement from others. Although people with low self-esteem have usually experienced less praise than others, the solution is not to simply give them more praise and recognition. Our self-esteem is greatly influenced by how well we have actually performed. Although the comments of others help us interpret our performance, how well we have actually done has a greater impact on our self-esteem. Therefore, in raising an individual's self-esteem, praise and compliments may not be as effective as actually helping the individual perform better.

Self-Efficacy

Self-efficacy refers to one's belief in one's capability to perform a specific task. In many respects the concept of self-efficacy is similar to the concepts of self-esteem and locus of control. However, self-efficacy is task-specific rather than a generalized perception of overall competence.

Self-efficacy emerged from the research on social cognitive theory and represents an important personality variable that explains variations in individual performance. Several studies suggest that self-efficacy is a better predictor of subsequent performance than past behavior is.[17] Although knowing how well people have performed in the past helps to predict their future performance, an even better predictor is knowing how capable they feel regarding a specific task.[18]

Self-efficacy has three dimensions: magnitude, strength, and generality. Magnitude refers to the level of task difficulty that a person believes he or she can attain, and is related to the concept of goal-setting. Some people think they can achieve very difficult goals. Strength refers to the amount of confidence one has in one's ability to perform, and it can be strong or weak. Some people have strong convictions that they will succeed even when they face difficult challenges. Generality indicates the degree to which one's expectations are generalized across many situations or restricted to an isolated instance. Some people believe they can succeed in a variety of situations.

Self-efficacy is a learned characteristic that is acquired by four kinds of information cues:

1. *Enactive mastery:* The most influential stimulus contributing to the development of self-efficacy is enactive mastery, which refers to the repeated performance or practicing of the task. For example, a nurse who has inserted many IV needles should have high self-efficacy in being able to do it again.
2. *Vicarious experience:* Observing the behavior of others (modeling) can be almost as effective as enactive mastery, especially when the person and the model are similar in terms of age, capability, and other characteristics, and when the model's behavior is clearly visible.
3. *Verbal persuasion:* In the development of self-efficacy, verbal persuasion is less effective than practicing or modeling; nevertheless, it can be an important source of efficacy information, especially if the source has high credibility and expertise, and if there are multiple sources who agree.
4. *Perceptions of one's physiological state:* Efficacy perceptions are influenced by momentary levels of arousal as illustrated by these statements of athletes: "We were ready for them," "They were really up for this game," "I was mentally prepared," and "He was really psyched for this match."

Efficacy perceptions appear to be self-reinforcing. Self-efficacy influences the kinds of activities and settings people choose to participate in, the skills they are willing to practice and learn, the amount of energy they are willing to exert, and the persistence of their coping efforts in the face of obstacles. People with high self-efficacy tend to engage more frequently in task-related activities and persist longer in coping efforts; this leads to more mastery experiences, which enhance their self-efficacy. People with low self-efficacy tend to engage in fewer coping efforts; they give up more easily under adversity and demonstrate less mastery, which in turn reinforces their low self-efficacy.[19]

Self-efficacy can predict performance in a variety of settings, as long as the efficacy measure is tailored to the specific tasks being performed. Consequently, efficacy perceptions are relevant in many organizational settings, such as employee selection, training and development, and vocational counseling. Employees with high self-efficacy would be expected to respond more favorably to most personnel programs, such as performance evaluation, financial incentives, and opportunities for promotion.[20]

Attitudes

Attitudes are involved in almost every aspect of organizational life. Employees have attitudes about hundreds of things, including their pay, their supervisors, top management, the work they do, and their co-workers. Outstanding employees are commended for their "good attitudes," while uncooperative workers are reprimanded for having "bad attitudes." Managers worry about how their decisions will influence employee attitudes, and whether the employees will resist change. Events that occur away from work influence the attitudes of employees, who carry these attitudes into the work setting. People can control their attitudes and how they react to them. When you are stuck in traffic you can choose to be angry and pound on the steering wheel or you can calmly accept the situation and listen to a radio program.

An attitude is a hypothetical construct; it is not a physical reality or something you can see, taste, or touch. Consequently, it is something that exists only because we can define it or infer it from the things people say or do. An attitude is defined as the positive or negative feelings we hold toward an object. Therefore, when we speak of positive job attitudes we refer to the pleasant feelings we have when we think about our jobs. It is possible to have positive feelings about some aspects of the job and negative feelings about other aspects. The early research on attitudes identified three attitude components: cognitive, affective, and behavioral tendency.

- The cognitive component consists of the beliefs and information a person possesses about the attitude object. This information includes descriptive data such as facts, figures, and other specific knowledge.
- The affective component consists of the person's feelings and emotions toward the attitude object. This component involves evaluation and reaction, and is often expressed as a liking or disliking for the attitude object.
- The behavioral tendency component refers to the way the person intends to behave toward the object, such as whether the person intends to follow, help, injure, abandon, or ignore the attitude object.

Emotions

The affective component of attitudes consists mostly of emotions and feelings. Our emotions are complex reactions that have both physiological and psychological implications. Emotions come from a different location in the brain than the location where cognitions are stored. In the formation of attitudes and perceptions, we often think that the cognitive component creates the affective component: that is, knowledge and beliefs come first, followed by feelings and emotions. According to neuroscience research, however, incoming information from our senses is routed to the emotional center as well as the cognitive (logical reasoning) center of our brain. Therefore, our emotions play an important role in determining how we process new information and anticipate responding to it.[21]

The process of attitude formation in influenced by the way emotions impact the perceptual interpretation process described earlier. When receiving incoming information, the emotional center quickly and *imprecisely* evaluates whether the new information supports or threatens our innate drives, and then attaches emotional markers to the information. These are not calculated feelings; they are automatic and unconscious emotional responses based on very transient sensory information. Positive emotions create positive attitudes.

Example

An employee who hears about a possible merger with a competitor may strongly object to the planned merger due to a fear of being replaced. Another employee may feel excited about the merger and welcome the potential changes. While the merger represents a threat to the first person, the second person perceives it as an opportunity.

An understanding of emotions helps us interpret our own behavior and analyze the reactions of others. Some people are much better than others when it comes to interpreting emotions and knowing how to manage them appropriately. Emotional intelligence (EI) refers to the set of competencies that allow us to perceive, understand, and regulate emotions in ourselves and others. People with high levels of emotional intelligence have the ability to express and perceive emotions, assimilate emotions in their thoughts, understand and reason with emotion, and regulate emotions in themselves and others. Emotional intelligence is organized into four dimensions representing (a) the *recognition* of emotions in ourselves versus others and (b) the *regulation* of emotions in ourselves versus others:

- *Self awareness:* Self-awareness refers to understanding our own emotions as well as our strengths, weaknesses, values, and motives. Self-aware people are better able to describe their emotional responses to specific situations, and to use this awareness as conscious information.
- *Self-management:* Self-management represents how consistently we control our internal feelings, impulses, and reactions. It includes keeping disruptive impulses in check, acting with honesty and integrity, having flexibility in times of change, maintaining the drive to perform well and to seize opportunities, and remaining optimistic even after failure.
- *Social awareness:* Social awareness is mainly about empathy, which involves understanding another person's situation, experiencing the other person's emotions, and knowing that person's needs even though they are unstated. Empathy is a crucial skill in effective communication, as we will learn in chapter 15.
- *Relationship management:* This dimension refers to managing other people's emotions. It is linked to a wide variety of interpersonal skills that are discussed in other chapters, such as developing other's capabilities (4), supporting teamwork and collaboration (11), resolving conflict (12), influencing people's beliefs and attitudes (15), inspiring others (17), and managing change (19).

The acquisition of these four competencies is mostly a sequential process that starts with acquiring self-awareness. Until you are aware of your own emotions and have some skill in recognizing them and talking about them, it is unlikely that you will be prepared to regulate your emotions or recognize the emotions of others. At the other extreme, relationship management cannot occur effectively until you have mastered the competencies of the other three dimensions; you cannot reasonably expect to manage other people's emotions unless you can recognize them and also know how to regulate your own emotions.

Although we still have much to learn about emotional intelligence, it appears to be an important attribute that contributes to a person's effectiveness on the job. People with higher levels of emotional intelligence are more skilled in interpersonal relations, they perform better in jobs requiring emotional understanding, and they are more successful in many aspects of job interviews. Teams with members who have high emotional intelligence initially perform better than teams with lower levels. Emotional intelligence appears to be a personality trait that is associated with conscientiousness; however, it can also be learned by training programs that describe and demonstrate various emotions.[22]

The Relationship between Attitudes and Behavior

We often assume that attitudes cause behavior; therefore, if you want to get people to change their behavior, you must first get them to change their attitudes. Unfortunately, the relationship is much more complex. The relationship between attitudes and behavior appears to be a reciprocal interaction in which each factor influences the other, as shown in Exhibit 8.4. Attitudes influence behavior by first influencing the behavioral intentions, whereas behavior influences attitudes by requiring individuals to justify their behavior.

Behavioral Intentions

Most of our attitudes do not have a direct impact on our behavior. We have an enormous number of attitudes about countless objects, and only a small percent of these attitudes ever

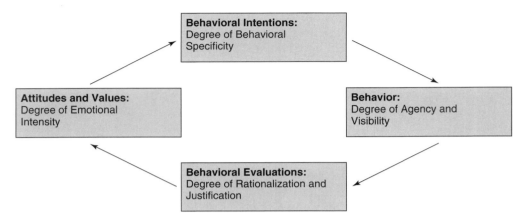

Exhibit 8.4 — **A Model Showing the Relationship between Attitudes and Behavior**

get translated into behavior. An intervening process between attitudes and behavior is behavioral intentions, a term that refers to the extent to which we actually expect to perform a given act.

Intentions are similar to motives or desires; they can be very specific, such as to call a client or to take a patient's blood pressure, or they can also be very general, such as to increase sales or to provide quality patient care. According to the model, attitudes affect behavior only to the extent that they influence our intentions to act.

How are behavioral intentions formed? The model indicates that behavioral intentions are influenced to some extent by attitudes, but they are also influenced by other situational forces that may be more important:

- Reinforcement contingencies providing specific rewards or punishments;
- Normative pressures from peer expectations and group norms;
- Random situational influences and alternative behaviors.

Specificity of Intentions

Goal setting and reward expectations have a sizable impact on our behavioral intentions and help us develop specific intentions to act. Specific intentions, once formed, are usually associated with specific behaviors. Four elements determine the degree of specificity:

1. How well the particular behavior has been visualized in clear detail;
2. Whether the target object toward which the behavior will be directed has been determined;
3. How clearly the situational context in which the behavior will be performed has been defined, including where and with whom;
4. Whether the time when the behavior should occur has been established.

Each of these elements helps to determine whether the behavior is specifically identified or only loosely contemplated. The most specific situation involves an intention to perform a clearly defined act toward a specific target in a defined place at a given time.

Example

The behavioral intention to "learn something about computers as soon as it's convenient" is a very loosely defined behavioral intention that would not have as much impact on behavior as the behavioral intention to "meet Larry in the computer lab tomorrow at 10:00 A.M. to learn how to download a program." To the extent that distinct behaviors are specifically articulated, the intentions are more closely tied to actual behavior.

This model contains some key insights into attitudes and behavior. To change the behavior of people, it is much more productive to focus directly on changing their behavioral intentions than indirectly trying to change their attitudes. Specific behavioral intentions are much more likely to lead to behavior than general intentions are.

Example

If employees have been negligent in accomplishing a task (e.g., accounting reports or safety inspections) it is more effective to help them set specific behavioral intentions to complete it than to lecture them about the importance of the task, which they probably already understand.

Behavioral Evaluations

The reciprocal interaction between attitudes and behaviors, as illustrated in Exhibit 8.4, illustrates the way our behavior changes our attitudes. The intervening process between behavior and attitudes, called behavioral evaluations, refers to the process of interpreting and making sense of our behavior. We do not view ourselves or others as capricious, random actors. We like to think of ourselves as rational beings whose behavior is conscious and planned. Therefore, we feel a need to explain and justify our behavior both to others and especially to ourselves. According to consistency theory and cognitive dissonance theory, our attitudes and behaviors need to be in harmony. When they are dissonant, the easiest way to create harmony is by changing our attitudes.

According to this model, the effects of behavior on attitudes depend on our felt need to justify our behavior. Therefore, the amount of attitude change increases as the need to justify behavior increases. This occurs when

- individuals are asked to explain their behavior;
- the explanation is a public declaration;
- there are alternative ways to behave;
- they are free to choose how to behave.

When people misbehave, they will probably rationalize and justify their misbehavior, which means their attitudes will change more than their behavior. Although people may have a negative emotional feeling the first time they misbehave, each succeeding time will be easier to justify. Employees who do things wrong (e.g., falsify an expense account or exceed the speed limit) may feel guilty the first time they do it. But, they will rationalize the mistake and feel less guilty in time as they continue doing it.

Example

The first time a partner in a law firm added a few hours to the billing statement that his firm submitted to the government for consulting work he felt a little guilty. But as he continued to add even more hours, he rationalized that his firm deserved the added revenue since the government rates for consulting were less than the rates for private industry. Eventually he was convicted of fraud although he claimed he had done nothing really wrong.

Job Satisfaction

Job satisfaction consists of the attitudes employees hold regarding factors in their work environment, particularly pay and benefits, the characteristics of the job, supervision, fellow workers, and opportunities for advancement. Managers are concerned about the job satisfaction of their employees because high job satisfaction contributes to organizational commitment, job involvement, improved physical and mental health, and a greater quality of life both on and off the job. On the other hand, job dissatisfaction contributes to absenteeism, turnover, labor problems, labor grievances, attempts to organize a labor union, and a negative organizational climate.

Satisfaction and Performance

Our primary interest in job satisfaction stems from the common belief that satisfaction is directly tied to productivity—that happy workers will be productive workers. To stimulate higher levels of productivity, therefore, managers need to create better jobs and a better work environment. Unfortunately, the relationship between satisfaction and productivity is not this simple. Lazy workers may also be highly satisfied, perhaps because they are allowed to laugh and loiter on the job without any pressure to change. Hundreds of studies examining the relationship between satisfaction and productivity have produced both positive and negative correlations, but most correlations have only been slightly positive and not statistically significant.[23] Some have even suggested reversing the direction of the relationship claiming that productivity determines satisfaction—that happiness comes from succeeding on the job and being highly productive.[24]

Rather than causing each other, both satisfaction and productivity are determined by the reward structure in each respective situation. Employees generally express high levels of job satisfaction when they feel rewarded and recognized at work and when their expectations are met or exceeded. Productivity depends on the reinforcement contingencies, as explained in Chapter 7. Employees tend to be highly productive when important rewards are directly tied to their job performance. This means that the correlations between satisfaction and productivity could be either positive or negative depending on how employees are rewarded. When employees are rewarded for their performance, the most productive employees will be the most satisfied because they receive the most rewards. When everyone is rewarded equally, however, the relationship may be zero or possibly negative because the most productive employees may be disappointed about not getting what they think they deserve.[25]

Attendance: Absenteeism and Tardiness

Absenteeism and tardiness are sometimes referred to as withdrawal or avoidance behaviors and they are consistently, although only moderately, related to job satisfaction. Individuals who are highly satisfied with their jobs are seldom absent from work, and faithfully see that their job is performed in spite of personal illnesses, family emergencies, or bad weather. Individuals who are unhappy or dissatisfied at work tend to miss work or come late more frequently than those who are satisfied.

Turnover

Turnover is caused mostly by job dissatisfaction and favorable economic conditions. The highest turnover levels are found in companies where employees report the greatest dissatisfaction. Employees also tend to leave their jobs when alternative jobs that better satisfy their needs become available. Consequently, turnover levels are generally high in companies with poor working conditions, undesirable jobs, wage inequities, poor communication, and limited opportunities for advancement.

Mental and Physical Health

Studies have found that job satisfaction contributes to better overall mental and physical health, while dissatisfaction caused by stress, conflict, and boredom at work contribute to higher incidences of death due to heart disease. The two most important job attributes for good mental and physical health seem to be (1) challenging work and (2) opportunities to use one's abilities and skills. Some research has even found that job satisfaction influences one's life expectancy. An analysis of numerous physical and attitudinal variables, including physical conditioning and tobacco use, revealed that the single best predictor of longevity was work satisfaction. Those who felt their work was meaningful and useful outlived their less satisfied co-workers.[26]

Job Involvement

Job involvement refers to the strength of the relationship between an individual's work and his or her self-concept. Individuals are said to be highly involved in their job if they actively participate in it, view it as a central life interest, and see their job and how well they perform it as a central part of their self-concept.[27]

People who are highly involved in their jobs tend to be ego-involved with their work. They spend long hours working at their jobs, and think about them when they are away from work. If a project they have completed fails, they may feel intense frustration and despair. When they perform poorly, they feel embarrassed and disappointed. Since they identify with their work, they want others to know them for their work and to know that they do it well. For them, work is the most important aspect of life.

Individuals tend to have greater job involvement if they are committed to the work ethic, and if they define their self-concepts according to their performance. Higher job involvement is also associated with how long they have performed their jobs and whether they have meaningful opportunities to make important decisions.

Individuals who are highly involved in their jobs tend to be more satisfied than those who are not as involved. They are also generally happier with the organization, more committed to it, and absent less frequently. This evidence suggests that job involvement is a desirable characteristic that managers ought to encourage.

Some individuals, however, become so highly involved in their job that they become workaholics. A workaholic is someone who is literally addicted to work, which by definition is an unhealthy condition.[28] This need to work incessantly can arise from many different sources. People may feel anxious or guilt ridden and turn to work as a means to salve their conscience; or they may suffer from feelings of insecurity and turn to work to obtain a sense of permanence, usefulness, and competence. Some people rely on their work to support their feelings of self-righteousness and self-worth.

Organizational Commitment

Organizational commitment refers to the relative strength of an individual's identification with and involvement in an organization. Three characteristics are associated with organizational commitment:[29]

- a strong belief in and acceptance of the organization's values and goals, called normative commitment;
- a strong emotional attachment to the organization and a willingness to exert considerable effort in behalf of it, called affective commitment;
- a strong desire to maintain membership in the organization, called continuance commitment.

These three characteristics suggest that organizational commitment involves more than mere passive loyalty to the organization. It involves an active relationship with the organization, in which employees are willing to give of themselves and make a personal contribution to help the organization succeed.

Studies on organizational commitment have identified four primary factors that contribute to organizational commitment.[30]

1. *Personal factors.* Organizational commitment is generally higher among older and more tenured employees. Those who have greater intrinsic work values are more committed. As a group, female employees tend to be more committed to organizations than males, and employees who have less education also tend to display more commitment than highly educated employees.
2. *Role-related characteristics.* Organizational commitment tends to be stronger among employees in enriched jobs and jobs that involve low levels of role conflict and ambiguity.
3. *Structural characteristics.* Organizational commitment is stronger among employees in worker-owned cooperatives and among employees in decentralized organizations, who are more involved in making critical organizational decisions.

4. *Work experiences.* Organizational commitment tends to be stronger among employees who have had favorable experiences at work, such as positive group attitudes among one's peers, feelings that the organization has met the employee's expectations, feelings that the organization could be relied upon to fulfill its commitments to its personnel, and feelings that the individual is important to the organization. Employees manifest higher levels of commitment when firms have well-developed recruitment and orientation procedures, and well defined organizational value systems.

Employees who have high levels of either affective or continuance commitment generally have better attendance records and are more likely to stay with the company. Job performance, however, is generally only correlated with affective commitment. Individuals who have high levels of affective commitment tend to be more satisfied with their jobs, they feel better about their opportunities for career advancement, and they find greater fulfillment in life away from work.

■ Endnotes

1. J. T. Malloy, *Dress for Success* (New York: Warner Books, 1975); M. Snyder, E. D. Tanke, E. Berscheid "Social perception and interpersonal behavior: on the self-fulfilling nature of social stereotypes" *Journal of Personality and Social Psychology*, vol. 35 (1977), pp. 656–666.
2. Douglas McGregor, *The Human Side of Enterprise* (New York: McGraw-Hill, 1960).
3. Rosabeth Moss Kanter, *Men and Women of the Corporation* (New York: Basic Books, 1977), Chapter 8.
4. Robert Rosenthal and L. Jacobson, *Pygmalion in the Classroom* (New York: Holt, Reinhardt, and Winston, 1968).
5. Ibid. See also Jack Horn "Pygmalion vs. Golem in a high school gym." *Psychology Today*, vol. 18, (July 1984), pp. 9–10.
6. J. Sterling Livingston, "Pygmalion in Management," *Harvard Business Review*, (July-August 1969), pp. 81–89; L. Sandler, "Self-fulfilling prophecy: Better training by Mayle." *Training: The Magazine of Human Resource Development*, vol. 23, (Feb. 1986), pp. 60–64.
7. Lee Ross and Richard E. Nisbett, *The Person and the Situation*. (New York: McGraw Hill, 1991).
8. F. Heider, *The Psychology of Interpersonal Behavior* (New York: Wiley, 1958); Steven E. Kaplan, "Improving Performance Evaluation", *CMA—The Management Accounting Magazine*, vol. 61, (May-June, 1987), pp. 56–59.
9. Jean M. Bartunek, "Why Did You Do That? Attribution Theory in Organizations," *Business Horizons*, vol. 24, No. 5, (1981) pp. 66–71; Edward E. Jones and Richard E. Naisbett, *The Actor and the Observer, Divergent Perceptions of the Causes of Behavior* (Morristown, N.J.: General Learning Press, 1971); J. C. McElroy and C. B. Shrader, "Attribution theories of leadership and network analysis," *Journal of Management*, vol. 12, (Fall 1986), pp. 35.
10. Harold H. Kelley and John L. Michela, "Attribution Theory and Research," *Annual Review of Psychology* (1980), pp. 457–501.; Terence R. Mitchell and Robert E. Wood, "Supervisors' Responses to Subordinate Poor Performance: A Test of an Attributional Model," *Organizational Behavior and Human Performance* (1980), pp. 123–128.
11. A. Witt, L. A. Burke, and M. R. Barrick, "The Interactive Effects of Conscientiousness and Agreeableness on Job Performance," *Journal of Applied Psychology* 87 (2002: 164–169.
12. Julian B. Rotter, "Generalized Expectancies for Internal Versus External Control of Reinforcement," *Psychological Monographs*, vol. 80, 1966, pp. 1–28.
13. Virginia T. Geurin and Gary F. Kohut, "The Relationship of Locus of Control and Participative Decision Making Among Managers and Business Students," *Mid-Atlantic Journal of Business*, vol. 25, (February 1989), pp. 57–66; Mia Lokman, "Participation in Budgetary Decision Making, Task Difficulty, Locus of Control, and Employee Behavior: An Empirical Study", *Decision Sciences*, vol. 18, (Fall 1987), pp. 547–561; Paul E. Spector, "Development of the Work Locus of Control Scale," *Journal of Occupational Psychology*, vol. 61, (December 1988), pp. 335–340.

14. C. Anderson, Donald Hellriegel, and John Slocum, "Managerial Response to Environmentally Induced Stress," *Academy of Management Journal*, vol. 20, 1977, pp. 260–272; see also Phillip L. Storms and Paul E. Spector, "Relationships of Organizational Frustration with Reported Behaviorial Reactions: The Moderating Effect of Locus of Control," *Journal of Occupational Psychology*, vol. 60, (December 1987), pp. 227–234.
15. S. Eitzen, "Impact of Behavior Modification Techniques on Locus of Control of Delinquent Boys," *Psychological Reports*, vol. 35 (1974), pp. 1317–1318; Charles J. Cox and Gary L. Cooper, "The Making of the British CEO: Childhood, Work Experience, Personality, and Management Style," *Academy of Management Executive*, vol. 3, (August 1989), pp. 241–245.
16. R. H. Combs and V. Davies, "Self-conception and the relationship between high school and college scholastic achievement," *Sociology and Social Research*, vol. 50, (1966), pp. 460–471; B. Borislow, "Self-evaluation and academic achievement," *Journal of Counseling Psychology*, vol. 9, (1962), pp. 246–254; D. E. Hamachek, ed. *The Self in Growth, Teaching, and Learning*. (Englewood Cliffs, N.J.: Prentice-Hall, 1965).
17. Albert Bandura, "Self-Efficacy: Toward a Unifying Theory of Behaviorial Change," *Psychological Review*, vol. 84, (1977), pp. 191–215; Albert Bandura, "Self-Efficacy Mechanism in Human Agency," *American Psychologist*, vol. 37, (1982), pp. 122–147; Albert Bandura, N. E. Adams, A. B. Hardy, G. N. Howells, "Tests of the Generality of Self-Efficacy Theory," *Cognitive Therapy and Research*, vol. 4, (1980), pp. 39–66.
18. John Lane and Peter Herriot, "Self-Ratings, Supervisor Ratings, Positions and Performance," *Journal of Occupational Psychology*, vol. 63, (March 1990), pp. 77–88; Robert Wood, Albert Bandura, and Trevor Bailey, "Mechanisms Governing Organizational Performance in Complex Decision-Making Environments," *Organizational Behavior and Human Decision Processes*, vol. 46, (August 1990), pp. 181–201.
19. Albert Bandura, D. H. Shunk, "Cultivating Confidence, Self-Efficacy, and Intrinsic Interest Through Proximal Self Motivation," *Journal of Personality and Social Psychology*, vol. 41, (1981), pp. 586–598.
20. Marilyn E. Gist, "Self-Efficacy: Implications for Organizational Behavior and Human Resource Management," *Academy of Management Review*, vol. 12, (July 1987), pp. 472–485.
21. R. H. Fazio, "On the Automatic Activation of Associated Evaluations: An Overview," *Cognition and Emotion* 15 (2001): 115–141.
22. P. N. Lopes et al., "Emotional Intelligence and Social Interaction," *Personality and Social Psychology Bulletin* 30, (2004): 1018–1034.
23. A. H. Brayfield and W. H. Crockett, "Employee Attitudes and Employee Performance," *Psychological Bulletin*, vol. 52 (1955), pp. 396–424; Dennis W. Organ, "A Restatement of the Satisfaction-Performance Hypothesis," *Journal of Management*, vol. 14 (December 1988), pp. 547–557.
24. Edward E. Lawler, III, and Lyman W. Porter, "The Effect of Performance on Job Satisfaction," *Industrial Relations, A Journal of Economy and Society*, vol. 7, no. 1 (October 1967), pp. 20–28.
25. David J. Cherrington, H. Joseph Reitz, and William E. Scott, Jr., "Effects of Contingent and Non-Contingent Reward on the Relationship between Satisfaction and Task Performance," *Journal of Applied Psychology*, vol. 55 (1971), pp. 531–537; Dennis W. Organ, "A Reappraisal and Reinterpretation of the Satisfaction-Causes-Performance Hypothesis," *Academy of Management Journal*, vol. 2, (no. 1, 1977), pp. 46–53.
26. E. Palmore, "Predicting Longevity: A Follow-Up Controlling for Age," *Gerontologist*, vol. 9 (1969), pp. 247–250.
27. S. D. Saleh and J. Hosek, "Job Involvement: Concepts and Measurements," *Academy of Management Journal*, vol. 19 (1976), pp. 213–224.
28. David J. Cherrington, *The Work Ethic: Working Values and Values That Work* (New York: AMACOM Publishing, 1980), Ch. 12.
29. Natalie J. Allen and John P. Meyer, "The Measurement and Antecedents of Affective, Continuance, and Normative Commitments to the Organization," *Journal of Occupational Psychology*, vol. 63 (1990), pp. 1–18.
30. Richard M. Steers, "Antecedents and Outcomes of Organizational Commitment," *Administrative Science Quarterly*, vol. 22 (1977), pp. 46–56.

Performance Management

Evaluating Performance

Performance evaluation programs represent a significant application of motivation theory. Performance feedback, plus the evaluation process itself, contain elements of both positive and negative reinforcement. How well people perform is largely determined by whether their performance is evaluated and rewarded.

Multidimensionality of Performance

What are the behavioral requirements of effective organizations and how do organizations want their members to behave? Effective organizations require three basic types of behavior:

1. *Attracting and retaining people.* The first requirement of every organization is to attract people and persuade them to stay for at least a reasonable period of time. Every organization (other than the military when the draft is in effect) depends on its ability to attract members: the failure to attract a sufficient number of new members could prevent it from functioning effectively and could even cause it to die. High turnover and absenteeism are very costly, and as a general rule, organizations that are more successful in attracting and retaining people are more effective.
2. *Dependable role performance.* Members are assigned to perform their individual roles; they are expected to know their responsibilities and achieve minimal levels of quantity and quality performance. Organizations are more effective when workers are motivated to do their jobs well.
3. *Extra-role behaviors.* In addition to the formal task requirements, many other behaviors profoundly influence the effectiveness of an organization. These extra-role behaviors are also called spontaneous and innovative behaviors, or above and beyond behaviors, because they are in addition to the formal task requirements. Since an organization cannot foresee all contingencies in its operations, its effectiveness is influenced by the willingness of its employees to perform spontaneous and innovative behaviors as the need arises. Some of the most important extra-role behaviors include these:

- *Cooperation:* assisting coworkers and helping them achieve the organization's goals;
- *Protective acts:* safeguarding the organization by removing hazards or eliminating threats;
- *Constructive ideas*: contributing creative ideas to improve the organization;
- *Self-training:* improving one's skills to fill the organization's ever present need for better-trained workers;
- *Favorable attitudes:* expressing positive comments about the organization to other employees, customers, and the public, thus facilitating recruitment, retention, and sales.

Extra-role behaviors are voluntary actions that benevolent employees choose to perform, similar to altruism and organizational citizenship behaviors. The conditions that encourage members to perform such helpful actions are described in Chapter 12. The important insight to remember here is that performance evaluation should include more than a simple assessment of quantity and quality; there are other important behaviors that contribute to organizational success.

From *Creating Effective Organizations,* 5th edition by David J. Cherrington and W. Gibb Dyer. Copyright © 2009 by Kendall/Hunt Publishing Company. Reprinted by permission.

Role of Performance Evaluation

Why should companies evaluate the performance of their employees? Many organizations, especially smaller ones, do not have formal evaluation programs because they do not see a need for them. However, performance evaluation programs serve at least five important organizational functions regardless of size.

1. *To reward and recognize performance.* Performance data allows high performers to be rewarded and recognized. With merit pay programs, for example, increases in pay are tied to performance levels. Without performance data, everyone has to be rewarded equally, or rewards must be distributed subjectively—conditions that are perceived as inequitable by the recipients. Performance appraisals also provide intrinsic rewards, since outstanding performers receive positive recognition for their efforts.
2. *To guide personnel actions such as hiring, firing, and promoting.* Performance information is necessary for making rational decisions about whom to promote or terminate. When this information is not available, personnel decisions are made by subjective impressions. It is better to make careful, defensible decisions based on good performance data. Organizations that fail to have a formal evaluation program are vulnerable to costly legal challenges, because without accurate performance data, they cannot show that their personnel decisions are free from illegal discrimination on the basis of race, religion, sex, national origin, or age.
3. *To provide individuals with information for their own personal development.* Individuals need performance feedback to help them improve; accurate and timely feedback facilitates the learning of new behavior. Furthermore, most people want to know how well they are doing and where they need to improve.
4. *To identify training needs for the organization.* A well-designed performance evaluation system identifies who could benefit from training, and what abilities and skills are needed for each job.
5. *To integrate human resource planning and coordinate other personnel functions.* The information obtained from a performance evaluation is essential for individual career planning and for organizational staffing. Performance information is used to identify high potential people, who are known as "fast-track" employees. It is also used in succession planning to identify the kinds of developmental experiences employees need for advancement.

Criticisms of Performance Evaluation

In spite of its importance, the evaluation process has been severely criticized. Many people, especially low performers and people who dislike work, simply dislike being evaluated. They are opposed to having anyone evaluate their performance because they are threatened by it.

The process of evaluating performance can also be intimidating to supervisors. Some supervisors do not like to evaluate their subordinates, and they feel threatened by having to justify their evaluations. These supervisors argue that having to evaluate subordinates creates role conflict by forcing them to be a judge, coach, and friend at the same time. Many supervisors do not have adequate interpersonal skills to handle evaluation interviews. Nevertheless, evaluating the performance of subordinates is a basic supervisory responsibility, and a supervisor who lacks the skills to provide performance feedback simply cannot be a good supervisor.

On some jobs, performance is difficult to define, especially jobs that do not produce a physical product. Managers provide leadership, engineers create new ideas, and trainers present information, but these "products" cannot be meaningfully counted. So how do we know what to measure?

While some people argue that intangible products such as new ideas, leadership, and training cannot be reliably measured, in reality everything can be measured even if it is only by a subjective rating scale. If an evaluator has an opinion about an employee's performance, this attitude can be evaluated like any other attitude, regardless of how subjective it is.

Organizations need to make certain that these subjective judgments are job-related, however. Because subjective evaluations can give rise to discrimination against protected groups, the federal courts have not been willing to accept evaluation procedures that allow "unfettered subjective judgments." In some instances, organizations have been required by the courts to establish objective guidelines for evaluation, promotion, and transfer.[1]

Evaluating performance and assigning a number to represent it often create feelings of anxiety in both the evaluator and the person being evaluated. Eight of the most frequent criticisms of performance evaluation are described in Exhibit 9.1. Although these criticisms represent legitimate problems, they should be treated as problems to resolve rather than insurmountable obstacles.

Criticisms of Performance Appraisals — Exhibit 9.1

1. *Halo Effect:* Sometimes one characteristic about a person, positive or negative, strongly influences all other attitudes about that person.

2. *Leniency-Strictness Effect:* Some evaluators give mostly favorable ratings, while other evaluators evaluate the same performance more unfavorably.

3. *Central Tendency Effect:* Some evaluators give average ratings to everyone to avoid sticking their necks out to identify marginal or outstanding performance.

4. *Interrater Reliability:* Two evaluators seeing the same behavior may disagree and give different ratings.

5. *Contrast Effect:* The evaluation of one employee's performance may be influenced by the relative performance of the preceding individual.

6. *Zero-Sum Problem:* Some appraisal systems require supervisors to balance high ratings given to some employees with low ratings given to others.

7. *Numbers Fetish:* An excessive focus is sometimes placed on numbers, which may be treated as though they possess unquestioned accuracy.

8. *Recency Effect:* Recent events are unduly reflected in the appraisal, to the exclusion of events earlier in the year.

Performance Evaluation Methods

Performance evaluations occur whether or not a formal evaluation program exists. The demands to hire, fire, promote, and compensate necessitate some form of evaluation. Supervisors have always evaluated their subordinates and formed impressions about each employee's work, and these informal, subjective evaluations have influenced personnel decisions just as much as formal written evaluations. The advantage of an informal system is that it is easier to design and administer; the advantage of a formal program is that it is more unbiased, defensible, and open to inspection.

The evaluation should focus on relevant behaviors that matter to the organization. The popular proverb "what you evaluate is what you get" emphasizes the importance of evaluating behaviors that are essential to organizational effectiveness.

Example

The importance of evaluating relevant behaviors was illustrated by the experience of a military officer who included "orderliness" as one of the criteria for evaluating a unit of clerk-typists. The officers who conducted the evaluation defined orderliness in terms of how clear and uncluttered the clerk-typists kept their desks. The clerk-typists responded by removing everything from the tops of their desks and keeping it in their desk drawers. Although the procedure was inefficient and the volume of work dramatically declined, the clerk-typists obtained high performance evaluations.[2]

Deciding what to evaluate is in part a value judgment; the personal values of those who design the evaluation system will be reflected in it. In deciding what to evaluate, an important issue is whether the evaluation should focus on outcomes (results) or behaviors (activities). For example, the performance evaluation of a salesclerk could focus on the number of products sold per hour or it could focus on the behaviors required to produce the sale, such as describing the product, arranging for financing, and making repeat calls. When asked, most people say outcomes are more important to measure than behaviors; they are primarily interested in measuring results. However, most performance evaluations focus more on behaviors than on results, especially when evaluating managers and supervisors.

The major advantage of focusing on outcomes is that attention is directed toward producing specific results. The primary objective of all employees should be to produce results, not behaviors. Unfortunately, some employees perform many of the right behaviors and still fail to produce results.

Example

Doing the right behaviors and not achieving the outcome can be illustrated by examining the behaviors of a student writing a research paper. The right behaviors include finding references, reading articles, making notes, and studying the materials. A student can perform all these activities very well and still fail to get the paper written.

A potential problem with exclusively evaluating outcomes is that results can sometimes be achieved by unethical or undesirable means. By exerting excessive pressure on subordinates, supervisors can increase performance, but over time, excessive pressure leads to turnover, dissatisfaction, and unethical conduct. In managing people, the way it is done (behaviors) is just as important as the result (outcomes).

Good performance evaluation programs depend more on the competence of the evaluator than on the specific evaluation technique. Nevertheless, some appraisal techniques are considerably better than others, depending on the purpose of the evaluation and the nature of the work being done. The primary techniques include ranking procedures, classification procedures, graphic rating scales, behaviorally anchored rating scales, and descriptive essays.

Ranking Procedures

The objective of a ranking procedure is to order a group of employees from highest to lowest along some performance dimension, usually overall performance. Ranking is frequently used when making promotion decisions and occasionally used when making compensation decisions, to decide which employees should get the largest financial bonuses. However, ranking is not helpful for providing personal feedback.

Classification Procedures

Classification procedures simply assign individuals to one of several categories based on their overall performance. Many evaluation systems classify employees as "greatly exceeds expectations," "exceeds expectations," "meets expectations," "below expectations," and "fails to meet expectations." Other labels are also used, such as "superior," "outstanding," "excellent," "average," "fair," and "poor."

Graphic Rating Scales

Graphic rating scales are the most frequently used method of evaluating performance for non-managerial workers. Some of the most popular characteristics measured by graphic rating scales include quantity of work, quality of work, cooperativeness, job knowledge, dependability, initiative, creativity, and overall performance. The scales used to measure these

Exhibit 9.2 — Illustration of a Graphic Rating Scale

Name of Employee _____ Job Title _____

Department _____

Rated By _____

Date _____

Instructions: Rate this employee on the basis of the actual work he or she is now doing. Read the definitions very carefully. Compare this employee with others in the same occupation in this company or elsewhere. In the space before each number, rate the employee according to the following scale.

1	2	3	4	5	6	7	8	9
Fair				**Average**				**Excellent**

☐ 1. *Quantity of Work:* How does the quantity of this employees work compare with what you expect? Is this employee energetic and industrious, or does he or she waste time?

☐ 2. *Quality of Work:* How does the quality of this employee's work compare with what you expect? Consider the degree of completeness and the number of errors and mistakes.

☐ 3. *Dependability and Responsibility:* Habits of punctuality and attendance. Can this employee be trusted to complete work with a minimum of supervision?

☐ 4. *Initiative, Resourcefulness, and Leadership:* Consider the employee's ability to proceed without supervision and achieve results without being told. How does this employee affect the output of coworkers? Does he or she have the ability to direct and train others, and utilize company resources and properties effectively?

☐ 5. *Judgment:* Does the employee impress you as a person whose judgment would be dependable, even under stress? Is the employee likely to be excitable or hasty when making decisions in an emergency? Are decisions objective and rational, or swayed by feelings and the opinions of others?

☐ 6. *Ability, Training, Skill, and Experience:* Does the employee have sufficient job knowledge to perform satisfactorily? Does the employee need additional training on the job?

☐ 7. *Personal Appearance and speech:* Does the employee make a good first impression? Is the employee well-groomed, or slovenly? Does the employee have a pleasant speaking voice? Does he or she express thoughts and ideas well?

characteristics are typically seven or ten point scales that are described by such words as *high* versus *low*, or *exceeds job requirements* versus *needs improvement,* as shown in Exhibit 9.2 The accuracy of graphic rating scales and their freedom from bias and subjectivity improve as the points along the scale are more accurately described in behavioral terms. Ideally, each point along the scale should be defined by a specific behavioral description.

Behaviorally Anchored Rating Scales

When the points along a graphic rating scale are clearly defined by specific behavioral descriptions, as shown in Exhibit 9.3, these scales are called behaviorally anchored rating scales (BARS). Research indicates that these scales are superior to regular graphic rating scales because they are more reliable, less ambiguous, and less biased; furthermore, they are more accurate measures of performance and provide better feedback to employees.[3] The disadvantage of using behaviorally anchored rating scales is that they require more time and effort to develop.

Descriptive Essays

Some performance evaluation forms simply provide a blank space for the evaluator to write a descriptive essay summarizing the employee's performance. New and inexperienced evaluators find this procedure extremely challenging and unpleasant; however,

Exhibit 9.3 — Illustration of a Behaviorally-Anchored Rating Scale

Cooperation and dependability refer to spontaneous and innovative behaviors beyond the formal job description that contribute significantly to the effectiveness of the company, e.g., dependability, willingness to accept assignments, cooperation in working with others, initiative in seeing what needs to be done and doing it willingly.

Excellent attitude	7	Positive and enthusiastic approach to work. Always pleasant, helpful, and cooperative. A self-starter. Strives to further the company's interests.
Good attitude	6	Excellent and enthusiastic worker, willing to do more than expected. Always pleasant and cooperative unless criticized or mistreated.
Slightly good attitude	5	Performs assigned work, but seldom goes beyond the normal job expectations.
Average attitude	4	Adequate worker, but occasionally allows personal problems to influence work much of the day.
Slightly poor attitude	3	Sometimes resistive; expresses a dislike for being asked to assist others.
Poor attitude	2	Openly resistive; may even resist performing tasks that are part of the normal job. Argumentative and sometimes nasty to coworkers.
Very poor attitude	1	Occasionally acts belligerently or hostile to supervisors.

experienced evaluators use it quite effectively. The essay description typically identifies the employee's job responsibilities on one side of the page, and the other side of the page contains a description of how well these duties have been performed. If they wish, evaluators are free to construct and use their own scales to facilitate their essay descriptions. One of the major benefits of a descriptive essay procedure is that it provides valuable feedback to help employees improve their performance. The major disadvantage is that the information cannot be used readily to make comparisons among employees.

Results-Oriented Appraisals

Many organizations emphasize individual accountability through a results-oriented approach to performance evaluation. Less emphasis is placed on the activities employees perform and more emphasis is placed on the results they are expected to produce. Many labels have been attached to these results-oriented evaluations. The most popular label is management by objectives (MBO).

Peter Drucker is credited with first publicizing MBO in his 1954 book *The Practice of Management*.[4] Drucker noted the advantages of managing people by "objectives" rather than by "drives." The advantages are that each manager from the highest level to the lowest level has clear objectives that reflect and support the objectives of the organization. All managers participate in the goal-setting process and then exercise self-control over their own performance; that is, they monitor their own performance and take corrective actions as necessary. To do this, their performance is measured and compared with their objectives. The measurements do not need to be rigidly quantitative or exact, but they must be clear and rational.

MBO is primarily a philosophy of management that reflects a positive, proactive way of managing, rather than a reactive way. The focus is on (1) predicting and shaping the future of the organization by developing long-range organizational objectives and strategic plans, (2) accomplishing results rather than performing activities, (3) improving both individual competence and organizational effectiveness, and (4) increasing the participation and involvement of employees in the affairs of the organization.

MBO is also a process consisting of a series of integrated management functions: (1) the development of clear, precise organizational objectives, (2) the formulation of coordinated individual objectives designed to achieve the overall organizational objectives, (3) the systematic measurement and review of performance, (4) the use of corrective action as needed to achieve the planned objectives.

MBO programs are typically implemented in three phases. The first phase focuses on evaluating managers by having them identify measurable objectives and recording how well they have achieved them at the end of a period. In phase two, MBO programs are integrated into an organization's planning and control processes so that the objectives are coordinated with the strategy and objectives of the company. Phase three fully integrates the MBO system with other organizational functions, including the development of strategic plans, budgeting and financial planning, staffing, performance evaluations, compensation, human resource development, and management training. This integration is achieved by emphasizing teamwork and flexibility during the goal-setting process, and by emphasizing individual growth and development during the performance review process.

Evaluation Process

Performance evaluations provide an excellent opportunity for supervisors to coach and mentor subordinates, regardless of the evaluation method that is used. Effective performance reviews can significantly improve employee performance and contribute greatly to their career development. Most supervisors and subordinates fail to see this as an opportunity for personal development. Good performance reviews should consist of a combination of goal setting, performance feedback, and recognition for their accomplishments.

Goal Setting

Goal setting is an important element in the evaluation process; effective supervisors help their team members set specific and measurable goals and then follow up by providing useful feedback. Individuals perform significantly better when they are attempting to achieve a specific goal, such as to complete a project before noon, increase productivity by 5 percent, work for the next hour without making a mistake, maintain 100 percent attendance, or get a research paper submitted on time.

Goal Setting Theory

In 1968 Edwin A. Locke first presented a theory of goal setting and a series of studies showing the effects of goal setting on performance. Continuing research in both laboratory and field studies supports Locke's theory and shows that goal setting has a powerful impact on motivation.[5] Reinforcement theory explains why goal setting has such a powerful influence on behavior.

Some of the earliest work on goal setting was performed by Frederick W. Taylor (1856–1915) in his work on scientific management. Taylor attempted to identify appropriate goals for workers, which he called standards, using time and motion studies and a careful task analysis. Taylor's work focused on teaching workers the ideal ways to perform their tasks using the appropriate physical motions, pacing, and tools.

The basic elements of goal setting theory are illustrated in Exhibit 9.4. The goals we seek are determined by our values. After examining our present circumstances, we compare our actual conditions with our desired conditions. If we are achieving success, we feel satisfied and continue on the same course. But if there is a discrepancy, we go through a goal setting process.

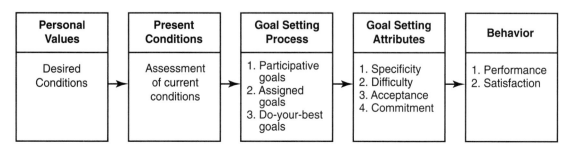

Exhibit 9.4 Goal-Setting Model

> **Example**
>
> *Students go through the goal-setting model frequently during their educational program. Based on their personal values, students have an idea of what they want, such as graduating from college, going on to graduate school, or securing an attractive job. As they assess their present conditions, however, they often discover that their test scores are low, their class attendance is down, and their term papers are behind schedule. These discrepancies between their desired and actual conditions frequently cause students to initiate a goal setting process. They establish such goals as raising their next test score from a C+ to an A−, attending every lecture, and having a first draft of that term paper written within the next two weeks.*

The process that is used to set goals seems to matter greatly in the success of a goal setting program. Supervisors need to carefully consider the maturity of their subordinates and their commitment to the organization when working with them in a goal setting program. Goal setting occurs in three ways.

Participative goals allow employees to participate in the process of setting goals by providing information and contributing to the goal selection. If they believe the goals are too high or too low, they can express their opinions and try to influence the goal statements.

Assigned goals are determined by management and simply assigned to the employees. In scientific management, the standards of performance are determined by industrial engineers with almost no input from the employees.

Do-your-best-goals allow employees to control their own goals; management simply asks the employees to do their best, without getting involved in approving or vetoing their goals.

Applying Goal Setting Theory

The effects of goal setting on behavior are influenced by four major goal setting attributes: goal specificity, goal difficulty, goal acceptance, and goal commitment.

- *Goal specificity.* When employees are working toward specific goals, they consistently perform better than when they are simply told to do their best, or are given no instructions at all. Since do-your-best goals are only loose guidelines, they have about the same effect on performance as no goals at all. A review by Locke and his associates of field experiments using a wide variety of jobs found that 99 out of the 110 studies they reviewed concluded that specific goals led to better performance than vague goals.[6]
- *Goal difficulty.* Studies on the effects of goal difficulty have found a direct linear relationship between goal difficulty and task performance: higher goals lead to higher performance. These studies investigated a wide variety of jobs with participants ranging in age from four years to adulthood. Similar results have been observed for brief one-time tasks lasting as little as one minute, and for ongoing tasks lasting as long as seven years.[7] However, the goals should not be unreasonably difficult. When a goal is perceived as so difficult that it is virtually impossible to attain, the result is often frustration rather than achievement, and performance may be only slightly better than it would have been with no goals at all. Dreaming the impossible dream does not improve performance as much as a difficult but realistic goal. Research on the achievement motive proposed that the probability of success was one minus the probability of failure. Therefore, the optimum levels of motivation occurred when the probability of success (.5) was equal to the probability of failure (.5). Since effort is the product of the probability of success times the probability of failure, other combinations of probabilities produce lower numbers (e.g. $.3 \times .7 = .21$, which is less than $.5 \times .5 = .25$). Therefore, to obtain high performance levels, goals should be difficult and challenging, but the difficulty should not be so great that individuals believe their chances of succeeding are less than 50/50.

- *Goal acceptance.* Goal acceptance refers to the degree to which individuals accept the goal as a reasonable target to work toward. Goals are typically resisted or ignored when they are too difficult and out of reach. They can also be rejected for a variety of other reasons, such as when the employees distrust management, when they feel they are being exploited by the organization, when the goals are not fair and consistent, or when the activity is meaningless and irrelevant. Unrealistically high goals are not always entirely rejected. There is some indication that unreachable goals are reinterpreted by employees rather than rejected altogether.[8]

Example

Employees in a training program who had been reading about 20 pages each night were told that they were expected to be reading at least 100 pages nightly. Although they considered 100 pages an absurd goal, they responded by increasing their reading to 30 pages nightly.

- *Goal commitment.* Goal commitment is determined by both situational variables (goal origin and public announcement) and personal variables (need for achievement and locus of control). Individuals need to feel that the goal belongs to them: "This is my goal." The evidence suggests that commitment to difficult goals is higher when (1) goals are self-set rather than assigned, (2) goals are made public rather than private, (3) the person has an internal locus of control, and (4) the person has a high need for achievement.[9] High levels of goal commitment can also be expected regarding goals associated with one's self-esteem. To the extent that individuals become ego-invested in achieving a goal, their level of goal commitment can be expected to be very high.

Performance Feedback

The importance of performance feedback is emphasized in learning theory. Operant conditioning explains that feedback is essential for acquiring new responses and that learning cannot occur without timely feedback. Feedback is also central to goal setting theory, since goals are meaningless when feedback is absent. There is no uncertainty about the importance of feedback, but there are questions about the most helpful way to give it.

Some recommendations for giving feedback are inconsistent with empirical research. For example, learning theory recommends that feedback occur immediately after the response for optimal learning. However, supervisors are cautioned to postpone telling employees what they did wrong until they can do so privately, to avoid public humiliation. Another popular recommendation is that supervisors should limit their feedback to positive comments and avoid criticism. Studies on discipline have shown, however, that criticism is useful and even necessary to improve performance.[10] The interesting paradox regarding criticism is that those who need it most are usually the most threatened by it and the least capable of benefiting from it. Research on the effects of performance feedback has produced these conclusions:

1. Supervisors give subordinates feedback more often after instances of good performance than after instances of poor performance. People dislike being criticized, and negative feedback creates an uncomfortable discussion. Consequently, many supervisors avoid giving negative feedback.[11]
2. When they are compelled to give negative feedback, supervisors tend to distort the feedback to make it less negative or convey the feedback in very specific terms in order to convince the subordinate that the evaluation was not biased.[12] While distorting the feedback is dysfunctional, giving specific comments is generally beneficial and helps the recipient know how to improve.
3. Supervisors are traditionally told that discussions about performance levels and pay increases should be separate. Research does not support this advice, however. Discussions

about pay increases represent a significant form of feedback that clarifies and reinforces other comments about performance. Therefore, performance reviews should include information about the recommended pay increase that accompanies a given performance level.[13]

4. Feedback tends to improve performance to the extent that it indicates that prior performance levels are inadequate for reaching the goal. Therefore, negative feedback that implicitly calls for greater effort tends to improve performance more than positive feedback that endorses current performance levels does.[14]
5. Individuals who have high self-efficacy and self-esteem can respond more adaptively to criticism than can individuals who have low self-efficacy and self-esteem. People with high self-efficacy and high self-esteem are likely to use the feedback to diagnose their performance and make adaptive changes, while people who are low in these traits are inclined to coast or quit.[15]

Performance interviews are usually uncomfortable experiences for both supervisors and subordinates, but they are also significant events that have an enormous impact on employee motivation, personal development, and job satisfaction. Good performance reviews require good interpersonal skills, accurate performance information, and careful preparation. The feedback is most helpful when supervisors describe behavior in a way that is direct, specific, and nonpunishing.

Who Should Evaluate Performance?

In most instances, the immediate superior should be responsible for evaluating an employee's performance, although information can also be obtained from subordinates, peers, clients, and customers. When data come from all of these sources, the appraisal is referred to as a 360 degree appraisal. As a general rule, performance appraisals are most accurate and useful when the evaluations come from sources closest to the person being rated.[16]

Supervisors

The hierarchical arrangement of formal authority gives supervisors the legitimate responsibility to evaluate subordinates. Generally there is a shared expectation that supervisors have the right and the obligation to evaluate performance. To behave otherwise would seem unnatural and inappropriate. Furthermore, since supervisors administer the rewards and punishments, they should be responsible for evaluating performance.

Subordinates

Although evaluations of superiors by subordinates might seem backward, they can be useful in some circumstances. Subordinates are being asked frequently to evaluate corporate officers in what are sometimes called upward appraisals or subordinate appraisals, and this information may be used to decide pay increases and promotions. There are at least three good reasons for using subordinate appraisals: (1) subordinates possess unique information about superiors that ought to be included in the evaluation process, (2) feedback from subordinates provides a powerful impetus for change, and (3) evaluations by subordinates tend to equalize the power differentials in organizations and make the workplace more democratic and responsive to human needs. Power equalization improves the flow of communication.

Subordinate evaluations of superiors have certain limitations. Subordinates can only evaluate what they observe, and so they generally evaluate their superiors based on their interactions with them. This means that supervisors are primarily evaluated on the basis of interpersonal skills rather than on organizational effectiveness. Some administrative decisions are not popular, and a desire to please their subordinates could cause managers to make bad decisions. Subordinate evaluations also have the potential to undermine the legitimate authority of supervisors and reduce their organizational effectiveness. For a two-way evaluation process to function effectively, both supervisors and subordinates must have adequate maturity to make responsible evaluations and accept feedback from one another.

Peers

In some situations, the most knowledgeable and capable evaluators are an employee's peers. Coworkers are sometimes in a better position than supervisors to evaluate each other's performance. Research on peer evaluations has found them to predict success and correlate with both objective and subjective ratings of success in numerous situations. A review of many studies examining the use of peer ratings in the military found that peer ratings were more valid predictors of leadership performance than were ratings by superiors. Peer ratings also have yielded good reliability and validity.[17] The conditions required for good peer appraisals are:

- a high level of interpersonal trust;
- a noncompetitive reward system;
- opportunities for peers to observe each other's performances.

When these conditions do not exist, the usefulness of peer appraisals is severely restricted. Peer appraisals are most frequently used among professional and technical employees in organizations that meet these conditions. The use of peer appraisals has the potential to increase the interaction and coordination among peers.

Self

People are always evaluating themselves; the question is how formally and systematically these self-evaluations should be recorded and acted on. In recent years a decline in authoritarian leadership has contributed to an increase in self-evaluations in both large and small companies. Some of the arguments in favor of self-evaluation are that self-evaluation results in:

more satisfying and constructive evaluation interviews;
less defensiveness regarding the evaluation process;
improved job performance through greater commitment to organizational goals.[18]

On the other hand, the arguments opposing self-evaluations center on the fact that low agreement usually exists between self and supervisory evaluations. Because of the systematic biases and distortions that can appear, self-evaluations must be used very carefully. Self-evaluations are very valuable for personal development and the identification of training needs, but they are not useful for evaluative purposes. Asking employees to evaluate themselves for purposes of promotions or pay increases is like asking students to grade themselves. It puts individuals in the awkward and uncomfortable situation of trying to guess how biased others will be in rating themselves.

Clients

As a general rule, everyone who can observe the behaviors or outcomes of an individual should be included in the evaluation process. According to this principle, there are occasions when clients and customers ought to be asked for their observations. This information could come from casual complaints or letters of appreciation, or companies could systematically survey their clients and consumers.

Performance Interviews

Performance evaluation interviews can be uncomfortable experiences for both supervisors and subordinates. Managers complain about the difficulties they encounter in the appraisal interview, such as explaining poor performance to marginal employees, providing feedback to poor performers who think they are doing a good job, and trying to find something fresh to say about an experienced employee's performance. They are especially threatening to insecure supervisors and new employees. Some supervisors tend to postpone an interview indefinitely, which means that the employees do not receive adequate, feedback on their performance. If the interview is handled poorly, feelings of disappointment, anger, and resentment may result. Rather than increasing performance and improving personal development, poor evaluation interviews can destroy initiative, creating feelings of defeat and despair. The effectiveness of evaluation interviews will be enhanced if managers and subordinates follow some simple guidelines.

1. Evaluators should develop their own styles so they feel comfortable in an interview. If the evaluator feels uncomfortable, the employee being evaluated probably will feel uncomfortable too. An evaluator should not try to copy someone else or follow a rigid format if it does not feel comfortable and natural.
2. Both parties should prepare for the interview beforehand. Employees should review their performance and document how well they have done. Evaluators should gather relevant information and compare it against the objectives for the period. Lack of preparation for the interview by either party is an obvious indication of lack of interest.
3. The evaluator should begin by clarifying the purpose of the interview. The employee should know whether it is a disciplinary session, a contributions appraisal (which focuses on employee results), or a personal development appraisal. In particular, the employee should understand the possible consequences of the interview so that he or she can prepare appropriate responses. For example, an employee's responses during a contributions appraisal can appropriately be a bit guarded and defensive, but in a personal development appraisal, such responses would greatly reduce the effectiveness of the interview.
4. Neither party should dominate the discussion. The supervisor should take the lead in initiating the discussion, but the employee should be encouraged to express opinions. The supervisor should budget time so that the employee has approximately half the time to discuss the evaluation.
5. The most popular format for the interview is the "sandwich" format—like bologna between two slices of buttered bread, criticism is sandwiched between compliments. The rationale for the sandwich interview format is that positive comments made at the beginning and end of the interview are intended to create a positive experience. The opening compliments should put the employee at ease and the closing compliments should leave the employee feeling good about the interview, and motivated to do better. However, most employees dislike the sandwich-interview format and report that it makes them feel manipulated.
6. An alternative format is to identify and discuss problems, then talk about future improvements, and finally express appreciation for good behaviors. This approach is very direct and to the point. The supervisor begins by saying, "There are problems I'd like to talk with you about:_____ , _____, and _____." Each problem is briefly identified at the beginning before the supervisor discusses the problems in detail. An employee immediately knows what the "charges" are and does not sit in uncertainty waiting for the next bomb to fall. After the problems have been discussed by both supervisor and subordinate, the discussion focuses on accomplishments for which the employee deserves recognition. The supervisor should describe specific actions that deserve recognition, and be as complimentary as the behavior merits. The interview should not end until the supervisor and subordinate have discussed plans for future performance. Future goals and objectives should be clarified, and plans for improvement should be discussed.

Employees should be encouraged to take an active role in the performance-evaluation process. Most employees wait until their supervisor initiates action and schedules an interview. Then they sit through the interview feeling as though they are being "chewed out," manipulated, or "run over." Instead, employees should take an active role by anticipating their evaluations, collecting data about their performance, scheduling interviews with their supervisor, taking the lead in interviews to discuss their strengths and weaknesses, and asking for feedback. An active role makes the evaluation process a dramatically different experience for subordinates. Rather than dreading the interviews, subordinates consciously plan for them and anticipate the experience.[19]

The evaluation interview should focus on behaviors and results rather than on personality factors. Performance feedback helps employees achieve better results, while discussions about personality characteristics are usually dysfunctional. Because personality factors are poorly defined, discussing them usually creates unnecessary conflict. Personality changes are difficult to achieve and are usually not necessary anyway. When supervisors think a personality change is needed, what they are actually concerned about are the behaviors caused by the personality. To correct such problems, the supervisor should describe the improper *behaviors* and help the employee change his or her *behavior*. If a personality change is indeed required, feedback about the specific behavior that needs to be changed is still the best approach to changing personality.

Some have suggested that appraisal interviews should include only the outstanding and poor performers, while the middle group should be excluded. Not only are the ones in the middle more difficult to evaluate, but it appears that telling people they are average is dysfunctional. Most people resent being labeled as average when they think they are members of an above-average group. Employees report a significant drop in organizational commitment when they are told that their performance is satisfactory, but below average. This suggestion, however, overlooks the important role that performance evaluations ought to play in improving performance. Supervisors should be actively involved in coaching and mentoring all employees by helping them set personal goals and advance their careers.

Rewarding Performance

Compensation systems are an important element in organizational strategy because pay has such an enormous influence on job satisfaction, productivity, and labor turnover. Compensation also has an enormous impact on all human resource functions, especially staffing, performance evaluation, training and development, and employee relations. Consequently, compensation decisions are very important to both people and organizations.

All employers have similar compensation objectives: to attract qualified employees, to retain them, and to motivate them to perform their duties in the most effective manner. Employers want their employees to feel financially secure; but they also want them to be highly motivated. To achieve security they must provide a predictable monthly income, regardless of performance; to motivate their employees they must tie pay levels to performance. Employees are more highly motivated if at least some of their pay depends on their performance. Obviously, these two objectives are inconsistent. Achieving an appropriate balance between security and motivation, called fine tuning, requires an appropriate balance between base pay and incentives.

Base Pay

Employees deserve to be paid an amount that is considered just and fair. An ethical principle regarding compensation, called a compensation maxim, is that *employees should be compensated first according to the requirements of the jobs they perform and how well they perform them, and second by labor market conditions (supply and demand) and the organization's ability to pay.* Ethical issues concerning compensation are especially sensitive because money is such an important reason why people work. People expect to be treated fairly, and our concept of fairness is greatly influenced by such issues as why managers deserve more than laborers, why older workers should be paid more than younger workers, and whether people who need more should get more.

Example

Although most people agree that managers deserve more than laborers, there is a growing concern that the enormous pay of chief executive officers cannot be morally justified. Fifty years ago, the average CEO received about thirty times as much as the average worker and now the multiple is about 450:1. Can their compensation be justified by the contribution they make or a scarcity of executive talent in the labor force? Most people think CEO pay is exorbitant, including many corporate board members who are trying to do a better job of tying pay to performance.

The development of a sound wage-and-salary system involves three basic decisions. Each decision answers a critical question regarding an organization's compensation program.

Wage-Level Decision

The first decision concerns the overall level of an organization's compensation. It answers this question: How much money do members of this organization receive relative to people in other organizations who perform similar work? This decision reflects the values of the leaders of a company, and expresses their desire to be wage leaders, to be wage followers, or to pay the going market rate. In a firm that has an average profit picture for its industry, the most compelling definition of an equitable wage is usually the "going market wage," as determined by a wage survey. Both employees and managers are inclined to accept such a wage level as equitable. The primary instruments for making wage-level decisions are wage surveys conducted by the Bureau of Labor Statistics, surveys conducted by professional organizations, and surveys conducted by individual companies. Wage surveys report data regarding wages and benefits for jobs in various industries and geographic areas.

Wage-Structure Decision

The second decision concerns the relative pay of different jobs in an organization: how much money is paid for one job, relative to other jobs in the same company? People typically receive more pay if their job requires greater skill, effort, and responsibility. Companies generally use either a classification system or the point method to make decisions about the wage structure. Classification systems classify jobs, from simple to complex, by describing different levels of skill, effort, and responsibility, and a pay range is associated with each classification. Classification systems are used extensively in public organizations, such as the GS system used by the United States government. The point method involves the evaluation of the job descriptions and the assignment of points to different degrees of skill, effort, and responsibility; the pay for each job is determined by how many points it receives. The point method is very useful for determining and defending the base pay assigned to jobs that may be very different.

Individual-Wage Decision

The third decision concerns individual pay rates and incentives. It answers this question: How much money does one employee receive relative to others who perform similar work? As a general rule, employees receive more money if their performance increases or if they have been with the company longer. Companies use a variety of incentive systems to reward employees for their performance, including individual, group, and company-wide incentive systems.

These three wage decisions illustrate the kinds of wage comparisons employees make when they evaluate their wages.

Example

Accountants in Company A compare their wages with the wages of accountants in other organizations, to see whether Company A has a higher or lower level of wages. The accountants also compare their wages with the pay of bookkeepers, computer programmers, and other members of Company A to learn whether the internal wage structure offers higher pay to jobs that involve more responsibility and greater difficulty. Finally, the accountants discuss their wages among themselves to determine whether each person's wage is the same, or whether differences in wages are related to productivity, seniority, education, or something else.

Financial Incentives

The effects of money on motivation depend primarily on whether pay is based on performance. Companies that use direct financial incentives, such as piece-rates or commission sales, discover that they have a greater impact on performance than any other variable. In spite of this relationship, however, it is surprising to observe how seldom pay is based on performance. For example, when employees are asked what would happen if they doubled their efforts and produced twice as much, very few say they would receive additional income. Some say their supervisors would recognize their efforts and commend them, and a few think they might eventually receive a pay increase. Most say that the consequences of doubling their effort would be negative: it would disrupt the flow of work, their coworkers would hassle them, and they would eventually be expected to work at that rate all the time without additional compensation.

Companies use a variety of incentive plans to motivate employees. Incentive compensation can be granted on the basis of individual performance, group performance, or company-wide performance.

Individual Incentives

The most popular forms of individual incentive pay include merit pay, piece-rate incentives, and commission sales. Merit pay plans are based on a subjective assessment of each employee's performance, and the merit pay is typically awarded by increasing base pay for the coming year. Merit pay increases are relevant to all jobs paid a fixed wage or salary. The most important requirement for an effective merit pay incentive program is the ability to measure performance against clearly defined objectives. To the extent that performance is more difficult to evaluate, the potential problems associated with tying pay to performance increase. For an effective merit pay plan to function smoothly, supervisors and managers must have the competence to evaluate employee performance and provide meaningful feedback. But even when performance can only be evaluated subjectively, most employees still believe that pay increases should be related to performance.[20]

The most direct relationship between pay and performance generally appears in the form of piece-rate incentives, where workers receive a specified amount of money for each unit of work. The effectiveness of piece-rate incentives has been studied for many years. Frederick W. Taylor recommended piece-rate incentives and defended them with research showing that workers paid on a piece-rate basis produced more work and earned more money. Taylor claimed that piece-rate incentive programs would increase productivity by at least 25 percent. Surveys of piece-rate plans over the past eighty years have suggested that Taylor underestimated the actual results. Most surveys have found that productivity under piece work has increased by 30 to 40 percent, and in some cases by greater than 60 percent.[21]

Although piece-work incentive systems predictably increase productivity, there is some question whether the increase is due to financial incentives alone or to other changes that accompany piece-work plans. Two variables that accompany piece-work programs are (1) changes in the design of the work and (2) higher performance goals. Before a piece-work plan is installed, a careful analysis of the job is usually conducted to ensure that it is being performed efficiently. A careful job analysis often identifies more efficient methods of performing the task. Moreover, when the task is being timed to establish pay rates, a goal-setting process occurs, followed by performance feedback. The question, then, is whether goal setting, measurement, and job redesign are more responsible than pay incentives for increasing productivity. Studies generally show that each factor alone has a positive influence on productivity, but that the impact is far greater when all three factors are present. Thus, incentive systems contribute to productivity increases because of improved work methods, higher performance goals with specific performance feedback, and monetary incentives that induce greater effort.[22]

An alternative to paying people for what they do is to pay them for what they are capable of doing. Skill-based pay encourages employees to acquire additional skills. Companies identify a list of valuable skills they would like to encourage their workers to acquire, and as the workers demonstrate mastery of each skill, they receive an increase in their base pay. Skill-based compensation plans reinforce employees for their growth and development and hopefully result in more creative ideas, organizational flexibility, and quality performance.

Another alternative, called pay for knowledge, provides incentives for employees to learn new information and demonstrate it by taking achievement tests. Specific dollar amounts are associated with each test, and employees receive an increase in their base pay after successfully passing each test. Pay for knowledge and skill-based pay systems are vital elements in the change strategies of organizations that experience rapid change and need to adapt to an uncertain environment.

Group Incentives and Bonuses

Although piece-work plans are typically based on individual performance, they can also be based on group production, with all members of the group sharing the money earned by the group. Group incentive plans have some important advantages over individual incentive plans, since they create greater cooperation among coworkers. This climate of cooperation usually reduces the need for direct supervision and control, since workers are supervised more by their coworkers than by their supervisors. In such a climate, slow workers are pressured by their coworkers to increase their productivity. Moreover, group incentives greatly facilitate the flow of work and flexibility in job assignments. When the normal work routine is disrupted because of unique problems such as illness or broken machines, individuals paid on a group incentive plan are willing to adapt to the problem and solve it themselves rather than complain to a manager or wait for the problem to solve itself.

Group incentives have certain limitations, however. When their jobs are independent, group members feel responsible only for their own jobs and think they should be paid individually. In this situation, group incentives provide little extra incentive to produce, since extra efforts by one worker will only result in a small increase in that worker's weekly pay. As the group gets larger, this problem becomes more severe. Thus, group incentives are most useful when jobs are interdependent, when the output of the group can be counted, and the group is small.

The powerful influence of group pressure explains why piece-rate incentives are sometimes not effective. Although many studies have shown that incentive pay systems increase productivity, other studies have found examples where groups restrict output to arbitrarily low levels. Group norms restricting productivity are very troublesome to managers, and they are particularly perplexing because they seem to be so irrational. Why should a group of workers collectively decide to restrict their productivity when they are paid only for what they produce? This behavior is not so irrational when it is examined from the workers' perspective. The problem centers on how the performance standards are established. Workers know that performance standards are some-what arbitrary. They believe that if they consistently produce more than the standard, the industrial engineer will return and retime the job; then they will be expected to produce more work for the same amount of pay.

Management has been guilty of retiming jobs often enough in some organizations to justify the workers' fears. Several interesting case studies have described the games played by workers and industrial engineers in setting performance standards. Since industrial engineers know that workers intentionally work slowly, they arbitrarily tighten the standards above the measured times. The workers know the industrial engineer suspects them of working slowly, so they add unnecessary and inefficient movements to look busy, which the industrial engineers expect and try to disregard.

Company-Wide Incentives

In some organizations, financial incentives are based on the performance of the entire organization. Three of the most popular forms of company-wide incentives include profit-sharing plans, Scanlon plans, and gainsharing.

Profit sharing is the most popular company-wide incentive, and in some companies the employees have been highly motivated to perform as a result of a generous profit-sharing plan. A typical profit-sharing plan distributes 25 percent of the pretax profit to the employees, according to an allocation formula that combines years of service and base wages. For example, in some plans, employees receive points for their base pay, such as one point for every $1000 of annual salary, and points for length of service, such as one point for every year of service. Profit-sharing money is then distributed to employees according to their percentage of the total points.

Profit-sharing plans can be either cash plans and deferred plans. Cash plans are more directly tied to performance because employees are paid annually. However, deferred plans are more popular because of tax considerations. Under a deferred plan, an employee's share of the profit is held in an individual account, where it grows without being taxed until it is received after, usually at retirement. Some deferred plans provide enormous wealth to their participants.

Profit-sharing plans generally reduce the conflict between managers and workers. Many companies claim that their plans have created a sense of partnership between employees and management, and have increased employee interest in the company. Profit-sharing plans typically increase productivity by increasing motivation; however, the impact of profit sharing is typically less than that for piece-rate plans, since each individual's profit share is not directly tied to individual productivity. Immediate rewards that are directly tied to specific individual behaviors are more effective than profit-sharing plans, especially for motivating employees who have short attention spans and cannot delay gratification. Deferred compensation plans, for example, are more effective for older workers than they are for younger workers, since retirement is not so distant. Scanlon plans were named after their founder, Joseph Scanlon, an accountant and union steward in a steel mill. While negotiating a new labor agreement, Scanlon proposed that the percent of revenue allocated to labor costs be maintained at a fixed ratio of what it had been over the past few years. Scanlon believed that the employees would be highly motivated to increase their productivity if they knew that a fixed percent of the revenue would be paid in wages. Scanlon believed that significantly higher revenues could be obtained without an increase in the number of employee hours by motivating the employees to work harder and submit suggestions of how to improve productivity. Since 1941, when Scanlon first proposed his idea, Scanlon plans have grown in popularity, and the results have shown that they tend to increase both company profits and employee wages.

Gainsharing is a company-wide incentive program similar to profit-sharing, but the bonuses are based on improved productivity rather than a percent of the profit. An effective gainsharing program requires managers to tie specific incentives to the strategic factors that determine a company's economic success, called business drivers. Some examples of business drivers are occupancy rates for hotels, turn-around time and vacant seats for airlines, and inventory shrinkage for retail companies. A successful gainsharing program at an oil refinery identified targeted goals for seven business drivers and promised to share the proceeds with the workers if they exceeded these goals. The goal for safety was an incident rate of 0.5, and for each accident that didn't happen the company would put $18,000 (the average cost of an accident) into the fund to be divided among employees. Gainsharing plans normally reward employees on a monthly or quarterly basis, depending on how productivity is measured, whereas profit-sharing is usually paid annually.

Bonuses

Executives and managers often participate in an additional bonus program designed specifically for them. The basic philosophy behind executive bonuses is to reward managers for good performance. When they are tied to the overall performance of a company, the bonuses are expected to create greater creativity and better cooperation among managers.

Executive bonuses are typically larger for upper-level managers than for middle-level managers, even when expressed as a percentage of salary. At upper levels of a company, a typical bonus might be 80 to 120 percent of salary. At lower levels of the company, supervisors typically receive bonuses that add only 15 to 40 percent of their salaries, if they receive bonuses at all.

The bonus plans of many companies are not carefully designed and administered. Although bonuses are intended to improve the performance of individual managers and the organization as a whole, the research evaluating bonuses does not entirely support their effectiveness.[23] Because management performance is difficult to evaluate, most bonus plans distribute money based on the manager's position rather than on the manager's performance. Consequently, these plans typically do little to motivate greater performance. Even though they are very expensive and the research evidence regarding their effectiveness is mostly negative, they are still widely used.

Fine-Tuning the Compensation Plan

In designing an effective compensation program, organizations need to find the proper balance between base pay and incentive pay, including individual incentives, group incentives, and company-wide incentives. The process of balancing the various incentives is called fine-tuning the compensation system.[24] Compensation managers must fine-tune the compensation system, just as a mechanic fine-tunes an engine. The engine needs to be adjusted for the load it must pull, the quality of fuel it will use, and even the altitude at which it will operate. Similarly, a compensation system needs to be fine-tuned to balance the employees' needs for security, equity, and motivation.

Employees who have a sizable base pay feel secure, but not motivated. However, if their total compensation consists of incentive pay without adequate base pay, several problems could develop, such as increased turnover because of inadequate security, dissatisfaction over inaccurate performance evaluations, and dysfunctional competition between coworkers.

The fine-tuning process consists of adjusting base pay, individual incentives, group incentives, and profit-sharing, to create feelings of security and motivation. Stable base pay that provides a dependable weekly or monthly income provides security. Equity and motivation, however, are provided through incentive plans. Some organizations choose to pay large base salaries and give small bonuses, while other organizations do just the opposite.

Recognition Awards

Nonmonetary reward systems have been used effectively to improve employee attitudes, motivation, and attendance.[25] Every motivation theory agrees that praise and recognition are effective rewards. Companies have created a variety of nonmonetary reward programs to recognize employees, and some have been more effective than monetary incentives. The following illustrations demonstrate the diversity of recognition rewards.

Example

A storage company paneled one of its walls inside the warehouse, and used it to display the photographs of the employee with the best safety record each month. The number of accidents in the warehouse was greatly reduced, and the forklift operators were pleased with the recognition they received, even though the public could not see their photographs.

Example

Sewing machine operators receive silver stars on their nameplates if they exceed 120 percent of their production quotas every day for a week. After they get ten silver stars, they receive a purple seal. Ribbons are awarded for high-quality production, and the operators display them with pride.

> **Example**
>
> *A hospital gives five-, ten-, fifteen-, twenty-, and twenty-five-year service pins to recognize employees for their years of service. The pins are top quality jewelry made with diamonds and gold that show the hospital's logo. When the price of gold increased, the hospital decided to give savings bonds rather than pins, but the administrators abandoned the idea when they discovered that the pins were far more important and valued by the employees than were the savings bonds.*

> **Example**
>
> *To reduce absenteeism and tardiness, a small apparel manufacturer decided to give gifts of ten to fifteen dollars to randomly selected employees who had perfect attendance. At the end of each week, the names of those who had perfect attendance records were placed in a drawing. For every twenty names in the drawing, one name was selected to receive a gift. After three months, tardiness was only a third of what it had been, and absenteeism was cut in half.*

Recognition awards, such as silver stars, purple seals, and photographs hung on a wall, are not inherently rewarding. Primary rewards such as food, water, rest, and the removal of pain are reinforcing because of their relationship to the innate physiology of the body. Secondary rewards such as recognition awards do not directly satisfy physiological needs. Instead, they become powerful reinforcers as people come to place value on them. Consequently, social approval, recognition, status, and feelings of pride and craftsmanship are secondary, or learned, rewards because their reinforcing properties are acquired through experience with them. Although a person may not immediately see the secondary reinforcer as a highly motivating award, over time it can become a powerful form of reinforcement. Recognition awards are often inconsequential to new employees, but as new workers observe their coworkers participate in meaningful recognition experiences, the reward comes to be a highly valued rein-forcer. For example, a twenty-five-year service pin can be an extremely motivating reward, not because of its financial worth but because of the symbolic meaning associated with it. In some organizations the service pins are distributed at an annual awards banquet where the recipients are recognized individually. Employees who observe this ritual year after year come to appreciate the ceremony and see the pin as a highly valued reward.[26]

Intrinsic versus Extrinsic Rewards

Some scholars are opposed to using any form of monetary incentives to motivate workers. Indeed, they adamantly condemn all extrinsic reward programs that are designed to motivate people or change their behavior, including piece-rate incentives in industry, grades in education, and gold stars in child rearing. Their argument is not that incentives do not work, because they admit that well-designed incentive programs can have an immediate and substantial impact on behavior. Their claim is that they work for all the wrong reasons. Six of the most important criticisms of extrinsic rewards are:[27]

1. *Rewards are used to control behavior.* Rather than encourage people to direct their lives according to their personal values, rewards manipulate and control them. Rewards are effective only for people who are dependent on them, and they only work if they continue to be received.
2. *Rewards punish.* Rewards and punishment are both elements of a common psychological model that views motivation as nothing more than the manipulation of behavior. To

not be rewarded, or to be rewarded less than last time, is to be punished. Therefore, all reward programs are also punishment programs.

3. *Rewards rupture relationships.* Competition for rewards within a group tends to destroy group cohesiveness. Likewise, the relationship between the person giving the rewards and the recipients is also damaged because of the unequal status inherent in the situation. The capacity of supervisors to give or withhold rewards inevitably places them in a position of power that automatically destroys feelings of equality.

4. *Rewards ignore reasons.* Successful performance is determined by both personal and situational factors, and when rewards are based strictly on performance, the uncontrolled situational factors that may have prevented success are ignored.

5. *Rewards discourage risk taking.* When people are competing for rewards, they focus primarily on customary methods that have worked in the past, and overlook new opportunities and creative insights for improving performance.

6. *Extrinsic rewards destroy intrinsic satisfaction.* The good feelings people have for performing a task or helping others are destroyed when they are given extrinsic rewards. This is the most serious and controversial criticism of using extrinsic rewards. If people who are performing a task because of the intrinsic satisfaction they get from doing it, what will happen to their motivation if they are paid for their efforts? More importantly, if the pay later ends what will happen to their motivation? Will they return to happily performing the task, or did the extrinsic reward destroy the intrinsic satisfaction? The research has produced mixed results; extrinsic rewards sometimes destroy intrinsic satisfaction, but not always.

These criticisms of extrinsic rewards are especially helpful for managers who want to strengthen the work values of their employees. The work ethic is not acquired by offering monetary incentives for good work; money may even distract employees from attending to the personal and social benefits of their labors. Feelings of pride and craftsmanship and a commitment to excellence are primarily stimulated by the intrinsic rewards of seeing the benefits that come from one's efforts and feeling that they are a reflection of one's self. Rather than using financial incentives to reward good work, supervisors need to help employees understand how their work benefits society.

Since people must be paid to work, and rewards serve many useful purposes, those opposed to the use of extrinsic rewards offer the following suggestions to minimize the damage caused by extrinsic rewards:

1. *Get rewards out of people's faces.* Encourage people to perform well without continually talking about the potential rewards. Focus on the intrinsic satisfaction of providing service and assistance.

2. *Offer rewards after the fact, as a surprise.* Rewarding excellence with unexpected rewards prevents people from feeling that they were only motivated by the rewards.

3. *Never turn the quest for rewards into a contest.* Contests reward some at the expense of others. Only have contests in which people compete against their own personal records.

4. *Make rewards as similar as possible to the task.* The best reward for good behavior is the opportunity to do it again and feel good about it.

5. *Give people as much choice as possible about how rewards are used.* If possible, let people suggest what will be given, to whom, and when.

Endnotes

1. *Baxter v. Savannah Sugar Refining Corp.*, 495 F2d 437 (1974); *Brito v. Zia Co.*, 478, F2d, 1200 (1973); *Albemarle Paper Company v. Moody*, 95 SCt 2362 (1974); *Rowe v. General Motors Corp.*, 457 F2d 348, 1972; *Wade v. Mississippi Cooperative Extension Service*, 528 F2d 508 (1976).

2. Personal communication from the commanding officer.

3. John P. Campbell, R. Darvey, Marvin D. Dunnette, and L. V. Hellervik, "The Development and Evaluation of Behaviorally Based Rating Scales," *Journal of Applied Psychology*,

vol. 57, (no. 1, 1973); Donald P. Schwab, Herbert G. Heneman, and T. A. DeCotis, "Behaviorally-Anchored Rating Scales: A Review of the Literature," *Personnel Psychology*, vol. 28, no. 4, (Winter, 1975), pp. 549–562.
4. Peter F. Drucker, *The Practice of Management* (New York: Harper and Row, 1954).
5. Edwin A. Locke, "Toward a Theory of Task Performance and Incentives," *Organizational Behavior and Human Performance*, vol. 3 (1968), pp. 157–189; Locke, Edwin A. and Latham, Gary P, "Building a Practically Useful Theory of Goal Setting and Task Motivation: A 35-year Odyssey," *American Psychologist*, vol. 57 (2002), pp. 705–717.
6. Edwin A. Locke, Karyll N. Shaw, Lise M. Saari, and Gary P. Latham, "Goal Setting and Task Performance: 1969–1980," *Technical Report*, GS1, Office of Naval Research, Washington, D.C., June 1980.
7. Edwin A. Locke and Gary P. Latham, *Goal Setting: A Motivational Technique That Works* (Englewood Cliffs, N.J.: Prentice-Hall, 1984); Locke, Edwin A. and Latham, Gary P, "Building a Practically Useful Theory of Goal Setting and Task Motivation: A 35-year Odyssey," *American Psychologist*, vol. 57 (2002), pp. 705–717.
8. H. Garland, "Influence of Ability Assigned Goals, and Normative Information of Personal Goals and Performance: A Challenge to the Goal Attainability Assumption," *Journal of Applied Psychology*, vol. 68, (1983), pp. 20–30; D. J. Cherrington and J. O. Cherrington, "Appropriate Reinforcement Contingencies in the Budgeting Process," *Empirical Research in Accounting: Selected Studies* (1973), pp. 225–253.
9. John R. Hollenbeck, Charles R. Williams, and Howard J. Kline, "An Empirical Examination of the Antecedents of Commitment to Difficult Goals," *Journal of Applied Psychology*, vol. 74, (February 1989), pp. 18–23; Andrew Li and Adam B. Butler. "The Effects of Participation in Goal Setting and Goal Rationales on Goal Commitment: An Exploration of Justice Mediators," *Journal of Business and Psychology*. Vol. 19 (No. 1, 2004), pp. 37–51.
10. Stephen G. Green, Gail T. Fairhurst and B. Kay Snavely, "Chains of Poor Performance and Supervisory Control," *Organizational Behavior and Human Decision Processes*, vol. 38, (1986), pp. 7–27.
11. James R. Larson, Jr., "Supervisors' Performance Feedback to Subordinates: The Impact of Subordinate Performance Valence and Outcome Dependence," *Organizational Behavior and Human Decision Processes*, vol. 37, (1986), pp. 391–408.
12. C. D. Fisher, "Transmission of Positive and Negative Feedback to Subordinates: A Laboratory Investigation," *Journal of Applied Psychology*, vol. 64, (1979), pp. 533–540; Daniel R. Ilgen and W. A. Knowlton, "Performance Attributional Effects on Feedback From Superiors," *Organizational Behavior and Human Performance*, vol. 25, (1980), pp. 441–456.
13. J. Bruce Prince and Edward E. Lawler, III, "Does Salary Discussion Hurt the Developmental Performance Appraisal?" *Organizational Behavior and Human Decision Processes*, vol. 37, (1986), pp. 357–375.
14. Tamao Matsui, Akinori Okada, and Osamu Inoshita, "Mechanism of Feedback Affecting Task Performance," *Organizational Behavior and Human Performance*, vol. 31, (1983), pp. 114–122.
15. Albert Bandura, "Self-efficacy Mechanism in Human Agency," *American Psychologist*, vol. 37, (February 1982), pp. 122–147.
16. Leanne E. Atwater and Joan F. Brett. "360-Degree Feedback to Leaders: Does It Relate To Changes In Employee Attitudes?" *Group & Organization Management*. Vol. 31 (2006), pp. 578–600.
17. Glenn M. McEvoy, Paul F. Buller and Steven R. Rognaar, "A Jury of One's Peers," *Personnel Administrator* 33 (May 1988): 94–101.
18. Edward J. Inderrieden, Robert E. Allen, Timothy J. Keaveny, "Managerial Discretion in the Use of Self-ratings in an Appraisal System: The Antecedents and Consequences," *Journal of Managerial Issues*, vol. 16 (2004), pp. 460–482.
19. Susan J. Ashford, Ruth Blatt and Don Vande Walle "Reflections on the Looking Glass: A Review of Research on Feedback-Seeking Behavior in Organizations," *Journal of Management*, vol. 29 (2003), pp. 773–799; Wing Lam, Xu Huang, Snape, Ed, "Feedback-Seeking Behavior and Leader-Member Exchange: Do Supervisor-Attributed Motives Matter?" *Academy of Management Journal*, vol. 50 (2007), pp. 348–363.

20. C. Bram Cadsby, Fei Song, and Francis Tapon, "Sorting and Incentive Effects of Pay for Performance: An Experimental Investigation," *Academy of Management Journal*, vol. 50 (2007), pp. 387–405.
21. Surveyed by Allan N. Nash and Stephen J. Carroll, Jr., *The Management of Compensation*, (Monterey, California: Brooks-Cole Publishing Company, 1975), p. 199.
22. James S. Devlin, "Wage Incentives: The Aetna Plan," Presented at the LOMA Work Measurement Seminar (April 1975).
23. J. Perham, "What's Wrong with Bonuses?" Dun's Review of *Modern Industry*, vol. 98, (1981), pp. 40–44.
24. David J. Cherrington and Laura Z. Middleton, *Human Resource Certification Preparation, Unit 4: Compensation and Benefits*, (Provo, UT: HRCP LLC, 2007), pp. 62–65.
25. Steven E. Markham, K. Dow Scott, and Gail H. McKee, "Recognizing Good Attendance: A Longitudinal, Quasi-Experimental Field Study," *Personnel Psychology*, vol. 55 (2002), pp. 639–660.
26. David J. Cherrington and B. Jackson Wixom, Jr., "Recognition is Still a Top Motivator," *Personnel Administrator*, (May 1983), pp. 87–91.
27. Alfie Kohn, *Punished by Rewards: The Trouble with Gold Stars, Incentive Plans, A's, Praise, and Other Bribes.* (Boston: Houghton Mifflin, 1993); Mark R. Lepper and David Greene, *The Hidden Costs of Rewards: New Perspectives on the Psychology of Human Motivation.* (Hillsdale, N.J.: Erlbaum, 1978).`

Effective Groups and Teams — 10

Group Formation

Groups and work teams are a central part of our everyday lives, and at any given time we are members of many groups, such as work teams, student clubs, church groups, athletic teams, professional associations, dormitory groups, political parties, and our families. At any one time the average individual belongs to five or six groups. The study of group dynamics is important for two reasons:

1. Groups exert an enormous influence on the attitudes, values, and behaviors of individuals. Groups teach us how to behave and help us understand who we are. Unique behavior occurs within groups because of group roles and norms;
2. Groups have a powerful influence on other groups and organizations. Much of the work that gets done in organizations is done by teams within the larger organization, and the success of an organization is limited by the effectiveness of its teams.

The collective action of a team of individuals can be much greater than the sum of individuals acting alone. Therefore, we need to know how to build effective teams.

Group Development

A group consists of two or more people interacting interdependently to achieve a common goal or objective. The principal characteristics of this definition are people, face-to-face interaction, and at least one common goal. A collection of people who use the same copy machine is not a group, even though they have face-to-face contact, because they are not interacting dependently. Members of a group must think they belong together; they must see themselves as forming a single unit. This feeling of self-awareness usually happens because the group members share common beliefs and attitudes and accept certain group norms. A cohesive group that has a common objective is often called a team.

Why People Join Groups

Formal groups, such as work teams and committees, are typically created to satisfy a particular organizational objective or to solve a specific problem. However, informal groups, such as friendship groups and reference groups, are created for personal reasons, and these reasons explain why people maintain their membership in them.

When individuals join a group, they voluntarily surrender part of their personal freedom, since they must be willing to accept the standards of the group and behave in prescribed ways that are sometimes very restrictive. Musical groups and athletic teams, for example, place heavy demands on members regarding attendance at practices and performances, dressing in the proper attire, and behaving in prescribed ways even outside the group. Although the loss of freedom varies from group to group, every individual voluntarily relinquishes at least some personal freedom as a member of a group. Why then do individuals want to join a group and sacrifice part of their personal freedom? People form groups for four primary reasons:

1. *Goal Accomplishment.* People work together in groups because they need the help of others to achieve important goals. Many goals require the cooperative efforts of other

From *Creating Effective Organizations*, 5th edition by David J. Cherrington and W. Gibb Dyer. Copyright © 2009 by Kendall/Hunt Publishing Company. Reprinted by permission.

people, such as building a high-rise tower, extinguishing a forest fire, and playing a basketball game. Some goals could be accomplished by individuals, but groups do them better, such as developing a new consumer product, restructuring the production process, and evaluating applications for college scholarships.

2. *Personal identity.* Membership in a group helps us know more about ourselves. Comments of peers generally have a great impact on our self-esteem because they come from people we respect; therefore, we have confidence in what they say. Their comments are also more credible because we assume they know us well and are concerned about our well-being.

3. *Affiliation.* People like to associate with other people, particularly if they have something in common. The mere presence of others provides friendship, social stimulation, and personal acceptance. College students and factory workers alike form informal peer groups simply to avoid the discomfort of being alone.

4. *Emotional Support.* To handle the pressures of daily living, and especially when situations are threatening or uncertain, people rely on others for emotional support. A person facing a stressful situation is comforted by the physical presence of another person facing the same stress.

Stages of Group Development

Most groups experience similar conflicts and challenges that need to be resolved as they strive to become effective. Groups do not immediately function as highly effective teams until they have gone through various stages of development and addressed the kinds of issues that separate effective from ineffective teams. Every work group, whether it is a surgical team, a quality control circle, or a production crew, has to resolve similar issues, and the way it resolves these issues determines the group's effectiveness.

Although the developmental process is not highly standardized, most effective groups go through four stages: orientation, confrontation, differentiation, and collaboration, as shown in Exhibit 10.1.[1] A useful mnemonic for remembering these developmental stages is forming, storming, norming, and performing. Groups may not necessarily advance through each of these four stages; indeed, some groups never advance to the later stages because of internal conflicts.

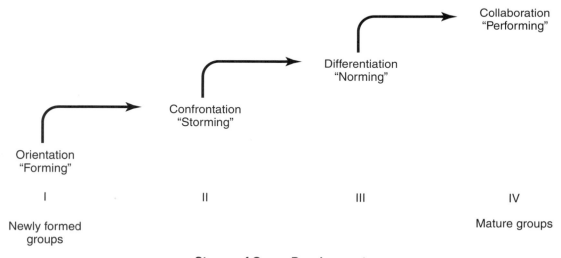

Exhibit 10.1 Stages of Group Development

Orientation ("Forming")

The first stage for almost every group is an orientation stage when members learn about the purposes of the group and the roles of each member. This stage is marked by caution, confusion, courtesy, and commonality. Individual members must decide how the group will be structured and how much they are willing to commit themselves to the group. The formal leader, or the person who assumes the leadership role, typically exerts great influence in structuring the group and shaping member expectations.

Members strive to discover the "rules of the game," and the biases and motives of other group members. During this stage, members should get acquainted with each other and share their expectations about the group's goals and objectives. Efforts to rush this process by expecting members to be fully open and express their real feelings can be very destructive, both to the individuals and the group. The trust and openness necessary for members to feel willing to share intimate details comes in later stages of development.

Confrontation ("Storming")

Although conflict is not a necessary phase of group development, the purposes of the group and the expectations of group members are eventually challenged in most groups. This stage contains conflict, confrontation, concern, and criticism. Struggles for individual power and influence are common. Challenging the group's goals can be a healthy process if the conflict results in greater cohesiveness and acceptance.[2] If the conflict becomes extremely intense and dysfunctional, the group may dissolve, or continue as an ineffective group that never advances to higher levels of group maturity.

Differentiation ("Norming")

The major issues at this stage of development are how the tasks and responsibilities will be divided among members and how members will evaluate each other's performance. Individual differences are recognized, and task assignments are based on skills and abilities. If a group can resolve its authority conflicts and create shared expectations regarding its goals and task assignments, it can become a cohesive group and achieve its goals. At this stage, the members often feel the group is successful as they pursue their group goals, and indeed their short-term effectiveness may look rather impressive. As unique situations arise that violate personal expectations, however, the long-term effectiveness of the group will require additional maturity in resolving conflicts and reestablishing shared expectations.

Collaboration ("Performing")

The highest level of group maturity is the stage of collaboration, where there is a feeling of cohesiveness and commitment to the group. Individual differences are accepted without being labeled good or bad. Conflict is neither eliminated nor squelched, but is identified and resolved through group discussion. Conflict concerns substantive issues relevant to the group task rather than emotional issues regarding group processes. Decisions are made through rational group discussion, and no attempts are made to force decisions or to present a false unanimity. The members of the group are aware of the group's processes and the extent of their own involvement in the group.

Separation ("Adjourning")

Some groups go through an "adjourning" stage by consciously deciding to disband, usually because the group has completed its tasks or because members choose to go their separate ways. This stage is typically characterized by feelings of closure and compromise as members prepare to leave, often with sentimental feelings.

Virtual Teams

A virtual team is a group that relies on technology to interact and accomplish its tasks. They may occasionally meet together in face-to-face interaction; but most of their interactions rely on various types of technology while their members are in different locations and possibly different time zones. The technologies they use can be either synchronous or asynchronous, depending on whether the interaction is in real time or delayed. Synchronous technologies allow team members to communicate with each other simultaneously in real time through teleconferencing, videoconferencing, instant messaging, and electronic meetings. Asynchronous technologies allow members to respond according to their own schedule, and include e-mail, electronic bulletin boards, and websites. The use of virtual teams in organizations has dramatically increased in recent years. Global teams are being used to collaborate with other countries, and technology has allowed for the increased use of global teams across a variety of industries.

Example

International Business Machines Corp. programmer Rob Nicholson has never met most of the 50 colleagues with whom he collaborates on writing software; they are scattered across three continents. But Mr. Nicholson feels part of a team from the moment he logs on each morning in Hursley, England. When his colleagues in India learn that he is online, they begin asking questions. Mr. Nicholson checks notes on interactive bulletin boards, or wikis, that his team shares. One day, for example, he found notes from team-mates in India suggesting changes to a proposed software design that he had posted the previous night; he revised the design that day.[3]

Characteristics of Effective Teams

Some teams are considerably more successful than others in accomplishing their goals and satisfying the needs of their members. Douglas McGregor identifies eleven dimensions of group functioning and argues that these dimensions make the difference between highly effective teams and ineffective teams.[4] Each dimension presents a continuum showing the differences between effective teams on the right and ineffective teams on the left.

1. *Atmosphere and relationships:* What kinds of relationships exist among team members?
   Formal and reserved ←——————→ Close and friendly
2. *Member participation:* Does everyone participate in the group activities and interactions?
   Some participate more ←——————→ There is equal
   than others participation
3. *Goal understanding and acceptance:* How well do members accept the objectives of the team and commit themselves to them?
   No commitment ←——————→ Total commitment
4. *Listening and sharing information:* Are people willing to listen to each other or are they afraid of looking foolish for suggesting creative ideas?
   There is no listening ←——————→ People listen and
   or sharing share
5. *Handling conflicts and disagreements:* Are conflict and disagreement tolerated and used to improve the group or are they avoided, brushed aside, or flamed into conflict?
   If they are not ignored, ←——————→ Conflict is dealt with
   they result in hostility and resolved
6. *Decision making:* How are decisions made? How many members participate in making group decisions and have an opportunity to provide input?
   Autocratically ←——————→ By consensus
7. *Evaluation of member performance:* What kind of feedback do members receive about their performance?
   Criticism and personal ←——————→ Frank, frequent, and
   attacks objective feedback
8. *Expressing feelings:* Do members feel free to express their feelings openly on more than just task issues?
   True feelings must ←——————→ Open expression
   remain hidden is welcomed

9. *Division of labor:* Are task assignments clearly made and willingly accepted?

    Poorly structured   ←————————→   Effective job
    job assignments   specialization

10. *Leadership:* How are the leaders selected? Are the leadership functions shared?

    Leadership is lacking   ←————————→   Leadership is shared
    or dominated by one   and effective
    person

11. *Attention to process:* Is the group conscious of its own operations? Can it monitor and improve its own processes?

    Unaware of group   ←————————→   Aware of operations
    operations   and monitors them

Effective teams share several important characteristics: the atmosphere is close and friendly; all members participate in the group; all members are committed to the team's goals; members listen to each other and share information; decisions are made by consensus; conflict is dealt with openly and resolved; members receive frank and objective feedback and feel free to express their feelings openly; there is a division of labor with shared leadership; and the team is aware of its own operations and able to monitor itself.

Group Structure

As a group develops, a structure emerges that influences what it does and how well it performs. Group structure is not an easy concept to explain because it does not refer to specific, observable objects. Group structure is the stable pattern of relationships among group members that maintain the group and help it achieve its goal. The major variables defining group structure are the group's roles and norms. Group roles are the task activities and responsibilities the group members perform; group norms are general expectations about how members ought to behave. Situational factors that alter the relationships among group members also influence group structure, and this section examines three of these situational factors: group size, social density, and nature of the task. Later sections examine group roles and group norms in greater detail.

Group Size

Perhaps the most visible factor influencing group structure is the size of the group. Groups vary enormously in size, from a dyad (two-person group) or a triad (three-person group) to as large as 400 to 500 members (such as the House of Representatives).

Size and Participation

Small groups provide opportunities for each member to be actively involved in the group. As the group gets larger, however, participation declines rather rapidly. A small graduate seminar with four students, for example, allows each student to participate freely in the discussion, while students in large classes have limited opportunities. Large, informal groups must develop a method that allows members to participate in an orderly manner so that everyone doesn't speak at once. When an informal group exceeds eight to twelve individuals, a significant part of the time, called process time, can be wasted simply trying to decide who should participate next.

Size and Satisfaction

As the size of a group increases, the satisfaction of the group members with the group and their involvement in it tend to increase—"the more the merrier"—but only up to a point. A five-person group provides twice as many opportunities for friendly interaction as a three-person group. Beyond a certain point, however (probably fewer than ten to fifteen members), increasing size results in reduced satisfaction. Members of an extremely large group cannot identify with the group's accomplishments nor experience the same degree of cohesiveness and participation as members of a smaller group.

Size and Performance

The relationship between group size and performance depends on whether the task is an additive task, conjunctive task, or disjunctive task.

On additive tasks the final group product is the sum of the individual contributions. Additive tasks are sometimes referred to as pooled interdependence, since the individual contribution of each member simply adds to the group product. On additive tasks, larger groups should produce more than smaller groups. However, as the size of the group increases, the average productivity of each member tends to decline due to social loafing, a concept that will be discussed later.

Example

Interviewing customers leaving a store as part of a consumer survey is an additive task. Three interviewers working together will survey more customers than one interviewer working alone, but the three working together in one location will probably not conduct as many interviews as they would have if they had been working alone in separate locations.

Conjunctive tasks are those that can be divided into interdependent subtasks and then assigned to various group members through a "division of labor." The overall performance depends on the successful completion of each subtask. The group's maximum performance is limited by the capacities of the least capable member. A chain, for example, is only as strong as its weakest link.

Example

The filming of an event by a television news team is a conjunctive task and each member's contribution is essential to the final product. A mistake by any member means failure for the whole group, whether it is a bad interview, a bad picture, or bad sound.

Disjunctive tasks are decision-making tasks that require the group to select the best solution. Disjunctive tasks include making simple dichotomous decisions (yes or no) as well as selecting the best solution from a list of alternatives.

Example

An early study on the performance of individuals and groups in performing a disjunctive task, asked individuals working alone or groups working together to arrive at a solution to the following problem: "On one side of a river are three wives and three very jealous husbands. All of the men but none of the women can row. Get them all across the river in the smallest number of trips by means of a boat carrying no more than three people at one time. No man will allow his wife to be in the presence of another man unless he is also there."[5]

Disjunctive tasks require at least one individual with sufficient insight to solve the problem. As a group gets larger, there is a greater probability that the group will contain at least one person with superior insight. In the study just mentioned, correct solutions to the problem of the three couples were produced by 60 percent of the groups, but only 14 percent of the individuals who worked alone.

On disjunctive tasks, therefore, the potential performance of the group depends on the performance of its best member. The term potential performance is used here instead of actual performance because the actual performance is usually something less than the potential performance. Although the potential performance of a group performing a disjunctive task increases with group size, the actual performance is typically less because the group suffers from process losses. Process losses are the inefficiencies that arise from having to organize and coordinate larger groups. The use of appropriate technology, such as computer mediated communication networks, can facilitate the flow of information in large groups and reduce the process losses to some extent. Large groups tend to restrict communication, inhibit creative thought processes, and reduce the personal commitment of group members.[6] Therefore, actual performance equals potential performance minus process losses.

Actual Performance = (Potential Performance − Process Losses)

Social Density

The interactions among group members are influenced by the physical or spatial locations of group members—whether they are physically separated or close together. Consequently, considerable interest has been expressed in the effects of modern architectural arrangements. Many modern offices use an open office plan with many desks in a large open room or small cubicles separated by partitions rather than separate rooms connected by long hallways. The concentration of people within an area is called social density, which is measured by square feet per person or the number of group members within a certain walking distance. Walking distance is used rather than straight-line distance since it is the distance someone must go to have face-to-face contact that is important.

Some organizational studies have found that greater social density improves performance because of greater accessibility. In a research-and-development organization, for example, reducing the distance between desks tended to improve performance by increasing the flow of technical information. In another technical organization, engineers reported less stress and tension when colleagues and other authority figures were located in close proximity. Likewise, the employees of a petroleum company reported greater feedback, friendship opportunities, and satisfaction with work when their social density was increased because of relocation.[7]

Obviously, the performance of a group will not endlessly increase as social density increases. At some point, the conditions become too crowded and people get in each other's way. The optimal social density depends on the nature of the task, the amount of feedback members need from each other, and their needs for privacy. Most studies of open office plans have found that employees generally dislike open office plans because of a lack of privacy. A large number of studies have shown that high levels of social density in organizations produce feelings of crowdedness, intentions to quit, high levels of stress, and low levels of satisfaction and performance. Although high social density normally has only a small effect on performance, the effects appear to be larger among employees who have a high need for privacy and who are performing complex tasks that require intense concentration.[8]

Nature of the Task

The kinds of interactions among group members depend on the kinds of tasks they are performing. Three types of tasks have already been described: additive, conjunctive, and disjunctive tasks. The need for coordination among group members is much greater for conjunctive tasks than it is for additive or disjunctive tasks.

> **Example**
>
> *If five students decided to sell tickets by telephone, they could divide the student directory into five sections, and each one could call the students in one section. Since this is an additive task, the need for coordination is minimal, and the performance of the group would simply be the sum of each individual's sales. Deciding how to divide the student directory would be a disjunctive task that could be done by one individual or a brief discussion, and it, too, requires minimal coordination.*

With a conjunctive task the need for coordination increases as the task becomes more complex.

> **Example**
>
> *Organizing and presenting a new product development conference is a conjunctive task that would require the coordinated efforts of many people from several departments, including research, sales, training, production, and finance. Playing basketball, another conjunctive task, is an even more complex activity that requires team members to constantly coordinate their efforts and even anticipate each other's moves.*

The relationships among group structure, the nature of the task, and task difficulty help to determine the best organizational structure. This topic will be discussed again in Chapter 13. There we will see that the structure of an organization needs to vary depending on the nature of the task and the need for coordination. Organizations that have highly specialized tasks require special structures to coordinate the activities of employees, especially when the activities change frequently. The same general conclusion applies here in the study of groups. Groups that perform complex conjunctive tasks require greater coordination among group members than groups performing simple additive or disjunctive tasks.

> **Example**
>
> *As a basketball team develops more complex offensive and defensive plays, team members are assigned to perform specialized activities, and the need for constant coordination among team members during the game increases.*

Group Roles

A *role* refers to the expected behaviors attached to a position or job. In organizations, roles are briefly described by position titles and more extensively described by job descriptions. In athletic teams, positions have designated titles, such as point guard, power forward, middle linebacker, and goalie. Informal groups usually do not have explicitly stated roles; one group member may perform several roles or several members may alternate performing the same role. In formal groups, however, roles are usually designated or assigned. These assigned roles are prescribed by the organization as a means of dividing the labor and assigning responsibility. Emergent roles develop naturally to meet the needs of group members or assist in achieving formal goals. The dynamics in many groups often result in emergent roles replacing assigned roles as people express their individuality and assertiveness.

Work Roles and Maintenance Roles

Group members may be expected to perform a variety of different behaviors. Exhibit 10.2 makes a distinction between three major kinds of group roles: work roles, maintenance roles, and blocking roles.[9]

Work roles are task-oriented activities involved in accomplishing the work and achieving the group objective. Work roles include such activities as clarifying the purpose of the group, developing a strategy for accomplishing the work, delegating job assignments, and evaluating progress.

Maintenance roles are the social-emotional activities of group members that maintain their involvement and personal commitment to the group. These roles include encouraging other members to participate, praising and rewarding others for their contributions, reconciling arguments and disagreements, and maintaining a friendly group atmosphere.

Blocking roles are activities that disrupt or destroy the group, such as dominating the discussion, attacking other group members, disagreeing unreasonably with other group members, and distracting the group with irrelevant issues or unnecessary humor.

Exhibit 10.2 Group Roles

Work Roles	Maintenance Roles	Blocking Roles
1. *Initiator:* Proposing tasks or actions; defining group problems; suggesting a procedure.	1. *Harmonizer:* Attempting to reconcile disagreements; reducing tension; getting people to explore differences.	1. *Aggressor:* Deflating another's status; attacking the group or its values; joking in a barbed or semi-concealed way.
2. *Informer:* Offering facts; giving expression of feeling; giving an opinion.	2. *Gatekeeper:* Helping to keep communication channels open; facilitating the participation of others; suggesting procedures that permit sharing remarks.	2. *Blocker:* Disagreeing and opposing beyond reason; resisting stubbornly the group's wish for personal reasons; using a hidden agenda to thwart the movement of a group.
3. *Clarifier:* Interpreting ideas or suggestions; defining terms; clarifying issues for the group.	3. *Consensus tester:* Asking if a group is nearing a decision; assessing whether there is agreement on a possible conclusion.	3. *Dominator:* Asserting authority or superiority to manipulate the group; interrupting contributions of others; controlling by means of flattery or patronizing behavior.
4. *Summarizer:* Pulling together related ideas; restating suggestions; offering a decision or conclusion for the group to consider.	4. *Encourager:* Being friendly, warm and responsive to others; indicating by facial expression or remark the acceptance of others' contributions.	4. *Comedian:* Making a comical display of others or one's lack of involvement; using sarcasm and humor to disrupt the group; seeking recognition in ways not relevant to the group task.
5. *Reality tester:* Making a critical assessment of the situation and problem; testing an idea against data to see if it would work.	5. *Compromiser:* Offering a compromise that yields status; admitting error; modifying the group's policies or objectives.	5. *Avoidance behavior:* Pursuing special interests not related to task; staying off the subject to avoid commitment; preventing group from facing controversy.

Source: Kenneth D. Benne and Paul Sheats, "Functional Roles of Group Members," *Journal of Social Issues,* 2 (1948), pp. 42–47.

Deciding whether someone is performing a blocking role is sometimes difficult because the behavior may not be intentional. For example, a member may question a conclusion to force the group to think more carefully about an issue. Other group members may feel that this person is stubbornly resisting the emerging consensus, simply trying to disrupt its progress. Likewise, a good joke may help to relieve tension and keep the group working together, or it may disrupt the group discussion and prevent the group from returning to a crucial issue.

Both work roles and maintenance roles are necessary for effective group functioning, and they can be performed either by a designated leader or as emergent roles by someone else. These two group roles will be discussed again in Chapter 17, where they will be used to examine leader behaviors.

Role Episode

Role expectations are communicated to individuals during a role episode, which is the interaction between role senders and the person receiving the role.[10] A role episode is diagrammed in Exhibit 10.3. A role sender may be anyone attempting to change the behavior of another individual, called the focal person. In formal groups, the most legitimate role senders are generally supervisors, project directors, and other organizational leaders responsible for delegating assignments. In reality, however, every group member participates as a role sender to other group members. Even subordinates tend to communicate how they expect their supervisors to behave.

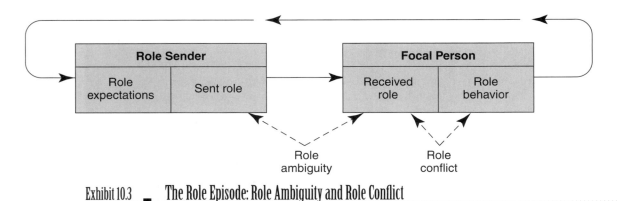

Exhibit 10.3 — The Role Episode: Role Ambiguity and Role Conflict

Source: Adapted from Daniel Katz and Robert Kahn, *The Social Psychology of Organizations*, 2nd ed. (New York: Wiley, 1978), p. 196.

Role senders typically communicate only a small percentage of their role expectations. Some expectations are so self-evident that they do not need to be communicated (such as answering your telephone when you hear it ring), while others are not communicated because of uncertainty on the part of the role sender (such as whether the supervisor should say anything to group members involved in horseplay).

The focal person may or may not respond to the role sender. Communication problems may create a discrepancy between the sent role and the received role. But even if the expectations are accurately received, the focal person may not respond because of a lack of motivation or inadequate ability. The feedback loop, going from the focal person back to the role sender, illustrates the ongoing nature of a role episode. A role episode is a continuous process of evaluating each other's behavior and communicating expectations, both overtly and covertly.

An important factor influencing how well the focal person will respond to a sent role is the focal person's state of role readiness. Role readiness concerns the focal person's ability and willingness to accept the responsibility associated with a new role.

> **Example**
>
> *A new employee who has had a broad background of relevant experience and is prepared to immediately perform a new job would have a high degree of role readiness. A lack of role readiness occurs when union stewards resist promotions to supervisory positions because they have difficulty changing their thinking from hourly wages, seniority, and job security to salary, merit pay, and raising productivity.*

Role Ambiguity

Role ambiguity occurs when there is a discrepancy between the sent role and the received role, as shown in Exhibit 10.3. Ambiguity often comes from confusion when delegating job responsibilities. Many jobs do not have written job descriptions and when employees are told what to do, their instructions are often unclear. Supervisors may contribute to the ambiguity because they may not understand how the job should be done, what the standards of acceptable performance are, how performance will be evaluated, or the limits of the employees' authority and responsibility. Even when supervisors know this information, the instructions usually overwhelm new employees.

The consequences of role ambiguity are frustration and other signs of stress. Moderate levels of ambiguity may be tolerable and even desirable, since some employees like to structure their own environment. However, extreme role ambiguity creates an unhealthy condition that contributes to dissatisfaction and turnover.

Role Conflict

Role conflict comes from inconsistency between the received role and role behavior, as shown in Exhibit 10.3, but role conflict is not the same as role ambiguity. The conditions that create role conflict and the amount of discomfort it creates seem to be unique to each person. The same situation may cause more stress for one person than for another. There are four major types of role conflict.[11]

- Intrasender role conflict occurs when a single role sender communicates incompatible role expectations to the focal person. For example, a manager could tell the staff members that they are each expected to perform the role of critical evaluator and challenge every decision, but they are also expected to work together cooperatively and be team players.

- Intersender role conflict occurs when two or more role senders communicate incompatible expectations to the focal person. The first-line supervisors in most organizations typically experience rather intense intersender role conflict. Upper management expects them to tighten the controls to increase productivity, reduce errors, and eliminate wasted time. In contrast, their subordinates send messages that the supervisors need to loosen the controls and be less interested in productivity, quality, and wasted time. Boundary role occupants, those who straddle the boundary between the organization and its clients and customers, are also prone to experience intersender role conflict. For example, salespeople, schoolteachers, and purchasing agents often receive incompatible instructions from people within the organization and external clients or customers.

- Person-role conflict occurs when people are asked to behave in ways that are inconsistent with their personal values. An administrative aide, for example, may be told that a report must be completed before going home, even if it means several hours of overtime. But working overtime would mean missing the school play, and the aide's daughter is the star of the play. Employees experience person-role conflict when they are asked to do something illegal or unethical, such as falsifying reports or lying to customers.

- Role overload is caused by the conflicting demands of too many roles (also called interrole conflict). People fill a variety of roles, both within the organization and in their personal lives. We cannot be in two places at one time, and conflicting time schedules often create severe role overload, forcing us to reassess which role should take precedence. A human resource manager, for example, may experience role overload because of the inconsistent demands accompanying numerous roles, such as affirmative action officer, safety director, facilitator of a quality control circle, career development counselor, and manager of the Human Resource planning system. In addition to the roles she fills in the organization are her roles outside the organization as a wife, mother, and fundraiser for the United Way campaign. These multiple roles contain conflicts of time, interests, and loyalty, because they cannot all be filled simultaneously.

Group Norms

Group norms are the commonly held beliefs of group members about appropriate conduct. As such, they represent general expectations or codes of conduct that imply a duty or obligation. Group norms identify the standards against which the behavior of group members will be evaluated and help group members know what they should or should not do. Group norms typically develop around the eleven issues presented earlier regarding group effectiveness. Every group creates its own norms and standards for evaluating the appropriateness of individual behavior.

Example

The members of a fraternity created a group norm that it wasn't "cool" to act like dedicated students—a little studying was OK, but it should not interfere with social activities. To get good grades, several fraternity members had to lie about how they spent their time and not admit that their dates and weekend trips were actually to the library.

Example

The norm in an engineering firm was that no one should leave before the supervisor leaves. None of the engineers actually accomplished very much after the regular working hours; but even though they quit working, they did not leave.

Group norms are essential to group effectiveness. Although norms limit individuality and restrict the creativity of individuals, they create greater predictability within the group by structuring its activities.

Example

In a typical classroom most students adhere to the norm of raising their hands when they want to comment. This hand-raising norm prevents some class members from making insightful comments, but it also provides for an orderly class discussion.

Development of Norms

Over time, groups develop a variety of norms regarding many aspects of behavior. The most crucial group norms are those regarding issues of central concern to the group. In general, groups tolerate less deviation from norms regarding important group concerns.

> **Example**
>
> *A highly enforced norm for the offensive unit of a football team is that no one talks in the huddle but the quarterback. Accuracy in listening to the quarterback's instructions is vital to the success of the team. Wearing wrist-bands or putting stickers on helmets, however, are not closely enforced norms because they are not as important to the team's success.*

Group norms are typically created and enforced for four reasons:

- they identify the "rules of the game" which helps the group survive;
- they teach group members how to behave and make their behavior more predictable;
- they help the group avoid embarrassing situations;
- they express the central values of the group and clarify what is distinctive about its identity.

> **Example**
>
> *The norms governing the use of elevators call for people leaving the elevator to exit before other passengers enter. This unwritten procedure may be slightly slower than when everyone moves at once, but it is more orderly.*

> **Example**
>
> *After weeks of confusion and conflict, the members of a department established a norm of going around the circle and allowing each member to make a report. This process allowed for a much more orderly flow of conversation than when the members competed to present their ideas first.*

Two almost opposite theories explain how group norms are developed. In one explanation, norms are viewed as the product of the shared attitudes and beliefs that group members bring to the group. These are called injunctive norms since they result from the influence attempts of group members and are enforced through peer pressure.[12] The norms emerge from the group consensus after the group discusses the issue or from a dominant group member who simply voices an opinion. If no one expresses a dissenting view, the group may adopt the dominant member's viewpoint.

> **Example**
>
> *A norm of no smoking during the weekly planning meetings was created when one of the division managers took the ashtray off the table, put it on the shelf behind her, and said, "There's no need to get lung cancer." Her action went uncontested and no one said anything; thereafter, a no-smoking norm existed.*

Another explanation for how group norms are created is that they are post-hoc (after the fact) justifications. These are called descriptive norms, since they emerge from watching how others behave and then adopting the same patterns. After the group has been functioning for a while, we observe certain patterns of behavior and explain them as being a group norm. Many performance norms are simply justifications for what has happened in the past.

> **Example**
>
> *At Quigley Refractory all of the machines are stopped twenty minutes early so workers can wash up, and 38 pallets are considered a full day's work. These standards have never been part of the labor agreement; they are simply norms that have evolved over time.*

Generally Accepted Norms

Our day-to-day behavior is influenced by so many general social norms that we often fail to recognize them. Most people are members of numerous groups, and these multiple memberships generate a lengthy list of norms, lending regularity and predictability to our behavior.

Social Conduct

Social conduct norms are designed to create a pleasant social atmosphere, such as smiling when you pass a friend in a hallway, answering the phone when it rings by saying hello, and saying goodbye before you hang up. When we are introduced, we shake hands and say, "I'm pleased to meet you," whether it's true or not. If someone asks, "How are you?" the norm is to say "Fine!" not to give a full medical report. Walking away while someone is talking to you is considered a norm violation, and leaving in the middle of a lecture or public address is generally considered impolite.

Dress Codes

Some organizations, such as the military, police, hospitals, restaurants, and hotels, have formal dress standards for their members. The dress codes in other organizations may be more informal and unwritten, but just as powerful. Many organizations, especially financial institutions and law firms, expect employees to wear conservative dresses, shirts, ties, and suits.

Performance Norms

How fast group members are expected to work and how much they should produce are important issues to most groups. Therefore, performance norms are created to guide individual efforts. Supervisors can become very frustrated with a group's performance norms when they are unreasonably low or inconsistent with the organization's goals. Sometimes they appear to be very irrational because they are not in the worker's best interests either. In many work groups, productivity is determined more by the group's performance norms than by the ability and skill of the employees.

> **Example**
>
> *In the bank-wiring experiment of the famous Hawthorne Studies, a group of men maintained an arbitrarily low production norm that restricted productivity, even though the workers were paid according to how much work they did, and this study was conducted during the Great Depression when the workers needed additional income.*

Reward Allocation Norms

Groups develop norms governing how rewards should be distributed to the group members. The most commonly studied reward allocation norms are equality, equity, and social responsibility.

- The norm of equality suggests that everyone should be treated the same. We all share equally in our status as group members; therefore, the rewards that come to the group should be distributed equally to everyone.
- The norm of equity suggests that the rewards should be allocated on the basis of merit according to each person's contribution to the group. Those who have made the largest contribution to the group's product, either through effort, skill, or ability, should receive a larger share of the rewards.
- The norm of social responsibility suggests that the rewards should be allocated on the basis of need. People who have special needs, especially those who are disadvantaged or disabled, should receive special consideration and a larger share of the rewards, regardless of their contribution.

Norm of Reciprocity

The norm of reciprocity suggests that when people make an effort to help you, you should feel an obligation to help them at a later time. Among some people, this norm is a very firmly held expectation, and they keep track of favors and who owes whom. Although some people feel that service should be rendered specifically to those who have helped them, others have a much broader interpretation of whom they should help. For example, a mentor may be very happy to help a new employee, not because the mentor expects help from the new employee in the future, but because of the help that the mentor received as a new employee from someone else in the past.

Norm Violation

Although group norms are a group product, they may not match the private beliefs of all members. Norms are accepted in various degrees by the group members. Some norms may be completely accepted by all group members, while other norms are only partially accepted. Norms vary according to their inclusivity, or the number of people to whom they apply. Some norms are nearly universal in nature while others apply only to specific group members.

Example

The prohibition against theft is so widely shared that it applies to all members of society, regardless of status or position. Production norms, however, may not equally apply to everyone, especially a lead worker who is expected to spend part of the time training other employees.

For a norm to be maintained there must be a shared awareness that the group supports it and thinks it is appropriate. Although some members may violate the norm, it will continue to survive as long as the majority uphold and accept it. If adherence to the norm continues to erode, it will eventually collapse and no longer serve as a standard for evaluating behavior.

Example

Most students have witnessed the disintegration of student conduct norms. One or two students may violate the norm of raising their hands without the norm being destroyed, but when three or four more students begin to violate the norm, the class dissolves into a shouting match where all the students are speaking at once rather than raising their hands and waiting to be acknowledged.

Conformity to the essential group norms is a requirement for sustained group membership. Group members who do not conform to important norms are excluded, ignored, or ridiculed by the group as punishment. The ultimate punishment is to be expelled from the group.

Because of their status, group leaders are in a better position to violate the norms than are other group members. Indeed, leaders sometimes deviate slightly from accepted group norms as a means of asserting their uniqueness or superiority over other group members.

Example

Group members must not come late to work and tardiness is often enforced by peer pressure. But, managers think they can come when they want as a privilege of being a manager and escape the censure of the group.

Group norms are difficult to change. Since they were created by the group, they must be changed by the group. Organizational leaders are sometimes successful in helping groups change norms by communicating new expectations of behavior. They are successful to the extent that they can get the group to accept what they say as the new standard of behavior.

Conformity

Group norms provide regularity and predictability to the behavior of group members, but only if members conform to them; norms do not exist without conformity. Unless the members create pressure to enforce the group norms, they will disappear and be replaced by other norms. Conformity means yielding to group influence by doing or saying something you might otherwise choose not to do. To say you have conformed means you have succumbed to social influence and behaved differently from how you would have behaved in the absence of the influence.

Why do people conform? Organizations have been criticized for needless pressures that force people to conform in their thinking, dress, and living habits. Although conformity does reduce variability in the ways people behave, it also increases individual freedom by providing greater predictability and regularity of behavior. Group norms help groups achieve their goals, and as conformity increases, the likelihood of success also increases. Therefore, conformity reduces individuality and personal autonomy, but it also contributes to greater success for both the group and its members.

Pressures to Conform

Groups use two major social influence processes to obtain conformity: reward dependence and information dependence.[13]

Reward Dependence

Groups have the capacity to reward or punish their members. Leaders of formal groups can use organizational rewards and punishments to induce conformity, such as promotions, pay increases, performance evaluations, and job assignments. Informal groups have powerful rewards for inducing conformity among group members, such as praise, recognition, and social approval for good behavior, or criticism, ridicule, and harassment for deviant behavior.

Information Dependence

Individuals also conform to group pressure because they depend on others for information about the appropriateness of their thoughts, feelings, and behavior. We are particularly dependent on others in novel situations. We rely heavily on others to know how to behave, to interpret our feelings, and to help us understand our emotions.

Levels of Conformity

People conform to social pressure at three very different levels depending on their motives. Walking on the right side of a sidewalk illustrates a very different level of conformity from refusing to accept a bribe from a client because it violates company policy. When you conform to these accepted norms, what are your motives? Conforming to group norms occurs for three significantly different motives: compliance, identification, and internalization.[14]

Compliance

At the lowest level of conformity, people comply with social pressure either to obtain rewards or to avoid punishment. Peer pressure and fear of harassment or criticism induce group members to comply. Compliance, however, is usually quite temporary and is limited to the specific situation. If a police officer is parked at an intersection, the fear of being ticketed will probably induce compliance to stop for the stop sign. If the fines for overdue library books are exorbitantly high, students will probably return them on time. If supervisors receive a $50 bonus for a good safety rating, they will probably conduct periodic safety inspections simply to obtain the reward.

Example

The members of a university's privacy committee decided that they did not understand the Family Educational Rights and Privacy Act (FERPA) adequately to properly monitor its implementation on campus. The committee members agreed that each member should read a training booklet explaining the act before the next meeting. To motivate them, the chair said that she would construct a short exam to test their knowledge at the next meeting. Not wanting to fail this exam was the primary motivation for several committee members to study the material.

Identification

The second level of conformity is called identification because the motive is the desire to be accepted by others who are perceived as important. Identification is the process of behaving like "significant others" and adopting their characteristics and personal attributes. Not only do we want to be like them and acquire their attributes, we also want them to think well of us and to approve of our attitudes and actions. Through imitative learning, we tend to model their behavior and accept what they say and how they behave. People who identify with a significant other will stop at stop signs, return library books, and work independently on take-home exams if that is the way they think the significant other expects them to behave.

Example

Some members of the FERPA Committee were motivated to study the act before the next meeting because they respected the committee chair and she asked them to do it. They knew that privacy violations at the university would reflect negatively on her because she had a legal responsibility to monitor compliance and they wanted to help her.

Internalization

At the highest level of conformity, the standards of behavior are internalized and become part of the person's basic character. At the internalization level of conformity norms are followed because the person accepts the beliefs, attitudes, and values supporting the norms.

Conformity does not occur because it achieves rewards, avoids punishment, or pleases others; it occurs because the behavior is perceived as morally right and proper. At this level you stop for stop signs, return library books, and avoid cheating on exams not to avoid punishment nor to receive the praise of others, but because you personally believe it is right and you are committed to abide by your own personal standards of right and wrong, which coincide with the group norms.

Example

A couple of FERPA Committee members were motivated to study the act and participate actively in the committee discussions because they strongly believed in the right of privacy and their obligation to help the university operate effectively and lawfully. Their desires were to ensure that the correct policies were established, that all faculty and administrators understood the policies, and that they were fairly administered.

Factors Influencing Conformity

Some situations exert greater pressures on group members to conform than others. As a general rule, the pressures to conform are greater in the following situations:

- Larger groups tend to exert greater pressure than smaller groups;
- Group members who are perceived as experts or as highly qualified or experienced persons exert greater pressures to conform than members who are not considered highly skilled;
- A united group exerts much greater pressure to conform than a group divided by dissension. In some cases, the presence of a single dissenter is enough to destroy the influence of the group;
- Conformity increases as the situation becomes more ambiguous. When people do not know what is expected of them, they become increasingly dependent on the influence of others;
- People who are insecure and lack self-confidence are more likely to conform than people who are confident in their judgments. When insecure people discover that their opinions do not agree with the majority opinion, they tend to question their own judgments and perceptions. People who are high in self-confidence, however, discredit the group when their opinions differ from the groups' opinions;
- The pressure to adhere to a social norm increases when conformity is essential to the group's success. As a group gets closer to achieving its goal, the anticipation of success increases the pressure to conform and makes nonconformity less acceptable. Deviation from the group norm becomes absolutely unacceptable at crucial times.

Example

During the playoff games at the end of a season, team members experience particularly strong pressures to abide by the group norms. As the probability of a strike increases, unions demand greater conformity among union members as a show of strength to management.

Effects of the Group on Individual Behavior

How does the presence of a group influence an individual's performance? Suppose you were laying bricks with four other bricklayers. Would more bricks get laid if the five of you worked together as a group along one side of a wall, or would it be better to assign each of you to different walls on the construction site? Two contrasting processes have been identified to explain the effects of the group on individual performance: social facilitation and social loafing. Another concept, called deindividuation, also explains the effects of a group on individual behavior.

Social Facilitation

Early studies in social psychology noted that people performed better as members of a group than they did when performing alone. It was observed, for example, that cyclists rode faster if they raced in head-to-head competition than when they raced alone to beat the clock. Subsequent research showed that the presence of an audience or crowd or simply the presence of other coworkers facilitated the performance of well-learned responses, such as crossing out letters and words, doing multiplication problems, and other simple tasks. This process, called the social facilitation effect, is caused by the mere presence of others rather than direct competition between individuals, since a number of studies found that subjects performed better even in front of a passive audience. The social facilitation effect has been observed not only on people, both adults and children, but also on an unusual assortment of other animals including, ants, fish, chickens, rats, and cockroaches.

One explanation for the social facilitation effect is called evaluation apprehension. According to this explanation, the presence of others creates a higher level of arousal and motivation because we expect others to evaluate our performance, and their opinions matter to us. When others are watching we want to look good, sometimes for no other reason than that we want others to think well of us.

Although the presence of others may improve performance, it can also inhibit performance on some tasks. This process, called social inhibition effect, has been observed on complex learning tasks such as learning a maze or a list of nonsense syllables. Since the social inhibition effect is the opposite of the social facilitation effect, it is important to know when the presence of others will inhibit and when it will facilitate an individual's performance.

Perhaps the best explanation of the contradictory results relies on an important distinction between learning a new task and performing a well-learned task. The presence of others increases our level of arousal and motivation, which helps us perform well-learned responses.[15] Therefore, the presence of others tends to improve our performance on well-learned responses such as walking, running, bicycling, or playing the piano (for a highly skilled pianist). However, if the response has not been well learned, which is the case with all new learning situations, then the presence of others produces higher levels of arousal which inhibits performance. Therefore, according to social facilitation the learning of complex new tasks is best accomplished in isolation, but the performance of well-learned tasks will be facilitated by an audience.

Example

Larry Bird (Indiana State 1977–1979; Boston Celtics 1979–1992) was an extremely talented basketball player who was such an excellent shooter that he excelled under pressure. During his 13-year career, his field goal percentage averaged .496 and his free throw percentage averaged .896. One season he made 71 consecutive free throws and he won three consecutive NBA Long Distance Shootout titles. Larger crowds and more intense competition motivated him to shoot better.[16]

Social Loafing

Social loafing occurs when the members of a group exert less effort while working as a group than when working as individuals. Social loafing is the opposite of social facilitation, but it is different than social inhibition. The social inhibition effect occurs when the presence of others leads to such high levels of arousal that it disrupts the person's limited abilities. Social loafing, in contrast, is not attributed to a decline in ability but to a decline in motivation.

> **Example**
>
> *One of the earliest studies in social loafing examined how much effort individuals exerted in pulling on a rope, either individually or in a group. The average pressure exerted by each individual was 63 kilograms, which was more than double the average pressure exerted by a group of eight people pulling together (248 kilograms per group, or 31 kilograms per person).*[17]

Social loafing occurs primarily because the presence of other group members reduces each individual's identifiability. When individuals cannot be identified, there is no relationship between their efforts and their outcomes; therefore, they cannot be individually recognized for good effort or punished for poor performance. The social loafing effect becomes increasingly apparent in larger groups because of reduced personal identifiability. Social loafing also occurs in decision-making groups with cognitive tasks: people in groups exert less effort and less concentration, and they also use less complex judgment strategies than do single judges or judges working in pairs.

Deindividuation

The issue of identifiability is related to another process of group dynamics: deindividuation. Individuals often become lost in crowds and perform acts they would not perform if they were alone. Unruly crowds at rock concerts have produced hysterical screaming and uncontrolled emotions, angry fans at athletic contests have thrown objects at athletes and assaulted referees, and groups of union picketers have destroyed property and committed acts of violence. Stories of lynch mobs illustrate how individuals in a group get carried away and do things they would not have done without the presence of the group. Crowds have the capacity to create a mental homogeneity, called a collective mind, that is frequently irrational and often functions at lower moral and intellectual levels than isolated individuals.

Three mechanisms have been proposed to explain the process of deindividuation in groups. First, people are anonymous because they lose their sense of individual identification. Second, the contagion of the group causes people to act differently by reducing their inhibitions and allowing them to behave like other group members. Third, people become more suggestible in groups where they feel greater pressures to conform.

The loss of individuality has often been associated with rather undesirable social consequences. In a study of the warfare patterns of many cultures, for example, it was found that in cultures where warriors deindividuate themselves by wearing masks and paint, there is a greater tendency to torture captives than in cultures whose warriors are not deindividuated. Another study of trick-or-treaters on Halloween found that they were more likely to steal when they wore masks and remained anonymous than when they were clearly identifiable.[18]

Perhaps the most shocking study of deindividuation was the Stanford Prison study, conducted by Phillip Zimbardo.[19] In this study, twenty-four male students who were described as mature, emotionally stable, normal, intelligent people were randomly assigned to play the roles of guards or prisoners. Both the prisoners and the guards were given appropriate uniforms, and the prisoners were placed in three-man cells for the duration of the experiment, which was to be two weeks. The guards were instructed to run the prison, and the experimenter served only as a warden. The guards wore silver reflector sunglasses, which increased the level of deindividuation. The prisoners made only meager attempts to escape, and their behavior was described as that of servile, dehumanized robots. The behavior of the guards became tyrannical and brutal, and the situation became so ugly and repressive that the experiment had to be terminated after only six days instead of the two weeks originally planned.

Deindividuation does not necessarily create undesirable social behavior; it can also be positive. Although they don't attract as much attention, many groups have noble purposes and worthwhile social goals that sweep people along in productive activities. Schools, charitable foundations, religious groups, and even business organizations frequently create groups where individuals lose a sense of their own personal identity and are carried along as part of the group in activities that contribute to their own growth and development and to the betterment of society. Therefore, although groups can be destructive and abusive, they don't necessarily need to be that way. Those who have enjoyed the exhilaration of wildly cheering for their favorite athletic teams know how much fun being "lost in the crowd" can be.

Endnotes

1. B. W. Tuckman, "Developmental Sequences in Small Groups," *Psychological Bulletin*, vol. 63 (1965), pp. 384–399; Toby Berman-Rossi, "My Love Affair with Stages of Group Development," *Social Work with Groups*, vol. 25 (no. 1/2, 2002), pp. 151–158; Diane L. Miller, "The Stages of Group Development: A Retrospective Study of Dynamic Team Processes," *Canadian Journal of Administrative Sciences*, vol. 20 (2003), pp. 121–134.
2. Karen A. Jehn and Elizabeth A. Mannix, "The Dynamic Nature of Conflict: A Longitudinal Study of Intragroup Conflict and Group Performance," *Academy of Management Journal*, vol. 44 (2001), pp. 238–251.
3. Phred Dvorak, "How Teams Can Work Well Together From Far Apart," *The Wall Street Journal*, 17 September 2007, B4.
4. Douglas McGregor, *The Human Side of Enterprise* (New York: McGraw-Hill, 1960), pp. 232–240; see also Anthony T. Pescosolido, "Group Efficacy and Group Effectiveness: The Effects of Group Efficacy Over Time on Group Performance and Development," *Small Group Research*, vol. 34 (2003), pp. 20–42.
5. Marjorie Shaw, "A Comparison of Individuals and Small Groups in the Rational Solution of Complex Problems," *American Journal of Psychology*, vol. 44 (1932), pp. 491–504.
6. Paul Benjamin Lowry, Tom L. Roberts, Nicholas C. Romano, Jr., Paul D. Cheney and Ross T. Hightower, "The Impact of Group Size and Social Presence on Small-Group Communication: Does Computer-Mediated Communication Make a Difference?" *Small Group Research*, vol. 37 (2006), pp. 631–661.
7. T. J. Allen and D. I. Cohen, "Information Flow in R&D Laboratories," *Administrative Science Quarterly*, vol. 14 (1969), pp. 12–25; Robert H. Miles, "Roles Set Configuration as a Predictor of Role Conflict and Ambiguity in Complex Organizations," *Sociometry*, vol. 40 (1977), pp. 21–34; Andrew D. Szilagyi and W. E. Holland, "Changes in Social Density: Relationships with Perceptions of Job Characteristics, Role Stress, and Work Satisfaction," *Journal of Applied Psychology*, vol. 65 (1980), pp. 28–33.
8. Greg R. Oldham, "Effects of Changes in Workspace Partitions and Spatial Density on Employee Reactions: A Quasi-Experiment," *Journal of Applied Psychology*, vol. 73 (1988), pp. 253–258; Eric Sundstrom, *Work Places* (Cambridge, England: Cambridge University Press), 1986; Eric Sundstrom, Robert E. Burt, and Douglas Kamp, "Privacy at Work: Architectural Correlates of Job Satisfaction and Job Performance," *Academy of Management Journal*, vol. 23 (1980), pp. 101–107.
9. Kenneth D. Benne and P. Sheats, "Functional Roles of Group Members," Journal of Social Issues, vol. 2 (1948), pp. 42–47; Hal B. Gregersen, "Group Observer Instructions," in J. B. Ritchie and Paul Thompson, *Organizations and People*, 3rd ed. (St. Paul, Minn.: West, 1984), pp. 231–234.
10. Daniel Katz and Robert L. Kahn, *The Social Psychology of Organizations*, 2nd ed. (New York: Wiley, 1978), chap. 7.
11. Robert L. Kahn, D. M. Wolfe, R. P. Quinn, J. D. Snoek, and R. A. Rosenthal, *Organizational Stress: Studies in Role Conflict and Ambiguity* (New York: Wiley, 1964).
12. Mark G. Ehrhart and Stefanie E. Naumann, "Organizational Citizenship Behavior in Work Groups: A Group Norms Approach," *Journal of Applied Psychology*, vol. 89 (2004), pp. 960–974; M. Deutsch and H. B. Gerard, "A Study of Normative and Informational Social Influences Upon Individual Judgment," *Journal of Abnormal and Social Psychology*, vol. 51 (1955), pp. 629–636.

13. Edward E. Jones and Harold B. Gerard, *Foundations of Social Psychology* (New York: Wiley, 1967), Chaps. 3 and 4; Rod Bond, "Group Size and Conformity," *Group Processes & Intergroup Relations*, vol. 8 (2005), pp. 331–354.
14. H. C. Kelman, "Compliance, Identification, and Internalization: Three Processes of Opinion Change," *Journal of Conflict Resolution*, vol. 2 (1958), pp. 51–60.
15. Robert Zajonc, "Social Facilitation," *Science*, vol. 149 (1965), pp. 269–274.
16. *http://www.nba.com/history/players/bird_bio.html* as of 28 September 2007.
17. This early study by Ringelmann is reported by J. F. Dashiel, "Experimental Studies of the Influence of Social Situations on the Behavior of Individual Human Adults," in Carl Murchison (ed.), *The Handbook of Social Psychology* (Worcester, Mass.: Clark University Press, 1935).
18. R. I. Watson, "Investigation into Deindividuation Using a Cross Cultural Survey Technique," *Journal of Personality and Social Psychology*, vol. 25 (1973), pp. 342–345; E. Diener, S. Fraser, A. Beaman, and Z. Kellem, "Effects of Deindividuation Variables on Stealing Among Halloween Trick-or-Treaters," *Journal of Personality and Social Psychology*, vol. 33 (1976), pp. 178–183.
19. Phillip Zimbardo, *The Psychological Power and Pathology of Imprisonment*, statement prepared for the U.S. House of Representatives Committee on the Judiciary, (Subcommittee No. 3, Robert Kastemeyer, Chairman, Hearings on Prison Reform). Unpublished paper, Stanford University, 1971; http://www.prisonexp.org/ as of 28 September 2007.

Managerial Control

11

The Role of Finance and Financial Managers

The central goal of this chapter is to answer two major questions: "What is finance?" and "What do financial managers do?" Finance is the function in a business that acquires funds for the firm and manages those funds within the firm. Finance activities include preparing budgets; doing cash flow analysis; and planning for the expenditure of funds on such assets as plant, equipment, and machinery. Financial management is the job of managing a firm's resources so it can meet its goals and objectives. Without a carefully calculated financial plan, the firm has little chance for survival, regardless of its product or marketing effectiveness. Let's review the role of an accountant and compare it with that of a financial manager.

An accountant could be compared to a skilled laboratory technician who takes blood samples and other measures of a person's health and writes the findings on a health report (in business, the equivalent of a set of financial statements).[1] A financial manager of a business is the doctor who interprets the report and makes recommendations to the patient regarding changes that will improve the patient's health. In short, financial managers examine the financial data prepared by accountants and make recommendations to top executives regarding strategies for improving the health (financial performance) of the firm.

It should be clear that financial managers can make sound financial decisions only if they understand accounting information. Similarly, a good accountant needs to understand finance. It's fair to say that accounting and finance go together like peanut butter and jelly. In large and medium-sized organizations, both the accounting and finance functions are generally under the control of a chief financial officer (CFO).[2] However, financial management could also be in the hands of a person who serves as the company treasurer or vice president of finance. A comptroller is the chief *accounting* officer.

A financial manager's two key responsibilities are to obtain funds and to control the use of those funds effectively. Controlling funds includes managing the firm's cash, credit accounts (accounts receivable), and inventory. Finance is a critical activity in both profit-seeking and nonprofit organizations.[3]

Finance is important no matter what the firm's size. Financing a small business is a difficult but essential function if a firm expects to survive its important first five years. But the need for careful financial management goes well beyond the early years and remains a challenge that a business, large or small, must face throughout its existence.[4] Even a market giant cannot afford to ignore finance. Chrysler Corporation, for example, faced extinction in the late 1970s because of severe financial problems. Had it not been for a government-backed loan in 1980 of $1 billion, Chrysler might have joined the ranks of defunct auto companies such as Packard and Hudson instead of becoming part of Daimler-Benz.[5] The following are three of the most common ways for a firm to fail financially:

1. Undercapitalization (lacking enough funds to start the business).
2. Poor control over cash flow.
3. Inadequate expense control.

From *Understanding Business*, 8th edition by William Nickels, James McHugh and Susan McHugh. Copyright © 2008 The McGraw-Hill Companies. Reprinted by permission of The McGraw-Hill Companies.

The Importance of Understanding Finance

You can see the issues involved with capitalization, control over cash flow, and expense control when you consider the financial problems encountered several years ago by a small organization called Parsley Patch. Two friends, Elizabeth Bertani and Pat Sherwood, started the company on what can best be described as a shoestring budget. It began when Bertani prepared salt-free seasonings for her husband, who was on a no-salt diet. Her friend Sherwood thought the seasonings were good enough to sell. Bertani agreed, and Parsley Patch Inc. was born.

The business began with an investment of $5,000, which was rapidly eaten up for a logo and a label design. Bertani and Sherwood quickly learned the importance of capital in getting a business going. Eventually, the two women personally invested more than $100,000 to keep the business from experiencing severe undercapitalization.

The partners believed that gourmet shops would be an ideal distribution point for their product. Everything started well, and hundreds of gourmet shops adopted the product line. But when sales failed to meet expectations, the women decided that the health-food market offered more potential than gourmet shops because salt-free seasonings were a natural for people with restricted diets. The choice was a good one. Sales soared, approaching $30,000 a month. Still, the company earned no profits.

Bertani and Sherwood were not trained in monitoring cash flow or in controlling expenses. In fact, they had been told not to worry about costs, and they hadn't. They eventually hired a certified public accountant (CPA) and an experienced financial manager, who taught them how to compute the costs of the various blends they produced and how to control their expenses. The financial specialists also offered insight into how to control cash coming in and out of the company (cash flow). Soon Parsley Patch earned a comfortable margin on operations that ran close to $1 million a year. Luckily, the owners were able to turn things around before it was too late.

If Bertani and Sherwood had understood finance before starting their business, they may have been able to avoid the problems they encountered. The key word here is *understood*. You do not have to pursue finance as a career to understand finance. Financial understanding is important to anyone who wants to start a Small business, invest in stocks and bonds, or plan a retirement fund. In short, finance and accounting are two areas everyone involved in business needs to study.

What Is Financial Management?

Financial managers are responsible for seeing that the company pays its bills. Finance functions such as buying merchandise on credit (accounts payable) and collecting payment from customers (accounts receivable) are responsibilities of financial managers. Therefore, financial managers are responsible for paying the company's bills at the appropriate time and for collecting overdue payments to make sure that the company does not lose too much money to bad debts (people or firms that don't pay their bills). While these functions are critical to all types of businesses, they are particularly critical to small- and medium-sized businesses, which typically have smaller cash or credit cushions than large corporations.

It's vital that financial managers stay abreast of changes or opportunities in finance and prepare to adjust to them. For example, tax payments represent an outflow of cash from the business. Therefore, financial managers must be involved in tax management and must keep abreast of changes in tax law. Financial managers also carefully analyze the tax implications of various managerial decisions in an attempt to minimize the taxes paid by the business. It's critical that businesses of all sizes concern themselves with managing taxes.

Usually a member of the firm's finance department, the internal auditor, checks on the journals, ledgers, and financial statements prepared by the accounting department to make sure that all transactions have been treated in accordance with generally accepted accounting principles (GAAP). [6] If such audits were not done, accounting statements would be less reliable. Therefore, it is important that internal auditors be objective and critical of any improprieties or deficiencies they might note in their evaluation.[7] Regular, thoroughly conducted internal audits offer the firm assistance in the important role of financial planning, which we'll look at next.

Financial Planning

Financial planning is a key responsibility of the financial manager in a business. Planning has been a recurring theme of this book. We've stressed planning's importance as a managerial function and offered insights into planning your career. Financial planning involves analyzing short-term and long-term money flows to and from the firm. The overall objective of financial planning is to optimize the firm's profitability and make the best use of its money.[8]

Financial planning involves three steps; (1) forecasting both short-term and long-term financial needs, (2) developing budgets to meet those needs, and (3) establishing financial control to see how well the company is doing what it set out to do. Let's look at each step and the role these steps play in improving the financial health of an organization.

Forecasting Financial Needs

Forecasting is an important part of any firm's financial plan. A short-term forecast predicts revenues, costs, and expenses for a period of one year or less. This forecast is the foundation for most other financial plans, so its accuracy is critical. Part of the short-term forecast may be in the form of a cash flow forecast, which predicts the cash inflows and outflows in future periods, usually months or quarters. The inflows and outflows of cash recorded in the cash flow forecast are based on expected sales revenues and on various costs and expenses incurred and when they'll come due.[9] The company's sales forecast estimates the firm's projected sales for a particular period. A business often uses its past financial statements as a basis for projecting expected sales and various costs and expenses.[10]

A long-term forecast predicts revenues, costs, and expenses for a period longer than 1 year, and sometimes as far as 5 or 10 years into the future. This forecast plays a crucial part in the company's long-term strategic plan which asks questions such as: What business are we in? Should we be in it five years from now? How much money should we invest in technology and new plant and equipment over the next decade? Will there be cash available to meet long-term obligations? Innovations in Web-based software today assist financial managers in dealing with these long-term forecasting questions.

The long-term financial forecast gives top management, as well as operations managers, some sense of the income or profit potential possible with different strategic plans. Additionally, long-term projections assist financial managers with the preparation of company budgets.

Working with the Budget Process

The budgeting process depends on the accuracy of the firm's financial statements. Put simply, a budget is a financial plan.[11] More specifically, a budget sets forth management's expectations for revenues and, on the basis of those expectations, allocates the use of specific resources throughout the firm. The key financial statements—the balance sheet, income statement, and statement of cash flows—form the basis for the budgeting process. Businesses use cost and revenue information derived from past financial statements as the basis for forecasting company budgets. The firm's budgets are compiled from short-term and long-term financial forecasts that need to be as accurate as possible. Since budgeting is clearly tied to forecasting, financial managers must take forecasting responsibilities seriously. A budget becomes the primary guide for the firm's financial operations and financial needs.

There are usually several types of budgets established in a firm's financial plan:

- A capital budget.
- A cash budget.
- An operating (master) budget.

A capital budget highlights a firm's spending plans for major asset purchases that often require large sums of money. The capital budget primarily concerns itself with the purchase of such assets as property, buildings, and equipment.

A cash budget estimates a firm's projected cash inflows and outflows that the firm can use to plan for any cash shortages or surpluses during a given period (e.g., monthly, quarterly). Cash budgets are important guidelines that help managers to anticipate borrowing, debt repayment, operating expenses, and short-term investments.[12] The cash budget is often the last budget that is prepared. A sample cash budget for our ongoing example company, Very Vegetarian, is provided in Exhibit 11.1.

VERY VEGETARIAN Monthly Cash Budget			
	January	February	March
Sales forecast	$50,000	$45,000	$40,000
Collections			
Cash sales (20%)		$ 9,000	$ 8,000
Credit sales (80% of past month)		$40,000	$36,000
Monthly cash collection		$49,000	$44,000
Payments schedule			
Supplies and material		$11,000	$10,000
Salaries		12,000	12,000
Direct labor		9,000	9,000
Taxes		3,000	3,000
Other expenses		7,000	6,000
Monthly cash payments		$42,000	$39,000
Cash budget			
Cash flow		$ 7,000	$ 5,000
Beginning cash		−1,000	6,000
Total cash		$ 6,000	$11,000
Less minimum cash balance		−6,000	−6,000
Excess cash to market securities		$ 0	$ 5,000
Loans needed for minimum balance		0	0

Exhibit 11.1 A Sample Cash Budget for Very Vegetarian

The operating budget (master budget) ties together all the firm's other budgets and summarizes the business's proposed financial activities. It can be defined more formally as the projection of dollar allocations to various costs and expenses needed to run or operate a business, given projected revenues.[13] How much the firm will spend on supplies, travel, rent, advertising, salaries, and so forth is determined in the operating, Or master, budget. The operating budget is generally the most detailed and most useful budget that a firm prepares.

Clearly, financial planning plays an important role in the operations of the firm. This planning often determines what long-term investments are made, when specific funds will be needed, and how the funds will be generated. Once a company has determined its short-term and long-term financial needs and established budgets to show how funds will be allocated, the final step in financial planning is to establish financial controls. Before you read about such controls, the Spotlight on Small Business box challenges you to check your personal financial-planning skill by developing a monthly budget for "You incorporated."

Establishing Financial Controls

Financial control is a process in which a firm periodically compares its actual revenues, costs, and expenses with its budget. Most companies hold at least monthly financial reviews as a way to ensure financial control. Such control procedures help managers identify variances to the financial plan and allow them to take corrective action if necessary. Financial controls also provide feedback to help reveal which accounts, which departments, and which people are varying from the financial plans.[14] Finance managers can judge if such variances may or may not be justified allowing them to make some financial adjustments to the plan when needed.

SPOTLIGHT ON small business www.dinkytown.net/java/HomeBudget.htm

You Incorporated Monthly Budget

Let's develop a monthly budget for You Inc. Be honest and think of everything that needs to be included for an accurate monthly budget for You!

	Expected	Actual	Difference
Monthly Income:			
Wages (net pay after taxes)			
Savings account withdrawal			
Family support			
Loans			
Other sources			
Total monthly Income			
Monthly expenses:			
Fixed expenses			
Rent or mortgage			
Car payment			
Health insurance			
Life Insurance			
Tuition or fees			
Other fixed expenses			
Subtotal of fixed expenses			
Variable expenses			
Food			
Clothing			
Entertainment			
Transportation			
Phone			
Utilities			
Publications			
Internet connection			
Cable television			
Other expenses			
Subtotal of variable expenses			
Total expenses			
Total income−Total expenses = Cash on hand/(Cash deficit)			

The Need for Operating Funds

In business, the need for operating funds never seems to cease. That's why sound financial management is essential to all businesses. Like our personal financial needs, the capital needs of a business change over time. For example, as a small business grows, its financial requirements shift considerably. (Remember the example of Parsley Patch.) The same is true with large corporations such as Intel, Johnson & Johnson, and PepsiCo. As they venture into new product areas or markets, their capital needs increase, causing a need for funds for different reasons. Virtually all organizations have certain operational needs for which funds must be available. Key areas include:

- Managing day-by-day needs of the business.
- Controlling credit operations.
- Acquiring needed inventory.
- Making capital expenditures.

Let's look carefully at these financial needs, which affect both the smallest and the largest of businesses.

Managing Day-by-Day Needs of the Business

If workers expect to be paid on Friday, they don't want to have to wait until Monday for their paychecks. If tax payments are due on the 15th of the month, the government expects the money on time. If the interest payment on a business loan is due on the 30th, the lender doesn't mean the 1st of the next month. As you can see, funds have to be available to meet the daily operational costs of the business.

The challenge of sound financial management is to see that funds are available to meet these daily cash needs without compromising the firm's investment potential.[15] Money has what is called a *time value*. In other words, if someone offered to give you $200 today or $200 one year from today, you would benefit by taking the $200 today. Why? It's very simple. You could start collecting interest or invest the $200 you receive today, and over a year's time your money would grow. The same thing is true in business; the interest gained on the firm's investments is important in maximizing the profit the company will gain. That's why financial managers encourage keeping a firm's cash expenditures to a minimum. By doing this, the firm can free up funds for investment in interest-bearing accounts. It's also not unusual for finance managers to suggest that a company pay its bills as late as possible (unless a cash discount is available) but try to collect what's owed to it as fast as possible. This way, they maximize the investment potential of the firm's funds. Efficient cash management is particularly important to small firms in conducting their daily operations because their access to capital is generally much more limited than that of larger businesses.[16]

Controlling Credit Operations

Financial managers know that making credit available helps keep current customers happy and attracts new customers. In today's highly competitive business environment, many businesses would have trouble surviving without making credit available to customers.

The major problem with selling on credit is that as much as 25 percent or more of the business's assets could be tied up in its credit accounts (accounts receivable). This means the firm needs to use some of its available funds to pay for the goods or services already sold to customers who bought on credit. Financial managers in such firms must develop efficient collection procedures, For example, businesses often provide cash or quantity discounts to buyers who pay their accounts by a certain time. Also, finance managers carefully scrutinize old and new credit customers to see if they have a favorable history of meeting their credit obligations on time.[17] In essence, the firm's credit policy reflects its financial position and its desire to expand into new markets.

One way to decrease the time, and therefore expense, involved in collecting accounts receivable is to accept bank credit cards such as MasterCard or Visa.[18] This is convenient for both the customer and the business. The banks that issue such credit cards have already established the customer's credit-worthiness, which reduces the business's risk. Businesses must pay a fee to accept credit cards, but the fees are generally not considered excessive compared to the benefits the cards provide.

Acquiring Needed Inventory

As we noted earlier in the text, effective marketing implies a clear customer orientation. This focus on the customer means that high-quality service and availability of goods are vital if a business expects to prosper in today's markets. Therefore, to satisfy customers, businesses must maintain inventories that often involve a sizable expenditure of funds. Although it's true that firms expect to recapture their investment in inventory through sales to customers, a carefully constructed inventory policy assists in managing the firm's available funds and maximizing profitability. For example, Take-a-Dip, a neighborhood ice cream parlor, ties up more funds in inventory (ice cream) in the summer than in the winter. It's obvious why. Demand for ice cream goes up in the summer.

Innovations such as just-in-time inventory control help reduce the amount of funds a firm must tie up in inventory. Also, by carefully evaluating its inventory turnover ratio a firm can better control its outflow of cash for inventory. It's important for a business of any size to understand that a poorly managed inventory system can seriously impact cash flow and drain its finances dry.

Making Capital Expenditures

Capital expenditures are major investments in either tangible long-term assets such as land, buildings, and equipment or intangible assets such as patents, trademarks, and copyrights. In many organizations the purchase of major assets—such as land, for future expansion, manufacturing plants to increase production capabilities, research to develop new-product ideas, and equipment to maintain or exceed current levels of output—is essential. As you can imagine, these expenditures often require a huge portion of the organization's funds.

Expansion into new markets can also cost large sums of money with no guarantee that the expansion will be commercially successful. Therefore, it's critical that companies weigh all the possible options before committing what may be a large portion of their available resources. For this reason, financial managers evaluate the appropriateness of such purchases or expenditures. Consider the situation in which a firm needs to expand its production capabilities due to increases in customer demand. One option is to buy land and build a new plant. Another option would be to purchase an existing plant or consider renting. Can you think of financial and accounting considerations that would come into play in this decision?

Obviously, the need for operating funds raises several questions in any firm: How does the firm obtain funds to finance operations and other business necessities? Will specific funds be needed by the firm in the long term or short term? How much will it cost to obtain these needed funds? Will these funds come from internal or external sources? We address these questions next.

Alternative Sources of Funds

Earlier in the chapter, finance was described as the function in a business responsible for acquiring and managing funds. Determining the amount of money needed and finding out the most appropriate sources from which to obtain it are fundamental steps in sound financial management. A firm can seek to raise needed capital through borrowing money (debt), selling ownership (equity), or earning profits (retained earnings). Debt financing refers to funds raised through various forms of borrowing that must be repaid. Equity financing is money raised from within the firm (from operations) or through the sale of ownership in the firm (e.g., the sale of stock). Firms can borrow funds either short-term or long-term. Short-term financing refers to funds needed for a period of one year or less. In contrast, long-term financing refers to funds needed for a period longer than one year (usually 2 to 10 years). Exhibit 11.2 highlights reasons why firms may need funds short-term and long-term.

Exhibit 11.2 Why Firms Need Funds

Short-Term Funds	Long-Term Funds
Meeting monthly expenses	New product development
Unanticipated emergencies	Replacing capital equipment
Cash-flow problems	Mergers or acquisitions
Expanding current inventory	Expansion into new markets (domestic or global)
Temporary promotional programs	Building new facilities

We'll explore the different sources of short- and long-term financing fully in the next sections. For now it's important to know that businesses can use different methods of raising money.

Obtaining Short-Term Financing

The bulk of a finance manager's job does not involve obtaining *long-term* funds, In fact, in small businesses, long-term financing is often out of the question. Instead, the day-to-day operation of the firm calls for the careful management of *short-term* financial needs. Firms may need to borrow short-term funds for purchasing additional inventory or for meeting bills that come due unexpectedly, Also, as we do in our personal lives, a business sometimes needs to obtain short-term funds when its cash reserves are low. This is particularly true, again, of small businesses.

Most small businesses are primarily concerned with just staying afloat until they are able to build capital and creditworthiness. Firms can obtain short-term financing in several different ways. Also, suppliers of short-term funds can require that the funds provided be secured or unsecured. Let's look at the major forms of short-term financing and what's meant by secured and unsecured financing with regard to different ways of obtaining needed funds.

Trade Credit

The most widely used source of short-term funding, trade credit (an account payable), is the least expensive and most convenient form of short-term financing. Trade credit is the practice of buying goods or services now and paying for them later. Small businesses rely heavily on trade credit from firms such as United Parcel Service, as do large firms such as Kmart. When a firm buys merchandise, it receives an invoice (a bill) much like the one you receive when you buy something with a credit card. As you will see, however, the terms businesses receive are often different.

It is common for business invoices to contain terms such as *2/10, net 30*. This means that the buyer can take a 2 percent discount for paying the invoice within 10 days. The total bill is due (net) in 30 days if the purchaser does not take advantage of the discount. Finance managers need to pay close attention to such discounts because they create opportunities to reduce the firm's costs. Think about it for a moment: If the discount offered to the customer is 2/10, net 30, the customer will pay 2 percent more for waiting an extra 20 days to pay the invoice.

Uninformed businesspeople may believe that 2 percent is insignificant, so they pay their bills after the discount period. By doing that, however, such firms lose a tremendous opportunity to save money—and it's much more than 2 percent! In the course of a year, 2 percent for 20 days adds up to a *36 percent* interest rate (because there are eighteen 20-day periods in the year). If the firm is capable of paying within 10 days, it is needlessly (and significantly) increasing its costs by not doing so.

Some suppliers hesitate to give trade credit to organizations with a poor credit rating, no credit history, or a history of slow payment. In such cases, the supplier may insist that the customer sign a promissory note as a condition for obtaining credit. A promissory note is a written contract with a promise to pay a supplier a specific sum of money at a definite time. Promissory notes can be sold by the supplier to a bank at a discount (the amount of the note less a fee for the bank's services in collecting the amount due).

Family and Friends

Many small firms obtain short-term, funds by borrowing money from family and friends. Because such funds are needed for periods of less than a year, friends or relatives are sometimes willing to help. Such loans can create problems, however, if the firm does not understand cash flow.[19] As we discussed earlier, the firm may suddenly find itself having several bills coming due at the same time with no sources of funds to pay them. It is better, therefore, not to borrow from friends or relatives; instead, go to a commercial bank that fully understands the business's risk and can help analyze your firm's future financial needs.[20]

Entrepreneurs appear to be listening to this advice. According to the National Federation of Independent Business, entrepreneurs today are relying less on family and friends as a source of borrowed funds than they have in the past. If an entrepreneur does decide to ask family or friends for financial assistance, it's important that both parties (1) agree on specific loan terms, (2) put the agreement in writing, and (3) arrange for repayment in the same way they would for a bank loan. Such actions help keep family relationships and friendships intact.

Commercial Banks

Banks are highly sensitive to risk and are often reluctant to lend money to small businesses. Nonetheless, a promising and well-organized venture may be able to get a bank loan. In fact, almost half of small business financing today is funded by commercial banks.[21] If a business is able to get such a loan, a small-or medium-sized business should have the person in charge of the finance function keep in close touch with the bank. It's also wise to see a banker periodically (as often as once a month) and send the banker all the firm's financial statements so that the bank is kept up-to-date and continues to supply funds when needed.

If you try to imagine the different types of businesspeople who go to banks for a loan, you'll get a better idea of the role of financial management. Picture, for example, a farmer going to the bank to borrow funds for seed, fertilizer, equipment, and other needs. The farmer may buy such supplies in the spring and pay for them after the fall harvest. Now picture a local toy store buying merchandise for Christmas sales. The store may borrow the money for such purchases in the summer and pay it back after Christmas. Restaurants may borrow funds at the beginning of the month and pay by the end of the month. It's evident that how much a business borrows and for how long depends often on the kind of business it is and how quickly the merchandise purchased with a bank loan can be resold or used to generate funds.

You can also imagine how important it is for specialists in a company's finance and accounting departments to do a cash flow forecast. Unfortunately, small-business owners generally lack the luxury of such specialists and must monitor cash flow themselves. By anticipating times when many bills will come due, a business can begin early to seek funds or sell other assets to prepare for a possible financial crunch. This is why it's important for business-people to keep friendly and close relations with their bankers. An experienced banker may spot cash flow problems early or be more willing to lend money in a crisis if a businessperson has established a strong, friendly relationship built on openness, trust, and sound management practices. It's important to remember that your banker wants you to succeed almost as much as you want to. Bankers can be an invaluable support to any business but especially to small, growing businesses.

Different Forms of Short-Term Loans

Commercial banks offer different types of loans to customers. A secured loan is a loan that's backed by something valuable, such as property. The item of value is called *collateral*. If the borrower fails to pay the loan, the lender may take possession of the collateral. For example, an automobile loan is a secured loan. If the borrower fails to pay the loan, the lender will repossess (take back) the car. Collateral thus takes some of the risk out of lending money.

Accounts receivable are assets that are often used by businesses as collateral for a loan; the process is called *pledging*. Some percentage of the value of accounts receivable pledged (usually about 75 percent) is advanced to the borrowing firm.[22] As customers pay of their accounts, the funds received are forwarded to the lender in repayment of the funds that were advanced. Inventory such as raw materials (e.g., coal, steel), is also often used as collateral or security for a business loan. Other assets that can be used as collateral include buildings, machinery, and company-owned stocks and bonds.

The most difficult kind of loan to get from a bank or other financial institution is an unsecured loan. An unsecured loan doesn't require the borrower to offer the lending institution any collateral to obtain the loan. In other words, the loan is not backed by any specific assets. Normally, a lender will give unsecured loans only to highly regarded customers (e.g., long-standing customers or customers considered financially stable).

If a business develops a good relationship with a bank, the bank may open a line of credit for the firm. A line of credit is a given amount of unsecured short-term funds a bank will lead to a business, provided the bank has the funds readily available. In other words, a line of credit is not guaranteed to a business; however, a line of credit can speed up the borrowing process so that a firm does not have to go through the hassle of applying for a new loan every time it needs funds. Generally, the funds requested are available as long as the credit limit set by the bank is not exceeded. As businesses mature and become more financially secure, the amount of credit often is increased. Some firms will even apply for a revolving credit agreement, which is a line of credit that's guaranteed. However, banks usually charge a fee for guaranteeing such an agreement. Both lines of credit and revolving credit agreements are particularly good sources of funds for unexpected cash needs.

If a business is unable to secure a short-term loan from a bank, the financial manager may seek short-term funds from commercial finance companies. These non-deposit-type organizations make short-term loans to borrowers who offer tangible assets (e.g., property, plant, and equipment) as collateral. Since commercial finance companies are willing to accept higher degrees of risk than commercial banks, they usually charge higher interest rates than banks. Commercial finance companies often make loans to businesses that cannot get funds elsewhere. General Electric Capital Corporation is the largest commercial finance company in the United States, with $425 billion in assets; GE Capital Corporation has operations in 47 countries around the world.[23]

Factoring Accounts Receivable

One relatively expensive source of short-term funds for a firm is factoring, which is the process of selling accounts receivable for cash. Factoring dates as far back as 4,000 years, during the days of ancient Babylon. Today, the Internet can help a firm find factors quickly so that they can solicit bids on the firm's accounts receivable promptly.[24] Here's how factoring works: Let's say that a firm sells many of its products on credit to consumers and other businesses, creating a number of accounts receivable. Some of the buyers may be slow in paying their bills, causing the firm to have a large amount of money due to it. A *factor* is a market intermediary (usually a financial institution like a commercial bank) that agrees to buy the firm's accounts receivable, at a discount, for cash. The discount rate charged depends on the age of the accounts receivable, the nature of the business, and the condition of the economy. The factor collects and keeps the money that was owed the firm when it collects the accounts receivable.

Even though factoring can be an expensive way of raising cash, it is popular among small businesses.[25] Factoring can also be used by large firms. Macy's, the department store chain, for example, used factoring during its reorganization several years ago. Factoring is common in the clothing and furniture businesses, and it is popular in financing growing numbers of global trade ventures.[26] The Reaching Beyond Our Borders box explains how firms use factoring to reduce the risk of selling products in global markets. What's important for you to note is that factoring is not a loan; factoring is the sale of an asset (accounts receivable). And while it's true that discount rates charged by factors are usually higher than loan rates charged by lending institutions, remember that many small businesses cannot qualify for a loan. A company can reduce the cost of factoring if it agrees to reimburse the factor for slow-paying accounts, and it can reduce costs even further if it assumes the risk of those customers who don't pay at all.

Commercial Paper

Sometimes a large corporation needs funds for just a few months and wants to get lower rates of interest than those charged by banks. One strategy is to sell commercial paper. Commercial paper consists of *unsecured* promissory notes, in amounts of $100,000 and up, that

Reaching Beyond (www.factoring.org)

Our Borders

Guaranteeing That the Deal Gets Done

With over 6 billion potential customers on planet Earth, the lure of global markets is just too enticing for businesses to ignore. Unfortunately, the path of would-be exporters is often blocked by financing constraints such as the complications of trading in foreign currencies and difficulty in collecting money owed from global accounts. Combine these financing challenges with political instability, high loan defaults, threats of terrorism, and unstable currencies, and the prospects of doing business globally look iffy at best. This shaky global environment requires U.S. companies to use creative financing methods such as International factoring (also called forfeiting), for protection in global markets. International factoring involves negotiating with intermediaries who make sure the payment for products gets from the foreign buyer back to the seller.

There are four parties involved in an international factoring transaction; the exporter (the seller), the U.S. factor (called the export factor), the foreign factor (called the import factor), and the importer (the buyer). It works like this: The exporter and the export factor sign a factoring agreement that transfers the exporter's accounts receivable to the U.S. factor in exchange for coverage against any credit losses that could be incurred globally. In other words, the export factor guarantees the exporter that it will receive the money it is owed (minus fees, of course). The export factor selects an import factor to act on the seller's behalf under the export factor's supervision. The import factor assists in finding local customers in global markets to whom the seller can sell its goods or services.

When an exporter receives an order from a customer, the import factor collects payment from the global buyer. The import factor deducts a fee and gives the remainder to the export factor. The export factor deducts a fee and gives that remainder to the selling company (exporter). Complicated? Yes, but by using these agreements U.S. exporters can do business even in risky global markets without the risk of suffering significant credit losses. Today, international factoring accounts for almost $1 trillion in global trade.

Sources: Michael Rudnick, "Shift Abroad Keeps Fueling Import-Factoring Demand," *Home Furnishing Network,* August 15, 2005, and Lisa Casabona, "Origins of Factoring Come Full Circle," *WWD,* September 19, 2005.

mature (come due) in 270 days or less. Commercial paper states a fixed amount of money the business agrees to repay to the lender (investor) on a specific date. The interest rate is stated in the agreement.

Still, because commercial paper is unsecured, only financially stable firms (mainly large corporations with excellent credit reputations) are able to sell it. For these companies it's a way to get short-term funds quickly and for less than the interest charged by commercial banks. Since most commercial paper matures in 30 to 90 days, it's also an investment opportunity for buyers who can afford to put up cash for short periods to earn some interest on their money.

Credit Cards

Letitia Mulzac seemed to have things going her way as she planned to open an imported gift and furniture shop. She had chosen a great location and lined up reliable business contacts in India, Indonesia, and Morocco. Unfortunately, she didn't have enough money in her savings to start the business.[27] She did, however, have a Small Business Credit Card with a high credit limit from American Express. According to the National Small Business Association, about half of all small businesses like Mulzac's finance their formation or first-level expansion with credit cards. Credit cards provide a readily available line of credit to a business that can save time and the likely embarrassment of being rejected for a bank loan.[28] Of course, in contrast to the convenience credit cards offer, they are extremely risky and costly. For example, interest rates can be exorbitant. There are also considerable penalties users must pay if they fail to make their payments on time. Credit cards are an expensive way to borrow money and are probably best used as a last resort.

Obtaining Long-Term Financing

Forecasting helps the firm to develop a financial plan. This plan specifies the amount of funding the firm will need over various time periods and the most appropriate sources for obtaining those funds. In setting long-term financing objectives, finance managers generally ask three questions:

1. What are the organization's long-term goals and objectives?
2. What are the financial requirements needed to achieve long-term goals and objectives?
3. What sources of long-term capital are available, and which will best fit our needs?

In business, long-term capital is used to buy expensive assets such as plant and equipment, to develop new products, and to finance expansion of the organization. In major corporations, decisions involving long-term financing normally involve the board of directors and top management, as well as finance and accounting managers. Take pharmaceutical giant Pfizer, for example. Pfizer spends over $8 billion a year researching and developing new products.[29] The actual development of a new innovative medicine can sometimes take 10 years and cost close to $1 billion in company funds before the product is ever introduced in the market. It's easy to see why long-term financing decisions involve high-level managers at Pfizer. In small- and medium-sized businesses, it's also obvious that the owners are always actively involved in analyzing long-term financing opportunities that affect their company.

As we noted earlier in the chapter, long-term funding comes from two major types of financing, debt financing or equity financing. Let's look at these two sources of long-term financing next.

Debt Financing

Debt financing involves borrowing money that the company has a legal obligation to repay. Firms can borrow funds by either getting a loan from a lending institution or possibly issuing bonds.

Debt Financing by Borrowing Money from Lending Institutions

Firms that establish and develop rapport with a bank, insurance company, pension fund, commercial finance company, or other financial institution often are able to secure a long-term loan. Long-term loans are usually repaid within 3 to 7 years but may extend to 15 or 20 years. For such loans, a business must sign what is called a term-loan agreement. A term-loan agreement is a promissory note that requires the borrower to repay the loan in specified installments (e.g., monthly or yearly). A major advantage of using this type of financing is that the interest paid on the long-term debt is tax deductible.

Because long-term loans involve larger amounts of funding than short-term loans, they are generally more expensive to the firm than short-term loans are. Also, since the repayment period could be quite long, lenders are not assured that their capital will be repaid in full. Therefore, most long-term loans require collateral, which may be in the form of real estate, machinery, equipment, company stock, or other items of value. Lenders may also require certain restrictions on a firm's operations to force it to act responsibly in its business practices. The interest rate for long-term loans is based on the adequacy of collateral, the firm's credit rating, and the general level of market interest rates. The greater the risk a lender takes in making a loan, the higher the rate of interest a lender requires. This principle is known as the risk/return trade-off.

Debt Financing by Issuing Bonds

If an organization is unable to obtain its long-term financing needs by getting a loan from a lending institution, it may try to issue bonds. A bond is a long-term debt obligation of a corporation or government. To put it simply, a bond is like an IOU with a promise to repay the amount borrowed on a certain date. To be more specific, a bond is a binding contract through which the organization issuing the bond agrees to specific terms with investors in return for the money those investors lend to the company. The terms of the agreement in a bond issue are referred to as the indenture terms.

You are probably somewhat familiar with bonds. For example, you may own investments like U.S. government savings bonds, or perhaps you have volunteered your time to help a local school district pass a bond issue. Maybe your community is building a new stadium or cultural center that requires selling bonds. It's fair to say that businesses compete with the government when issuing bonds. Potential investors (individuals and institutions) in bonds measure the risk involved in purchasing a bond against the return (interest) the bond promises to pay and the company's ability to repay the bond when promised.

Like other forms of long-term debt, bonds can be secured or unsecured. A secured bond is issued with some form of collateral, such as real estate, equipment, or other pledged assets. If the bond's indenture terms are violated, the bondholder can issue a claim on the collateral. An unsecured bond (called a debenture bond) is a bond backed only by the reputation of the issuer. Investors in such bonds simply trust that the organization issuing the bond will make good on its financial commitments. Bonds are a key means of long-term financing for many organizations. They can also be valuable investments for private individuals or institutions.

Equity Financing

If a firm cannot obtain a long-term loan from a lending institution, or if it is unable to sell bonds to investors, it may look for long-term funding from equity financing. Equity financing comes from the owners of the firm. Therefore, equity financing involves selling ownership in the firm in the form of stock, or using earnings that have been retained by the company to reinvest in the business (retained earnings). A business can also seek equity financing by selling ownership in the firm to venture capitalists. Exhibit 11.3 compares debt and equity financing options.

Equity Financing by Selling Stock

Regardless of whether or not a firm can obtain debt financing, there usually comes a time when it needs additional funds. One way to obtain such funds is to sell ownership shares

Exhibit 11.3 Differences between Debt and Equity Financing

Conditions	Debt	Equity
Management influence	There's usually none unless special conditions have been agreed on.	Common stockholders have voting rights.
Repayment	Debt has a maturity date. Principal must be repaid.	Stock has no maturity date. The company is never required to repay equity.
Yearly obligations	Payment of interest is a contractual obligation.	The firm isn't legally liable to pay dividends.
Tax benefits	Interest is tax deductible.	Dividends are paid from after-tax income and aren't deductible.

(called *stock*) in the firm to private investors. The key word to remember here is *ownership*. The purchasers of stock become owners in the organization. The number of shares of stock that will be available for purchase is generally decided by the corporation's board of directors. The first time a company offers to sell its stock to the general public is called an *initial public offering (IPO)*.

Selling stock to the public to obtain funds is by no means easy or automatic, U.S. companies can issue stock for public purchase only if they meet requirements set by the Securities and Exchange Commission (SEC) as well as by various state agencies.[30] Companies can issue different types of stock, such as common and preferred stock.

Equity Financing from Retained Earnings

Have you ever heard a businessperson say that he or she reinvests the firm's profits right back into the business? The profits the company keeps and reinvests in the firm are called *retained earnings*. Retained earnings often are a major source of long-term funds, especially for small businesses, which have fewer financing alternatives, such as selling bonds or stock, than large businesses do. However, large corporations also depend on retained earnings for needed long-term funding. In fact, retained earnings are usually the most favored source of meeting long-term capital needs since a company that uses them saves interest payments, dividends (payments for investing in stock), and any possible underwriting fees for issuing bonds or stock. Also, if a firm uses retained earnings, there is no new ownership created in the firm, as occurs with selling stock.

Unfortunately, many organizations do not have sufficient retained earnings on hand to finance extensive capital improvements or business expansion. If you think about it for a moment, it makes sense. What if you wanted to buy an expensive personal asset such as a new car? The ideal way to purchase the car would be to go to your personal savings account and take out the necessary cash. No hassle! No interest! Unfortunately, few people have such large amounts of cash available. Most businesses are no different. Even though they would like to finance long-term needs from operations, few have the resources on hand to accomplish this.

Equity Financing from Venture Capital

The hardest time for a business to raise money is when it is just starting or moving into early stages of expansion. A start-up business typically has few assets and no market track record, so the chances of borrowing significant amounts of money from a bank are slim. Venture capital is money that is invested in new or emerging companies that are perceived as having great profit potential. Venture capital has helped dozens of firms—such as Intel, Apple Computer, and Cisco Systems—get started. Venture capital firms are a potential source of start-up capital for new companies or companies moving into expanding stages of business.

The venture capital industry originally began as an alternative investment vehicle for wealthy families. The Rockefeller family, for example (whose vast fortune came from John D. Rockefeller's Standard Oil Company, started in the 19th century), financed Sanford McDonnell when he was operating his company from an airplane hangar. That small venture grew into McDonnell Douglas, a large aerospace and defense contractor that merged with Boeing Corporation in 1997. The venture capital industry grew significantly in the 1980s, when many high-tech companies such as Intel and Apple were being started. In the 1990s the industry grew immensely, especially in high-tech centers such as California's Silicon Valley, where venture capitalists concentrated primarily on Internet-related companies. In the early 2000s, however, problems in the technology industry and the slowdown in the overall economy reduced venture capital expenditures considerably. Today, venture capitalists are treading cautiously and holding companies to strict standards before investing their capital.[31]

An entrepreneur or finance manager must remember that venture capitalists invest in a business in return for part ownership of the business. Venture capitalists admit that they expect higher-than-average returns and competent management performance for their investment. Therefore, a start-up company has to be careful when choosing a venture capital firm. The dangers of financing with venture capitalists can be illustrated by the experience of Jon Birck, who started Northwest Instrument Systems with venture capital money. Birck worked until 11:00 or 12:00 each night to build the company. After having dedicated three years to the company, he was asked to leave by the venture capital firm, which wanted a more experienced chief executive officer to protect its investment. Birck had left a secure job, put his marriage on the line, taken out a second mortgage on his house, and given himself a below-average salary to get Northwest on its feet; then, just when the firm was ready for rapid growth, he was asked to resign.

As this story shows, financing a firm's long-term needs through venture capital can involve a high degree of risk. Still, it's obvious there are risks whenever firms borrow funds. Knowing this, you might be inclined to ask: Why do firms borrow funds at all? Why not just use the other forms of equity funding, especially selling stock? The reason involves the use of leverage (debt). Next, let's look briefly at why companies use leverage.

Making Decisions on Using Financial Leverage

Raising needed funds through borrowing to increase the firm's rate of return is referred to as leverage. While it's true that debt increases the risk of the firm, it also enhances the firm's ability to increase profits. Remember, two key jobs of the finance manager or chief financial officer (CFO) are to forecast the need for borrowed funds and to plan how to manage these funds once they are obtained.

Firms are concerned with the cost of capital. Cost of capital is the rate of return a company must earn in order to meet the demands of its lenders and expectations of its equity holders (stockholders or venture capitalists). If the firm's earnings are larger than the interest payments on the funds borrowed, business owners can realize a higher rate of return than if they used equity financing. Exhibit 11.4 describes an example involving a vegetarian restaurant, Very Vegetarian. If Very Vegetarian needed $500,000 in financing, it could consider selling bonds (debt) or stock (equity) to raise funds. Comparing the two options in this situation, you can see that Very Vegetarian would benefit by selling bonds since the company's earnings are greater than the interest paid on borrowed funds (bonds). However, if the firm's earnings were less than the interest paid on borrowed funds (bonds), the owners could lose money on their investment. It's also important to remember that bonds, like all debt, have to be repaid at a specific time.

Normally, it's up to each individual firm to determine exactly how to balance debt and equity financing. For example, Trump Hotels and Casino deals with billions of dollars of debt in financing its operations. In contrast, chewing-gum maker Wm. Wrigley Jr. Company

Exhibit 11.4 Using Leverage versus Equity Financing

VERY VEGETARIAN NEEDS TO RAISE $500,000; COMPARE ITS TWO OPTIONS FOR DOING SO

Option A		Option B	
Raise 10% by selling stock (equity); raise 90% by issuing bonds (debt).		Raise 100% by selling stock (equity).	
Common stock	$ 50,000	Common stock	$500,000
Bonds (@ 10% interest)	450,000		
	$500,000		$500,000
Earnings	$125,000	Earnings	$125,000
Less bond interest	45,000		
Net earnings/income	$ 80,000	Net earnings/income	$125,000
Return to stockholders	$80,000 / $50,000 = 160%	Return to stockholders	$125,000 / $500,000 = 25%

carried no long-term debt until it issued bonds to help finance the company's purchase of Kraft Food's candy business in 2005.[32] Leverage ratios give companies a standard of the comparative leverage of firms in their industries. According to Standard & Poor's and Moody's Investor Services (firms that provide corporate and financial research), the debt of a large industrial corporation typically ranges between 33 and 40 percent of its total assets. Small-business debt varies considerably.

As the requirements of financial institutions become more stringent and investors more demanding, it's certain that the job of the finance manager will become more challenging. In your career, you will likely be taking a closer look at bonds (debt) and stocks (equity) both as financing tools for businesses and as investment options for private investors. You will learn about bond and stock issues, the securities exchanges, how to buy and sell stock, how to choose the right investment strategy, how to read stock and bond quotations, and more. Finance takes on a whole new dimension when you see how you can participate in financial markets yourself.

■ Endnotes

1. Jane von Bergen, "Calling All Accountants," *Philadelphia Enquirer*, October 12, 2005; David Simanoff, "Accountants Can Count on More Job Offers," *Tampa Tribune*, June 26, 2005; and Mike Allen, "Supply and Demand Works in Accountants' Favor: Firms Are Desperately Seeking Skilled CPAs," *San Diego Business Journal*, January 16, 2006.
2. Tom Lowry, "The CFO Behind Adelphia's Rescue," *BusinessWeek*, April 11, 2005; and Gregory J. Millman, "Two Generations of CFOs: How Different Are They?," *Financial Executive*, November 1, 2005; "Paradigm Shifts," *CFO*, March 2005, pp. 37–54; and Terry Maxon, "EDS Loses CFO to eBay: Swan, Who Helped Lead Turnaround, to Take Similar Job at eBay," *Dallas Morning News*, February 22, 2006.
3. Tom Herman, "Charities May See More Scrutiny," *The Wall Street Journal*, March 2, 2005, p. D3.
4. Don Durfee, "The Top Spot," *CFO*, October 2005, pp. 52–60.
5. Fara Warner, "Keeping the Crisis in Chrysler," *Fast Company*, September 1, 2005, pp. 68–73.
6. Chris Cather, "The World According to GAAP," *Motley Fool*, April 25, 2005; Robert Tie, "The Case for Private Company GAAP," *Journal of Accountancy*, May 1, 2005; and William A. Grimm, "Raising Capital? Then Make Sure to Mind the GAAP," *Orlando Business Journal*, February 17, 2006.

7. Joseph V. Hermanson and Dana R. Raghunandan, "Factors Associated with U.S. Companies' Investment in Internal Auditing," *Accounting Horizons*, June 1, 2005.
8. Gary McWilliams, "Dell Puts Cash Flow to Work," *The Wall Street Journal*, April 25, 2005, p. C3.
9. Michael Hunstad, "Better Forecasting: Know Your Cash Flows," *Financial Executive*, May 1, 2005, and Kenneth L. Parkinson, "Cash Flow Forecasting: Do It Better and Save," *Financial Executive*, January 1, 2006.
10. Patrick Kilts, "Effective Cash Flow Management Improves Investment Outlook," *Crain's Cleveland Business*, September 19, 2005; Bruce Perryman, "Grow with the Flow," *Stitches Magazine*, January 1, 2005; and Andi Gray, "The Optimum Growth Model," *Fairfield County Business Journal*, January 30, 2006.
11. Tim Reason, "Budgeting in the Real World," *CFO*, July 2005, pp. 43–48.
12. Charles Mulford, "A Best Practices Approach to Cash Flow Reporting: Implications for Analysis," *Business Credit*, January 1, 2005.
13. Jordan I. Shifrin, "All Boards Must Grapple with Budget Issues," *Daily Herald*, June 4, 2005.
14. Jennifer M. Mueller, "Evaluating Internal Financial Reporting Controls," *Health Care Financial Management*, August 1, 2005; Andrea Morrow, "Financial Solutions for Nonprofit Organizations: Out of Control," *Michigan Chronicle*, July 12, 2005; and "Financial Executives Research Foundation Issues Study of Internal Controls Reporting," PR Newswire, May 27, 2005.
15. Andrew Ashby, "Do's and Don'ts for Good Cash Management," *Financial Executive*, October 1, 2005.
16. Nathan Parmelee, "Why Free Cash Flow Matters," *Motley Fool*, August 28, 2005, and Chris Cather, "Operating Cash Flow Tricks," *Motley Fool*, March 28, 2005.
17. Phyllis Micahnik, "Credit Collection and Cash Flow," *Contracting Business*, August 1, 2005, and Tom Diana, "Changing Ways of Managing Collection and Deduction," *Business Credit*, September 1, 2005.
18. "Visa Says Its Check Card Is Transforming the Way People Pay for Goods," *Wireless News*, September 27, 2005; Jeff DeMoss, "Credit Card Companies Increase Minimum Monthly Payment Requirements," *Standard-Examiner*, January 1, 2006; and Yasmin Assemi, "Credit, Debit Cards Helped Revolutionize Shopping," *Stockton (California) Record*, February 12, 2006.
19. Susan C. Thompson, "Mixing Personal, Business Funds Is a Formula for Bankruptcy," *St. Louis Post-Dispatch*, August 5, 2005, and Carolyn M. Brown, "Borrowing from Dad: Financing from Relatives and Friends Has Risks and Rewards," *Black Enterprise*, January 1, 2005.
20. Kate Ashford, "Lend to a Friend (Without Regret): Four Things to Do When a Pal Asks for a Loan," *Money*, November 1, 2005.
21. Deanna Galbraith, "Borrowing Money Effectively," *San Fernando Valley Business Journal*, August 29, 2005, and Kerry Hall, "Stable Financing Is a Constant Concern for Small Businesses," *Charlotte Observer*, January 11, 2006.
22. David Barkholz, "Delphi Crisis May Hurt Vendors: CEO Miller Says Company Can Pay Its Bills—Even If It Is Bankrupt," *Automotive News*, September 26, 2005, and Marc Heller, "Despite Co-Op's Bankruptcy, Executive Says Farmers Served Best by DFA, Others," *Watertown Daily Times*, January 1, 2006.
23. www.gecapital.com.
24. Liza Casabona, "Origins of Factoring Come Full Circle," *WWD*, September 19, 2005, and "Texas Oil Drill Bit Manufacturer Taps into a $1 Million Factoring Credit Line," PR Newswire, February 1, 2006.
25. Jan Norman, "Accounts Receivable Financing Helps Some Small Businesses Grow," *Orange County Register*, August 9, 2005, and Joseph Ingrassia, "Venture Merchant Banking: Financing 'Sales' vs. 'Assets,'" *Financial Executive*, January 1, 2006.
26. Paulette Thomas, "For Sale: Unpaid Invoices," *Crain's Chicago Business*, May 9, 2005, and Liza Casabona, "CIT: Consolidation Remains a 'Huge Issue,'" *WWD*, February 13, 2006.

27. Jean Ende, "Card Issuers Charge After Owners," *Crain's New York Business*, July 18, 2005.
28. James C. Johnson, "Plastic Debt," *Black Enterprise*, September 1, 2005; Rick Archer, "Credit Card Issuers Targeting Small Businesses," *Westchester County Business Journal*, May 23, 2005; and Mark Calvey, "Small Biz Charge Is On," *San Francisco Business Times*, January 20, 2006.
29. Amy Barrett, "Pfizer's Funk," *BusinessWeek*, February 28, 2005, and Jennifer Bayot, "Pfizer's Pain Inflamed by Weak Sales," *International Herald Tribune*, April 6, 2005.
30. Amy Borrus, "The SEC: Cracking Down on Spin," *BusinessWeek*, September 26, 2005.
31. Randy Myers, "Stuck on Yellow," *CFO*, October 2005, pp. 81–86; and "Venture Capital: Not-So-Easy Money," *CFO*, October 2005, p. 20; and Michael Liedtke, "Venture Capital Investment Remained Level in 2005," AP Worldstream, January 24, 2006.
32. Suzette Parmley, "Trump Banking on Bankruptcy Reorganization Approval Tuesday," *Philadelphia Inquirer*, April 4, 2005, and James P. Miller, "Wrigley Bond Issue Would Come with a Pleasant Flavor," *Chicago Tribune*, April 7, 2005.

Operations and Services Management 12

Speed and Flexibility Rule Global Competition

Even in the world of high fashion you can't be competitive if you aren't fast and flexible. Pressures from upstart retailers like Zara International and others that excel at "fast fashion"—getting new designs into stores quickly, have even brought changes to Louis Vuitton. The maker of high-fashion handbags and other accessories has revamped production techniques to increase speed without sacrificing quality.

A Louis Vuitton tote bag used to take up to 30 craft persons some 8 days to make. The bag was passed from hand to hand, with each worker performing a separate and highly specialized task.

That all changed when Vuitton executives, advised by consultants from McKinsey & Company, turned to the automobile industry, believe it or not, for ideas. They benchmarked Toyota's production processes and decided that things at the fashion house could be done a lot faster. The company reorganized workers into teams of 6 to 12 people, working at U-shaped workstations. Workers in each team perform more than one task and pass the in-process tote bag back and forth. They complete a tote bag in just one day.

Vuitton calls its production system "Pégase" after the mythical flying horse that is a symbol of speed and power. Since Pégase was introduced, Louis Vuitton has been able to ship new designs every 6 weeks, more than twice as fast as previously shipped. Says Patrick Louis Vuitton of the founding family: "It's about finding the best ratio between quality and speed." Yves Carcelle, chief executive officer for the Pégase brand, says: " Behind the creative magic of Louis Vuitton is an extremely efficient supply chain."

This is quite a set of statements from a firm that thrived for years on fashion alone—a business strategy once described in the *Wall Street Journal* as "celebrity advertising, lavish fashion shows, and the star-power of its top designer." To compete today with fast rivals and global competitors, even Louis Vuitton has now recognized that without the best execution, even a great design can't guarantee success.[1]

Benchmark

Workers in Louis Vuitton's Pégase teams are less specialized than before, working on a broader set of individual tasks and as part of a team. They swap tasks and team roles while making different kinds of bags, allowing production to switch quickly from one design to another. Take a look around the next time you are in a service establishment or in a production facility. How much productivity could be gained by following similar ideas?

Self-Management

This chapter is about the management of operations—getting things right for organizations as they deal with lots of complexities. We face similar challenges in many ways; we're complex systems too, and we also need to be managed.

Career success today depends significantly upon one's capacities for self-management—the ability to understand yourself individually and in the social context, to assess personal

From *Management*, 10th edition by John R. Schermerhorn. Copyright © 2009 by John Wiley & Sons, Inc. Reproduced with permission of John Wiley & Sons, Inc.

strengths and weaknesses, to exercise initiative, to accept responsibility for accomplishments, to work well with others, and to adapt by continually learning from experience in the quest for self-improvement. Self-management is an essential skill that asks you to dig deep and continually learn from experience.

Some self-management ideas for career success are shown in the box. They are within everyone's grasp. But the motivation to succeed must come from within. Only you can make this commitment, and it is best made right from the beginning.

We all need to take charge of our destinies and become self-managers. You can help move your career forward by behaving like an entrepreneur, seeking feedback on your performance continually, setting up your own mentoring systems, getting comfortable with teamwork, taking risks to gain experience and learn new skills, being a problem solver, and keeping your life in balance.[2]

Self-Management for Career Success

- *Lesson one:* There is no substitute for high performance. No matter what the assignment, you must work hard to establish and maintain your credibility and work value.
- *Lesson two:* Be and stay flexible. Don't hide from ambiguity; don't wait for structure. You must adapt to new work demands, new situations, and new people.
- *Lesson three:* Keep the focus. You can't go forward without talent. You must be a talent builder—someone who is always adding to and refining your talents to make them valuable to an employer.

As the opening example of Louis Vuitton suggests organizations today operate in a world that places a premium on productivity, technology utilization, quality, customer service, and speed. Businesses large and small are struggling and innovating as they try to succeed in a world of intense competition, continued globalization of markets and business activities, and rapid technological change. Just how top executives approach these challenges differs from one organization to the next, but they all focus on moving services and products into the hands of customers in ways that create loyalty and profits.[3]

At Xerox Corporation, CEO Anne Mulcahy believes that competition is an opportunity to focus one's operations and keep employees' eyes on the target—winning ground against strong competitors. And she believes customers are center-stage, saying: "The toughest customers are the ones that embed themselves in *customer relationships*—that's what we're trying to do." When in the field, she advises her sales force to emphasize Xerox's strengths rather than bad-mouthing the competition.

At BMW, where customers are also foremost, a major thrust is on continuous innovation. CEO Norbert Reithofer says: "We push change through the organization to ensure its strength. There are always better solutions." One of those solutions is state-of-the-art manufacturing: the firm's facilities produce 1.3 million customized vehicles a year.

At Ann Taylor stores, when the firm was struggling to reassert its women's clothing brand and market position, newly-appointed CEO Kay Krill started with a 54-point action plan. It covered everything from processes to products to marketing. Although criticized for identifying so many things to address, she said: "There were 54 things we needed to fix. We fixed every one of them. All 54 were important to me."

Operations Management Essentials

In one way or another, all organizations must master the challenges of operations management—getting work done by managing the systems through which organizations transform resources into finished products, goods, and services for customers and clients.[4]

The span of operations management covers the full input-throughput-output cycle. Typical operations management decisions address such things as resource acquisition, inventories, facilities, workflows, technologies, and product quality.

Manufacturing and Services Settings

The essentials of operations management apply to all types of organizations, not just to product manufacturers. Yes, Xerox transforms resource inputs into quality photocopy machines; BMW transforms them into attractive, high-performance automobiles; and Ann Taylor stores transforms them into fashionable clothing and accessories. But also in the services sector. Southwest Airlines transforms resource inputs into low-cost, dependable air travel: American Express transforms them into financial services; the Mayo Clinic transforms them into health care services; and governments transform them into public services.

Productivity and Competitive Advantage

The core issues in operations and services management boil down to how "productivity" and "competitive advantage" are achieved. This focuses management attention on the various processes and activities that turn resources—in the form of people, materials, equipment, and capital—into finished goods and services.

Productivity

Operations management in both manufacturing and services is very concerned with productivity—a quantitative measure of the efficiency with which inputs are transformed into outputs. The basic productivity equation is:

$$\text{Productivity} = \text{Output/Input}$$

If, for example, a local Red Cross center collects 100 units of donated blood in one 8-hour day, its productivity would be 10.25 units per hour. If we were in charge of centers in several locations, the productivity of the centers could be compared on this measure. Alternatively, one might compare the centers using a productivity measure based not on hours of inputs, but on numbers of full-time staff. Using this input measure, a center that collects 500 units per week with two full-time staff members (250 units per person) is more productive than one that collects 600 units per week with three (200 units per person).

When Microsoft studied productivity of office workers in an online survey of 38,000+ people across 200 countries, results showed a variety of productivity shortfalls.[5] Although people reported working 47 hours per week, they were unproductive during 17 of the hours: 69 percent said time spent in meetings was unproductive. Productivity obstacles included unclear objectives and priorities, as well as procrastination and poor communication.

Competitive Advantage

Inefficiencies like those reported by Microsoft are costly; lost productivity by any measure is a drain on organizational competitiveness. Operating efficiencies that increase productivity, by contrast, are among the ways organizations may gain competitive advantage—defined earlier in the book as a core competency that allows an organization to outperform competitors.[6] Potential drivers of competitive advantage include such things as the ability to outperform based on product innovation, customer service, speed to market manufacturing flexibility, and product or service quality. But regardless of how competitive advantage is achieved, the key result is the same; an ability to consistently do something of high value that one's competitors cannot replicate quickly or do as well.

Consider the example of Matsushita Electric Industries—maker of telephones, fax machines, security cameras, and other electronics. When productivity at Matsushita's plant in Saga, Japan, doubled in a four year period, the executives didn't sit back and celebrate. They wanted still more. A huge set of conveyers was removed and robots were brought in along with sophisticated software to operate them. Plant manager Hitoshi Hirata says: "It used to be 2.5 days into a production run before we had our first finished product. But now the first is done in 40 minutes." And one might be tempted to compliment Hirata on a job well done and sit back to watch the results. Not so. He goes on to say: "Next year we'll try to shorten the cycle even more."[7]

Operations Technologies

The foundation of any transformation process is technology—the combination of knowledge, skills, equipment, and work methods used to transform resource inputs into organizational outputs. It is the way tasks are accomplished using tools, machines, techniques, and human know-how. The availability of appropriate technology is a cornerstone of productivity, and the nature of the core technologies in use is an important element in competitive advantage.

Manufacturing Technology

It is common to classify manufacturing technology into three categories; small-batch production, mass production, and continuous-process production.[8] In small-batch production, such as in a racing bicycle shop, a variety of custom products are tailor-made to order. Each item or batch of items is made somewhat differently to fit customer specifications. The equipment used may not be elaborate, but a high level of worker skill is often needed. In mass production, such as manufacturing the popular brands of recreational bicycles, the firm produces a large number of uniform products in an assembly-line system. Workers are highly dependent on one another as the product passes from stage to stage until completion. Equipment may be sophisticated, and workers often follow detailed instructions while performing simplified jobs.

Organizations using continuous-process production continuously feed raw materials—such as liquids, solids, and gases—through a highly automated production system with largely computerized controls. Such systems are equipment intensive, but they can often be operated by a relatively small labor force. Classic examples are oil refineries and power plants.

Among the directions in manufacturing technology today, the following trends are evident.[9]

- There is increased use of *robotics*, where computer-controlled machines perform physically repetitive work with consistency and efficiency. If you visit any automobile manufacturer today, chances are that robotics is a major feature of the operations.
- There is increased use of *flexible manufacturing systems* that allow automated operations to quickly shift from one task or product type to another. The goal is to combine flexibility with efficiency, allowing what is sometimes called *mass customization*—efficient mass production of products meeting specific customer requirements.
- There is increased use of *cellular layouts* that place machines doing different work together, so that the movement of materials from one to the other is as efficient as possible. Cellular layouts also accommodate more teamwork on the part of machine operators.
- There is increased use of *computer-integrated manufacturing*, in which product designs, process plans, and manufacturing are driven from a common computer platform. Such CIM approaches are now integrated with the Internet, so that customer purchasing trends in retail locations can be spotted and immediately integrated into production schedules at a manufacturing location.
- There is increased focus on *lean production* that continuously innovates and employs best practices to keep increasing production efficiencies. A master is Toyota, featured in the end-of-chapter case. A *BusinessWeek* headline once said "no one does lean like the Japanese."[10]

- There is increased attention to *design for disassembly.* The goal here is to design and manufacture products in ways that consider how their component parts will be recycled at the end of their lives.
- There is increased value to be found in *remanufacturing.* Instead of putting things together, remanufacturing takes used items apart and rebuilds them as products to be used again. One estimate is that using remanufactured materials saves up to 30 percent on costs.

Service Technology

When it comes to service technology, the classifications are slightly different.[11] In health care, education, and related services, intensive technology focuses the efforts of many people with special expertise on the needs of patients, students, or clients. In banks, real estate firms, insurance companies, employment agencies, and others like them, mediating technology links together parties seeking a mutually beneficial exchange of values—typically a buyer and a seller. And, long-linked technology can function like mass production, where a client is passed from point to point for various aspects of service delivery.

Value Chain Management

Whereas productivity may be considered the major efficiency measure in both manufacturing and services, "value creation" should be the target effectiveness measure. And in this sense, value creation means that the end result of a task or activity or work process is worth more than the effort and resources invested to accomplish it. In a manufacturing operation, for example, value is created when a raw material such as copper wire is combined with transistors and other electrical components to create a computer chip. In a service setting, value is created when a trained financial analyst provides a customer with advice that leads to profitable brokerage transactions in a stock portfolio.

Value Chain Analysis

You should recall that an organization's value chain, as shown in Exhibit 12.1 is the specific sequence of activities that result in the creation of product or services with value for customers. The value chain includes all *primar activities*—from inbound logistics to operations to outbound logistics to marketing and sales to after sales service, as well as *support activities*—such a procurement, human resource management, technology development an support, and financial and infrastructure maintenance.[12]

Analysis of any organization's value chain will show an intricate sequence of activities that step-by-step adds value to inputs, right up to the point at which finished goods or services are delivered to customers or clients. The essence of value chain management is

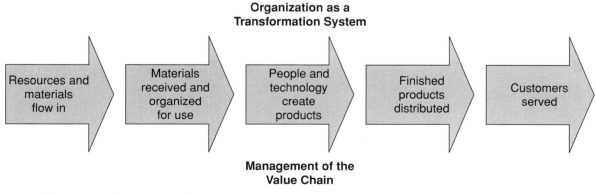

Exhibit 12.1 — Elements in an Organization's Value Chain

to manage each of these steps to maximum efficiency and effectiveness. Part of the logic of being able to identify and diagram a value chain is to focus management attention on three major questions. First: what value is being created for customers in each step? Second: how efficient is each step as a contributor to overall organizational productivity? Third: how can value creation be improved overall?

As the customer of an online retailer such as Amazon.com. for example, you can think of this value in such terms as the price you pay, the quality you receive, and the timeliness of the delivery. From the standpoint of value chain management. Amazon's value creation process can be examined from the point where books are purchased, to their transportation and warehousing, to electronic inventorying and order processing, and to packaging and distribution to the ultimate customer.

Supply Chain Management

An essential element in any value chain is the relationship between the organization and the many people and businesses that supply it with needed resources and materials. All of these supplier relationships on the input side of the input-throughput-output action cycle must be well managed for productivity.

The concept of supply chain management, or SCM, involves strategy management of all operations linking an organization and its suppliers including such areas as purchasing, manufacturing, transportation, and distribution.[13] The goals of supply chain management are to achieve efficiency in all aspects of the supply chain while ensuring on-time availability of quality resources and products. And, Wal-Mart is still considered a master of supply chain management. As one example, the firm uses an advanced information system that continually updates inventory records and sales forecasts based on point-of-sale computerized information. Suppliers access this information electronically, allowing them to adjust their operations and rapidly ship replacement products to meet the retailer's needs.

Purchasing plays an important role in supply chain management. Just as any individual tries to control how much they spend, a thrifty organization must be concerned about how much it pays for what it buys. To leverage buying power, more organizations are centralizing purchasing to allow buying in volume. They are trimming supply chains and focusing on a small number of suppliers with whom they negotiate special contracts, gain quality assurances, and get preferred service. They are also finding ways to work together in supplier-purchaser partnerships. It is now more common, for example, that parts suppliers maintain warehouses in their customer's facilities. The customer provides the space; the supplier does the rest. The benefits to the customer are lower purchasing costs and preferred service; the supplier gains an exclusive customer contract and more sales volume.

Inventory Management

Another important issue in the value chain is management of inventory the amount of materials or products kept in storage. Organizations maintain a variety of inventories of raw material, work in process, and finished goods. Whenever anything is held in inventory there is cost associated with it, and controlling these costs is an important productivity tool.

Fair Trade Fashion

Perhaps you're one of a growing number of consumers that like to shop "fair trade." Doesn't it feel good when you buy coffee, for example, that is certified as grown by persons who were paid fairly for their labors? But can we say the same about clothing? How do we know that what we're wearing right now wasn't made under sweatshop conditions or by children?

(continued)

There is at least one retailer that wants to be considered as selling fair trade fashion. Fair Indigo, launched by former executives of major fashion retailers, presents itself as "a new clothing company with a different way of doing business" that wants to "create stylish, high-quality clothes while paying a fair and meaningful wage to the people who produce them." Pointing out that there is no certifying body for fair trade apparel, Fair Indigo offers this guarantee: "We will therefore guarantee that every employee who makes our clothing is paid a fair wage, not just a legal minimum wage, as is the benchmark in the industry."

The firm's representatives travel the globe searching for small factories and cooperatives that meet their standards. By doing so, they're bucking industry trends in outsourcing and contract manufacturing. Fair Indigo's CEO, Bill Bass, says: "The whole evolution of the clothing and manufacturing industry has been to drive prices and wages down, shut factories and move work to countries with lower wages. We said, 'we're going to reverse this and push wages up.'"

You Decide

How do you define "fair," as in "fair trade"? Are you willing to pay a bit more for a fair trade product? And what do you think about Fair Indigo's business model? Is it "fashion" that sells apparel: or factory and conditions of origin? Will consumers pay more for fair trade fashion? Is Fair Indigo on the forefront of the next new wave of value creation in fashion retailing?

Economic Order Quantity

The goal of inventory control is to make sure that an inventory is just the right size to meet performance needs, thus minimizing the cost. The economic order quantity (EOQ) method of inventory control involves ordering a fixed number of items every time an inventory level falls to a predetermined point. When this point is reached, as shown in Exhibit 12.2, a decision is automatically made (typically by computer) to place a standard order to replenish the stock. The order sizes are mathematically calculated to minimize costs of inventory. The best example is the local supermarket, where hundreds of daily orders are routinely made on this basis.

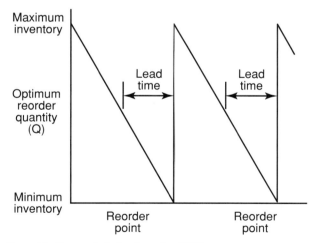

Exhibit 12.2 Inventory Control by Economic Order Quantity (EOQ)

Just-in-Time Systems

Another approach to inventory control is just-in-time scheduling (JIT), made popular by the Japanese. JIT systems reduce costs and improve workflow by scheduling materials to arrive at a workstation or facility "just in time" to be used. Since almost no inventories are maintained, the just-in-time approach is an important productivity tool. When a major hurricane was predicted to hit Florida, for example, Wal-Mart's computer database anticipated high demand for, of all things, strawberry Pop-Tarts. JIT kicked in to deliver them to the stores "just in time" for the storm.[14]

Break-Even Analysis

Another important value chain management issue relates to capacity planning for the production of products or services, and the pricing of them for sales. In basic business terms: too much capacity raises costs, and too little capacity means unmet sales: too low a price fails to deliver revenues that cover costs, and too high a price drives away customers. Thus, when business executives are deliberating new products or projects, a frequent question is: "What is the `break-even point?"

The graph in Exhibit 12.3 shows that the break-even point is where revenues just equal costs. You can also think of it as the point where losses end and profit begins. The formula for calculating break-even points is:

Break-even point = Fixed costs/(Price − Variable costs)

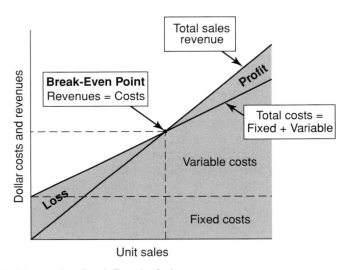

Exhibit 12.3 ■ Graphical Approach to Break-Even Analysis

Managers use break-even analysis to improve control and perform "what if" calculations under different projected cost and revenue conditions. See if you can calculate some break-even points, doing the types of analyses that business executives perform every day. Suppose the proposed target price for a new product is $8 per unit, fixed costs are $10,000, and variable costs are $4 per unit? What sales volume is required to break even? (Answer: the break-even point is at 2,500 units.) What happens if you are good at cost control and can keep variable costs to $3 per unit? (Answer: the break-even point is at 2,000 units.) Now, suppose you can only produce 1,000 units in the beginning and at the original costs. At what price must you sell them to break even? (Answer: $14.)

Service and Product Quality

Some years ago, at a time when American industry was first coming to grips with fierce competition from Japanese products, American quality pioneer J. M. Juran challenged an audience of Japanese executives with a prediction. He warned them against complacency, suggesting that America would bounce back in business competitiveness and that the words "Made in America" would once again symbolize world-class quality.[15] American businesses have since done a lot to live up to Juran's prediction, but the challenges of delivering consistent quality are still apparent in the news . . . and in our personal experiences. Have you ever heard conversations like this one?

"Here we go again—cut costs, cut costs, cut costs. How far can you cut costs and still have a viable operation? I think these top managers must have all graduated from the same MBA program, one that was dominated by 'number crunchers.' All they seem to know is how to cut costs. But where is it getting us? I see low morale, increasing problems meeting targets because we're all so overloaded, and corners being trimmed that could well turn into major quality problems at some point. I don't know about you, but I'm about fed up with it all."

"I know, just look at the wait lines at some service establishments. How long does it take you to get to the car rental counter or to cash a check at the bank? Most service establishments these days are cutting back so far on staff that there are few people left to actually serve their customers. And the next time you're in a restaurant, keep your eyes open. The chances are that the servers are being run ragged because there just aren't enough of them. Don't you wonder how much could be added to the bottom lines of these firms if they would just pay more to add staff at levels that customers would appreciate?"

A *Harvard Business Review* survey reports that American business leaders rank customer service and product quality as the first and second most important goals in the success of their organizations.[16] But notwithstanding the goals, there is often a disconnection between intentions and results—back to the prior conversations so to speak. In a survey by the market research firm Michelson & Associates, poor service and product dissatisfaction were also ranked number 1 and number 2, respectively, as reasons why customers abandon a retail store.[17]

Issues and Situations

Bloggers have arrived in the world of customer service complaints. There are many people who take pleasure in sharing their travails and disasters with anyone who can type the offending company's name into a Web address. And there's a lot of energy flowing through those stories.

When Justin Callaway didn't get satisfaction from Cingular (now AT&T) over a complaint that interference from his phone ruined his speakers, he used his experience as a freelance video editor to start a campaign. Along with friends he recorded a song about Cingular and then added an animated bandit based on the company's logo to create a video short—"Feeling Cingular"—posted on YouTube. A vice-president from AT&T then wrote him offering to buy him new speakers to settle his complaint. Callaway refused, claiming the firm should do better at informing customers of potential interference problems. "It wasn't about the speakers anymore," he said.

A *BusinessWeek* report claims that "good customer service" isn't that hard to deliver "Don't force customers to play 'call-center' tag . . . hire friendly people, train them well, and reward them with healthy pay and benefits."

In the last chapter we talked about "market control"—basically using responses from customers as a means of controlling behavior in and by organizations. What do you think? In this age of YouTube and blogger mania, does market control mean that organizations hold themselves more accountable for customer service, and will the suggestions from *BusinessWeek* become everyday business realities? Or will firms continue to respond to situations like Callaway's case-by-case, and without any major adjustments to their operations?

Reaching the twin goals of providing great service and quality products isn't always easy. But when pursued relentlessly, striving to reach these goals can be an important source of competitive advantage. Bill Gates once said: "Your most unhappy customers are your greatest source of learning." Just imagine what would happen if every customer or client contact for an organization was positive. Not only would these customers and clients return again and again, but they would also tell others and expand the customer base.

Customer Relationship Management

Without any doubt, customers put today's organizations to a very stiff test. Like you, most want three things: (1) high quality, (2) low price, and (3) on-time delivery of the goods and services they buy. And, these are the types of customer stories that cause headaches for managers.[18]

> *Dell Computer* suffered a major customer backlash when some 3,000 callers to its customer service lines during one week had to wait at least 30 minutes before being able to speak with a real person.
>
> *Northwest* Airlines had a lot to explain to potential customers after leaving passengers stranded inside a plane for 8 hours because of a snowstorm in Detroit.
>
> *Home Depot* saw customer satisfaction fall 8.2% while sales surged at its rival Lowe's, known for its top customer service.

Essentials of CRM

Many organizations now use the principles of customer relationship management to establish and maintain high standards of customer service.[19] Known as CRM, this approach uses the latest information technologies to maintain intense communication with customers as well as to gather and utilize data regarding their needs and desires. At Marriott International, for example. CRM is supported by special customer management software that tracks information on customer preferences. When you check in, the likelihood is that your past requests for things like a king-size bed, no smoking room, and computer modern access are already in your record. Says Marriott's chairman: "It's a big competitive advantage."[20]

There are probably many times in your experiences as a customer that you wonder why more managers don't get this message. Consider, for example, the case of Mona Shaw, a 76-year-old retired nurse. After arriving at a Comcast office to complain about poor installation of cable service to her home, she sat on a bench for two hours waiting to see a manager. She then left and came back with a hammer. She smashed a keyboard and telephone in the office, yelling: "Have I got your attention now?" it cost Shaw an arrest and $375 fine, but she became a media sensation and a rallying point for unhappy customers everywhere. As for Comcast, a spokesperson said: "We apologize for any customer service issues that Ms. Shaw experienced."[21]

Comcast's apology is nice, but don't you also wonder: Did the system change as a result of this incident? Was customer relationship management activated so that service improved for Shaw and other customers in the future? Was the experience of this branch incident reviewed by top management and the learning disseminated throughout Comcast operations nation-wide? Or, did things quickly slide back into business-as-usual?

External and Internal Customers

Customer relationship management applies equally well to external and internal customers. Exhibit 12.4 expands the open-systems view of organizations to depict the complex internal operations of the organization, as well as its interdependence with the external environment. In this Exhibit the organization's *external customers* purchase the goods produced or utilize the services provided. They may be industrial customers—other firms that buy a company's products for use in their own operations—or they may be retail customers or clients who purchase or use the goods and services directly. *Internal customers*, by contrast, are found within the organization. They are the individuals and groups who use or otherwise depend on one another's work in order to do their own jobs well.

Quality Management

World class organizations embed quality in all aspects of their operations.[22] ISO certification by the International Standards Organization in Geneva, Switzerland, serves as a major indicator of quality accomplishments. Another benchmark is the Malcolm Baldrige award. It is

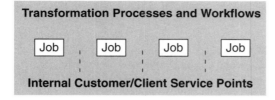

Exhibit 12.4 ■ The Importance of External and Internal Customers

given by the President of the United States to business, health care, education and non-profit organizations that meet quality criteria in the following areas: leadership, strategic planning, customer and market focus, measurement and knowledge management, human resource focus, process management, and results.[23]

The work of W. Edwards Deming is a cornerstone of the quality movement. His approach to quality emphasizes constant innovation, use of statistical methods, and commitment to training in the fundamentals of quality assurance. One outgrowth of his work is total quality management, or TQM. This is a process that makes quality principles part of the organization's strategic objectives, applying them to all aspects of operations and striving to meet customers' needs by doing things right the first time.

Most TQM approaches insist that the total quality commitment applies to everyone in an organization and throughout the value chain—from resource acquisition and supply chain management, through production and into the distribution of finished goods and services, and ultimately to customer relationship management. Both TQM and the Deming approach are also closely tied to the emphasis on continuous improvement—always looking for new ways to improve on current performance. Again, this applies throughout the value chain.[24] The basic notion driving continuous improvement is that one can never be satisfied: something always can and should be improved on.

Statistical Quality Control

For Deming, quality principles are straightforward: tally defects, analyze and trace them to the sources, make corrections, and keep records of what happens afterwards.[25] He championed statistical quality control that takes samples of work, measures quality in the samples, and determines acceptability of results. Unacceptable results trigger investigation and corrective action. An easy way to apply this notion is through control charts, such as the one shown in Exhibit 12.5.

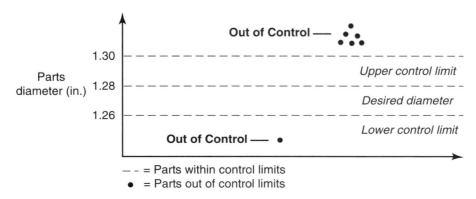

Exhibit 12.5 ■ Sample Control Chart Showing Upper and Lower Control Limits

Control charts are graphical ways of displaying trends so that exceptions to quality standards can be identified for special attention. In the Exhibit, for example, an upper control limit and a lower control limit specify the allowable tolerances for measurements of a machine part. As long as the manufacturing process produces parts that fall within these limits, things are "in control." As soon as parts fall outside the limits, it is clear that something is going wrong that is affecting quality. The process can then be investigated—even shut down—to identify the source of the errors and correct them.

The logic of tallying and analyzing defects can be further extended with a variety of sophisticated statistical techniques. For example, many manufacturers now use a Six Sigma program, meaning that statistically the firm's quality performance standard will tolerate no more than 3.4 defects per million units of goods produced or services completed.[26] This translates to a perfection rate of 99.9997 percent.

Work Processes

The emphasis on productivity and competitive advantage through operations management includes business process reengineering.[27] This is defined as the systematic and complete analysis of work processes and the design of new and better ones.[28] The goal is to break old work habits and focus attention on better ways of doing things.

Work Process Analysis

In his book, *Beyond Reengineering*, Michael Hammer defines a work process as "a related group of tasks that together create a result of value for the customer."[29] These tasks are what people do to turn resource inputs into goods or services for customers. Hammer highlights the following key words as essential elements of his definition: *group*—tasks are viewed as part of a group rather than in isolation: *together*—everyone must share a common goal: *result*—the focus is on what is accomplished, not on activities: *customer*—processes serve customers, and their perspectives are the ones that really count.

The concept of workflow, or the way work moves from one point to another in manufacturing or service delivery, is central to the understanding of processes.[30] The various parts of a work process must all be completed to achieve the desired results, and they must typically be completed in a given order. An important starting point for a reengineering effort is to diagram or map these workflows as they actually take place. Then each step can be systematically analyzed to determine whether it is adding value, to consider ways of eliminating or combining steps, and to find ways to use technology to improve efficiency.

Process Reengineering

Process reengineering can be used to regularly assess and fine-tune work processes to ensure that they directly add value to operations. Through a technique called process value analysis, core processes are identified and carefully evaluated for their performance contributions. Each step in a work-flow is examined. Unless a step is found to be important, useful, and contributing to value-added results, it is eliminated. Process value analysis typically involves the following.[31]

1. Identify the core processes.
2. Map the core processes with respect to workflows.
3. Evaluate all core process tasks.
4. Search for ways to eliminate unnecessary tasks or work.
5. Search for ways to eliminate delays, errors, and misunderstandings.
6. Search for efficiencies in how work is shared and transferred among people and departments.

Research Brief

How do you improve the productivity of a sales force?

That's the question asked by Dianne Ledingham, Mark Kovac, and Heidi Locke Simon. Writing in the *Harvard Business Review*, they use a series of case examples to illustrate how companies have used data and analytical methods to raise sales. They contrast the newer, data-driven approaches with what they call a "wing-and-a-prayer" style, in which salespersons are given goals and then simply told to go out and meet them.

One case involves U.S. Equipment Financing, a division of GE Commercial Finance headed by Michael Pilot. Pilot's approach was to focus on raising the performance of existing sales representatives by helping them sell more—the "productivity improvement approach"—in contrast to simply hiring more reps—the "capacity increase approach." Pilot attributes some $300 million in new business to his scientific approach to sales force productivity. He began with a new database that inventoried past transactions. He then asked sales reps to come up with criteria that would indicate the likelihood of a customer doing business with GE. He next ran regression analyses that tested these criteria against the past transactions. The result was a set of six criteria that correlated well with past successes.

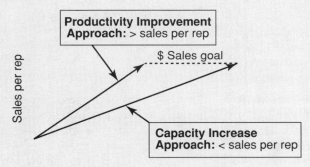

When new prospects were scored using the criteria, Pilot found 50 percent more top-prospect sales candidates than had previously been identified. Using this set of top prospects, he redesigned the sales force to maximize attention to those prospects, and he provided reps with information and tools to better deal with their customers. The result was a 19% increase in the "conversion" rate, or sales closings.

Researchers consider Pilot's scientific method a "best practice" approach to improving sales force productivity. They recommend the TOPSales approach, focusing on (1) targeted offerings by market segment, (2) optimized technology tools and procedures, (3) performance management metrics and systems, and (4) systematic sales force deployment.

You be the researcher

This article, by Ledingham et al., describes a vigorous productivity improvement approach to reaching a higher sales goal. Can you find examples in your experience or community where goals are reached, but the costs of doing so are very high? What would you propose so that the same goals could be reached with lower costs and higher productivity?

Reference: Dianne Ledingham, Mark Kovac, and Heidi Locke Simon. "The New Science of Sales Force Productivity." *Harvard Business Review*, vol. 84 (September 2006), pp. 124–33.

Exhibit 12.6 shows an example of how reengineering and better use of computer technology can streamline a purchasing operation. Ideally, a purchase order should result in at least three value-added outcomes: order fulfillment, a paid bill, and a satisfied supplier. For this to happen things like ordering, shipping, receiving, billing, and payment must all be well handled. A traditional business system might have purchasing, receiving, and accounts payable as separate functions, with each function communicating with each other and with the supplier. As the Exhibit shows, there are lots of inefficiencies here. Alternatively, process value analysis might result in reengineering the workflow and redesigning it to include a new purchasing support team. Its members can handle the same work more efficiently with the support of the latest computer technology.[32]

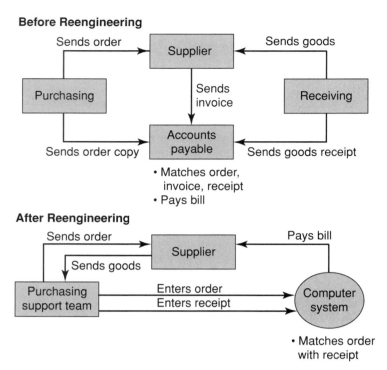

Exhibit 12.6 — How Reengineering can Streamline Work Processes

Process-Driven Organizations

Customers, teamwork, and efficiency are central to Hammer's notion of process reengineering. He describes the case of Aetna Life & Casualty Company, where a complex system of tasks and processes once took as long as 28 days to accomplish.[33] Customer service requests were handled in a step-by-step fashion by many different people. After an analysis of workflows, the process was redesigned into a "one and done" format, where a single customer service provider handled each request from start to finish. After the change was made, an Aetna customer account manager said: "Now we can see the customers as individual people. It's no longer 'us' and 'them.'"[34]

Hammer also describes reengineering at a unit of Verizon Communications. Before reengineering, customer inquiries for telephone service and repairs required extensive consultation between technicians and their supervisors. After process value analysis, technicians were formed into geographical teams that handled their own scheduling, service delivery, and reporting. They were given cellular telephones and laptop computers to assist in managing their work, resulting in the elimination of a number of costly supervisory jobs. The technicians enthusiastically responded to the changes and opportunities. "The fact that you've got four or five people zoned in a certain geographical area," said one, "means that we get personally familiar with our customers' equipment and problems."[35]

The essence of process reengineering is to locate control for processes with an identifiable group of people, and to focus each person and the entire system on meeting customer needs and expectations. It tries to eliminate duplication of work and systems bottlenecks so as to reduce costs, increase efficiency, and build capacity for change. The result is to create a process-driven organization that Hammer describes this way.[36]

> *Its intrinsic customer focus and its commitment to outcome measurement make it vigilant and proactive in perceiving the need for change; the process owner, freed from other responsibilities and wielding the power of process design, is an institutionalized agent of change; and employees who have an appreciation for customers and who are measured on outcomes are flexible and adaptable.*

Endnotes

1. Christina Passariello, "Louis Vuitton Tries Modern Methods on Assembly Line," *Wall Street Journal* (October 9, 2006).
2. Stephen Covey, "How to Succeed in Today's Workplace," *USA Weekend* (August 29–31, 1997), pp. 4–5.
3. Examples from Anne Mulcahy, "How I Compete," *BusinessWeek* (August 21/28, 2006), p. 55. Gail Edmondson, "BMW's Dream Factory," *BusinessWeek* (October 16, 2006), pp. 68–80. Amy Merrick, "Asking 'What Would Ann Do?'" *Wall Street Journal* (September 16, 2006), pp. B1, B2.
4. Good overviews are available in R. Dan Reid and Nada R. Sanders, *Operations Management: An Integrated Approach*, 2nd ed. (Hoboken, NJ: John Wiley & Sons, 2006); and Roberta S. Russell and Bernard W. Taylor III, *Operations Management: Quality and Competitiveness in a Global Environment* (Hoboken, NJ: John Wiley & Sons, 2005).
5. "Survey Finds Workers Average Only Three Productive Days Per Week," www.microsoft.com/press/2005/mar05 (retrieved October 20, 2006).
6. See Michael E. Porter, *Competitive Strategy: Techniques for Analyzing Industries and Competitors* (New York: Free Press, 1998) and *Competitive Advantage: Creating and Sustaining Superior Performance* (New York: Free Press, 1990); see also Richard A. D'Aveni, *Hyper-Competition: Managing the Dynamics of Strategic Maneuvering* (New York: Free Press, 1994).
7. Information from Ibid.
8. Joan Woodward, *Industrial Organization: Theory and Practice* (London: Oxford University Press, 1965; republished by Oxford University Press, 1994).
9. Brian Hindo, "Everything Old Is New Again," *BusinessWeek* (September 25, 2006), p. 70.
10. Kenji Hall, "No One Does Lean Like the Japanese," *BusinessWeek* (July 10, 2006), pp. 40–41.
11. This treatment is from James D. Thompson, *Organizations in Action* (New York: McGraw-Hill, 1967).
12. Porter, op. cit., 1998.
13. See Michael Hugos, *Essentials of Supply Chain Management*, 2nd ed. (Hoboken, NJ: John Wiley & Sons, 2006).
14. "Gauging the Wal-Mart Effect," *Wall Street Journal* (December 3–4, 2005), pp. A1, A9.
15. See Joseph M. Juran, *Quality Control Handbook*, 3rd ed. (New York: McGraw-Hill, 1979) and "The Quality Trilogy: A Universal Approach to Managing for Quality," in *Total Quality Management*, H. Costin, ed. (New York: Dryden, 1994): W. Edwards Deming, *Out of Crisis* (Cambridge, MA: MIT Press, 1986) and "Deming's Quality Manifesto," *Best of Business Quarterly*, vol. 12 (Winter 1990–1991), pp. 6–10. See also Howard S. Gitlow and Shelly J. Gitlow. *The Deming Guide to Quality and Competitive Position* (Englewood Cliffs, NJ: Prentice-Hall, 1987), and Juran, op. cit. (1993).
16. Rosabeth Moss Kanter, "Transcending Business Boundaries: 12,000 World Managers View Change," *Harvard Business Review* (May–June 1991), pp. 151–64.
17. Dale Dauten, "Which One Would You Rather Be?" *St. Louis Dispatch* (October 8, 2006), p. C2.
18. Information from Brian Hindo, "Satisfaction Not Guaranteed," *BusinessWeek* (June 19, 2006), pp. 32–38.
19. See C. K. Prahalad, Patricia B. Ramaswamy, Jon R. Katzenbach, Chris Lederer, and Sam Hill, *Harvard Business Review on Customer Relationship Management* (Boston, MA: Harvard Business School Publishing, 1998–2001).
20. Information from "How Marriott Never Forgets a Guest," *BusinessWeek* (February 21, 2000), p. 74.
21. Example and quote from Jena McGregor, "Customer Service Champs," *BusinessWeek* (March 3, 2008), pp. 37–42.
22. For the classics, see W. Edwards Deming, *Quality, Productivity, and Competitive Position* (Cambridge, MA: MIT Press, 1982) and Juran, op. cit.

23. http://www.nist.gov/public_affairs/factsheet/baldfaqs.htm
24. See Edward E. Lawler III, Susan Albers Mohrman, and Gerald E. Ledford Jr., *Employee Involvement and Total Quality Management: Practices and Results in Fortune 1000 Companies* (San Francisco: Jossey-Bass, 1992).
25. Rafael Aguay, *Dr. Deming: The American Who Taught the Japanese about Quality* (New York: Free Press, 1997): W. Edwards Deming, op. cit. (1986).
26. For pros and cons of (this approach see "Six Sigma: So Yesterday?" *BusinessWeek* (June, 2007), Special Edition, p. IN 11.
27. Michael Hammer, *Beyond Reengineering* (New York: Harper Business, 1997).
28. Michael Hammer and James Champy, *Reengineering the Corporation: A Manifesto for Business Revolution,* rev. ed. (New York: Harper Business, 1999).
29. Hammer, *Beyond Reengineering,* op. cit., p. 5; see also the discussion of processes in Gary Hamel, Leading the Revolution (Boston. MA: Harvard Business School Press, 2000).
30. Thomas M. Koulopoulos, *The Workflow Imperative* (New York: Van Nostrand Reinhold, 1995): Hammer, *Beyond Reengineering,* op. cit.
31. Ronni T. Marshak, "Workflow Business Process Reengineering," special advertising section, *Fortune* (1997).
32. A similar example is found in Hammer, *Beyond Reengineering,* op. cit., pp. 9, 10.
33. Ibid., pp. 28–30.
34. Ibid., p. 29.
35. Ibid., p. 27.
36. Quotation from Hammer and Company Web site: www.hammerandco.com/WhatIsAProcessOrgFrames.html.

Feature Notes

Real Ethics: Information and quotes from Susan Chandler, "'Fair Trade' Label Enters Retail Market," *Columbus Dispatch* (October 16, 2006), p. G6: and www.fairindigo.com/about.

Issues and Situations: Information and quote from Jena McGregor, "Customer Service Champs," *BusinessWeek* (March 3, 2008), pp. 37–42.

APPENDIX A
Chapter Exercises

Name _____   Date _____

Chapter 1   The Nature of Management

Closing Exercise

Visit a website that discusses business and management topics. Some of the most popular sites are:

Wall Street Journal	http://online.wsj.com/home-page
BusinessWeek	http://www.businessweek.com/
Fortune	http://money.cnn.com/magazines/fortune/
Forbes	http://www.forbes.com/
Inc.	http://inc.com/
New York Times	http://www.nytimes.com/
Atlanta Journal Constitution	http://www.ajc.com/

Find an article about an issue that you feel impacts a manager's decision-making process and summarize it in a few sentences. Think broadly here, such as the legal, political, and environmental issues that a manager must face. What are the issues in the macro environment that a manager must pay attention to? Are there industry issues? How about the more immediate environment, say within a state or a city? Are there issues within a company?

Name _____ Date _____

Chapter 2 The Basics of Planning and Project Management

Closing Exercise

Refer to the sample flowchart in this chapter. Come up with a strategy for finding an internship or a full-time job. Think about the steps that are required in this process. Map out the sequence with appropriate questions to be asked at each stage, along with "Yes" and "No" decisions. Ask only the necessary questions. Keep your flowchart straightforward, so that anyone can pick it up and understand your thought process.

Name _____   Date _____

Chapter 3 Strategy
Opening Exercise

1. Visit the Starbucks website: http://www.starbucks.com/mission/default.asp.

2. Who are the stakeholders?

3. Using Porter's Five Forces Model for industry analysis in the text, which force do you think is the most important to Starbucks' future success? Why?

4. What type of strategy is Starbucks pursuing? Cost leadership? Differentiation? Focus?

5. Which phrases in the language of the mission statement clue you to Starbucks' strategy?

239

Name _____ Date _____

Chapter 3   Strategy
Closing Exercise

After spending some time looking over Starbucks' website, how would you describe Howard Schultz's vision for the culture of the company?

Name _____ Date _____

Chapter 4 International Management
Closing Exercise

Go to the Central Intelligence Agency website: https://www.cia.gov/. Browse through the World Factbook and choose a country that interests you. Scroll down to the "People" and "Economy" sections and get a feel for the important characteristics of your country. Summarize the important features, including:

A. **People:**

   Population

   Median age

   Population growth rate

   Total fertility rate

   School life expectancy

B. **Economy:**

   Gross Domestic Product (GDP)

   GDP growth rate

   Purchasing Power Parity (PPP) GDP per capita

   Unemployment rate

   Inflation rate

   Central bank discount rate

What are some other interesting features outside of the "People" and "Economy" sections?

Name _____   Date _____

Chapter 5   The Nature of Entrepreneurship
Closing Exercise

1. Go to the *Franchise Business Review* website: http://www.fbr50.com/.

2. Find a franchise that piques your interest. Answer the following for your franchise:

    a. Franchise name

    b. Brief description of the business

    c. Year founded

    d. Total locations

    e. Start-up investment

    f. Cash required

    g. Net worth required

Name _____ Date _____

Chapter 6   Organizational Design
Closing Exercise

1. Visit the company overview website for Martha Stewart Living: http://phx.corporate-ir.net/phoenix.zhtml?c=96022&p=irol-homeprofile.

Spend a few minutes reading through the Web pages. Cite an example of an employee (other than a wedding expert) who works in this matrix organization. Describe how this employee likely contributes to the major divisions and project teams (groups) across the organization. What are the potential conflicts for the employee you chose?

Name _____   Date _____

Chapter 7 Leadership
Opening Exercise

1. Is there a 4th of July in England?

2. Some months have 30 days and some have 31 days. How many months have 28 days?

3. A doctor gives you 3 pills and prescribes 1 pill to be taken every half hour. How long will the pills last?

4. How many birthdays does the average woman have?

5. Divide 40 by $\frac{1}{2}$ and add 10. What is the result?

6. How much dirt is there in a ditch that is 2 ft by 3 ft by 10 ft?

7. A raccoon climbs into a well that is 30 ft deep. Each night it climbs up 3 feet and slips down 2 feet. How many days will it take the raccoon to climb out of the well?

8. A farmer had 17 head of cattle. All but 9 of them died. How many live sheep were left?

9. How many 3-cent stamps are there in a dozen?

Name _____   Date _____

Chapter 7 Leadership

Closing Exercise

Leadership Orientation

Directions. The following statements describe aspects of leadership behavior. Think about the way you usually act when you are the leader of a group. Respond to each item according to the way you would most likely act if you were the leader of a work group. Circle whether you would most likely behave in the described way: *always* (A), *frequently* (F), *occasionally* (O), *seldom* (S), or *never* (N).

A F O S N   1. I would consult the group before making any changes.
A F O S N   2. I would encourage the group to set specific performance standards.
A F O S N   3. I would trust the group to exercise its own good judgment.
A F O S N   4. I would urge the group to beat its previous record.
A F O S N   5. I would try to make certain all group members were comfortable and happy.
A F O S N   6. I would assign group members to specific tasks.
A F O S N   7. I would represent the group and defend them at outside meetings.
A F O S N   8. I would be the one to decide what should be done and how it should be done.
A F O S N   9. I would permit group members to use their own judgment in solving problems.
A F O S N   10. I would try to keep the work moving at a rapid pace.
A F O S N   11. I would invite group members to share their personal concerns with me.
A F O S N   12. I would carefully plan how to do the work most efficiently.
A F O S N   13. I would eliminate conflicts and make certain there were friendly feelings in the group.
A F O S N   14. I would encourage overtime work.
A F O S N   15. I would allow members complete freedom in their work.
A F O S N   16. I would encourage members to follow the standard procedures.
A F O S N   17. I would encourage members to get to know each other.
A F O S N   18. I would establish a schedule for getting the work done.
A F O S N   19. I would encourage members to share their ideas with me.
A F O S N   20. I would emphasize quality and insist that all mistakes be corrected.

Scoring. These 20 items measure two leadership orientations: the odd-numbered items measure concern for people and the even-numbered items measure concern for the task.

The responses to each item are scored as follows: A = four points, F = three points, O = two points, S = one point, and N = zero points. Calculate your score for both leadership orientations by adding the points for the odd items and then adding your points for the even items. Your score for each variable will be a number between 0 and 40.

Sum of the odd items: _____   Concern for People score
Sum of the even items: _____   Concern for the Task score

From *Creating Effective Organizations*, 5th edition by David J. Cherrington and W. Gibb Dyer. Copyright © 2009 by Kendall/Hunt Publishing Company. Reprinted by permission.

Name _____   Date _____

Chapter 8   Analyzing Individual Behavior

Opening Exercise

Introduction: As more women enter the workforce, communication between men and women will increase. Research shows that men and women often have trouble communicating effectively with one another because they have contrasting values and beliefs about differences between the sexes. The following assessment surveys your beliefs and values about each sex. **Instructions:** Mark each statement as either true or false. In some cases, you may find making a decision difficult, but you should force yourself to make a choice.

True/False Questions

_____ 1. Women are more intuitive than men. They have a sixth sense, which is typically called "women's intuition."

_____ 2. At business meetings, coworkers are more likely to listen to men than they are to women.

_____ 3. Women are the "talkers." They talk much more than men in group conversations.

_____ 4. Men are the "fast talkers." They talk much more quickly than women.

_____ 5. Men are more outwardly open than women. They use more eye contact and exhibit more friendliness when first meeting someone than do women.

_____ 6. Women are more complimentary and give more praise than men.

_____ 7. Men interrupt more than women and will answer a question even when it is not addressed to them.

_____ 8. Women give more orders and are more demanding in the way they communicate than are men.

_____ 9. In general, men and women laugh at the same things.

_____ 10. When making love, both men and women want to hear the same things from their partner.

_____ 11. Men ask for assistance less often than do women.

_____ 12. Men are harder on themselves and blame themselves more often than do women.

_____ 13. Through their body language, women make themselves less confrontational than men.

_____ 14. Men tend to explain things in greater detail when discussing an incident than do women.

_____ 15. Women tend to touch others more often than men.

_____ 16. Men appear to be more attentive than women when they are listening.

_____ 17. Women and men are equally emotional when they speak.

_____ 18. Men are more likely than women to discuss personal issues.

_____ 19. Men bring up more topics of conversation than do women.

_____ 20. Today we tend to raise our male children the same way we do our female children.

_____ 21. Women tend to confront problems more directly and are likely to bring up the problem first.

_____ 22. Men are livelier speakers who use more body language and facial animation than do women.

_____ 23. Men ask more questions than women.

_____ 24. In general, men and women enjoy talking about similar things.

_____ 25. When asking whether their partner has had an AIDS test or when discussing safe sex, a woman will likely bring up the topic before a man.

Reprinted by permission of Dr. Lillian Glass.

Name _____ Date _____

Chapter 9 Performance Management

Opening Exercise

1. Spend some time on the following United States Bureau of Labor Statistics http://www.bls.gov/websites:

   a. http://www.bls.gov/ncs/ocs/sp/nctb0220.pdf

   How does pay in the Atlanta area compare to pay in these metropolitan areas?

   Boston

   Oklahoma City

   b. http://www.bls.gov/ncs/ocs/sp/ncbl1148.pdf

   What is the mean hourly earnings rate for a sales manager in Atlanta?

   c. http://www.bls.gov/news.release/archives/ncspay_07252008.pdf

   Which is the highest paying metropolitan area?

   The lowest?

Chapter 9   Performance Management

Closing Exercise

Supervising an Obnoxious Employee

Michelle Boyd is the supervisor of the customer support department and she wants to fire one of her six staff members, Donald Harrison. She thinks Don's behavior is rude and obnoxious, and she wants to terminate him. Michelle is required to evaluate the performance of her staff and she thinks this is a good time to get rid of him.

Don has more seniority than Michelle: he has been with the company for two and a half years while Michelle was hired two years ago. She has been a supervisor for nine months. Don is probably the most technically competent member of the staff and he is usually the one who solves the most difficult customer problems. But he is also very arrogant and self-centered and he brags about the difficult problems he solves.

Between customer calls, Don dominates the group conversation with discussions of politics, current events, or personal feelings. Some staff members enjoy listening to him, but Michelle finds him argumentative and abrasive. What she objects to most are his teasing and questions about personal topics. While some staff members seem to enjoy discussing intimate feelings and personal opinions, Michelle finds it very threatening and does not like being questioned. Don is a master of practical jokes that are harmless but usually embarrassing.

When she announced her decision to terminate Don to the Human Resource manager, he did not support her decision. The Human Resource manager says Don has a record of excellent performance reviews, including the one Michelle submitted six months ago as a new supervisor. According to the company's Human Resource policies, Don should not be terminated without a warning and a hearing.

Michelle's supervisor also disagrees with firing Don for a different reason: she thinks Don's conversations are interesting and intellectually stimulating. She thinks Don should only be fired if he is incompetent. Since Don is highly competent, her supervisor thinks Michelle should either tolerate Don's personality and teasing or get him to change.

Questions

1. Should Michelle be allowed to fire Don? Since she also recommends semi-annual pay increases should she withhold Don's pay increase to punish Don?
2. Is being obnoxious a legitimate reason to fire an employee? What process should a company follow to terminate employees who deserve to be fired?
3. Can supervisors change the personality of subordinates? If so, how?

From *Creating Effective Organizations*, 5th edition by David J. Cherrington and W. Gibb Dyer. Copyright © 2009 by Kendall/Hunt Publishing Company. Reprinted by permission.

Name _____ Date _____

Chapter 9   Performance Management

Closing Exercise

Deciding Pay Increases

In the College of Business, all salary changes, including merit increases and cost-of-living adjustments, are decided by the department heads. This year, the dean's office has allocated $22,000 for salary increases to the six members of one department. The six faculty members, and information about their performances, are shown in the following table.

Professor	Present Salary	Years of Teaching	Performance Information
Brooks	$84,800	15	Students say he is a horrible teacher. Never keeps his office hours, spends most of his time doing outside consulting, and hasn't written anything but consulting project reports for nine years.
Falk	$76,100	3	Excellent researcher; good teacher of graduate classes; receives mixed evaluations from undergraduate students because most class activities are used to collect research data. Published six articles last year in leading journals.
Hunter	$92,100	12	Students say she is a very good teacher and is very helpful to students; a member of the College Advisory Council; published three articles last year in practitioner journals and one article in an academic journal.
Moore	$70,200	2	New to the job; students say she is entertaining in class, but her lectures are weak because she lacks experience; spent first year finishing dissertation and has been working on other research projects since then, but nothing is finished.
Stephens	$106,600	28	Former associate dean and department head, influential in college politics but is not on any committees; author of three books, including a textbook that he revised eight years ago. Has written nothing in the last four years. Students complain that his lectures are boring and obsolete. He spends much of his time at his hobby, training dogs.
Walker	$98,200	26	Considered an outstanding teacher at both graduate and undergraduate levels. Served on several thesis committees last year; involved in two major research projects; has authored two and coauthored six research articles; wrote about 40 percent of a textbook last year; serves on the editorial review board for a research journal.

From *Creating Effective Organizations*, 5th edition by David J. Cherrington and W. Gibb Dyer. Copyright © 2009 by Kendall/Hunt Publishing Company. Reprinted by permission.

In the past, pay increases have largely been tied to the rate of inflation, and everyone has received about the same percentage increase. The rate of inflation this year has been about 3 percent, and everyone would normally receive a cost-of-living adjustment of at least that amount. However, during its fall retreat, the college executive committee decided that pay increases should be based primarily on performance rather than on cost-of-living increases. The committee concluded that greater efforts should be made to reward outstanding faculty members for teaching, research, and professional service to the university or to society. When this decision was announced some of the faculty members objected. The dean said publicly that everyone would probably receive some increase, but that weak faculty members might not keep up with inflation.

Directions

Decide how you would allocate the $22,000 salary increases. After you have made your own decisions, discuss your recommendations with four or five other students and try to reach a group consensus based on similar arguments. Imagine that you are the department head who must justify these decisions to the faculty members.

Name _____ Date _____

Chapter 10 Effective Groups and Teams

Closing Exercise ■ ■ ■

Covering the Reception Desk

In their weekly productivity improvement meeting, the twelve committee members listened to a recommendation from Karen Nichols, one of the lead interviewers. The twelve committee members work for the placement division of the Job Service Agency. The purpose of the committee is to improve the performance of the agency by eliminating inefficiencies. Three weeks earlier, the committee identified the problem of inadequate staffing of the reception desk during the heavy midday demand. The busiest part of the day is from 12 to 2, and the receptionist's lunch break is scheduled at noon. Before the recent budget cuts, two receptionists worked at the desk and scheduled their lunch breaks so they were usually both there.

Karen proposed to have the five employer relations representatives assigned to work at the reception desk on a rotating schedule. "You can't expect us to do that," replied Janet Andrus, one of the employer relations representatives. "That's not part of our job. As ER reps we have our own responsibilities."

"So who should do it?" Karen asked. "Do you have a better idea?"

"I think the interviewers should do it. We have fourteen interviewers, and one or two of them should be able to handle it," Janet responded.

"But if you take them away from interviewing," Karen persisted, "the whole process slows down. We've got to keep the interviewers talking to the applicants. I think the ER reps could fill in one day a week without hindering their work very much."

"If we have to do it, then I think everyone should have to take a turn, including Barry," said another ER rep. Barry Walker, the placement director, smiled at the suggestion and his smile was all the encouragement Paul and Ernest needed. Suddenly, the meeting degenerated into a comedy as Paul and Ernest began to mimic Barry's voice and facial expressions. "Could ah hep ya pleeze?" "Have ya filled out yer blue card, partner?"

Karen was disappointed that the committee had dismissed her proposal without really considering it. Janet thought the committee was wasting time with silly jokes, but she was glad no one was taking the proposal seriously.

Paul enjoyed making the group laugh at his antics and he tried to have them imagine how Barry would look in a wig, a skirt, false eyelashes, and long fingernails. Louise, the receptionist,* was not amused at his humor. After listening to three or four of Paul's comments, Louise quietly left the room.

After she saw Louise leave, Janet decided the group had been clowning long enough. Turning to Paul and Ernest, she announced that it was time to quit fooling around. Stunned by Janet's reproof, they listened quietly as she redirected the group to the reception desk problem. Janet summarized Karen's proposal, explained her objection to it, and suggested they go around the room and each express his or her opinion.

*They were mimicing.

From *Creating Effective Organizations*, 5th edition by David J. Cherrington and W. Gibb Dyer. Copyright © 2009 by Kendall/Hunt Publishing Company. Reprinted by permission.

Questions

1. Although Barry is the official leader of this group, who seems to be the real leader in this episode? Why do groups need leaders? What purposes do they serve?
2. What happens to the performance of a group when one or more members begin to act like comedians?
3. What are the other positions or roles that group members played in this episode?
4. Relate the concepts of group dynamics—types of groups, group roles, group norms, conformity, and status—to this case.

Name _____   Date _____

Chapter 11   Managerial Control
Closing Exercise

Visit the website Bankrate.com and check current terms on home equity loans. Pick one of the banks' current offerings. For this loan, list

    a.   the maximum loan amount

    b.   the interest rate

    c.   the maximum loan to value ratio

    d.   the FICO score range

    e.   the fees and conditions

Chapter 12 Operations and Services Management

Closing Exercise

How Amazon Aims to Keep You Clicking
Maintaining Good Customer "Experience" is Key, even when it's an Outside Merchant Making the Sale

By Heather Green

Last summer, Lisa Dias was poking around the Amazon.com (AMZN) Web site for books that could help her start a home business. The 45-year-old found a used workbook for would-be entrepreneurs that sounded promising and was described as "like new." The seller wasn't Amazon itself, but one of the merchants that market through its Web site. Still, Dias went ahead and dished out $24.95 for the paperback.

When the book arrived at her New Jersey home, though, it wasn't anywhere close to new. The worksheets were already filled in with someone else's scrawlings. She felt burned but didn't do anything about it until November. She first tried the merchant and didn't get any response. Then Dias called Amazon. The company immediately gave her a refund, without her having to return the book. She's still a bit baffled that Amazon paid her money the company never received in the first place. "I felt like they stood up for me," says Dias.

For the most part, Amazon has earned a reputation for strong service by letting customers get what they want without ever talking to an employee. Sales clerks are nonexistent. Orders ship with a few mouse clicks. Packages arrive on doorsteps quickly. It all happens with monotonous regularity even as the number of customers has doubled in the past five years to 88 million. But when things go wrong at Amazon—and they occasionally do—the company's employees get involved. That may be where Amazon stands out most markedly from other companies, and helps explain how the company earned the No. 1 spot on *BusinessWeek's* customer service ranking this year.

One recent February day in Manhattan, Jeff Bezos, Amazon's excitable 45-year-old founder and chief executive, sat still long enough to explain the ideas behind his company's approach. He talked about the distinctions Amazon makes between customer experience and customer service. The latter is only when customers deal with Amazon employees—and Bezos wants that to be the exception rather than the rule. "Internally, customer service is a component of customer experience," he says. "Customer experience includes having the lowest price, having the fastest delivery, having it reliable enough so that you don't need to contact [anyone]. Then you save customer service for those truly unusual situations. You know, I got my book and it's missing pages 47 through 58," he says, breaking into a booming laugh.

Fixing customers' problems builds loyalty with people like Dias, says Bezos. But it's also a good way to spot recurring issues that need to be addressed more systematically.

From *Business Week Magazine*, February 19, 2009 by Heather Green. Reprinted by permission of The McGraw-Hill Companies.

Outside merchants, like the one Dias dealt with, are a prime example. For years, Amazon has allowed other retailers to sell through its Web site to broaden the selection of products it offers. But these companies can be an Achilles' heel. At eBay (EBAY), which also lets merchants sell through its site, there have been complaints about poor service and fraud.

Quality Controls

So Bezos is trying something that no other retailer has been able to pull off: He wants to bring the quality of service from Amazon's outside merchants up to the same level as its own. The company has long let customers rate their experience with merchants, as they can on eBay. But Amazon also has instituted many internal safeguards to track the behavior of merchants. For instance, retailers have to use an e-mail service on the Amazon site to communicate with customers so Amazon can monitor conversations.

The company also uses metrics such as how frequently customers complain about a merchant and how often a merchant cancels an order because the product isn't in stock. Partners who have problems with more than 1% of their orders can get booted off the site.

To refine the experience with outside merchants, Amazon in 2006 launched an initiative called Fulfillment by Amazon. Merchants simply send boxes of their products to Amazon's warehouses, and Amazon does the rest. It takes the orders online, packs the box, answers questions, and processes returns. Last quarter, Amazon shipped 3 million units for Fulfillment by Amazon partners, up from 500,000 a year earlier.

Though Amazon charges the merchants, Bezos says that's not why it launched the service. "It's important because it improves the consumer experience so much," he says. "It doesn't make us more money; it's heavy lifting. If you think long-term, I think it's very important for us." It might seem counterintuitive to help small merchants, including ones that undercut you, be more competitive. But for Amazon, the ultimate goal is to gain more control over the shopping experience, making it more consistent and reliable. The idea is that more people will use the online retailer and spend more.

Michael DuGally runs NorAm International Partners, a used book, DVD, and video game reseller in Hudson, Mass. He signed up for the program a few months ago. "I can't deliver the kind of customer experience that Amazon can," says DuGally. For instance, Amazon's customer service people are trained to provide consistent answers, while NorAm's four service employees often provide different responses, DuGally says. Amazon's people are drilled in what steps to follow when they get everyday questions, like "Where's my package?" as well as fielding more unusual requests. Amazon's people tend to be more prepared than most, because they try to answer customer questions through e-mail or a service where customers enter their phone numbers and wait for a call back after Amazon's reps have gathered data on them. (There is an 800 number to call Amazon, but it's not easy to find on the Web site.) To make sure that everyone at Amazon understands how customer service works, each employee, even Bezos, spends two days on the service desk every two years. "It's both fun and useful," says Bezos. "One call I took many years ago was from a customer who had bought 11 things from 11 sellers—and typed in the wrong shipping address."

DuGally says that Fulfillment by Amazon produces results. He says that sales are up 40% on the items he sells through the program, and return rates are down 70%. He also expects to save between $550,000 and $700,000 this year, primarily because Amazon can negotiate lower shipping rates.

Taking the Wheel

Amazon has gotten many ideas from trying to address customer complaints. One gripe from years past was that popular items—think Tickle Me Elmo or Crocs (CROX) Mammoth clog shoes—were at times out of stock. The last thing Amazon wants is for a frustrated shopper to then head to another site or the mall.

During the past two years, Amazon developed new programs to keep hot items in stock and ready for quick delivery. One initiative is something Amazon calls the Milk Run. Instead of waiting for suppliers to deliver to Amazon's warehouses, Amazon sends its own trucks out to pick up top-selling goods. That reduces the number of late or incomplete orders the company receives. The program is "very forward-thinking," says Simon Fleming-Wood, vice-president for marketing at Pure Digital Technologies, whose Flip camcorder has been included in weekly Milk Runs.

One of the drawbacks to shopping online, of course, is that people don't feel the instant gratification of getting their purchases right when they buy them. Albert Ko, an online marketer in Irvine, Calif., always wants his packages as fast as possible. "I'm always pushing them," he says. That's one reason Bezos is expanding Amazon Prime, the program for which customers pay $79 a year to get free two-day shipping on many in-stock products. During the past two years, Bezos has taken it international and increased the number of products that qualify for Prime. "Our vision is to have every item made anywhere in the world in stock and available for free two-day delivery," he says.

Still, as carefully as Amazon plots and plans, sometimes things go wrong. Last November, 23-year-old Lindsey Smolan splurged on an iPod and a pink case from Amazon. The iPod arrived, but the case didn't. Two weeks later, Smolan e-mailed Amazon and asked for a refund. After a little thought, she e-mailed again, asking for a free cover. "I didn't use my iPod because I was waiting for my case, and I'm a valuable customer," she says. Amazon agreed. She got the iPod case gratis.

How would you summarize Amazon's approach to customer relationship management (CRM)? How does Amazon treat customer complaints? What are the specific strategies it uses to stay on top of customer service? Have you or someone you know had a personal experience dealing with Amazon's CRM?

APPENDIX B
Valley Real Estate Fund 2006

The real estate industry was booming at the end of 2005. The mortgage brokerage business had expanded dramatically as well, fueled by unprecedented wealth creation in the United States over the previous decade. The level of liquidity in the system created the opportunity for creative real estate investments. This case examines a real estate investment opportunity in Rockbridge County, Virginia.

Investment Opportunity Memo

January 3, 2006

To: Fred Craven
From: George Dunhill
Re: Real Estate Opportunity

Dear Fred,

Enclosed is the information we discussed at breakfast last week. I have lived in Rockbridge County for 20 years and have never seen prices escalate as they have in the last few years. The partners in this fund are well known and respected in this area. I think it is a great opportunity to get in on a recession-proof market. Let me know if you are interested. I plan on investing and I am sure the units will be sold pretty quickly.

Valley Real Estate Fund 2006

Executive Summary

Valley Real Estate Fund, LLC (VREF) is being offered by Shenandoah Valley Mortgage Brokers Inc. (SVMB), a privately held company operating in Rockbridge County, Virginia. SVMB was organized in 2004 by two individuals with extensive loan experience in Rockbridge County.

Rockbridge County has experienced an extraordinary growth in home values over the past six years. Between 2000 and 2006, the median house price increased 61.1% from $124,167 to $200,000 [Crawford, 2007]. Lexington and Rockbridge County have become highly desirable locations for retirees looking for a quiet university town. The mountainous rural setting has been identified in several rankings as one the best retirement spots in the United States, generating a significant jump in demand for housing in all price ranges.

SVMB has identified an opportunity for providing superior returns based on the growth of the Rockbridge County real estate market. The number of retirees moving to the area, along with the normal local turnover, has produced a strong need for transition, or bridge capital in the residential housing market.

VREF proposes raising $1.2 million, through a limited partnership, for investment in mortgages in Rockbridge County and nearby markets. The investments will be sold in $100,000 units and will be managed by the general partners, Ralph Peifer and Amanda Highsmith.

Issuer

SVMB Inc., a privately held company, is incorporated in and licensed by the State of Virginia to broker all forms of mortgage loans.

Purpose

SVMB Inc. is seeking investor funds to be placed in short-term residential construction loans in and around Rockbridge County Virginia.

Overview

SVMB Inc. has a successful history of selling the loan products of many of the largest mortgage lenders in the country. While doing so, the company has created a wide network of working relationships, including satisfied customers, real estate professionals, architects, attorneys, builders, bankers, and insurers.

With an expertise in the national mortgage loan market, and a well-earned local reputation for integrity and competence, SVMB is uniquely positioned to place private capital in short-term residential construction loans with superior risk-adjusted returns.

The long-term financing for the finished home will be pre-approved through SVMB Inc., the essentials of which will be completed prior to the beginning of the building work.

The target return on the invested funds will benchmarked to the U.S. prime interest rate plus one and a half percentage points. At the current prime rate of 7.25%, the target return would be 8.75%. An additional 0.5% of each loan will be distributed to the investors.

All invested funds will be secured by a deed of trust on real estate in Rockbridge County Virginia and managed by SVMB.

Mortgage Industry Background

Consumers will take out $2.8 trillion in mortgages in 2006, and two thirds of homebuyers will turn to mortgage brokers to find financing for the biggest purchase of their lives. Mortgage brokers will earn approximately $33 billion in commissions this year, the vast majority of which will be paid to them by lenders and investors as an incentive for selling their loan products [Streitfeld, 2005].

In the past 30 years the industry has undergone a major transition, as the old savings and loan model has been phased out, replaced by the emerging brokerage system. The big lenders/investors such as Citi Group, Bank of America, and ABN Amro, are heavily invested in the broker network and compete vigorously to have their products sold through these relationships.

This dynamic works to the consumer/borrower's benefit as well. The broker's ability to shop nationally in a wider market enhances the product and price selection for the local consumer.

When a local brokerage has established trusting relationships with lenders/investors and the community of borrowers they service, the broker is able to carve out a major share of the mortgage lending market.

SVMB Inc. is a customer-focused and principle-driven brokerage. As a result, the company has developed quality relationships with lenders and borrowers alike. The specific location in which the company has nurtured a reputation for integrity and competence, Rockbridge County, Virginia, is a further enhancement to this investment offering and will be expanded upon in this summary.

Local savings and loans have been replaced by a variety of regional banks offering a wider menu of products and services. These regional banks generally act as brokers for long-term, fixed mortgage loans, serving on the front line, "originating" loans with consumers. The regional banks then sell the loan to, or close the loan in the name of, one of the large lenders/investors, competing directly with SVMB.

SVMB is well positioned in this market segment. However, the regional banks do make in-house, short-term residential construction loans, which are products that mortgage brokerages have historically not participated in. When a regional bank provides a short-term residential construction loan, the borrower will typically return to the bank for the placement of the long-term mortgage. This is the business that SVMB is intent on capturing and is a primary factor behind this investment offering.

Short-term residential construction loans are based on the prime interest rate, which has increased from 4.00% to 7.25% over the last 24 months. This fund will target a return of prime plus 1.5%, based on an in-house underwriting and management process, providing investors an excellent return compared to similar risk class investments. The key for investor returns is the ability to shorten the funding and construction cycle, thereby increasing the number of turns of the investment pool per year. SVMB will benefit from the placement of the final mortgages, which also guarantees the payoff of the privately placed construction loan.

Shenandoah Valley Mortgage Brokers

SVMB was formed in January 2004, when two of the most successful mortgage loan originators in Rockbridge County joined forces to start the company. Ralph Peifer was a branch manager and top producer with The Mortgage Group, and Amanda Highsmith was a branch manager and top producer with Hometown Mortgage, a division of Mortgage International. Both Ralph and Amanda are Rockbridge County natives with deep ties to the community.

SVMB is licensed by the state of Virginia to originate and place real estate-secured mortgages with a variety of national lenders, such as Citi Group, Bank of America, Chase Manhattan Bank, Lehman Brothers, Interfirst, and First National Bank. The brokerage also works with a number of specialty lenders focused on the sub-prime market (where loans are made available to borrowers with less than perfect credit at higher interest rates).

Through this network of lender relationships, SVMB has access to the complete range of loan products available in the marketplace and is constantly updated on new products and trends in the industry.

Having collectively placed over 2000 mortgages in the past five years, Ralph and Amanda have developed a deep understanding of both the mortgage industry on a national level and the real estate market on a local level. It is this valuable knowledge that provides the foundation for this investment offering. Selectively placing private funds in lieu of funds from large national lenders provides an attractive rate of return with minimal risk for interested investors.

Management

Ralph Peifer is President, cofounder, and managing partner of SVMB Inc. Ralph is a 1989 graduate of the University of Virginia with a degree in Economics and Business. He spent four years on active duty in the Army where he achieved the rank of Captain. Ralph completed his MBA while serving in Washington, D.C. Upon returning to Virginia in 1995, Ralph opened a branch for a local mortgage company and quickly became a top performer and multi-branch manager. Ralph founded SVMB Inc. in 2003.

Amanda Highsmith is Treasurer and cofounder of SVMB Inc. Amanda has worked in the banking industry for seven years and opened the first exclusively mortgage-focused office in Rockbridge County. Amanda was the sales manager of Hometown Mortgage and a top national sales person when she left to found SVMB Inc.

Sherry Gravely is Vice President and senior loan consultant with SVMB Inc. Sherry has worked in the banking and lending business for twenty years. Previously, she was a branch manager and lending specialist at a local bank for eight years and has extensive experience in construction, commercial, small business and consumer lending.

Rockbridge Country, Virginia

Indian Legend has it that the beauty of the Shenandoah Valley so awed the heavens that each star cast the brightest jewel from its own crown into the valley's sparkling waters, there to shine ever after in a gesture of celestial benediction. Thus arose the valley's name: Shenandoah, "clear eyed daughter of the stars" [Lexington, Virginia, 2007].

Rockbridge County is located in the heart of the valley, approximately 200 miles south and west of Washington D.C. It takes its name from the famed stone arch bridge (The Natural Bridge) located in the southern end of the county, which was once owned by Thomas Jefferson. Its approximately 600 square miles are bordered by the Blue Ridge Mountains to the east and the Alleghenies to the west. Over 40% of the area is farmland, and much of the remaining acreage is national- and state-owned forestland. The rural character and scenic vistas are a hallmark of the county.

The County Seat is located in the city of Lexington. This name was chosen for the city by the Virginia Legislature in the spring of 1778 to honor the first battle of the Revolutionary War, the battle of Lexington, Massachusetts, which occurred three years earlier.

The city of Lexington is home to two historically significant colleges, which both have a large influence on the town and the surrounding communities.

Washington & Lee University

Liberty Hall Academy was established in 1749 just to the north of town. When George Washington made a sizable gift to the college's endowment, the institution's name was changed to Washington College so as to honor the nation's first President. At the end of the Civil War, the presidency of the college was offered to General Robert E. Lee, who presided over the school for five years. Upon Lee's death in 1870, the trustees renamed the school Washington & Lee University. Today, it enjoys a reputation as one of the finest coeducational centers of learning in the country. Its enrollment is in excess of 1700 undergraduates and 350 law students [Washington & Lee: A History, 2007].

Virginia Military Institute

In 1816, the General Assembly of Virginia established three arsenals for the housing of arms. One of these was built in Lexington. By the mid 1830s, a prominent local attorney and graduate of Washington College, John T.L. Preston, advocated the establishment of a state military school at the arsenal. The Virginia Military Institute enrolled its first students in November of 1839 and prospered in the years prior to the Civil War. Among its faculty was Major Thomas J. Jackson, soon to be known as "Stonewall Jackson" and noted as one of the South's most famous and revered heroes. The disciplined military lifestyle, together with its reputation for academic excellence in engineering and the sciences, has earned VMI a national reputation for producing graduates who consistently go on to achievements in the military, engineering, and the business world [Virginia Military Institute, 2007].

These two storied institutions, combined with a bustling downtown historic district, have long attracted those seeking the "small town" lifestyle with the cultural amenities of a much larger city.

Lexington has netted its share of tourist interest as one of the best small towns in America. In 1997, Time magazine selected Lexington as one of the "Top 10 Small Towns" [Pooley, 1997] and Money Magazine chose Lexington as one its "Best Places to Vacation" in its summer 2001 issue [Daragahi, 2001]. Consumer Reports has anointed Lexington as one of six "perfect places to retire." On CBS's The Early Show, which aired October 4 2005, Consumer Reports Deputy Editor Lisa Freeman announced the results of an extensive review of the best places to retire in North America. Lexington, Virginia, was included on a list of six towns that were singled out as "outstanding in terms of climate, housing prices and entertainment opportunities" [Freeman, 2005].

On Veterans Day 2002, ABC's Good Morning America crew was on hand for a parade, followed by visits to VMI and the campus of Washington & Lee University in their "50 States, One Nation, One Year" broadcast [Washington & Lee, 2002]. In 2001 Lexington was recognized in a book entitled The 50 Best Small Southern Towns by Gerald W. Sweitzer and Kathy M. Fields. This book depicts 50 southern towns that are charming, livable places affording a gentler way of life [Sweitzer, 2001].

Lexington is home to a thriving arts community, featuring Sally Mann, selected by Time Magazine as the most influential photographer working today [Lacayo, 2005], as well as Cy Twombly, one of the 20th century's most prominent modern artists.

Additionally, tourism represents a $100 million per year industry in the Rockbridge County area, according to the Virginia Tourism Corporation [Virginia Tourism Corporation, 2007].

The total population of the Rockbridge area is estimated at approximately 35,000. According to the U.S. Census Bureau, the population increased by 10.4% from 1990 to 2005. This was a marked change from the previous 50 years, during which there was no significant increase in population [CSVPD, 2007].

The town of Buena Vista also lies within the county, only five miles east of Lexington. Southern Virginia University, a growing university recently associated with the Mormon Church, is located here and is a significant addition to the county. Buena Visa is home to a number of manufacturing facilities.

The Rockbridge Area has a diversified economy, with strong manufacturing, trade, services, and agricultural sectors. Manufacturing activity centers around natural resources including timber, textiles, and a variety of industrial, commercial, and residential goods. The unemployment rate is currently estimated at 3%, which is below the state and national average of 3.5% and 4.9%, respectively [CSVPD, 2007].

Rockbridge County has experienced significant increases in overall property values during the past decade. Rockbridge County led the Commonwealth of Virginia in the increase in the median value of real estate from 1997–2003. To put that in perspective, Fairfax County, Virginia—a major metropolitan area near the nation's capital—saw an increase of 65%, while Rockbridge County was up 71% over the same period. Between 2000 and 2006, the median price increased 61.1% from $124,167 to $200,000 [Crawford, 2007].

The demographics driving increased home values are predictable. A steadily growing number of retirees are drawn to the area's scenic beauty, vibrant cultural life, Lexington's pristine downtown district, historic educational institutions, and attractive quality of life. For instance, Kendal at Lexington, a non-profit retirement community opened in 2000, has plans for expansion that will increase its independent living capacity by 70% [Kendal at Lexington, 2007]. Between 1989 and 1999, the number of households in Rockbridge County with incomes greater than $100,000 increased by 408% (compared with a statewide increase of 286%). Lexington boasts one of the highest percentages of college graduates in the state at 42.6% (compared to a statewide rate of 29.5%) and retail sales per capita of $14,952 (compared to a statewide $9,293) [US Census Bureau, 2007]. As wealth has flowed to Rockbridge County (bank deposits increased from $120 million to $347 million from 2000 to 2006), real estate demand and prices have followed suit.

One result of these demographic trends is that a significant number of homebuyers and homebuilders here in the county are not dependent on the local job market, but instead bring accumulated resources into the county. Consequently, the local real estate market is far less sensitive to fluctuations in both the local and national economy. Therefore, while Rockbridge County has experienced an increase in property values, it is less vulnerable to sudden property value decreases associated with economic downturns and job layoffs.

With more people arriving every day, the inventory of existing homes for sale in Rockbridge County is not adequate to meet the demand. According to Rick Reeves, owner/broker of the local RE/MAX Real Estate office, "In the market that we find ourselves presently, with high asking prices on the limited inventory of existing homes, many buyers feel that they are better off building exactly what they want in a location of their own choosing."

The lack of adequate existing inventory is generating an increase in the number of homebuyers who are choosing to build at all levels of the market in Rockbridge County. SVMB Inc. wants to grow its presence and participation in this increasingly important market segment and, in particular, the placement of permanent mortgages.

Modular Construction Focus

The primary market for SVMBs privately placed loans will be the rapidly growing modular home segment of the construction market. The investor/lender network now does not distinguish between a modular home and a traditional stick-built house, whereas in years past a rate premium was added to loans made on modular homes. The premium was based on the perceived difference in quality and the confusion with mobile homes. Modular homes are not mobile homes and have none of the lender/investor restrictions associated with mobile homes. In fact, modular home construction has gained mainstream acceptance and earlier quality issues have long since disappeared. Modular homes are built with the same materials as "stick-built" homes, but the building process occurs indoors in a controlled environment, and the completed modules are then transported to the home site and assembled. The modular process reduces construction time by as much as half and minimizes the chances for errors and delays. The reduced construction time allows for quicker turnover of invested funds, increasing the bottom line for both the private investor and SVMB.

The Loan Process

SVMB currently receives applications for a wide variety of loan products, including construction loans. At present, SVMB Inc. matches these borrowers with the national lenders whose products best meet their needs. With an in-house construction funding capability, SVMB Inc. would select the most appropriate applications for private placement.

Once a construction project has been selected for in-house funding, the architectural plans and the building lot will be appraised in order to establish the value of the project and the amount of the loan relative to the project.

SVMB will get approval for the permanent financing via the lender/investor network, based on the established loan to value ratio. Therefore the permanent mortgage, which will pay off the construction loan, is already in place before the construction work begins.

Once the value and loan amounts have been established, and the final long-term financing has been approved, the construction loan can be closed with SVMB Inc.'s local attorney, who will complete a title search and create a loan note and a deed of trust. From this point, the first draw can be advanced, and construction can begin. Once the building project is under way, SVMB will work closely with the builder to monitor progress and provide the appropriate draws as each phase of the project is completed and inspected.

Upon completion of the house:

- SVMB will request a final title policy through its settlement agent.
- SVMB will schedule a final inspection by the appraiser, which assures that the property has been built according to plans and specifications.
- The Rockbridge County building inspector issues the certificate of occupancy.
- As these final project sequences are occurring, the placement of the permanent financing is proceeding toward closing.
- Once the permanent loan closes, the funds provided by the national lender are distributed to pay off the construction loan.

The Decision

Fred Craven moved to Rockbridge County six years ago, after an All Pro career in the NFL. He has been approached with an opportunity by an old friend, George Dunhill. The two spend time together with family and friends, and have been partners in several successful business ventures. Fred has been an astute investor, growing his wealth substantially over the course of his career. He has been mulling over this latest investment, but needs to give George a call by the end of the week.

Appendix A Financial Assumptions

1. Returns are based on the current short-term interest rate environment. Valley Real Estate Fund will charge its borrowers prime (7.25%) plus 1.5% for a total of 8.75%.
2. Borrowers will pay a 1% origination fee, collected on Day 1 of the construction loan. VREF and SVMB will share the 1% origination fee on a 50-50 basis.
3. The typical construction loan amount is assumed to be $150,000, drawn as follows:

    Day 1 (Draw 1): $35,000

    For the modular home process, a down payment of 10% is required at the time the house is ordered from the factory. The house is ready for delivery approximately 60 days later. So on Day 1, Draw 1 of $15,000 will go to the factory as a deposit. The remainder of $20,000 is used for site preparation and foundation work.

    Day 60 (Draw 2): $100,000

    This draw pays the balance at the factory for completed/shippable house.

    Day 110 (Draw 3): $15,000

    This draw completes the construction loan.

    Day 120:

    The construction loan is paid off by permanent financing. VREF collects $150,000 in principal plus all accrued interest.

4. VREF will close three construction loans per month on average.
5. VREF will earn 3% on all idle cash balances.
6. VREF investors will receive a pro rata share of 90% of each year's profit, assuming cash is available. This payment will be net of any expenses incurred in the event of collection or foreclosure costs. This model assumes all borrowers make scheduled payments in a timely manner.
7. SVMB will absorb any start-up costs and monthly administrative costs incurred.

APPENDIX B

Valley Real Estate Fund, LLC
Year 1 Cash Projections

	Start-up	Month 1	Month 2	Month 3	Month 4	Month 5	Month 6	Month 7	Month 8	Month 9	Month 10	Month 11	Month 12	Totals
Revenue:														
Origination Fees		2250	2250	2250	2250	2250	2250	2250	2250	2250	2250	2250	2250	27000
Draw 1 Interest						3021	3021	3021	3021	3021	3021	3021	3021	24164
Draw 2 Interest						4315	4315	4315	4315	4315	4315	4315	4315	34521
Draw 3 Interest						108	108	108	108	108	108	108	108	863
Return on Interest-bearing Account		3000	2751	2501	1500	497	522	548	573	599	625	651	677	14443
Monthly Revenue		5250	5001	4751	3750	10190	10216	10241	10267	10293	10318	10344	10370	100991
Cumulative Revenue		5250	10251	15001	18751	28942	39157	49399	59666	69959	80277	90621	100991	
LLC Funds, Beginning Balance	1200000	1200000	1100250	1000251	600001	198751	208942	219157	229399	239666	249959	260277	270621	1200000
LLC Principal Loaned Out: Draw 1		105000	105000	105000	105000	105000	105000	105000	105000	105000	105000	105000	105000	1260000
LLC Principal Loaned Out: Draw 2				300000	300000	300000	300000	300000	300000	300000	300000	300000	300000	3000000
LLC Principal Loaned Out: Draw 3						45000	45000	45000	45000	45000	45000	45000	45000	360000
LLC Principal Repaid						450000	450000	450000	450000	450000	450000	450000	450000	3600000
LLC Funds, Subtotal	1200000	1100250	1000251	600001	198751	208942	219157	229399	239666	249959	260277	270621	280991	
Payment to LLC Investors													90892	90892
LLC Funds, Ending Balance	1200000	1100250	1000251	600001	198751	208942	219157	229399	239666	249959	260277	270621	190099	190099
LLC Investors' Return														7.57%

APPENDIX B

Valley Real Estate Fund, LLC
Year 2 Cash Projections

	Month 1	Month 2	Month 3	Month 4	Month 5	Month 6	Month 7	Month 8	Month 9	Month 10	Month 11	Month 12	Totals
Revenue:													
Origination Fees	2250	2250	2250	2250	2250	2250	2250	2250	2250	2250	2250	2250	27000
Draw 1 Interest	3021	3021	3021	3021	3021	3021	3021	3021	3021	3021	3021	3021	36247
Draw 2 Interest	4315	4315	4315	4315	4315	4315	4315	4315	4315	4315	4315	4315	51781
Draw 3 Interest	108	108	108	108	108	108	108	108	108	108	108	108	1295
Return on Interest-bearing Account	475	501	526	552	577	603	629	655	680	706	732	758	7395
Monthly Revenue	10169	10194	10220	10245	10271	10296	10322	10348	10374	10400	10426	10452	123717
Cumulative Revenue	10169	20363	30583	40828	51099	61395	71717	82065	92439	102839	113265	123717	
LLC Funds, Beginning Balance	190099	200268	210462	220682	230927	241198	251494	261816	272164	282538	292938	303364	190099
LLC Principal Loaned Out: Draw 1	105000	105000	105000	105000	105000	105000	105000	105000	105000	105000	105000	105000	1260000
LLC Principal Loaned Out: Draw 2	300000	300000	300000	300000	300000	300000	300000	300000	300000	300000	300000	300000	3600000
LLC Principal Loaned Out: Draw 3	45000	45000	45000	45000	45000	45000	45000	45000	45000	45000	45000	45000	540000
LLC Principal Repaid	450000	450000	450000	450000	450000	450000	450000	450000	450000	450000	450000	450000	5400000
LLC Funds, Subtotal	200268	210462	220682	230927	241198	251494	261816	272164	282538	292938	303364	313816	
Payment to LLC Investors												111345	111345
LLC Funds, Ending Balance	200268	210462	220682	230927	241198	251494	261816	272164	282538	292938	303364	202471	202471
LLC Investors' Return												9.20%	

Case Questions

1. Describe the general environment surrounding the residential real estate industry in the United States in 2006.
2. Describe the role a mortgage broker played in the residential real estate market.
3. Describe the role commercial banks and the financial services industry in general played in the residential real estate market.
4. What are the key elements of the financial projections for this investment?
5. Which assumptions might you challenge?
6. What advice would you give to Fred Craven?

References

Central Shenandoah Valley Planning District (CSVPD), http://www.cspdc.org/DesktopDefault.aspx?tabid=80, September 20, 2007.

Crawford, Darryl, "Virginia Housing Cost Comparisons," Commission, February 28, 2007.

Daragahi, Borzou Rafi, Natasha and Rob Turner, Best Places to Vacation, Money, April 2001, p. 116.

Freeman, Lisa, Interview on CBS' The Early Show, October 4, 2005, http://www.cbsnews.com/stories/2005/10/04/earlyshow/series/main907091.shtml.

Kendal at Lexington, Phase II Expansion, http://kalex.kendal.org/living/PhaseIIExpansion.aspx, July 26, 2007.

Lacayo, Richard, 5 Snappy Photo Books, Time Magazine Online, December 12, 2005, http://www. time.com/time/magazine/article/0,9171,1137685,00.html, July 25, 2007.

Lexington, Virginia, A Brief History, http://www.lexva.com/index.htm, September 18, 2007.

McCance, McGregor, Roanoke Times, February 15, 2004.

Pooley, Eric, "A Small Town Sampler," Time Magazine Online, December 8, 1997, http://www.time.com/time/magazine/article/0,9171,987490,00.html.

Streitfeld, David, "Real Estate Fraud On Rise," Los Angeles Times, December 5, 2005.

Sweitzer, Gerald W. and Kathy M. Fields, The Best Small Southern Towns, (Peachtree Publishers, 2001).

U.S. Census Bureau, http://quickfacts.census.gov/qfd/states/51000.html, July 26, 2007.

Virginia Military Institute: A Brief History, http://www.vmi.edu/show.asp?durki=1792, October 5, 2007.

Virginia Tourism Corporation, http://reports.yesvirginia.org/LocalSpending/GenerateReport.aspx, October 6, 2007.

Washington & Lee: A History, http://www2.wlu.edu/web/page/normal/174.html, October 12, 2007.

Washington & Lee University News Office, ABC's "Good Morning America" Will Go Live from W&L, October 28, 2002, http://newsoffice.wlu.edu/NewsReleases/4248.html.

Index

A

A-B-C priority system 26
Accounts receivable, factoring, 208–209
Acquisitions, 72
Advertising, 62
Aetna Life & Casualty Co., 230
Altria Group, 71
Amazon.com Inc., 20–21
American Express, 26, 219
Analyzers, 20, 21
Angel investors, 88
Ann Taylor, 218, 219
Apple Computer, 12, 213
Art of War, The (Tsu), 5
Assimilation, 139
Attention, 133–134
Attitudes, 146–149
Attribution theory, 141–142
Authoritarian leadership, 120–121
Authority, delegation of, 96–97
Authority-compliance leadership, 123

B

Banks, loans from commercial, 207–208
Barnard, Chester, 5
Barney, Jay, 55
Bartlett, Christopher, 74
Bass, Bill, 223
Behavior, relationship between attitudes and, 147–149
Behaviorally anchored rating scales (BARS), 159, 160
Benevolent-authoritative style, 106
Benmark Inc., 49
Bertani, Elizabeth, 200
Beyond Reengineering (Hammer), 228
Bezo, Jeffrey P., 20–21
Big Five Personality Model, 142–143
Birck, Jon, 213
Black Enterprise, 82
Blake, Robert, 122
Blanchard, Ken, 124
BMW, 4, 218, 219
Body Shop, 82
Bonds, debt financing by issuing, 211
Bonuses, 171–172
Borrowing. *See* Loans, sources for
Brabeck-Letmathe, P., 6
Branson, Richard, 82
Brazil, 66
Break-even analysis
　algebraic method, 38
　fixed versus variable costs, 38
　formula, 224
　graphical method, 39
　price planning, 39
　profit planning, 39
　strengths and limitations of, 40
Budgets, developing, 201–202
Bureaucracy
　advantages of, 103–104
　characteristics of, 102
　defined, 102
　disadvantages of, 104–106
Burnett, Iris, 81
Business plan, writing a, 87
Business trap, avoiding the, 27
Buyers, 58

C

California Custom Sport Trucks, 87
Callaway, Justin, 225
Canadian Tire, 48
Capital budget, 202
Capital expenditures, making, 205
Cash budget, 202
Cemex, 74
Centralized authority, 96–97
Change, managing, 2
Charismatic leadership, 116–117
China, 65–66
　acquisitions, 72
　emerging economy, 67
　government regulations, 67
　licensing, 71
　subsidiaries, 73
Chrysler Corp., 199
Cingular, 225
Cisco Systems, 213
Clinton, Bill, 117
CNOOC, 72
Cobb, Liz, 88
Collaboration (performing) stage of group development, 179
Collateral, 208
Collectiveness, versus individualism, 69
Comcast, 226
Commercial finance companies, 208
Commercial paper, 209–210
Compensation
　base pay, 167–168
　bonuses, 171–172
　incentives, financial, 169–171
　recognition awards, 172–173
　rewarding performance, 167–174
Competitive advantage, 219–220

Competitor analysis, 58–60
Conceptual skills, needed by managers, 12
Conformity, 192–194
Confrontation (storming) stage of group development, 179
Consultative style, 106
Consumer markets sector, 57
Contingency theory of leadership, 124
Contrast, 139
Controlling, 7
Controls, financial, 203
Cooptation, 61–62
Core competencies, 55
Corporation, 88
Cost leadership strategy, 48
Count-Me-In for Women's Economic Independence, 81
Country club leadership, 123
Credit cards, loans using, 210
Credit operations, controlling, 204–205
Culture, 53–54
    globalization and role of, 69–70
Customer departmentalization, 94
Customer relationship management (CRM), 226
Customers, external and internal, 226, 227
Customer service, 225
Cypress Semiconductor Corp., 28

D

Daewoo Group, 47
Daily financial needs, 204
Debt financing, 88, 210
    differences between equity financing and, 212
    by issuing bonds, 211
    from lending institutions, 211
Decentralized authority, 96–97
Decisional roles, 9–10
Decision making, group, 107
Decision-making model of leadership, 124
Defenders, 20
Deindividuation, 196–197
Dell Computer, 71, 226
Delta Airlines, 49
Deming, W. Edwards, 29, 227
Democratic leadership, 120–121
Departmentalization
    customer, 94
    functional, 92–93
    geographic, 94
    product, 93–94
Descriptive essays, 159–160
DeSio, Tony, 83
Differentiation (norming) stage of group development, 179
Differentiation strategy, 48–49
Directing, 6–7
Discrimination and prejudice, 138–141
Disney, 55
Disseminator role, 9
Disturbance handler role, 9
Division of labor, 91–92
Dress codes, 190
Drucker, Peter, 27, 28, 160
DuPont, 52

E

Eachnet.com, 73
Eastman Kodak, 21–22
eBay, 73, 84
Economic development, global, 67
Economic order quantity (EOQ), 223
Economics sector, 57
80/20 principle, 26–27
Emotions, 146–147
Employee-centered leader behavior, 121
Enron, 67
Entrepreneurial management, 4
Entrepreneurial role, 9
Entrepreneurs/entrepreneurship
    business plan, writing the, 87
    characteristics of, 82–83
    diversity and, 83–84
    examples of, 81–82
    failure, reasons for, 85–86
    family businesses, 85
    financing, 88
    how to get started, 84
    Internet, 84–85
    life cycles, 86–87
    ownership, forms of, 87–88
Environment
    institutional, 67–68
    understanding a country's, 66–68
Environmental analysis, 55–57
Environmental influences, on leadership, 125–127
Environmental sectors, 56–57
Environmental uncertainty, 60–62, 108–109
Equity financing, 88
    differences between debt financing and, 212
    retained earnings, 212
    by selling stock, 211–212
    from venture capital, 212–213
Exploitive-authoritative style, 106
Exporting, 70–71

F

Factoring accounts receivable, 208–209
Fair Indigo, 223
Family and friends, borrowing from, 207
Family businesses, 85
Federkeil, Ed, 87
FedEx, 73
Feedback, 163–164
Fiedler, Fred, 124, 126, 127
Figurehead role, 8
Financial leverage, 213–214
Financial management
    See also Loans, sources for
    budgets, developing, 201–202
    controls, establishing, 203
    defined, 200–201
    forecasting needs, 201
    importance of, 200
    long-term financing, obtaining, 210–214
    operating funds, 204–206

role of, 199
short-term financing, obtaining, 206–210
Financial managers, role of, 199
Financial planning, 201–203
Financial resources sector, 56
Financing entrepreneurs, 88
Firm analysis, 51–55
Five-forces model, 58–59
Flow charts, 34–35
Focus strategy, 49
Follett, Mary Parker, 5
Ford, Gerald, 116
Forecasting, 61, 201
Francais, Geneva, 81
Friedman, Thomas, 65, 66
Functional departmentalization, 92–93

G

Gantt, Henry L., 35
Gantt charts, 35–36
Gates, Bill, 12, 225
Gender focus, 69–70
General Electric (GE), 12
General Electric Capital Corp., 208
General Motors (GM), 52
Geographic departmentalization, 94
Ghoshal, Sumantra, 74
Ghosn, Carlos, 75
Gilbreth, Frank, 5
Gilbreth, Lillian, 5
Globalization
   country's environment, understanding a, 66–68
   culture, role of, 69–70
   defined, 65
   economic development, 67
   global focus, 74
   government rules and regulations, 67–68
   growth of, 66
   impact of, 2–3, 57
   managing operations, 73–76
   market-entry strategies, 70–73
   multicultural teams, 76
   physical infrastructure, 68
   region-country focus, 74
   transnational focus, 74–75
Global mind-set, 76–77
GLOBE, 69
Goals. *See* Objectives (goals)
Goal setting theory, 161–163
Government regulations, global, 67–68
Government sector, 57
Graphic rating scales, 158–159
Graves, Earl, 82
Greenfield venture, 73
Group roles
   ambiguity, 187
   blocking, 185
   conflict, 187
   episode, 186–188
   maintenance, 185
   work, 185

Groups
   See also Teams
   conformity, 192–194
   development, stages of, 178–180
   individual behavior affected by, 194–197
   norms, 188–192
   reasons for joining, 177–178
   size, 181–182
   social density, 183
   tasks and, 183–184

H

Halo effect, 137
Hammer, Michael, 228, 230
Harley-Davidson, 20
Hayes International, 55
Hersey, Paul, 124
Herzberg, Frederick, 5
Hewlett-Packard, 46
Hirata, Hitoshi, 220
Hofstede, Geert, 69
Home Depot, 26, 226
House, Robert, 69, 124
Huizenga, H. Wayne, 81
Human resources sector, 56

I

IBM, 72
Illegal activities, 62
Impoverished leadership, 123
Impressions, first, 138
Incentives, financial, 169–171
Incentive Systems, 88
India, 66
   outsourcing, 71
Individual behavior
   attitudes, 146–149
   discrimination and prejudice, 138–141
   group effects on, 194–197
   job satisfaction, 149–152
   perception, 133–138
   personality, 141–145
Individualism, versus collectivism, 69
Industry analysis, 58–59
Industry sector, 57
Informational roles, 9
Information processing, organizational design and, 109–110
ING Bank, 27
Initial public offering (IPO), 88, 212
Initiating structure and consideration, 121–122
Institutional environment
   economic development, 67
   importance of, 68
   physical infrastructure, 68
   political-legal rules and regulations, 67–68
Intel, 213
Intellectual property rights, 68
Intelligence, of leaders, 119
International management. *See* Globalization

Internet
    entrepreneurship, 84–85
    impact of, 2
Interpersonal roles, 8
Interpersonal skills, needed by managers, 12
Inventory control, 205
Inventory management, 222–224
ISO (International Standards Organization), 226
Iwata, Satoru, 17–18

J

Job involvement, 151
Jobs, Steve, 11
Job satisfaction, 149
    absenteeism and tardiness and, 150
    involvement and, 151
    mental and physical health and, 150
    organizational commitment, 151–152
    performance and, 150
    turnover and, 150
Juran, J. M., 224
Just-in-time, 223–224

K

Krill, Kay, 218

L

Lafley, A. G., 77
Laissez-faire leadership, 120–122
Lawrence, Paul, 108–109
Leadership (leaders)
    authoritarian, democratic, and
        laissez-faire, 120–121
    behaviors, 120–122
    charismatic, 116–117
    constraints on, 128–129
    defined, 113
    effectiveness, determinants of, 127–128
    environmental influences, 125–127
    followers, characteristics, 125
    followers, influence of, 126
    Grid, 122–123
    initiating structure and consideration, 121–122
    intelligence, 119
    management versus, 113–115
    personality traits, 119–120
    physical traits, 118
    production-centered versus employee-
        centered, 121
    roles, 8, 123
    situational theories, 123–124
    strategies for improving, 127–128
    styles, selecting, 124–125
    substitutes, 129
    training, 127–128
    traits, 118–120
    transactional, 115–116
    transformational, 116–117
Ledingham, Dianne, 229
Legal rules and regulations, global, 67–68

Lenova, 72
Leverage, 213–214
Lewin, Kurt, 120–121
Liaison role, 8
Licensing, 71
Life cycle theory of leadership, 124
Likert, Rensis, 106–107
Limited liability corporation (LLC), 88
Loans, sources for
    banks, commercial, 207–208
    commercial paper, 209–210
    credit cards, 210
    debt financing, 210–211, 212
    equity financing, 211–213
    factoring accounts receivable, 208–209
    family and friends, 207
    forms of short-term, 208
    tax credit, 206–207
Locke, Edwin A., 161
Locus of control, 143–144
Lorsch, Jay, 108–109
Louis Vuitton, 217

M

Macy's, 209
Mail Boxes Etc., 83
Malcolm Baldrige award, 226–227
Management
    choices permitted by, 10, 11
    constraints on, 10, 11
    defined, 1
    demands on, 10, 11
    entrepreneurial, 4
    historical approaches to, 5
    leadership versus, 113–115
    of resources, 3
    strategic, 3–4
Management by objectives (MBO)
    cycle, 28–29
    defined, 160–161
    strengths and limitations of, 29–30
Managers
    leaders versus, 113–115
    responsibilities of, 5–7
    roles of, 8–11
    skills needed by, 11–12
Manufacturing technology, 220–221
Market-entry strategies
    acquisitions, 72
    exporting, 70–71
    licensing, 71
    strategic alliances, 71–72
    subsidiaries, 73
Market Line Associates, 26
Marlboro, 71
Marriott International, 226
Mary Kay Cosmetics, 49, 81–82
Maslow, Abraham, 5
Matrix structures, 99–100
Matsushita Electric Industries, 54, 219–220
Mayo Clinic, 219

Maytag, 49
McCartney, Heather, 81
McDonald's Corp., 61
McDonnell Douglas, 213
McGregor, Douglas, 5, 136–137, 180–181
Mechanistic versus organic organizational structure, 100–102
Mergers and acquisitions, 61
Merlino, Nell, 81
Michelson & Associates, 225
Microsoft, 4, 12, 219
    Project for Windows, 32
Middle-of-the-road leadership 123
Mintzberg, Henry, 8
Mission statements, 22–23
    value of, 45
    writing, 45–46
Miyamoto, Shigeru, 17
Monitor role, 9
Mouton, Jane, 122
Mulcahy, Anne, 3, 218
Multicultural teams, managing, 76

N

National Foundation for Women Business Owners (NFWBO), 83, 84
Negotiator role, 9
Nestlé, 6
New entrants, 59
Nintendo, 17–18
Nissan, 75
Nordstrom, 49
Norms
    group, 188–192
    of reciprocity, 191
    violations, 191–192
Northwest Airlines, 226
Northwest Instrument Systems, 213

O

Objectives (goals)
    defined, 24
    goal setting theory, 161–163
    importance of, 25
    means-ends chain of, 25
    performance, 107
    writing, 24–25
Operating budget, 202
Operating funds, 204–206
Operations management
    customer relationship management, 226
    customer service, 225
    essentials, 218–219
    inventory management, 222–224
    productivity and competitive advantage, 219–220
    quality control, 224–225, 226–228
    technology, 220–221
    value chain management, 221–222

Organic versus mechanistic organizational structure, 100–102
Organizational commitment, 151–152
Organizational design (structure)
    bureaucratic, 102–106
    coordinating mechanisms, 97–98
    defined, 91
    delegation of authority, 96–97
    departmentalization, 92–94
    division of labor, 91–92
    environmental uncertainty, 108–109
    information processing, 109–110
    matrix structures, 99–100
    mechanistic versus organic, 100–102
    span of control, 94–96
    System Four, 106–107
    technology and, 107–108
    theories, contingency, 107–110
    theories, universal, 100–107
Organizing, 6
Orientation (forming) stage of group development, 178–179
Outsourcing, 71
Ownership, forms of, 87–88

P

Participative-group style, 106
Parsley Patch Inc., 200
Partnership, 87–88
Path-goal leadership theory, 124
Peers, evaluation by, 165
Perception, 134–136
Perceptual process
    attention, 133–134
    errors, 137–138
    perception, 134–136
    sensation, 133
Performance
    feedback, 163–164
    goals, 107, 161–163
    group size and, 182–183
    interviews, 165–167
    management by objectives, 160–161
    norms, 190
    rewarding, 167–174
Performance evaluation
    behaviorally anchored rating scales, 159, 160
    criticisms of, 156–157
    descriptive essays, 159–160
    goal setting theory, 161–163
    graphic rating scales, 158–159
    methods, 157–160
    multidimensionality of, 155
    process, 161–163
    ranking procedures, 158
    role of, 156
    who conducts, 164–165
Personality
    attribution theory, 141–142
    Big Five Model, 142–143
    locus of control, 143–144

Personality (*continued*)
   self-efficacy, 145
   self-esteem, 144–145
   theories, 137
   traits, of leaders, 119–120
PERT (Program Evaluation and Review Technique)
   development of, 36
   example of, 36–37
   positive and negatives aspects of, 37
   terminology, 36
Peter Principle, 106
Pfizer, 210
Philip Morris, 71
Philips, 54
Physical infrastructure, 68
Physical traits, of leaders, 118
Pilot, Michael, 229
PixArts, 83
Planning, 6
   control cycle, 27
   defined, 22
   financial, 201–203
   horizons, 24
   mission statement, 22–23
   objectives, 24–25
   priorities, 26–27
   strategic, intermediate, and operational, 23–24
Pledging, 208
Political activities, 62
Political rules and regulations, global, 67–68
Porter, Michael, 58
Power distance, 69
Practice of Management, The (Drucker), 160
Prejudice, 138–141
Priorities, 26–27
Processes, 54
Process reengineering, 228–230
Procter & Gamble, 77, 94
Product departmentalization, 93–94
Production-centered leader behavior, 121
Productivity, 219
Projection, 137
Project managers, roles of, 32, 33
Project planning and management, 30
   guidelines, 32–33
   life cycle, 31–32
   software, 32
Promissory notes, 207
Prospectors (pioneers), 20–21
Public relations, 62
Pygmalion effect, 139–141

Q

Quality control, 224–225, 226–228

R

Raw materials sector, 56
Reactors, 20, 21–22

Reagan, Ronald, 117
Recognition awards, 172–173
Reengineering, 228–230
Reithofer, Norbert, 218
Resource allocator role, 9
Resource-based theory, 55
Resources, management of, 3
Retained earnings, 212
Rewards
   See also Compensation
   allocation norms, 190–191
   criticism of, 173–174
   incentives, financial, 169–171
   recognition, 172–173
Risk/return trade-off, 211
Rivals, 58–59
Rockefeller family, 213
Roddick, Anita, 82
Rodgers, T. J., 28
Role
   See also Group roles
   defined, 184
Roosevelt, Franklin D., 117
Russia, 66

S

S&S Sportscards, 84–85
Sarbanes-Oxley Act (SOX) (2002), 67–68
Schmidt, Warren, 124
Scholastic, 30
Selective perception, 137
Self-efficacy, 145
Self-esteem, 144–145
Self-evaluation, 165
Self-fulfilling prophecy, 139–141
Self-management, 217–218
Sensation, 133
Separation (adjourning) stage of group development, 179
Service technology, 221
Sherwood, Pat, 200
Sheth, Jagdish, 77
Situational leadership, 123–124
Sloan, Alfred P., 5
Social conduct, 190
Social density, 183
Social facilitation, 195
Social loafing, 195–196
Sole proprietorship, 87
Southwest Airlines, 48, 219
Span of control, 94–96
Specialization, job, 91–92
Spencer, Rod, 84–85
Spokesperson role, 9
Starbucks, 18, 73
Statistical quality control, 227–228
Stereotyping, 138
Stewart, Rosemary, 10
Stock, equity financing by selling, 211–212
Stogdill, Ralph, 119
Strategic alliances, 71–72
Strategic management, 3–4

Strategies
    competitor analysis, 59–60
    cost leadership, 48
    differentiation, 48–49
    environmental analysis, 55–57
    firm analysis, 51–55
    focus, 49
    formulating, 50–51
    goals of, 47
    industry analysis, 58–59
    selecting, 46–47
Structure, strategy and, 52
Subsidiaries, 73
Substitute products, 59
Sullivan, Dan, 24
Suppliers, 58
Supply chain management (SCM), 222
Supportive relationships, principle of, 107
SWOT (Strengths, Weaknesses, Opportunities, and Threats) method, 50–51
System Four, 106–107
Systems, 52–53

T

Tannenbaum, Robert, 124
Taobao, 73
Taylor, Frederick W., 5, 35, 161, 169
Teams
    See also Groups
    characteristics of effective, 180–181
    leadership, 123
    multicultural, 76
    virtual, 179–180
Technical skills, needed by managers, 11–12
Technology
    impact of, 2
    manufacturing, 220–221
    organizational design and, 107
    sector, 57
    service, 221
Teva Pharmaceuticals, 21
Theory X and Y, 136–137
3M, 22
Time value, 204
Total quality management (TQM), 227
Toyota Motors, 49, 66
Trade credit, 206–207
Transactional leadership, 115–116
Transformational leadership, 116–117
Transnational focus, 74–75
Trump Hotels and Casino, 214
Tsu, Sun, 5

U

Uncertainty, 18
    avoidance, 69
    environmental, 60–62, 108–109
    organizational responses to, 19–22
    reducing, 61–62
    types of, 19
Unilever, 74
Unocal, 72
UPS, 73
U.S. Equipment Financing, 229
United States, government regulations, 67–68
US Steel, 51

V

Value chain management, 221–222
Venture capital, 88
    equity financing from, 212–213
Verizon Communications, 230
Virgin Group, 82
Visibility, 139
Vodaphone, 74
Vroom, Victor, 124

W

Wal-Mart, 48, 66–67, 72, 222, 224
Weber, Max, 102
Welch, Jack, 12
Whitman, Meg, 4, 10, 73
Woodward, Joan, 107–108
Work processes
    analysis, 228
    process reengineering, 228–230
WorldCom, 67
World Is Flat, The (Friedman), 65, 66
Wozniak, Steve, 12
Wrigley Jr. Co., 213–214

X

Xerox, 3, 218, 219

Y

Yetton, Philip, 124

Z

Zara International, 217
Zimbardo, Phillip, 196